Investigative Interviewing

Investigative Interviewing
Rights, research and regulation

Edited by

Tom Williamson

WILLAN
PUBLISHING

Published by

Willan Publishing
Culmcott House
Mill Street, Uffculme
Cullompton, Devon
EX15 3AT, UK
Tel: +44(0)1884 840337
Fax: +44(0)1884 840251
e-mail: info@willanpublishing.co.uk
website: www.willanpublishing.co.uk

Published simultaneously in the USA and Canada by

Willan Publishing
c/o ISBS, 920 NE 58th Ave, Suite 300
Portland, Oregon 97213-3786, USA
Tel: +001(0)503 287 3093
Fax: +001(0)503 280 8832
e-mail: info@isbs.com
website: www.isbs.com

Hardback
ISBN-13: 978-1-84392-124-0
ISBN-10: 1-84392-124-3

British Library Cataloguing-in-Publication Data

A catalogue record for this book is available from the British Library

Project management by Deer Park Productions, Tavistock, Devon
Typeset by GCS, Leighton Buzzard, Beds
Printed and bound by T.J. International, Padstow, Cornwall

Contents

Foreword

The Honourable Justice Peter Cory

If society did not already have grave concerns for the well-being of society, recent events have given rise to still greater concerns relating to the administration of justice. Let us consider but a few of these events.

To mention terrorist activity leads to thoughts of the alleged terrorists confined at Guatanamo Bay for extended periods of time while investigations are undertaken. For all this time they are held in captivity without knowing the charge or charges that they may eventually face. This seems to violate the provisions of Magna Carta, perhaps the earliest declaration of human rights in the western world. How does such an extended detention affect the prisoner and his response to interrogation? What safeguards, if any, should be imposed on the manner of interrogating the prisoners?

What of false confessions. Case studies have determined that false confessions leading to the conviction of innocent prisoners have all too often been made. Was it the manner of interrogation that led to these confessions and, if so, how should an interrogation be conducted of those who it appears are likely to make such confessions?

As well, studies have demonstrated that tunnel vision of investigators can affect the investigation of a crime and those involved in the interrogation of suspects. Once again, what can be done to correct tunnel vision during the interrogation of suspects?

A great deal of the investigation of crimes and terrorist activities will be done by means of interrogation. This excellent book deals with methods of interrogation and aspects such as tunnel vision which may affect the manner in which an interrogation is conducted which in turn may result in false confessions and wrongful convictions.

This book will be helpful to all those who conduct interrogations and to all who are interested in the manner and methods used in questioning and the effect it may have on the subject of interrogation. I believe this book will be frequently read and should be referred to by all who interrogate and all who are interested in the reliability and fairness of the interrogation.

The Honourable Peter Cory, C.C., C.D., Q.C.

Acknowledgements

This book has its origins in the presentations given at the first International Conference on Police Interviewing, held at the École nationale de police du Québec, Québec, Canada from 9 to 11 February 2004. The conference was the brainchild of Michel St-Yves, a forensic psychologist with the Sûreté du Québec, and of his colleagues Jaques Landry and Michel Pilon who are police officers with the Sûreté, and they all share a particular interest in investigative interviewing. In pursuit of this interest they have visited several countries and closely examined various models of teaching people skills in interviewing. They observed that there was much in common with the various approaches and also areas of considerable disagreement. It was their vision to hold a conference that would allow the various interested parties to explain and defend their respective positions. To this end the conference can be considered a success in that, although creative tension was built into the design of the conference and disagreements were discussed, the atmosphere was constructive and never became disagreeable. Those of us who were privileged to take part in the conference owe a debt of gratitude to the Sûreté du Québec for the vision to hold the conference and for their excellent arrangements. It is hoped that this will be the first of a continuing series of international conferences on investigative interviewing, with others planned for Portsmouth, England, in 2006 and Hong Kong in 2008.

Introduction

Tom Williamson

The aim of this book is to bring together academics and practitioners from different countries with different types of criminal justice system to discuss the central position occupied by police questioning in conducting investigations and eliciting information for intelligence or prosecution purposes. The book highlights the skills deficit frequently found in this area and it sets out a remedial framework for investigative interviewing based on respect for human rights, sound psychological research and effective, but positive, regulation.

Part I: Developments in rights

In Part I we examine developments in human rights in relation to interrogation as a response to the war on terror. This is addressed in Chapter 1 by Tom Williamson. Williamson argues that the growing post-war consensus for the principle of human rights is facing serious challenges from the response to the war on terror and especially from the militarization of criminal justice processes. The chapter draws on experience in the UK of military interrogation practices, which led to the abandonment of these practices and the beginning of a process leading to the professionalizing of investigative interviewing. He considers the constitutional arrangements for custodial questioning and the limited influence of judges over the processes employed to obtain information. Two models for dealing with terrorism are discussed but it is argued that both require investigators to be trained so that they have a sound understanding of the psychology of custody and acquire skills in humane methods of interviewing.

In Chapter 2, Michael G. Gelles and his colleagues commence from the premise that the object of questioning for both criminal justice and intelligence purposes should be to gather accurate and reliable information. Their chapter addresses the difficulties of doing so when interviewing suspects in the war on terrorism whose beliefs, ideologies, cultures and life experiences differ markedly from those of their interrogators. This chapter is based on extensive interviews with al-Qaeda operatives and describes approaches to interrogation that have proven to be effective.

In Chapter 3, David Rose, based on interviews with key personnel involved in the interrogation of suspects detained at Guantánamo Bay, Cuba, critically examines the steps taken by the US government to put in place procedures for the detention, interrogation and trial of suspects in the war on terror which fundamentally erode international standards for human rights. Moreover, Rose questions whether these interrogation methods actually resulted in the production of valuable intelligence.

Part I concludes with Chapter 4, by John J. Pearse. Pearse addresses the importance of gaining an understanding of terrorists and adopting the position of 'the other' and being aware of cultural considerations. He then goes on to examine the psychological research relating to interrogator bias and the impact of the physical environment. This is followed by an examination of the interrogation tactics at Abu Ghraib and Guantánamo Bay. He concludes by reflecting, as others have done, on the banality of torture.

Part II: Developments in research

Part II considers developments in investigative interviewing and psychological research. In this part we begin to examine the research evidence that would help in developing effective interviewing strategies and skills. It begins with acknowledging the importance of being able to establish a rapport between the interviewee and interviewer. In Chapter 5, Michel St-Yves draws on extensive experience of analyzing interviews in Canada, and he describes a model that he and his colleagues have developed which emphasizes the importance to an investigation of establishing a positive rapport with the interviewee. The model is based on an analysis of psychological research and is built around five rules: keeping an open mind; building up rapport;

paying attention; keeping a professional attitude; and knowing how to conclude. The chapter identifies areas for further research. A theme that emerges in the chapter is the danger of over-reliance on confession evidence.

In Chapter 6, again by Michel St-Yves, and this time based on interviews with prisoners convicted of sexual offences St-Yves examines the factors that correlate with a confession. He demonstrates that the perception formed by the suspect of the manner in which he or she is being addressed and questioned is a key factor in determining the outcome of the interview. Those suspects who have acknowledged their guilt say that an interviewing style that they considered humane and respectful was helpful in enabling them to disclose to the interviewer what they had done.

The psychological factors present during custodial questioning are considered in Chapter 7, by Gisli H. Gudjonsson. This chapter is based on Gudjonsson's extensive experience of miscarriage of justice cases over 20 years in many countries. The chapter begins with a critical appraisal of police interrogation training manuals. It then addresses the special factors relating to the interrogation of terrorist suspects. Various models of the interrogation process are examined. Gudjonsson concludes by examining the factors that contribute to false confessions by explaining how interrogation can go wrong.

Tom Williamson is another contributor who points to the dangers that arise from an over-reliance on confession evidence. In Chapter 8 he draws on research showing the correlation between the weight of evidence in the case and the outcome of the interview with a suspect. A set of ethical principles for investigative interviewing is described, together with an introduction to the PEACE model of investigative interviewing now being taught in England and many other countries. Miscarriage of justice cases in several countries are examined and many commonly recurring contributing factors are identified, including 'tunnel vision'. Williamson concludes by arguing for sound, scientifically based training programmes and continuous professional development pathways leading to academic qualifications and 'licence to practise' regulations, as essential steps in professionalizing investigative interviewing.

Chapter 9, by Andrew Griffiths and Becky Milne is based on an analysis of the performance of police officers who received training in advanced investigative interviewing. It demonstrates that the skills acquired on the course were maintained in the workplace. A model of analyzing interviews, the Griffiths Question Map, is described.

Probably the most popular interviewing and interrogation training course in the world is presented in Chapter 10 by Joseph P. Buckley who describes the programme and discusses recent developments to take account of concerns regarding some aspects of the methodology. He demonstrates that the model operates within the jurisprudence currently established by the higher courts in Canada and the USA. This method is not without its critics and, in Chapter 11, Saul M. Kassin examines contemporary interrogation practices in the USA and in particular provides a critical analysis of the Reid technique. By drawing on recent case studies, he shows that the dangers of false confessions have been underestimated.

The detection of deception is a subject that has been studied by psychologists, and this is addressed in Chapter 12 by Mark G. Frank, John D. Yarbrough and Paul Ekman who describe a model of investigative interviewing and, in particular, examine the psychology of emotion and facial micro-expressions of emotion.

Part III: Developments in regulation

In Part III we consider the arrival of new phenomena that have caused considerable controversy and concern regarding the reliability of evidence provided by victims in cases of historical sexual abuse. This is explored in Chapter 13 by James Ost, who examines the controversy in many countries regarding the phenomenon of so-called 'recovered memories' where people have been encouraged during psychological therapy to recall sexual abuse in childhood. This has led to a number of prosecutions and growing concern regarding the possibility of miscarriages of justice. This chapter demonstrates the need for constant vigilance in monitoring developments that can have a profound effect on the reliability of evidence obtained through questioning, and points to the need for further education and regulation.

The issue of what is the best way to regulate custodial questioning is considered in Chapter 14 by Robert Roy. This chapter is based on extensive research in Canada and Switzerland of the ethical challenges faced by investigators in trying to obtain information through questioning. A methodology based on applied ethics is used to consider how investigative interviewing can best be regulated. It considers the influence of rules and concludes that they are insufficient, as rules cannot be developed to cover every eventuality. Instead, there is a need to develop processes that improve the exercise of moral judgement by investigators. Using custodial interviewing as a case study, a set of ethical criteria is developed, including when and where deception can be used. The chapter concludes that legislation should be considered to prevent a miscarriage of justice occurring whereby the guilty in serious cases go free if society is to achieve a better balance between the rights of suspects and those of victims.

Chapter 15, by David Dixon, considers the possibilities and problems in the regulation of police interrogation. Dixon draws on a critical appraisal of the limitations of legal regulation of audio-visual records of interrogations, and he situates this analysis in recent developments in regulatory theory. Regulation is described as a sustained attempt to alter the behaviour of others according to defined standards or purposes with the intention of producing a broadly defined outcome, including mechanisms of standard setting, information gathering and behaviour modification. This approach is further discussed in the context of governance where regulation should seek to foster good interviewing and not merely to sanction bad practice. Good regulation positively encourages, shapes and directs.

In the concluding chapter, Tom Williamson briefly pulls together themes from the earlier discussions of rights, research and regulation and indicates the future of investigative interviewing.

Notes on contributors

Randy Borum is Associate Professor, Department of Mental Health Law and Policy, University of South Florida, and a diplomate of the American Board of Forensic Psychology. He has a doctorate in clinical psychology. He has published extensively in forensic and clinical psychology journals. He has provided consultancy on a wide range of justice matters, including terrorism, counterterrorism, violence and threat assessment.

Joseph P. Buckley is President of John E. Reid and Associates in Chicago. He is a forensic interviewer, detection of deception examiner, lecturer and consultant. He has written numerous articles and papers and is co-author of three books on interrogation and confessions. He lectures extensively to law enforcement, government and business groups.

David Dixon is Profesor of Law at the University of New South Wales in Sydney, Australia. He has researched and published widely on policing and crime control, focusing on the policing of illegal markets, comparative crime control strategies, legal regulation of police practices, and police interrogation in Britain and Australia.

Paul Ekman is Emeritus Professor of Psychology at the University of California and internationally renowned for his research on facial expressions, emotion and nonverbal communication. He has published extensively on lying and methods for uncovering lies. He works with police, law enforcement and intelligence agencies.

His book *Telling Lies: Clues to Deceit in the Marketplace, Politics and Marriage*, first published in 1991, has been widely acclaimed.

Mark G. Frank is Professor of Communication at Rutgers University. He has an international reputation for his research into the detection of deception. He has published in this area and trains law enforcement personnel in many countries.

Michael G. Gelles is the Chief Psychologist for the US Naval Criminal Investigative Service. He holds a doctorate in psychology and is a member of many academic societies, and he publishes regularly. He has an international reputation for his study into the questioning of al-Qaeda suspects.

Andy Griffiths is a detective chief inspector with Sussex Police and is a member of the Association of Chief Police Officers' advisory board on investigative interviewing. He has broad operational and training experience in interviewing and is being supported by his force to research for a PhD. He has developed a new system to analyze question usage in interviews.

Gisli H. Gudjonsson is a professor of forensic psychology at the Institute of Psychiatry, King's College London and Head of Forensic Psychology Services, Maudsley Hospital, London. He has published extensively in the areas of forensic psychology, including violence, psychological vulnerability, false confession, police interviewing and recovered memories. He pioneered the empirical measurement of suggestibility. He has provided expert psychological testimony in high-profile cases in many countries. He is co-editor-in-chief of *Personality and Individual Differences*.

Saul M. Kassin is a professor of psychology at Williams College, Massachusetts. He has written extensively on police interviewing in the USA and has conducted laboratory studies on the risk of false confessions and their influence on juries.

Robert McFadden is a member of the Naval Criminal Investigative Services with extensive experience in the interviewing of al-Qaeda suspects.

Becky Milne is a principal lecturer at the Institute of Criminal Justice Studies, University of Portsmouth, and a chartered forensic psychologist. She holds a doctorate for her research into investigative interviewing and teaches police officers and is recognized for her expertise with regard to the cognitive interview. She publishes regularly and is the co-author of recent texts on investigative interviewing. She is a member of the Association of Chief Police Officers' advisory board on investigative interviewing.

James Ost is a chartered psychologist and senior lecturer in the International Centre for Research in Forensic Psychology at the University of Portsmouth. He is a member of the scientific board of the BFMS, a charity offering support to families and professionals in cases of contested accusations of abuse. He has published extensively on this subject.

John J. Pearse has recently retired as a detective superintendent at Scotland Yard where he was actively involved in the interviewing of terrorist suspects. He holds a doctorate in investigative interviewing from the University of London and is a chartered forensic psychologist. He is currently conducting research into the detection of deception and examining the effectiveness of police interviews with terrorists in the UK. He is a member of the Association of Chief Police Officers' advisory board on investigative interviewing in the UK.

David Rose has been an investigative reporter for 24 years. His latest book is *Guantanamo: America's War on Human Rights* (Faber 2004). Currently a contributing editor for the international magazine *Vanity Fair*, and a writer for the *Observer*, he has also made numerous documentaries for the BBC. He has pursued a special interest in miscarriages of justice for many years, and among other cases, helped to uncover new evidence which led the Court of Appeal to quash the convictions of the Tottenham Three, the men wrongly convicted of murdering PC Keith Blakelock in the 1987 riot at Broadwater Farm, North London.

Robert Roy is full-time lecturer of ethics at Sherbrooke University, Quebec, Canada, and is currently attached to the Sûreté du Québec, as part of a police reform programme. He is an expert in the methodology of applied ethics and is a consultant to the police department in Lausanne, Switzerland.

Michel St-Yves is a forensic psychologist with the Behavioral Science Unit of the Sûreté du Québec, Canada, and previously worked for the Correctional Services of Canada for 13 years as a specialist in risk assessment for adult offenders, including sexual offenders. He has published on sexual offences, crisis negotiations and police interviewing. He has an extensive network of contacts in the francophone world who share his interest in investigative interviewing.

Bryan Vossekuil is a member of the CounterIntelligence Field Activity, US Department of Defense, with extensive experience in the interviewing of al-Qaeda suspects.

Tom Williamson is a visiting professor at the Institute of Criminal Justice Studies, University of Portsmouth. He is a chartered forensic psychologist and has a doctorate from the University of Kent for his research into investigative interviewing. He is one of the founders of the PEACE method of interviewing. He is a former police officer who retired from the post of Deputy Chief Constable of the Nottinghamshire Police in 2001 and was previously a commander at New Scotland Yard.

John D. Yarbrough was a sworn peace officer for nearly 30 years, specializing in homicide investigations for 16 years. He served as his department's criminal profiler for eight years, and was certified in criminal investigative profiling and crime scene analysis by the Federal Bureau of Investigation and the International Criminal Investigative Analysis Fellowship in 1995. In 1998, he served on a technical working group that developed and published *Crime Scene Investigation: A Guide for Law Enforcement* for the National Institute of Justice in Washington, DC. In 2001, he joined Park Dietz and Associates, an internationally recognized firm of consultants in forensic medicine and the behavioural sciences.

List of figures and tables

Figures

Tables

Part I

Developments in Rights

Chapter 1

Investigative interviewing and human rights in the war on terrorism

Tom Williamson

Introduction

The growing post-war consensus around the principle of respect for human rights is breaking down. Old threats are diminishing and new threats such as international terrorism have arrived resulting in the so-called 'war on terror'. One characteristic of this has been a deliberate undermining of human rights and a legitimizing of deviance through government-sanctioned and intentional abuses with dreadful consequences, particularly for those who have been detained and questioned as terrorist suspects. The erosion of human rights has been exacerbated by the process of militarization of criminal justice as a response to terrorism.

A natural experiment has been occurring in the UK which has over 30 years of experience of dealing with terrorism, including the use of military interrogation techniques. It is acknowledged that there are considerable difficulties in balancing the needs of the state for achieving security for its people and simultaneously respecting human rights. The responses of the UK and US governments will be considered together with the limited influence that judges have over the constitutional arrangements for regulating the questioning of suspects in terrorist cases. Ultimately parliaments must choose the legal frameworks that they consider to be appropriate to the threat, but their choice will determine whether their country develops into a security state with restrictions on freedoms and rights or retains the freedoms normally associated with a democracy. It is a choice for parliaments, not just governments. The difference is constitutionally important, if sustaining democracy is a primary concern. The ability of military, intelligence and police agencies to develop effective investigative interviewing and elicitation procedures and skills for the war on terror is central to the question of which should be the preferred option.

It is argued that democracies can balance the security needs of the state with respect for human rights and that there is no need for them to develop the apparatus of a security state with the erosion of personal freedoms that would inevitably occur. Two models for dealing with terrorism are in contention, one based on traditional criminal investigation and the justice process and the other based on new intelligence-led approaches which do not consider successful prosecution a necessary outcome. Both models rely heavily on investigative interviewing skills to furnish reliable information. Ironically at a time when there is renewed interest in human, as opposed to electronic, sources of information, military, intelligence and police organizations are currently suffering from a lack of skilled practitioners and investment in formal training which provides a sound understanding of the psychology of custody and skills in humane methods of interviewing.

Human rights, globalization and risk

The postmodern world is changing dramatically and in complex ways that have raised concerns about custodial questioning to unprecedented levels. The questioning of victims, witnesses and suspects lies at the heart of any information-gathering exercise, investigation and criminal justice system. Two arguments against the abuse of human rights are made in this chapter: first, the moral argument that interviewers should demonstrate respect for individual human rights as this is morally superior to the abuse of rights; and, secondly, the empirical claim that the most effective way of eliciting *reliable information* is through humane techniques (see Chapters 5–7, this volume). Until recently this would have been considered an irrefutable proposition in most democracies. That perception appears to be changing. States' reactions to the threat of terrorism can result in the militarization of criminal justice processes with the intentional abuse or erosion of human rights. When states are faced with a terrorist threat it is not unusual for them to respond by suspending or significantly altering existing systems of justice. Primacy for dealing with the terrorist threat is passed from the civil police to the military.

Suspects are interrogated by the military in ways that would never be accepted by the ordinary courts with criminal suspects. Denial of access to legal representation, detention without trial and trial by special tribunal form part of the process of the militarization of justice. This trend should be resisted because respect for rights provides a basis for trust and reciprocity between governments; their military, intelligence and police agencies; and the population being policed. Ultimately, the solutions to the causes of terrorism are political not military. The metaphor 'war on terror' is, therefore, misleading as there can never be a purely military solution. The militarization of justice processes is inimical to the goal of democracy. The systematic abuse of human rights over the long term breeds more terrorists not fewer. It is questionable whether any instrumental short-term gains believed to come from coercive interrogation methods are worth the long-term damage to the prospects for peace and democracy.

The end of the twentieth century was marked by the growth of the phenomenon of globalization, a term which sociologists use to describe those processes which are intensifying worldwide social relations and interdependence. The rapid connections between the local and the global are quite new in human history and driven by ever quicker advances in communications technology and transportation (Giddens 1999, 2002: 48–76). The impact of globalization has been reflected in the rise of individualism and the gradual spread of democracy, dramatically illustrated in the fall of communism. These developments have also provided new opportunities for criminal networks and cross-border crime flows which are putting strains on organizational structures designed in the nineteenth century (Loader and Sparks 2002: 97–8; Williamson 2004).

Even prior to the events of 9/11, criminologists were arguing that we inhabit what has been characterized as the 'risk society', which Beck considers to be a way of dealing with hazards and insecurities brought about by the process of modernization and globalization (1992: 21, see also Giddens 2002: 65–8). These processes identify 'which risks are selected for particular attention, which categories of person and which places come to be regarded as bearers or containers of intolerable risk' (Loader and Sparks 2002: 95). That we all live in a risk society can be conveyed by our sharing of an ambient sense of risk, including the risk of victimization. When is my car going to be stolen, my house broken into, or am I to get assaulted, robbed or raped? This ambient sense of risk is amplified by the risk stories that form the staple diet of the news media.

The elevation of perceptions of risk has led to heated debates about crime and punishment and the state's capacity to deliver levels of security that may once have been taken for granted. Fear of the risk or threat is coupled with fear that the state will fail to respond effectively and this is driving a demand for greater accountability. Law enforcement agencies, as agents of the state, operating in this environment find themselves facing greater pressures for accountability and transparency. The global communications revolution has created a mass-mediated society in which blame is instantly attributed whenever the media identify a particular risk. In this environment, according to Loader and Sparks (2002), 'every failure of propriety or competence in risk management is potentially a scandal'. In policing this can be seen through the steady growth of independent civilian oversight bodies for policing the police, such as Independent Police Complaints Commission in England and Wales and the Ombudsman for the Police Service of Northern Ireland. Such bodies vary enormously in their effectiveness, resources and powers at their disposal but that they exist at all is evidence of the demand for accountability for individual officers and police organizations.

Key challenges for organizations operating in democratic states in the twenth-first century risk society are:

- risk identification, assessment and management;
- managing propriety or ethical values;
- developing professional competence; and
- managing public perceptions.

The undermining of human rights law and legitimizing of deviance

These new challenges arise at a time when there is increasing public pressure on states to react in more penal ways to the perception of threats from terrorism or rising crime than was the case for democracies in the post-war period (Young 1999). This growing penality is in conflict with other efforts aimed at extending respect for individual human rights.

The concept of rights has been slowly developing over the last 300 years from the philosophical debates occurring during the Enlightenment. Countries that rejected monarchies, such as France and the USA, incorporated the concept of rights into their constitutions. The Constitution of the USA speaks of certain 'inalienable rights'. More recently, following the Second World War the countries of the world came together under the newly constituted United Nations and one of their first actions was to endorse at their meeting on 10 December 1948 in San Francisco the Universal Declaration of Human Rights. The first 50 years has been spent in gaining international acceptance of the *principle* of human rights and if that process continued unhindered the next 50 years would have to be spent achieving in every member state of the United Nations compliance with the *practice* of human rights. There is much to commend this approach, rights form a basis for the relationship of trust and reciprocity between the state and state's parties, including intelligence and law enforcement agencies and the individual. Respect for citizens' rights are a solid basis for reciprocity in policing (Wright 2002: 44–6). Investigations and interviews conducted in ways that respect these rights will strengthen reciprocity, accountability and democracy.

History and academic research show that all too frequently military and police investigations have been associated with a deviant culture where the ends have been thought to justify the means (Klockars 1980; Williamson 1990; see also Chapter 15, this volume). For example, in an interview training course conducted in a newly democratized European country a detective explained that torture was not a problem in his country because they only tortured 'guilty' people. He decided whether or not a person was guilty or innocent, and if they were guilty and don't confess he tortures them to get their confession (Crawshaw, pers. comm. 2003). In countries where torture is not practised, there can be a temptation to abuse the psychological process inherent in custodial questioning in a similar 'ends justifies the means' way in order to obtain confession evidence (Kassin and Wrightsman 1985; Ofshe and Leo 1997; Kassin 1998; Gudjonsson 2003; Rose 2004). Both approaches involve an abuse of human rights. States can be complicit and culpable in condoning physical and psychological abuse and have a responsibility to provide a regulatory framework that encourages public confidence that people questioned in custody will be treated professionally. There was a steady but growing acknowledgement of these issues, and torture was both condemned and becoming, in many countries, an increasingly rare event. This changed after the events of 11 September 2001.

The international legal regulatory framework

The events of 11 September 2001 mark a watershed in international governance, disturbing extant legal cultures that once appeared to vouchsafe international human rights law, and this is creating confusion about how states should respond to the threat of terrorism. According to a British academic lawyer:

> International law has been revealed as feeble, constitutional law as insecure, while human rights law has become negotiable. Law's apparent stable edifice has been exposed as being as fragile as our world order. International legal doctrines, treaties and constitutional texts seem superseded by the political expediency of alleged international and national security concerns in the face of terrorist threats... The actions of Al Qa'ida and the responses to them challenge the carefully crafted system of international relations in the second half of the last century (Strawson 2002: xi, xix).

Farer, an American lawyer, argues that, once this international frame of order is broken and states slip out of the normative restraints on their tools for safeguarding their security: 'we can reasonably anticipate increasingly norm-less violence, pitiless blows followed by monstrous retaliation in a descending spiral of hardly imaginable depths' (2002: 354). What is unfolding has been described as the degradation of international law:

> International law is no longer accepted as a legitimate curb on the use of force by Western powers, while coercive intervention by Western powers against other States is increasingly legitimised through the framework of 'international justice'. The gap between 'justice' and what is 'legal' has led to the degradation of international law rather than to its development (Chandler 2002: 158).

The issue at stake is respect for the sovereignty, equality and legal parity of nation-states, regardless of their wealth or power, in order to establish the rule of 'right' over 'might' in regulating interstate affairs (Chandler 2000: 55).

One result is that investigators in many countries find themselves caught between the narratives of crime and war (Hayward and

Morrison 2002: 140–57), with military, security and police organizations operating in the same areas. The rules of engagement may be unclear but are likely to have changed, resulting in extension of police powers, the sudden arrival of military and intelligence personnel, and the militarization of criminal justice structures in what previously would have been considered the bailiwick of criminal investigators. After all, terrorism is a crime. This raises a fundamental question as to whether we are fighting a war or investigating a crime. International humanitarian law covers both: if it is a war, the Geneva Convention applies, and if it is a crime, human rights treaties and domestic law apply. Both forms of engagement also rely heavily on human sources of information. If, as will subsequently be demonstrated, investigators were not getting interviewing right before 11 September (see Chapter 8, this volume) it is even more likely that they and their military and intelligence colleagues were likely to repeat these mistakes when acting under legislation and policies that provide an extension of powers and suspension of internationally guaranteed human rights obligations, thereby legitimizing deviance.

The erosion of human rights through the militarization of justice: the UK experience

Some lessons can be learnt from a natural experiment that has been taking place in Britain which has a recent history of dealing with terrorism. One of the first responses to terrorism is for the state to bring in the military. Between 1966 and 1999 there were 3,636 deaths in Northern Ireland from political violence, in a population of 1.5 million. By 1971 the scale of the violence grew beyond the capabilities of the para-military police force, the Royal Ulster Constabulary, and the army became the prime security force and legislation was passed permitting internment without trial. These emergency powers also led to the ill-treatment of detainees and lethal confrontations between the army and civilian population which directly contributed to the continuation of terrorist activity.

Legislation was often event driven in response to the latest terrorist attack. In a review of the legislation in 1996 four principles were set out against which terrorism legislation should be judged:

1. Legislation against terrorism should approximate as closely as possible to the ordinary criminal law and procedure.

2. Additional statutory offences and powers may be justified, but only if they are necessary to meet the anticipated threat. They must then strike the right balance between the needs of security and the rights and liberties of the individual.

3. The need for additional safeguards should be considered alongside additional powers.

4. The law should comply with the UK's obligations in international law (Lloyd 1996).

Emergency powers to deal with terrorism often fail to meet these principles. The human rights problems associated with the militarization of criminal justice through abusive interrogations and indeterminate detention were eventually recognized and resulted in the police regaining primacy for security in 1975. The Lloyd Review to consider the legal procedures to deal with terrorist activities resulted in the carefully considered Terrorism Act 2000 which provided an extensive counter-terrorist code but with diminished rates of abuse and complaint. In response to 11 September the UK government hastily passed the Anti-terrorism, Crime and Security Act 2001 which contains new powers, including that of indefinite detention which has required the UK to derogate from Article 5 of the European Convention required by its own Human Rights Act 1998 (cf. Walker 2002 for text and discussion of the legislation).

It did not follow the USA in creating military tribunals for dealing with persons suspected of terrorism (US Presidential Order, *Detention, Treatment, and Trial of Certain Non-citizens in the War against Terrorism,* 13 November 2001 (66 Federal Register 57831) s. 4).

Military interrogation techniques

The purpose of investigative interviewing is to obtain evidence. In criminal investigation there is no legal power to detain people in custody for the purpose of obtaining intelligence. Military and security service interviewers are different: they may want to interview purely for intelligence to be used to disrupt the enemy or, in the case of the US military tribunals, to obtain evidence, including confession for use in a prosecution.

The erosion of rights is particularly prone to happen at times of national emergencies. The use of military interrogation techniques on suspects detained in Northern Ireland led to the government of the

Republic of Ireland successfully taking action against the government of the UK in the European Court of Justice in what became known as the 'hooded men' case because of the way bags were put over the heads of detainees. The court found that the men had not been tortured but that they had been subjected to degrading and inhuman treatment (*Ireland* v. *United Kingdom*, App. No. 5310/71, Ser. A. 25 (1979–80) 2 EHRR 25). This court finding led to a government inquiry which brought about far-reaching changes in the detention and treatment of suspects for custodial questioning (Bennett 1979). More recently the link between rights and policing was made explicit in another government inquiry in Northern Ireland, the Patten Commission, as part of the peace process, which has led to fundamental changes in the police structure in Northern Ireland with a process of change from para-military policing to human rights-based civil policing: 'It is a central proposition of this report that the fundamental purpose of policing should be the protection and vindication of the human rights of all, *policing means protecting human rights*' (Patten 1999: 18, emphasis added).

It is important therefore to understand certain key characteristics that apply to rights. Notwithstanding the earlier equivocation voiced by lawyers regarding international human rights law, rights are still internationally guaranteed through binding agreements signed at the governmental level. They are legally protected. They focus on the dignity of the human being. They protect both individuals and groups. They place obligations on states and organizations such as the police, intelligence agencies and the military. As articulated in the Preamble to the Universal Declaration of Human Rights they are the equal and inalienable rights of all members of the human family and the basis for freedom, justice and peace in the world. They are universal. Some, such as the right not to be tortured, are absolute rights and cannot be subject to any qualification or derogation by the state.

The Universal Declaration of Human Rights articulated 30 rights and these have been addressed through two conventions published in 1976. The first convention relates to economic and social rights, such as the right to work, social security, health and education. The second convention relates to civil rights and includes the right to life and prohibitions against arbitrary detention and torture. A *Code of Conduct for Law Enforcement Officials* was published in 1979 as the basis for policing in ways that respect human rights. This is a work in progress but it has given rise to additional conventions which spell out what this means in practice – for example, *The Right* to *Life and the Use of Force by Law Enforcement Officials* published in 1990 (see Crawshaw and Holmstrom 2001 for a compilation of the various relevant international instruments). At present the codes have something to say about custodial conditions but nothing on how to interrogate people in ways that respect their universal rights. There is therefore a need for international best practice in relation to investigative interviewing to be collected and for it to acquire the status of a convention or code of conduct. This process is likely to take several years (Crawshaw *et al.* 1998).

The treatment of detainees at Guantánamo Bay appears to be similar to the military interrogation techniques that resulted in the European Court finding against the government of the UK in the case of the hooded men. We still do not know sufficient about how the 660 men and boy(s) in Guantánamo Bay are being treated to know whether it amounts to torture, but it certainly appears to amount to inhuman and degrading treatment. There is some suggestion that all interrogations have been videotape recorded, but this has yet to be confirmed and, if so, the tapes are not yet in the public domain. The focus on Guantánamo Bay may have diverted attention from other locations where suspects have been detained indefinitely and subjected to the planned use of coercive techniques. Human rights organizations have criticized the detention and interrogation of detainees at Guantánamo Bay and have identified the principal violations of international human rights as follows:

- The creation by the US government of zones where people are considered to be outside the law and have no legal channels to assert their rights.

- People are being kept in indefinite detention without charge or trial.

- They are being held in conditions that may amount to cruel, inhuman or degrading treatment and that violate other minimum standards relating to detention.

- Those who do go on trial will be tried by military commissions which are not independent of the executive.

- The military commissions will allow a lower standard of evidence than is admissible in courts, including hearsay evidence.

- The commissions will have the power to hand down death sentences without the right of appeal to an independent and impartial court.

- Detainees have only a limited right to effective defence being restricted to US military lawyers (although this has now been overturned by a federal court in Washington and is being appealed to the Supreme Court).

- There is a concern that people in US custody may have been transferred for interrogation in another country where there is a likelihood of unfair trial, torture, the death penalty and inadequate human rights protection, which is a breach of the principle of *non-refoulement* (Amnesty International 2002: 1).

Given those conditions and the militarization of justice, it is not clear what reliability, if any, can be placed on evidence obtained through custodial questioning in these conditions (see Chapters 3 and 7, this volume). The militarization of criminal justice has often been associated with torture and extra-judicial executions rather than the elicitation of information and the subjugation of its own people (or some of them) by the state. The purpose was punishment not intelligence (Huggins *et al.* 2002). The unilateralist approach of the US government may be a serious threat to a human rights basis for investigation and custodial questioning. Their new approach is unlikely to be overturned by the US Supreme Court, although it has provided some limited access to legal representation for detainees. The coercive regime appears to have continued, notwithstanding its international condemnation. What is happening may not be a temporary aberration following the disastrous events of 11 September 2001 (Koh 2003); we may have entered a new era which has been criticized by Kofi Annan, Secretary General of the United Nations:

> There is no trade-off between effective action against terrorism and the protection of human rights. On the contrary, I believe that in the long term we shall find that human rights, along with democracy and social justice, are one of the best prophylactics against terrorism (statement at United Nations' Security Council meeting on counter-terrorism, 18 Janauary 2002).

Apart from attracting criticism from human rights non-governmental bodies, the treatment of prisoners, including British subjects, at Guantánamo Bay has attracted criticism from Lord Steyn, one of the most senior judges who sits in the House of Lords, Britain's final court of appeal. He said (2003): 'the blanket presidential order deprives them all of any rights whatever. As a lawyer brought up to admire the ideas of American democracy and justice, I would have to say that I would regard this as a monstrous failure of justice.'

Is it a monstrous failure of justice or has the world changed so much that torture should now be permitted? (see Chapters 14 and 15, this volume, for further discussion of this point). Not so long ago this would have been considered a rhetorical question for a British police officer. Article 5 of the Universal Declaration of Human Rights expressly states that 'No one shall be subjected to torture or to cruel, inhuman degrading treatment or punishment'. Similar wording is to be found in Article 3 of the European Convention for the Prevention of Torture and Inhuman or Degrading Treatment or Punishment. Countries that are state parties to the European convention cannot derogate from the requirement not to torture. The UK is a party to the convention and is bound by its provisions.

A case, however, has been made by the UK government to the British Court of Appeal that the convention against torture does not explicitly prohibit the use of information obtained by torture. This is correct in that the convention does not contain a prohibition of torture but a range of measures to make the prevention of torture more effective. It includes such things as a definition of torture, the requirements on states to take measures to prevent torture and a prohibition on returning people to places where they may be tortured. Under Article 15 it does contain a provision that no statement obtained as a result of torture should be invoked as evidence in any proceedings, except against a person accused of torture.

In August 2004 in a two-to-one ruling, the Court of Appeal said that evidence obtained under torture in third countries may be used in special terrorism cases, under structures established by the Anti-terrorism, Crime and Security Act 2001, provided that the British government has 'neither procured the torture nor connived at it'. The Home Secretary can use evidence obtained under torture outside the country when deciding to detain indefinitely foreign terrorism suspects providing Britain was not involved in the torture or encouraged it. Such information can be considered by the Special Immigration Appeals Commission that hears appeals by these suspects against indefinite detention, allowed under Part 4 of the Anti-terrorism, Crime and Security Act 2001. Such evidence is heard in closed proceedings to which the detainees and their lawyers have no access; instead they are represented by lawyers appointed by the government. The Joint Human Rights Committee of Parliament has called for indefinite detention to be scrapped.

In his dissenting judgment, Lord Justice Neuberger made clear that, in his view, the consequence of the Court of Appeal's decision was that 'by using torture, or even adopting the fruits of torture, a democratic state is weakening its case against terrorists, by adopting their methods, thereby losing the moral high ground an open democratic society enjoys'.[1] The case is now before the House of Lords.

The British legislation was passed in the immediate aftermath of 9/11. (For a discussion of the way the government of the USA sought to get around international human rights law relating to interrogation see Rose 2004 and Chapter 3, this volume.) In the USA the President intended to create a legal back hole in Guantánamo where human rights entitlements could apparently be suspended.

The relaxation of safeguards for human rights was exacerbated by the fact that it is now alleged that untrained interrogators were deployed in order to obtain 'enormously valuable intelligence' (Rose 2004). The officer in charge of Guantánamo had no previous intelligence experience. Under pressure for more results he decided to combine the roles of gaoler and intelligence gatherer, a system that was then adopted in Abu Ghraib. In October 2004, Staff Sergeant Ivan Frederick, an army reservist and military policeman, pleaded guilty to eight counts of abusing and humiliating Iraqi detainees at Abu Ghraib prison. He had attached wires to a detainee's hands and told him that he would be electrocuted if he fell off a box. He also forced prisoners to masturbate. His only mitigation was that he was apparently doing what military intelligence told him to do (see Chapter 5, this volume, for a discussion of Zimbardo's famous experiment of abuse by prison guards).

In Britain the separation of the roles of supervision of people in custody from that of custodial questioning was incorporated into the Police and Criminal Evidence Act (PACE) 1984 which was quite prescient in the light of the massive reform of police question practices that has occurred following the introduction of PACE. Faced with the possibility of nuclear, biological or chemical attack, PACE may seem to some people to be rather like boxing to the Marquess of Queensberry Rules. A number of pundits are now advocating the use of torture under controlled conditions (see Chapter 15, this volume). The fears generated by the threat of terrorism are stoking up an increasingly penal public reaction. It is unlikely that torture would ever be allowed in Britain. On the other hand, if the intelligence was obtained as a result of torture in another country, should we not use that? No one would wish to underestimate the enormous challenges that police officers and the intelligence community face in dealing with global terrorism. But accepting evidence obtained through torture appears a bit like saying you did not steal anything you only received it from someone who, you had reason to believe, had stolen it. Is this really an essential part of the solution to international terrorism?

Three consequences flow from the use of torture or information obtained from other people using torture. One is that it could affect the treatment of US, UK and Coalition soldiers, police officers and civilian hostages captured in future armed conflicts. Secondly, it would remove the restraints of human rights law on other states that would be able to invoke the precedent of US policy at Guantánamo Bay and in British tribunals. Thirdly, it would be likely to make martyrs in the moderate Muslim world, with whom the West must work to ensure peace and stability, of the prisoners treated in this way.

The limited influence of the judges

The weakness of the judges in curtailing these recent developments is most worrying. Even if the judges were minded to act in support of human rights it is questionable what effect they could have. Although the criminal justice systems in England and parts of North America share many similarities due to their common law heritage the responses will reflect the way their particular constitutions operate. Unlike Britain's unwritten constitution that allows for state intervention, the US Constitution confers little opportunity for state intervention and regulation, including in the field of custodial questioning. This is neatly summed up by Lazare (1998), who argues that, because the US constitution is almost impossible to rewrite, it has been amended only 15 times since 1791, and that arguments over civil liberties and social progress are frozen: 'By externalising civil liberties in the form of an untouchable Bill of Rights, US constitutionalism has prevented their internationalisation as part of the democratic political process.'

Britain in contrast has addressed these issues through legislation whereby the state can and has prescribed the regulatory framework for custodial questioning in non-terrorist cases that complies with human rights standards and proscribes certain behaviours in a code of practice. Some states' constitutions would prevent a similar model being introduced and so the British experience is not always transferable.

The result of these developments in response to the threat of terrorism is to create a gap between those countries that have reacted by restricting human rights and liberal democracies which have not. It may be symptomatic of a divergence of values between the USA and Europe (Hutton 2003: 101–2).

The militarization of criminal justice is a strategy that fails on moral, legal and utilitarian grounds, and bitter experience. The response to the threat of terrorism and the legal frameworks chosen ultimately defines the kind of country we each live in and the means adopted to ensure our security.

Governments' choice of legal frameworks for the war on terrorism: security state or democracy?

British officers working within the existing anti-terrorism legislation can find it very frustrating. It is not as though they have not had their share of successes. Some of the frustration that officers engaged in combating terrorism face include the requirement for terrorist suspects to be detained for limited periods of time and that they are entitled to a legal representative being present when they are questioned with the result that most will exercise their right of silence. The issue of who can be detained by whom purely for the purposes of intelligence gathering as opposed to questioning for evidence to be used in a criminal prosecution remains ambiguous.

The British government incorporated the European Convention on Human Rights into its domestic law in the Human Rights Act 1998, which meant that all new legislation relating to terrorism should have successfully passed a human rights audit. The passing of the Terrorism Act 2000 appears to have achieved that and the government claimed that the law was compatible with European convention rights and they therefore rescinded a previous derogation relating to the detention of people suspected of terrorist offences. No sooner was this legislation on the statute book than the events of 9/11 led the government to pass the Anti-terrorism, Crime and Security Act 2001. This legislation contains provisions that would fail a human rights audit and in consequence the government was required yet again to derogate from its responsibilities under Article 5 of the convention, which guarantees the right to life, liberty and security. If the Terrorism Act 2000 appeared to get close to achieving a balance between the level of the threat and the powers to restrict human rights, the more recent legislation contains powers that go well beyond that. It is of interest that Britain is the only country of

Council of Europe member states that felt it was necessary to respond to 9/11 by bringing forward this kind of legislation. The government argued that Britain was more at risk than other European countries. The Committee of Privy Counsellors set up by the Anti-terrorism Act to review its provisions argued for the removal of the 'internment provisions' and proposed a more 'proportionate response' involving house arrest, intensive surveillance and other measures.

A further review of the terrorism legislation is under way. The outcome of this will have serious implications for democracy in the UK. If the war on terrorism requires that all terrorism in the world be eradicated the war will go on for ever and therefore the emergency legislation will never be dismantled and we will inevitably move towards living in a security state, a trend that criminologists have been predicting. This is not the only option available. There is an alternative. The Terrorism Act 2000, together with the Regulation of Investigatory Powers Act 2000 and the Human Rights Act 1998, demonstrated that it was possible to have workable legislation that enabled the police to deal with threats in an intelligence-led way rather than resort to preventative detention. Police and security organizations will need legislation to enable them to do their job but the form of the legislation they are given will reflect the kind of organization they become and determine whether their country becomes more like a security state than a democracy.

Conclusion

The choice between a security state where personal freedoms are inevitably eroded and a democracy achieving a proportionate balance between individual rights and threats to national security is not a false dichotomy. It may be that we are at a watershed in terms of a new approach to managing the threat of third-millennium terrorism and other international crimes. The world of law enforcement is rapidly changing. Instead of the public police there is now a multitude of other public and private providers. Many people employed as interrogators in Iraq are private contractors. According to Newburn (in Jones and Newburn 2002):

> Policing has changed, as has the society being policed. The increasing visibility of a plurality of providers of security will mean, one way or another, that we will be forced to consider once again what it is we want policing in general, and the

police service in particular, to achieve, and in what way we feel that it is appropriate to achieve these things.

Bayley and Shearing (1996) consider that a paradigmatic shift is taking place. If that is the case, are we likely to see traditional approaches of constructing a case for a prosecution based largely on confession evidence and the shaping of the narratives provided by victims and witnesses with some form of penal sanction as the intended outcome being replaced? Are we witnessing instead the emergence of an approach based on proactive risk management where intelligence gathering and disruption of criminal networks become more important than conviction? Is a twenty-first-century risk model more fitted for a global 'risk society' instead of a nineteenth-century criminal justice model designed to operate within the borders of a nation-state?

Others have argued that concepts such as globalization and risk have been overstated and suggest instead continuity with the past, but do so in recognition that important shifts have been taking place in policing arrangements that will necessitate radical, but evolutionary reform in the near future in order to meet what are acknowledged to be dramatic new challenges (Jones and Newburn 2002).

One important aspect for either model will be the issue of governance. The public police face growing forms of regulation, as do private security contractors in some jurisdictions. However, for those engaged in the war on terrorism, especially when they are operating outside the borders of their own nation-state, there appears to be little in the way of formal accountability, regulation and governance. If the trend is away from old law enforcement models to new intelligence-led risk models, are new oversight arrangements going to be developed on a statutory basis or will the current democratic deficit continue indefinitely?

Whichever model comes to dominate in the third millennium or whether, as I believe, they will continue in some form to coexist, both currently suffer from fundamental weaknesses in the level of skills, knowledge and understanding of how to elicit information from people. Time will prove that investigative interviewing, not torture, degrading or inhuman treatment, produces reliable information that either model requires for their very different purposes. Interviewing people in a humane way that establishes rapport, elicits and examines whatever account that may be given, will remain a core competence. Recent publicity has not only revealed breaches in propriety but it is also evidence of a shocking lack of skilled interviewers. What is striking, in my experience, is that this can be applied generally across military, intelligence and police agencies. Interviewing is not valued as an important skill and there has been a chronic underinvestment in training and research. There are obviously some exceptionally gifted interviewers and there is much that we can learn from each other but this is not to gainsay the value of acquiring through formal training a greater understanding of the psychology of custody and skills in methods of eliciting information through humane interviewing (cf. Philips 1981: 195).

Note

1. Case of A, B, C, D, E, F, G, H, Mahmoud abu Rideh, Jamal Ajouaou and Secretary of State for Home Department, 11 August 2004 ([2004], EWCA 1123).

References

Amnesty International (2002) *United States of America. Memorandum to the US Government on the Rights of People in US Custody in Afghanistan and Guantanamo Bay*. London: Amnesty International (http://web.amnesty. org/library/print/ENGAMR51042002).

Bayley, D. and Shearing, C. (1996) 'The future of policing', *Law and Society Review*, 30: 585–606.

Beck, U. (1992) *Risk Society: Towards a New Modernity*. London: Sage.

Bennett Report (1979) *Report of the Committee of Inquiry into Police Interrogation Procedures in Northern Ireland* (Cmnd 9497). London: HMSO.

Chandler, D. (2000) 'International justice', *NLR*, 55: 6.

Chandler, D. (2002) *From Kosovo to Kabul: Human Rights and Humanitarian Intervention*. London: Pluto.

Crawshaw, R., Devlin, B. and Williamson, T. (1998) *Human Rights and Policing: Standards for Good Behaviour and a Strategy for Change*. The Hague: Kluwer Law International.

Crawshaw, R. and Holmstrom, L. (2001) 'Essential texts on human rights for the police: a compilation of international instruments', in R. Crawshaw and L. Holmstrom (eds) *Essential Texts for Human Rights for the Police*. The Hague: Kluwer Law International.

Farer, J. (2002) in J. Strawson (ed.) *Law after Ground Zero*. London: Glasshouse Press.

Giddens, A. (1999) *Runaway World: How Globalisation is Reshaping our Lives*. London: Profile Books.

Giddens, A. (2002) *Sociology* (4th edn). Cambridge: Polity Press.

Gudjonsson, G.H. (2003) *The Psychology of Interrogations and Confessions. A Handbook.* Chichester: Wiley.

Hayward, K. and Morrison, W. (2002) 'Locating "Ground Zero": caught between the narratives of crime and war', in J. Strawson (ed.) *Law after Ground Zero.* London: Glasshouse Press.

Huggins, M.K., Haritos-Fatouros, M. and Zimbardo, P.G. (2002) *Violence Workers: Police Torturers and Murderers Reconstruct Brazilian Atrocities.* London: University of California Press.

Hutton, W. (2003) *The World We're In.* London: Abacus.

Jones, T. and Newburn, T. (2002) 'The transformation of policing? Understanding current trends in policing systems', *British Journal of Criminology,* 42: 129–46.

Kassin, S.M. (1998) 'More on the psychology of false confessions', *American Psychologist,* March: 320–1.

Kassin, S.M. and Wrightsman, L.S. (1985) 'Confession evidence', in S.M. Kassin and L.S. Wrightsman (eds) *The Psychology of Evidence and Trial Procedures.* London: Sage.

Klockars, C.B. (1980) 'The Dirty Harry problem', *Annals of the American Academy of Political and Social Science,* 452: 33–47.

Koh, H.H. (2003) 'Rights to remember', *The Economist,* 1–7 November.

Lazare, D. (1998) 'America the undemocratic', *New Left Review,* December.

Lloyd, Lord (1996) *Inquiry into Legislation against Terrorism* (Cm 3420). London: HMSO.

Loader, I. and Sparks, R. (2002) 'Contemporary landscapes of crime, order, and control: governance, risk, and globalization', in M. Maguire *et al.* (eds) *The Oxford Handbook of Criminology.* Oxford: Oxford University Press.

Ofshe, R.J. and Leo, R.A. (1997) 'The social psychology of police interrogation. The theory and classification of true and false confessions', *Studies in Law, Politics and Society,* 16: 189–251.

Patten, C. (1999) *A New Beginning: Policing in Northern Ireland: The Report of the Independent Commission on Policing for Northern Ireland.* London: HMSO.

Philips, Sir C. (1981) *The Royal Commission on Criminal Procedure* (Cmnd 8092). London: HMSO.

Rose, D. (2004) *Guantanamo, America's War on Human Rights.* London: Faber & Faber.

Steyn, Lord (2003) 'F.A. Mann lecture. Report', *The Times,* 26 November.

Strawson, J. (2002) 'In the name of the law', in J. Strawson (ed.) *Law after Ground Zero.* London: Glasshouse Press.

Walker, C. (2002) *Blackstone's Guide to the Anti-Terrorism Legislation.* Oxford: Oxford University Press.

Williamson, T.M. (1990) 'Strategic changes in police interrogation: an examination of police and suspect behaviour in the Metropolitan Police in order to determine the effects of new legislation, technology and organisational policies.' Unpublished PhD thesis, University of Kent at Canterbury.

Williamson, T.M. (2004) *The War on Terror: Developments in Intelligence and Homeland Security. Police Professional.* Reigate: NSI Professional Media.

Wright, A. (2002) *Policing: an Introduction to Concepts and Practice.* Cullompton: Willan Publishing.

Young, J. (1999) *The Exclusive Society: Social Exclusion, Crime and Difference in Late Modernity.* London: Sage.

Zander, M. (1994) 'Ethics and crime investigation by the police', *Policing*, 10, 39–48.

Chapter 2

Al-Qaeda-related subjects: a law enforcement perspective

Michael G. Gelles, Robert McFadden,
Randy Borum and Bryan Vossekuil

Introduction

National security and public safety are primary concerns for all professionals who investigate terrorism (White 2003; Borum 2004). These investigations frequently involve questioning subjects, either for purposes of intelligence gathering or for investigations that may lead to criminal prosecution. The objective of these interviews/interrogations is to gather accurate and reliable information that furthers security, safety, intelligence and investigative interests. The current threat environment, however, poses some particular challenges for law enforcement professionals investigating terrorism (Hoffman 1999; Laqueur 1999; Simon 2003; Borum *et al.* 2004).

Many 'adversaries' in the global war on terrorism have beliefs, ideologies, cultures and life experiences that differ markedly from those of their interrogators – and often differ from those of criminals with whom law enforcement professionals more typically interact. Terrorist groups and networks affiliated with al-Qaeda, in particular, pose ominous threats and present enormous challenges to the investigative and intelligence personnel who pursue them. Al-Qaeda and related operatives are committed to a cause: not just to their own personal interests, but to the interests of the 'brothers' (group) of Islam. They may be trained to withstand questioning and to utilize counter-interrogation techniques (Gunaratna 2001).

Various interrogation strategies have been employed with success against al-Qaeda-affiliated subjects since the first attack on the World Trade Center in 1993. These approaches were refined over the ensuing decade, incorporating lessons learnt along the way. They have proven effective in the interrogation and/or prosecutions of al-Qaeda terrorists associated with the Africa Embassy bombings in 1998, the attack on the *USS Cole* in 2000 and the 11 September 2001 attacks.

To date, the most extensive interviews with al-Qaeda operatives have been conducted with Sunni extremists from Middle Eastern Arab societies who are held in detainee status. Just as there are differences, however, in how one might approach a custodial versus a non-custodial interview, there may be features and effects of the detainee situation that are unique and may not generalize well to other kinds of law enforcement interviews with people of investigative concern.

Nevertheless, the collective experience of professionals involved in detainee interviews and interrogations may offer insights into the thinking and behaviours of al-Qaeda-related individuals, especially those who are from, or have roots in, Middle Eastern Arab countries. Knowledge about the expectations, communications and behaviours of these persons may aid other investigators to improve interrogation efforts. In addition, what has been learnt about gathering information from these people may inform the efforts of law enforcement and intelligence professionals who work with other al-Qaeda-related people (Einesman 1999).

To state immediately the central theme of this paper: a relationship/rapport-based approach with Middle Eastern Arab subjects who may be affiliated with al-Qaeda networks will generally result in more truthful and reliable information than will an aggressive approach. This is an approach that is advocated in almost all interrogations, not just with Middle Eastern subjects. The following guidelines are offered as an interrogation approach that works well with national security cases and criminal cases. In all instances where interrogation is conducted for the purpose of eliciting reliable and non-coerced confessions, a rapport-based approach is recommended. In the specific case of terrorism, in the opinion of the authors aggressive strategies have been ineffective and, whilst yielding information, the information is often not reliable or actionable. Aggressive and forceful interrogation of a subject who may be trained to anticipate torture and to resist questioning is likely to be counterproductive to the goal of eliciting accurate, reliable and useful information (Arrigo 2003).

Clearly differences exist between subjects of al-Qaeda-related terrorist investigations and subjects of other investigations more commonly conducted by law enforcement (Navarro 2002). This chapter seeks to highlight some of these differences and to provide some suggestions, based on experience, about how best to deal with them. The chapter offers background information and context for interrogating Middle Eastern Arab al-Qaeda-affiliated detainees and subjects of investigation. It also suggests what has been learnt about general interview approaches during detention. The chapter recommends ways to navigate interviews: preparation, development of rapport, development of themes, management of resistance, and detection of deception.

This is not a 'how to' chapter. There is much to be learnt about interrogation, especially with regard to strategies that take cognizance of the culture, background and expectations of the subject being interviewed (Gudjonnsson 2003). The goal of this chapter is to outline some themes and ideas that may result in more effective and useful interrogation strategies and practices.

Understanding contexts for interrogating subjects of al-Qaeda-related investigations

Successful strategies recognize that Arab culture is one that is built on relationships, oriented towards a larger collective, and focused on impression management (Nydell 2002). Within much Arab culture is an acceptance of conspiracy theories as a means of explaining the reasons behind certain events. Osama Bin Laden has reinforced these long-standing beliefs that Americans and Jews and their Western allies are seeking to control and dominate the Middle East and attack the faith of Islam. In accepting these theories, it could be said that al-Qaeda supporters and sympathizers have suspended critical thinking. They might have done so in order to find meaning, direction and structure through a strong affiliation with a radical Islamist view of the West and a commitment to the jihad (Borum and Gelles 2004).

Knowledge of these underlining factors may help an investigator to assess deception during an interrogation and to elicit accurate and useful information from al-Qaeda operatives and supporters. For example, many Middle Eastern Arab males think associatively. From a Western point of view, their thinking may appear to jump from point to point and from place to place in a discussion. Associative thinking differs from Western 'linear' thinking (Nydell 2002). Linear thinking is goal oriented, with one point following the next in logical order. Understanding the manner in which information is communicated is critical in analyzing the reliability and usefulness of information offered during an interview or interrogation.

Understanding motivation and the importance of relationship

In our exploration of the motivation of al-Qaeda-affiliated extremists, we must rely heavily on our own observations, assessments and experiences with subjects who have been captured, detained and interrogated. At the time of writing, there has been no systematic study of personal pathways to militant Islamist ideology or of recruitment into its terrorist factions. The existing social science literature and our own appraisals, however, do suggest several vulnerabilities that frequently appear in these subjects. Understanding these vulnerabilities may inform an examination of what may motivate these men to commit to an extremist view of Islam and to waging jihad against the West.

Perhaps we first should clarify that the constellation of these motivational themes does not comprise a 'profile' of the Islamic extremist. In fact, there is no such profile that can reliably be based on demographic, psychological or social characteristics (Borum *et al.* 2003). The extremists of whom we have knowledge come from a range of social classes and possess varying levels of intellect and education. Instead, the thematic consistency we have observed is that many of these men, prior to their involvement with militant Islamist ideas, were actively seeking meaning, direction, structure and connection in their lives. This pursuit often appeared to be related to their radicalization (Borum and Gelles 2004).

It is not uncommon to hear stories amongst al-Qaeda-affiliated detainees of how they were drawn into a jihadist group through others in their social network. Marc Sageman (2004) estimates that more than two thirds of his sample of al-Qaeda-associated extremists had already formed into a social collective (in Western terms 'a bunch of guys') before they committed their terrorist acts. Social networks and relationships are particularly powerful in collectivist societies – such as in Asian and Middle Eastern cultures – where Islam and the presence of al-Qaeda also tend to be most prevalent. People raised with collectivist values quite naturally and normatively see themselves (and other individuals) as being part of a larger meaningful cause. The identities and perceptions of self-worth amongst many in the Middle East – and to some extent in Asia –

are influenced strongly by the idea that 'who I am is part of whom I am with'. Seeking connections is critical in a world where one's value is defined by whom you know and who is in your network (in Arabic, *Wasta*; Cunningham and Sarayrah 1993). These priorities are distinctly different from traditional Western values that tend to emphasize individual achievement and self-worth (Nydell 2002).

Thus, in his quest for personal meaning, direction and structure (particularly in an environment where extremist sects and ideologies are prevalent), a man will often suspend critical thinking, commit to a particular mosque, leader or collective that advocates militant jihad and then, by making that commitment, develop the capabilities and connections to participate in potential terrorist attacks against Western interests (Borum and Gelles 2004). The extremist mosque is generally small, private and, in many cases, found just by happenstance. For example, one extremist told an interviewer that it just happened to be in his 'patch.' Once connected, however, they are powerful vehicles of jihadist ideology. Sageman (2004) found that nearly half of the 400 al-Qaeda extremists he studied came from just 10 mosques.

The mosque may provide a refuge from the turmoil of inner psychological conflicts and crisis. For all people, participating with a group meets an initial need for affiliation and belonging, particularly for those who have failed to affiliate and be validated elsewhere or who have not lived up to the expectations of their families (Luckabaugh *et al.* 1997). Islam – and jihadist ideology – provides structure, meaning and identity (Monroe and Kreidie 1997). *Shuriu* (Islamic law) and the teachings of the imam impart a needed structure, and the unequivocal rules are defined by the *Koran* and *Hadith*. Status is achieved through memorization of the *Koran*, not by analysis of ambiguities and nuances.

The radical collective fosters and maintains an unquestioning adherence to its tenets and to one another as 'brothers'. These individuals learn quickly that questioning beliefs leads to rejection, whilst embracing them reinforces the primary motive of affiliation and connectivity (Marsella 2003). Those who question may be marginalized or even shunned by others.

Understanding jihad and the history of Sunni extremism: the path to commitment

The Arabic language root of jihad (the verb *j-h-d*) is defined as 'to endeavor, strive, labor, take great pains' (*Dictionary of Modern*

Written Arabic). The noun form is sometimes – depending on one's perspective – defined as a great effort in the struggle to maintain the straight path of Islam. Bernard Lewis (2003), an eminent historian of Islam and the Middle East, notes the concept of jihad in the great majority of topics in the Arabic language, and the context of Islamic issues refers to a religious duty to wage holy war against infidels or non-believers, for the sake of God Almighty (Allah). Understandably, in the current context of radical Islam, some moderate Muslims have claimed that jihad is misunderstood in the West, and that the word and concept are intended to characterize the effort a Muslim must exert to live a good life. A fair reading, though, of orthodox Sunni and Shia teachings – even setting aside extremist variants – supports Lewis's contention that jihad almost always refers to the duty to fight against 'the enemies of Islam'. Modern-day extremists such as Osama Bin Laden have been profoundly influenced by the notion of this 'neglected duty' – i.e. jihad (*al-farida al-gha'iba*) – as were the Egyptian Islamist philosophers of the 1950s and 1960s, Sayyad Qutb and Muhammad al-Farraj. Qutb and al-Farraj averred that after faith in God (iman) and the belief in only one true God (tawhid), there is no more important duty for *all* Muslims than jihad against the unbelievers (Lewis 2003).

Within US government security and intelligence circles, discussions of Islamic extremism usually distinguish between the two major branches of the religion, Sunni and Shia. Militant extremism amongst Shia Muslims is most often associated in the Western public's mind with the Iranian US embassy hostage crisis of 1979, and with terrorist acts of the Lebanese Hizballah. In contrast to the current form of Sunni extremism, Shia terrorism has been motivated primarily by nationalist objectives, not by strivings for a worldwide Islamic utopia (Ridell and Cotterell 2003).

In the current security environment, however, there is consensus amongst counterterrorism experts and policy-makers, at least in America, that Sunni extremism currently poses the greatest threat to Western interests. The voice of these jihadists is most aptly represented in the words and deeds of al-Qaeda and its associated groups, and of men such as Osama Bin Laden, Ayman al-Zawahiri and a number of lesser known shaykhs. These jihadist groups and the men behind them have a rigid view of Islam and have little tolerance for those whose beliefs diverge from them. They oppose Jews, Christians and less devout Muslims (Borum and Gelles 2004). Their world is divided between 'us' and 'them'. The proponents of this ideology, including Sayyad Qutb, Muhammad 'Abd al-Salam al-Farraj and

'Abdallah Azzam, as well as their contemporary counterparts such as Bin Laden, believe two competing forces seek to dominate the condition of the world. Since the time the *Koran* was revealed to the Prophet Muhammad, the states of Dar al-Islam (the abode of Islam) and Dar al-Harb (abode of war or conflict) have been in conflict and will remain so until the end of time (Lewis 2003).

In the current state of Dar al-Harb, true believers of Islam are impelled to wage defensive jihad in order to reclaim lands once under the control of pious Muslims. These territories include parts of Spain and other areas of Europe 'up to the gates of Rome' and, of course, Israel. Once Muslims reclaim the land, then the struggle (jihad) moves to an offensive mode of conquest to ensure the remainder of the world is safe for Islam. In recent times, the USA has been viewed as the primary opponent in the Dar al-Harb because al-Qaeda and recognized Sunni religious leaders believe it has sided and conspired 'against Muslims' in numerous conflicts around the world (e.g. Israel, East Timor, Serbia, the South Philippines, etc.) (Lewis 2003).

Sunni extremism, however, is not a monolithic movement. It includes a number of different groups with varying philosophies. For example, the Salafiun or the Salafi (an affiliation claimed by many in al-Qaeda), are part of a modern reform movement of Islam, founded by the Egyptian Muhammad 'Abduh (1849–1905). Salafism was preceded by the doctrine of Muhammad Ibn 'Abd al-Wahhab (currently referred to as 'Wahhabism' or Unitarians), another fundamental ideology.[1]

The severity and exclusiveness of the Salafiun and the earlier extremist Wahhabiun are arguably surpassed by movements such as Takfir wal-Hijra and Takfir wal-Hikma. The principal adherents to this highly militant brand of extremism tend to be concentrated in Algeria, Morocco and Tunisia. The 'takfiris' believe that the pre-eminent jihad calls for the death, first and foremost, of Muslims born of the faith but who reject their narrowly literal application of the *Koran* and the *Hadith*. This has been referred to as a sort of modern-day 'outing' movement in the sense that takfiris have a duty to identify and accuse non-takfiri Muslims of being non-Muslim. From Egyptian president Husni Mubarrak to the entirety of Shia Islam, all have been designated by takfiris as deserving nothing less than death for their un-Islamic ways (Elliott 2004).

It is important to emphasize that to conduct an interrogation of a subject with an extremist ideology and a commitment to jihad, the interviewer must have some understanding of the subject's ideology and the history associated with his thinking, commitments and beliefs if he or she is to manage an interview better. In a rapport-based approach it is critical to demonstrate respect for the subject. Without a knowledge of the subject's ideology it is difficult to interpret and manage the subject during the interview. The content of his communications will reflect where he stands, when he is being co-operative and when he is using his beliefs to engage in a personal jihad during the course of the interrogation. For some subjects, resisting the interrogator is a continuance of his personal jihad. During the course of an interrogation, adherence to his beliefs reinforces the subject's expectations about the interrogator that influence his perceptions of the interrogator. He may use his beliefs to provoke the interrogator to react in a manner that confirms his established or preconceived expectation of the interrogator as an apostate and infidel. We have found that, by understanding his beliefs, we are better able to anticipate his communications and provocations, to react neutrally with a degree of respect and, eventually, to erode his expectations and perceptions through a rapport-based approach.

A final caveat before moving on to more direct interrogation strategies is to address the issue of competing identities. Competing identities is a concept that is applied to individuals who are born, and to some degree raised, in a country that is different from where they reside and where they have been detained. Many people from the Middle East immigrate to Western and first-world industrialized nations. These people are different from people who have lived their whole lives in their native country and who therefore reflect more strongly that country's ethnic and cultural behaviours and attitudes. An individual who has lived in the West and, in particular has lived most of his life in the West will have assimilated some of the characteristics of his new-found homeland. This will, of course, vary based on the length of time he has lived in a Western country, the community he has lived in and the manner in which he has been raised. In many cases the degree of assimilation can be assessed by where people live, the peer group they have interacted with and the diversity of their experiences beyond the more ethnic or cultural activities indigenous to their native country. For example, we have found during the course of an interrogation that people who have lived in the West for a considerable period of time have a more in-depth understanding of Westerners and therefore a different set of expectations. Additionally, depending on the degree of assimilation to Western thought and activities, immigrants from the Middle East who become subjects of terrorist investigations and interrogations tend to be more linear in their thinking. In some cases, the interrogations are easier if the subject has lived in the West for a considerable period of time; in other cases, more difficult, based on the subject's expectation of what will occur and his knowledge of the laws.

Foundations of the rapport-based interview approach

The cornerstone of an interrogation that will yield the most reliable information is an effective, ongoing assessment of the subject. Before and during the interviews, the interview team should evaluate factors that are unique to the subject, or at least that distinguish him from other individuals who may be the subject of al-Qaeda-related investigations.

A rapport-building (or relationship-based) approach will yield the best results in an interview/interrogation that occurs over days/ weeks/months. Rapport building is designed to develop a common understanding and respect between the interviewer and subject. The interviewer works to build a bond between the two of them based on commonalities and shared experiences in the interview room.

Although sometimes difficult to do, the interviewer should exhibit at least an apparent empathy for the subject's beliefs, motivations and circumstances. Such an approach facilitates the information gathering process for two reasons. First, people tend to share their experiences with someone who is empathic, who values them and who, they feel, can understand them (Schafer and Navarro 2004). Secondly, the importance of relationships is fundamental to many people raised or with roots in the Middle East (Nydell 2002) – relationships are a vital part of a subject's developmental and cultural experience. The relationship that develops during hours spent together between interviewer and subject may, in certain cases, approach or approximate a friendship. That friendship may be genuine or contrived, but the interviewer's goal is always to elicit truthful and reliable information.

Whilst a relationship-based approach has generally been most effective with al-Qaeda-related subjects, individual cases may require a different strategy. No single interrogation or debriefing technique will be successful in all situations. Interrogators tailor their approach to an interview and interrogation based on the current context and the background of the witness or subject. Ongoing assessment of continuously collected information about a subject's behaviour and ideology will assist in identifying or creating moments of vulnerability for optimal elicitation. Each interviewee requires an individualized approach that is dynamic and modified according to behavioural data collected from different sources (Schafer and Navarro 2004). The interviewer should build flexibility into any interview plan. Changes in interview strategies and techniques should be guided by data from the ongoing assessment.

Preparing for the interview

The attributes generally seen as desirable for a law enforcement interrogator (e.g. good intelligence, an understanding of human nature, an ability to get along well with others, patience and persistence) apply equally to interrogations of al-Qaeda detainees. There are some other specific considerations, however, that can affect the 'fit' between interviewer and a Middle Eastern Arab al-Qaeda-related subject. For example, age should be a consideration when matching or assigning an interviewer to a subject because of Arabic respect for elders and seniority (Nydell 2002). (The more experienced interviewers should similarly be assigned to those subjects who, it is believed, have the most important information). In general, care should be given to selecting an interviewer who can relate to the subject. If possible, the interviewer should speak the subject's native language (or at least know some key terms of the language).

Interrogations are most productive when the interrogator and subject can be paired consistently. Arabic people tend to respond best when interviewed by the same interrogator rather than with a round robin or 'whoever is available' assignment process (Nydell 2002). Consistency allows the interrogator to become familiar with the subject's history and to see how he responds to various questions and approaches. The subjects of investigations are not mechanical objects who can be turned on to pump out information. They require constant care and understanding if they are to respond.

Members of the interview team should read all the available background information and be aware of all evidence seized with or associated with the subject. Sometimes 'pocket litter' in the subject's possession at the time of apprehension, evidence seized during searches and statements from others can be helpful in assessing who the subject is (if his identity is in doubt) or what he has been doing. Pocket litter may also help to corroborate or disconfirm the subject's statements and to help the interviewer assess whether the subject is being deceptive.

Collateral informants can also be a valuable source of information. Arresting officers, guards, corrections officers or other law enforcement professionals who have observed the subject's behaviour can assist the interviewer/interrogator to understand the subject. Correctional or detention staff, in particular, can provide information about how the subject behaves in detention and can help measure the impact of the prison environment on an interrogation plan. In a custodial environment, guards see and spend more time with a subject than does an interviewer. Therefore, they may be in an excellent position to monitor a subject's behaviour and to observe comments and activities. Observations by the guards about whether a subject keeps to himself, gets support and counsel from others, about how and what he communicates to others, what he likes to eat, whether he exercises, etc., can greatly assist the interviewers in formulating interview strategies and building relationships with the subject (Walters 2002).

The interrogator should not impose a time limit on an interview or an expectation of the frequency of interviews. The length of the interviews should vary. Having a set, routine block of time for interviews allows a subject to anticipate events better and thus to attempt to manipulate the interrogator and the process. For example, if in a confined setting interviewing takes place for a specified amount of time for each subject, the remaining detainees can anticipate how long they will need to defend themselves and can practise steeling themselves to outlast the interviewer.

Operating with a translator

If a translator is needed, the translator's role must be clearly defined and continually reinforced so that he or she does not slide into the role of a surrogate interrogator. The interviewers must control the interrogation, not the interpreters. The interpreter must appear subordinate to the interviewer – someone working with and for the interviewer. As a practical matter, some have found it helpful to have the translator sit behind the subject.

Developing rapport

Developing rapport involves more than simply 'being nice' to a subject or giving him what he wants just to gain information. It requires a series of give-and-take interactions, under circumstances controlled by the interviewer. The interrogator needs to engage the subject in an extended conversation and to develop a relationship that helps to provide insight into the subject's motivations and, perhaps, deceptive practices or resistance techniques if he or she is to elicit accurate information (Walters 2002).

To build rapport, the interviewer engages in dialogue with the subject, during which he or she identifies and assesses potential motivations, interests and vulnerabilities. Rapport is founded on a *quid pro quo* basis (the perceived ability of an interviewer to help the subject), on commonalities (family, wife, education, adversity), personality and mutual respect. Often, rapport-based approaches include adversarial arguments, disagreements, admonishments, criticism and challenging questions. These are always tempered with the fact that the subject knows that the interviewer is concerned about his future and is fair to him (Schafer and Navarro 2004).

In a rapport-based interview process, the interviewer shapes the relationship, using a variety of interpersonal, cognitive and emotional strategies and techniques, to gain critical information – or a confession – from the subject. The subject shares critical information with the interviewer because this collaborative relationship with the interrogator leads him to value the relationship more than the information he is perhaps trying to withhold.

At the beginning of the relationship, questions of an investigative nature are purposely avoided. This is done to allow the subject and the interviewer to develop a bond on matters unrelated to the investigation. News unrelated to terrorism that may be of interest to the subject has served as a good ice-breaker – for example, news about the World Cup. Offers of food and beverages may be used to build goodwill and, later, to be used as an incentive. Another productive line of inquiry involves having the subject talk about his country of origin and the interviewer showing an interest in learning about his country. In some cases, subjects have seemed particularly interested in maps and graphics (such as National Geographic maps). These might be used to point out significant cities/towns/villages and paths of travel.

Regardless of an interviewer's own style, it is important to remember that a major goal of relationship building is for the subject to see the interviewer as a person (a 'Rob' rather than as an enemy). If a subject sees an interviewer as a person rather than an instrument of an 'enemy' government, when the subject refuses to talk, lies or is deceitful, he is offending that personal relationship. Because the relationship may matter more to the subject at the time than 'doing his duty against the enemy' (as he may have been trained to do), he may choose to share accurate information with the interview team.

Gathering information

The interview team should approach each interview with positive expectations. The interrogator – and team – should enter every interview session with confidence that, over time, they will make a breakthrough with the subject. As noted above, rapport is probably the single most important element in creating a climate for eliciting information. The interviewer should not engage in a sensitive or probing inquiry at the beginning of the interview process or at the beginning of an individual session. This should only be done once rapport has been established or re-established. When getting to the essence of the interrogation, the interviewer should focus on the general and work towards the specific, all the while emphasizing the relationship – that is, the interviewer should concentrate on the relationship before mining for facts.

Once initial rapport has been established, a technique that has worked well for some investigators is to listen to the subject's story with what appears to be an open mind. The interviewer should listen carefully both for content and for emotional and motivational cues. With such active listening, the interviewer can learn about the subject's primary motivations (Walters 2002) (e.g. concerns about family, a son, a daughter, wife, money, coming to the West in the future, spreading the word of Islam or fatigue with the 'jihad life', etc.).

During the initial storytelling phase, the interviewer does not interrupt or criticize as the subject lays out what may, in reality, be his cover story. Once he has laid out his full story, the interviewer can go back and ask him to go over it again in more detail and in a systematic manner, perhaps alternating queries from the general to the specific (Walters 2002).

In reviewing the story, the interviewer should ask detailed questions about every element. It may be that the subject will attempt to give as little information as possible to satisfy the interviewer. The challenge, then, is to identify meaningful, important or inconsistent details and sequences from the subject's outline or story. The greater the level of the detail queried, the greater the likelihood that the subject will eventually 'stumble' over errors or inconsistencies in his cover story. Questions need to be very specific to guard against omission. This process may seem tedious – asking ten questions when it should only take two – but it is an important part of gathering reliable and accurate information.

In the detailed inquiry phase, the interviewer should insert or suggest some type of context or time-line reference, possibly using as markers, seasons and Islamic holidays rather than Western calendar dates if the subject has not lived in the West or is not familiar with Western conventions about dates and time. When establishing locations with some subjects, the interviewer might use geographic descriptors: direction of prayer, geographic landmarks, valleys, rivers, mountains, lakes, etc. (e.g. along the road, across a bridge over a river, then along the riverbank).

When a timeline has been established, the interviewer should have the subject explain all the details provided across the timeline. As noted earlier, a Middle Eastern Arab male's usual way of thinking is associative rather than linear. Holding him to a 'common sense' timeline of when various events happened may increase the conflict he experiences if he is giving a cover story. The subject may not be able to maintain consistency in the details of a fabricated timeline. Recognizing the subject's inconsistencies and confronting him with these in the context of a relationship that has developed between the subject and the interviewer may force the subject to recognize that the interviewer knows he is not telling the truth.

Finally, the interview team should develop skills in assessing non-verbal cues (Knapp and Hall 1997). There should be a mechanism for members of the team to report significant observations to the interrogator. Some reactions, such as 'cotton mouth' (i.e. the white foamy saliva that collects at the corners of the mouth), are autonomic or physiological responses and may be regarded as stress reactions common to all peoples. Other non-verbal behaviours, such as crossing one's arms or glancing away, may have particular cultural meanings.

Developing themes

Much interrogation theory and practice relies heavily on the strategy of 'theme development'. In the West, a 'theme' is an excuse or justification for behaviour that the subject can acknowledge to save face. Theme development in Western criminal interrogation often involves mitigating the subject's fear and/or guilt by helping the subject to justify the behaviour in his or her own mind or by diverting blame (e.g. to another person or to uncontrollable circumstances) (Inbau et al. 2001). These themes may require substantial modification for use with subjects of Middle Eastern Arab al-Qaeda-related investigations.

Al-Qaeda operatives, members and supporters may not feel shame or guilt in the Western sense for what they believe or for what they have done. If they experience shame, it may be out of concern for what parents, family or others they respect are thinking about them. Other than this, Middle Eastern Arab subjects of al-Qaeda-related investigations are unlikely to feel shame as it is conceived in the West. Instead, they may feel honoured for what they have done or not done (for example, co-operated with the interrogators). The interviewer should understand and at least acknowledge a subject's sense of honour.

It is generally not productive for the interviewer to try to manipulate Western feelings of shame. If appropriate, however, the interviewer may express concern for the 'trouble' caused to the family at home or to others in the subject's relationship world.

Other modifications of traditional interrogation practices may be required to develop themes of 'justification' or themes not based on the subject's anxiety or negative emotions. For example, one common interrogation strategy is to confront the subject with information that is inconsistent with what he has said. It is believed, however, that people affiliated with al-Qaeda often suspend critical thinking. They ignore information that contradicts their beliefs. Thus confronting a subject who has justified his actions by referring to the *Koran* with opposing viewpoints similarly based upon a study of the *Koran* may be ineffective. In general, it is not helpful or productive to argue with the subject about religion or to engage in a battle of wits (or quotes) regarding Islam. Instead, the interviewer can emphasize that he or she is determined to understand fully the matters at hand and is prepared to spend the time to do so. These matters – will and time – are squarely in the interviewer's domain.

Other traditional Western interrogation strategies involve the condemnation of accomplices or playing subjects off against their co-offenders (Leo 1996). Amongst members of al-Qaeda, however, loyalty to the brotherhood is paramount. Confronting a subject with the statements of another co-operating subject is not likely to be effective, especially in the early stages of an interrogation.

The strength of the relationship between interviewer and subject is critical as the interview team develops themes that may facilitate disclosure of concealed information. At this point, the interview may assume some characteristics common to a negotiation. Two points are central. First, when the relationship has developed effectively, the subject becomes dependent on the interviewer. The interviewer is in control of what happens, and the subject is aware of this. Secondly, because the interviewer maintains the real power, he or she is in a position to do favours or to grant requests. Accordingly, the subject's disclosure of information often evolves on a *quid pro quo* basis.

Favours, privileges or honoured requests should be contingent upon the subject's co-operation. By granting/attempting to grant a request, the interviewer makes the subject feel obligated to 'repay the favour' (e.g. to co-operate with the interrogation process). The interviewer should expect and ask for a *quid pro quo*, whereby the subject demonstrates an appropriately co-operative response.

Managing resistance

The interview team needs to prepare for resistance. The team should have a plan for dealing with subjects who refuse to answer questions. For example, a subject who is supported by his network in a detention facility is likely to be prepared and to have several strategies that he plans to employ as resistance in the initial phases of the interview. The interviewer and support team need to be prepared to work through these resistances.

Recognizing and managing deception

Subjects of al-Qaeda-related investigations may lie or may try to conceal information at some point in the interview, particularly at the beginning when given the open-ended opportunity to tell their story. It is critical, whenever possible, to recognize and address possibly deceptive communications.

False information provided by a subject may lead to significant fiscal and personnel resources being wasted. Time and energy are expended on attempts to corroborate inaccurate reports or to deal with non-existing threats. Disinformation may also obscure potentially real threats by creating a confusing intelligence picture.

Moreover, if a subject lies successfully to the interviewer, the interviewer will lose credibility and the subject's respect. Subsequent information provided by the subject will be less and less valuable. The subject learns that that he can deceive without any consequences and will be motivated to continue to manipulate and lie.

The interviewer must recognize the lie (if possible) and not tolerate it. The key objective is to condition the subject to tell the truth. When the subject attempts deception, omission or other straying, the interviewer should discuss the fact that what the subject is saying is illogical or does not make sense, and should work to get the subject to acknowledge this. If the subject digresses or attempts to obfuscate (an anti-interrogation technique), the interrogator should firmly and immediately redirect him. When confronted with generalities or inconsistencies, the interviewer can attempt to force the content into a timeline, offering facts that refute what a subject is saying and slowly and incrementally backing him into a corner of admission. In the context of the relationship that has been developed, the interviewer may exhibit disappointment or express a sense of feeling disrespected for being provided with false information.

Conclusion

In this chapter we have outlined an approach for interviewing subjects of al-Qaeda-related investigations. The rapport-based approach described here appears to be the best and most effective approach to elicit reliable and accurate strategic information. Whilst there is debate regarding the use of more aggressive tactics in the face of critical intelligence that might impact on a nation's security and safety, it is our opinion such techniques are morally and strategically inappropriate. Moreover, how we choose to treat suspects may affect how Westerner suspects are treated. Even in the popular 'ticking time bomb' scenario (Dershowitz 2002), aggressive tactics that humiliate, intimidate and cause physical pain and suffering, in our opinion, are unlikely to be effective. Such mistreatment merely reinforces the jihadists' expectations of Western abuses. Of course, some subjects may provide information in response to aggressive tactics, but the information may be unreliable and misleading. Nevertheless, such tactics may at times be employed in ticking-bomb scenarios in a desperate attempt to do something rather than nothing.

When possible, it is held in this chapter that the use of a relationship-based approach is more likely to yield accurate and useful information. The essence of this approach is to lever the relationship between the subject and interrogator. Its tone typically is not sympathetic and supportive but, rather, direct and at times confrontational. The interrogator begins strategic inquiry only after rapport and a relationship have been established. This general approach has been effective in many terrorism investigations and has often produced reliable and actionable information that could be corroborated, validated and subsequently used at trial.

Note

1. See Dore Gold's *Hatred's Kingdom* for the accounts of the plundering of and killing in Shia cities of Najaf and Karbala c. 1799–1803 by the descendents of the Muhammad Ibn 'Abd al-Wahhab and the Muhammad Ibn Sa'ud alliance. This early period of 'Wahhabism' was characterized by death and destruction in the name of God, and not just for the worst of the apostates. According to this belief system, those deserving of death included Shia and Sunni 'brothers' in Mecca and Medina who would challenge the Wahhabi brand of Islam.

References

Arrigo, J. (2003) 'A consequentialist argument against torture interrogation of terrorists.' Paper presented at the Joint Services Conference on Professional Ethics, 30–31 January, Springfield, VA (retrieved online 23 September 2004 at http://www.usafa.af.mil/jscope/JSCOPE03/Arrigo03.html).

Borum, R. (2004) 'Counterterrorism training post-9/11', in R. Gunaratna (ed.) *The Changing Face of Terrorism*. Singapore: Eastern Universities Press.

Borum, R., Fein, R., Vossekuil, B. and Gelles, M. (2003) 'Profiling hazards: profiling in counterterrorism and homeland security', *Counterterrorism and Homeland Security Reports*, 10: 12–13.

Borum, R., Fein, R., Vossekuil, B., Gelles, M. and Shumate, S. (2004) 'The role of operational research in counterterrorism', *International Journal of Intelligence and Counterintelligence*, 17: 420–34.

Borum, R. and Gelles, M. (2004) 'Al-Qaeda's organizational and operational evolution' (manuscript under review).

Cunningham, R. and Sarayrah, Y. (1993) *Wasta: The Hidden Force in Middle Eastern Society*. Wesport, CT: Praeger.

Dershowitz, A. (2002) 'Torture of terrorists: is it necessary to do and to lie about it?', in *Shouting Fire: Civil Liberties in a Turbulent Age*. Boston, MA: Little, Brown.

Einesman, F. (1999) 'Confessions and culture: the interaction of Miranda and diversity', *Journal of Criminal Law and Criminology*, 90.

Elliott, M. (2004) Hate club: Al-Qaeda's web of terror. Accessed online August 13, 2004 at http://www.time.com/time/nation/article/0,8599,182746,00.html

Gudjonnsson, G. (2003) *The Psychology of Interrogations and Confessions: A Handbook*. New York, NY: Wiley.

Hoffman, B. (1999) *Inside Terrorism*. New York, NY: Columbia University Press.

Inbau, F., Reid, J., Buckley, J. and Jayne, B. (2001) *Criminal Interrogation and Confessions* (4th edn). Gaithersburg, MD: Aspen.

Knapp, M. and Hall, J. (1997) *Nonverbal Communication in Human Interaction* (4th edn). Orlando, FL: Harcourt Brace.

Laqueur, W. (1999) *The New Terrorism*. New York, NY: Oxrord University Press.

Leo, R. (1996) 'Inside the interrogation room', *Journal of Criminal Law and Criminology*, 86: 266.

Lewis, B. (2003) *The Crisis of Islam: Holy War and Unholy Terror*. New York, NY: Modern Library.

Luckabaugh, R., Fuqua, H.E., Cangemi, J.P. and Kowalski, C.J. (1997) 'Terrorist behavior and United States Foreign Policy: Who is the enemy?: Some psychological and political perspectives', *Psychology*, 34(2): 1–15.

Marsella, A.J. (2003) 'Terrorism: reflections on issues, concepts, and directions', in F.M. Moghaddam and A.J. Marsella (eds) *Understanding Terrorism: Psychosocial Roots, Consequents and Interventions*.

Monroe, K.R. and Kreidic, L.H. (1997) 'The perspective of Islamic fundamentalists and the limits of rational choice theory', *Political Psychology*, 18(1): 19–43, 11–48. Washington, DC: American Psychological Association.

Navarro, J. (2002) 'Interacting with Arabs and Muslims', *FBI Law Enforcement Bulletin*, 71: 20.

Nydell, M. (2002) *Understanding Arabs: A Guide for Westerners* (3rd edn). Yarmouth, MA: Intercultural Press.

Riddell, P. and Cotterell, P. (2003) *Islam in Context: Past, Present, and Future*. Grand Rapids, MI: Baker Academic.

Sageman, M. (2004) *Understanding Terror Networks*. University of Pennsylvania Press.

Schafer, J. and Navarro, J. (2004) *Advanced Interviewing Techniques: Proven Strategies for Law Enforcement* Springfield, IL: Charles C. Thomas.

Simon, S. (2003) 'The new terrorism: Securing the nation against a messianic foe', *Brookings Review*, 21: 18–24.

Walters, S. (2002) *Principles of Kinesic Interview and Interrogation* (2nd edn). Boca Raton, FL: CRC Press.

White, J. (2003) *Defending the Homeland: Domestic Intelligence, Law Enforcement, and Security*. New York, NY: Wadsworth.

Chapter 3

American interrogation methods in the war on terror

David Rose

This chapter is based on my work as an investigative reporter who has specialized in the coverage of criminal justice, intelligence and human rights for many years. In October 2003, I visited the US detention camp at Guantánamo Bay, Cuba, where I interviewed guards, doctors and other officials, including Major-General Geoffrey Miller, then Guantánamo's commandant. I followed this up with further interviews with intelligence officials in America and with a study of formerly classified memoranda on interrogation from the White House, Defense Department and Justice Department. These were published by the administration in May 2004, in the wake of the disclosure of the abuse of detainees at Abu Ghraib, Iraq.[1] Finally, I was able to conduct long interviews with four British Guantánamo detainees who were released in March 2004 – Shafiq Rasul, Asif Iqbal, Rhuhel Ahmed and Tarek Dergoul. This chapter argues that, since 2001, during the so-called 'Global War on Terror', US interrogators have used a variety of coercive techniques which had previously been abandoned by most democratic societies. These techniques, it suggests, contravene both the international law of war and the laws and Constitution of the USA. However, they have not produced (to use Major-General Miller's phrase) 'enormously valuable intelligence'. In practical terms, they can be considered to have been a failure.

As they reeled from the shock of the terrorist attacks on New York and Washington of 11 September 2001, it was swiftly apparent both to America's political leadership and its intelligence chiefs that they were ill-equipped to deal with their enemy. Although some clues to the impending blow had crossed the intelligence radar screen, and there was a vague and generalized awareness that the Islamist network known as al-Qaeda sought to attack American targets, 9/11 took the USA by surprise (National Commission on Terrorist Attacks upon the United States 2004). Moreover, its intelligence agencies were both structurally and operationally deficient to deal with further threats of this type. Since the end of the Vietnam War, the HUMINT (human intelligence) skills of agent recruitment, debriefing and prisoner interrogation had been neglected in favour of SIGINT (intelligence derived from electronic interception) and what American military intelligence termed CEWI (combat electronic warfare intelligence). As the British had learnt long before in Northern Ireland, these techniques are, by definition, of limited use against well organized terrorist conspiracies. 'We became over-enamoured with technology, and failed to teach people skills,' Lieutenant-Colonel Anthony Christino, a 20-year-old intelligence officer who worked at the heart of the Pentagon's intelligence effort in the war on terror, told me in an interview. According to Christino, by mid-2004 (after his own retirement) there were simply *no* military intelligence personnel of officer rank in the US army who specialized in interrogation. A similar neglect was also apparent within the CIA.

Against this background, American intelligence found itself handicapped more specifically in attempting to penetrate terrorist networks based in the wilder parts of rural Asia. Just a month before the attacks, the former CIA officer Reuel Marc Gerecht warned that US intelligence was dangerously reliant on agents who worked under the comfortable cover of day jobs in embassies, and that its staff had long been reluctant to accept assignments where dysentery was likely to be an operational hazard (Gerecht 2001). At the same time, as a senior German official later told me, 'you cannot recruit a convinced and fanatical jihadi,' and attempts to do so might easily result in the death of the would-be recruiter. In the wounded, shocked and vengeful climate which enveloped the USA in the wake of 9/11, these handicaps drove policy-makers to seek to fill intelligence gaps using all available means. One of their principal methods rapidly became coercive interrogations of prisoners. At every location in the global war on terror, from Washington, DC to Afghanistan, previous restraints on the treatment of prisoners were reconsidered, and in significant ways abandoned.

During the late spring of 2004, a series of leaks to the US media persuaded the administration to publish much of the internal legal paper trail which preceded and endorsed the introduction of such methods. Its first important milestone was a memo dated 9 January

2002, by the then Deputy Assistant Attorney-General John Yoo to the Pentagon's general counsel, William J. Haynes. 'Restricting the President's plenary power over military operations (including the treatment of prisoners) would be constitutionally dubious,' Yoo wrote. Even at this early stage, the administration was prepared to consider disregarding the hitherto sacrosanct provisions of the Third Geneva Convention of 1949, whose Article 17 states:

> No physical or mental torture, nor any other form of coercion, may be inflicted on prisoners of war to secure from them information of any kind whatever. Prisoners of war who refuse to answer may not be threatened, insulted, or exposed to unpleasant or disadvantageous treatment of any kind.

Two days after Yoo wrote his memo, Guantánamo accepted its first prisoner transport from Afghanistan, where the Taliban regime had recently been crushed. Over the following three weeks, an intense debate raged within the administration. Eventually, the Pentagon and Justice Department were able to defeat the arguments made by Colin Powell and his colleagues at the State Department, who said that to abandon Geneva would place captured US troops at risk in future conflicts. On 7 February 2002, President Bush formally announced that America did not consider itself bound by Geneva in respect of detainees at Guantánamo, nor in its treatment of Taliban and al-Qaeda detainees elsewhere. Having been 'captured on the battlefield' of the war on terror, these prisoners were to be designated 'unlawful combatants',[2] and therefore did not deserve the convention's shield. The USA would, Bush said, respect the 'spirit' of the convention, but even this was qualified – this indefinable quality would only be observed 'so far as military necessity allows'. There would be no tribunals to determine whether detainees really had been terrorists or unlawful combatants, as Geneva's Article 5 appears to require in the case of irregular fighters of all kinds. At the stroke of a pen, the international law of war had effectively been cast aside.

The implications of this decision, and of Yoo's doctrine of unrestricted presidential power, were developed over the next few months by a broad interagency group chaired by Jay S. Bybee, then Assistant Attorney-General. Its classified report was issued on 1 August 2002. When this was leaked almost two years later, and its frank readiness to countenance torture revealed, the White House claimed the document was 'irrelevant', saying it would now be 'rewritten'. No rewritten version has, at the time of writing in

December 2004, emerged. Large parts of its text and analysis were to be reproduced verbatim in subsequent memos drawn up at the Pentagon.

Bybee and his colleagues appear not to have questioned the premise that torture and coercion will be more effective at finding out what a prisoner knows than other forms of interrogation. Having accepted this, the memorandum sought to establish an extremely narrow view of what torture meant. If the pain inflicted were physical, it 'must rise to the level of death, organ failure, or the permanent impairment of a significant bodily function'. If it were mental, 'it must result in significant psychological harm of significant duration, e.g., lasting for months or even years'. According to the memo, America's domestic law against torture, a Congressional Act of 1994 and the UN Convention against Torture to which the USA was a signatory 'prohibit only the most extreme forms of physical or mental harm'. Anything less would be merely 'cruel, inhuman or degrading treatment'. Whilst this too was banned by the convention, those responsible for such treatment would not be liable to criminal penalties.

Bybee and his colleagues based this definition – which was reproduced in many subsequent documents – on the fact that both the American statute and the UN convention described torture as the infliction of 'severe' pain, but did not specify what 'severe' meant. They went on to adopt a curious reading of the definition in Webster's dictionary, which lists the meanings of 'severe' pain as 'hard to endure; sharp; afflictive; distressing; violent; extreme'. They were clearly being highly selective, for pain might well be sharp, afflictive and hard to endure without rising to the level of organ failure or death – indeed, there would be little point in administering any coercive technique if it were *easy* to endure. Bybee's team therefore tried to buttress their definition from a strange source: US laws governing the payment of health insurance benefits. These laws, the memo stated, 'treat severe pain as an indicator of ailments that are likely to result in permanent and serious physical damage in the absence of immediate medical treatment'. If insurance companies had to pay out in cases where patients were at risk of organ failure or death, their logic ran, then to count as torture the methods used by interrogators 'must rise to a similarly high level'.

Echoing the argument made by Yoo, the memo went on to state that it would be improper to rule *any* interrogation method out, because any attempt to apply the law in a way which would interfere with the President's right to determine the conduct of a war would be unconstitutional: 'As Commander-in-Chief, the President has the constitutional authority to order interrogations of enemy combatants to gain intelligence information about the plans of the enemy.' These powers were:

> especially pronounced in the middle of a war in which the nation has already suffered a direct attack... it may be that only successful interrogations can provide the information necessary to prevent the success of covert terrorist attacks on the United States and its citizens. Congress can no more interfere with the President's conduct of interrogations of enemy combatants than it can dictate strategy or tactical decisions on the battlefield.

Moreover, if an interrogator were later to be accused of torture, he or she would have two lines of defence: that it was 'necessary' to prevent a terrorist attack or that it had been performed in self-defence.

Against this background, from October 2002 until April 2003, the Pentagon and its lawyers developed a menu of coercive techniques for Guantánamo and other detention camps in response to requests for guidance as to what might be permissible. 'We'd been at this for a year-plus and got nothing out of them,' one official told the *Wall Street Journal*. 'We need[ed] to have a less-cramped view of what torture is and is not.' Before the official menu was developed, 'people were trying like hell to ratchet up the pressure', and had used methods which included placing women's underwear on prisoners' heads. On 11 October 2002, the interrogators' frustration at their lack of success was set down in a memo passed up the chain of command from Guantánamo's Lieutenant Colonel Jerald Phifer. 'PROBLEM,' he wrote. 'The current guidelines for interrogation procedures at GTMO limit the ability of interrogators to counter advanced resistance.'

Their difficulties stemmed from the standard rulebook for American military interrogators, a document known as *Field Manual 34-52*, which begins with a clear prohibition against the use of coercive techniques: 'The use of force, mental torture, threats, insults, or exposure to unpleasant and inhumane treatment of any kind is prohibited by law and is neither authorized nor condoned by the US Government.' Not only is this unnecessary, the manual states, it is ineffective: 'The use of force is a poor technique, as it yields unreliable results, may damage subsequent collection efforts, and can induce the source to say whatever he thinks the interrogator wants to hear.' The manual does authorize psychological techniques, including deception and inducing fear. But in the war on terror, wrote Phifer, they were not enough to break resistance. He sought authorization for a range of 'category two' techniques, including prolonged solitary confinement, to be given in successive doses of 30 days at a time; the use of painful 'stress positions,' in which prisoners would be forced to stand or sit chained doubled up for hours; continuous interrogations for periods of up to 20 hours; the removal of clothing; and 'forced grooming' (shaving of facial hair, etc.). He also asked for permission to 'use detainees' individual phobias (such as fear of dogs) to induce stress'.

Even these methods would not always be sufficient, Phifer wrote. He also sought permission for still tougher 'category three' techniques, which were 'required for a very small percentage of the most uncooperative detainees' and 'may be utilized in a carefully coordinated manner to help interrogate exceptionally resistant detainees'. They included convincing a detainee that 'death or severely painful consequences are imminent for him and/or his family', exposure to both water and extreme cold and, perhaps most horrifying of all, 'use of a wet towel and dripping water to induce the misperception of suffocation'. The CIA calls this technique 'water-boarding,' and has reportedly deployed it against 'high value' terrorist prisoners in places other than Guantánamo. In China, Pinochet's Chile, Robert Mugabe's Zimbawe and elsewhere it has more usually been termed 'the submarine'.

Defence Secretary Donald Rumsfeld issued his response to Phifer's request on 27 November 2002. Having discussed it with his deputy, Paul Wolfowitz, Under Secretary Douglas Feith and General Richard Myers, Chairman of the Joint Chiefs of Staff, he was prepared to authorize all the 'category two' techniques, including forcible shaving, dogs, the replacement of hot meals with cold military rations, the removal of all 'comfort items', even copies of the *Koran*, and stress positions. 'I stand for 8–10 hours,' Rumsfeld scrawled at the bottom of his order. 'Why is standing limited to four hours?' For the time being, he would not permit the 'submarine'. The only category-three method he would allow would be 'use of mild non-injurious physical contact,' such as 'grabbing, poking in the chest, and pushing'.

Six weeks later, after concerns were raised by some of the Pentagon's military lawyers, Rumsfeld unexpectedly rescinded this order, and set up another legal 'working group' to reconsider what techniques were appropriate. Chaired by the Defence Department's general counsel, and comprising representatives of the armed services, the Joint Chiefs of Staff and the CIA, this produced at least two long memoranda. The first, dated 6 March 2003, drew heavily on the earlier Bybee document, and echoed both its definition of torture and the claim that the President had a free hand in wartime. It suggested that torture could be justified as a form of self-defence:

> The nation's right to self-defense has been triggered by the events of September 11. If a government defendant were to harm an enemy combatant during an interrogation in a manner that might arguably violate criminal prohibition, he would be doing so in order to prevent further terrorist attacks on the United States by the al-Qaeda network... He could argue that the executive branch's constitutional authority to protect the nation from attack justified his actions.

The memo's authors were well aware of the dark territory into which their arguments led: the war criminal's claim that he was 'only following orders', and thus could not be held accountable. They even quoted the charter of the Nuremburg Nazi War Crimes Tribunal: 'The fact that the defendant acted pursuant to the order of his government or of a superior shall not free him from responsibility.' But an interrogator accused of torture could argue that his or her orders 'may be inferred to be lawful', they suggested, and would have been 'disobeyed at the peril of the subordinate'. In other words, an interrogator ordered to inflict torture could justify his or her actions by saying he or she was frightened of the consequences of disobedience.

The group's last memorandum on interrogation methods at Guantánamo emerged six weeks later. It took a pragmatic approach, arguing that the 'choice of interrogation techniques involves a risk benefit analysis in each case'. When assessing whether 'exceptional' methods were appropriate, 'consideration should be given to the possible adverse effects on US armed forces culture and self-image, which at times past may have suffered due to perceived law of war violations'. There was also a risk that extracting a confession by harsher means 'may produce a statement that might be argued to be involuntary for purposes of criminal proceedings... the more coercive the method, the greater the likelihood that the method will be met with significant domestic and international resistance'.

On 16 April 2003, Rumsfeld issued his revised menu of 'counter-resistance techniques' for interrogators. In addition to psychological methods, detainees could be placed in 'less comfortable' settings and deprived of proper meals for long periods. All comfort items, including the *Koran,* could be confiscated. The use of 'sleep adjustment' was permitted – this meant 'adjusting the sleeping times of the detainee [e.g. reversing sleep cycles from night to day]'. Rumsfeld claimed: 'This technique is NOT sleep deprivation.' Also included was 'environmental manipulation: altering the environment to create moderate discomfort [e.g. adjusting the temperature or introducing an unpleasant smell].' This, Rumsfeld acknowledged, would be regarded by some nations as 'inhumane'.

Finally, and perhaps most important, came isolation in solitary confinement. Rumsfeld placed no limit on the length of time prisoners might have to endure this. 'Those nations that believe detainees are subject to POW protections may view use of this technique as inconsistent with the requirements of Geneva III,' he admitted. But since 'the provisions of Geneva are not applicable to the interrogation of unlawful combatants', this was no obstacle.

Before examining what have been the operational consequences of this official lead, it is worth considering the radical nature of this policy's fracture with the recent past. In Europe, a sense that torture is both morally abhorrent and ineffective dates back to the Enlightenment and beyond. Friedrich Spee, a Jesuit academic from Trier, issued his polemic against the use of torture in witch hunts, the *Cautio Criminalis*, in 1631. The point at which different individuals will break will vary, he wrote: the end of endurance to pressure and pain is a subjective, not an objective phenomenon. Eventually, however, all would: 'It is incredible what people say under the compulsion of torture, and how many lies they will tell about themselves and about others; in the end whatever the torturers want to be true, is true.' If he were an inquisitor, Spee wrote, he could exact confessions from priests and bishops. He had met an inquisitor who boasted that he could wring a confession to devil-worship out of the Pope himself.

Cesare Beccaria also knew that torture is not only repugnant, it doesn't 'work', in the sense of providing discernibly accurate information. 'The only difference between torture and trials by fire and boiling water is, that the event of the first depends on the will of the accused, and of the second on a fact entirely physical and external: but this difference is apparent only, not real,' he wrote in his *On Crimes and Punishments* in 1764. 'A man on the rack, in the convulsions of torture, has it as little in his power to declare the truth, as, in former times, to prevent without fraud the effects of fire or boiling water.' The greater the pressure, the less reliable the testimony: 'The very means employed to distinguish the innocent from the guilty will most effectually destroy all difference between them.' Frederick the Great of Prussia had banned torture even before

Beccaria's book, in 1754. Its publication is generally held responsible for abolition in Baden (1767), by Gustavus II of Sweden (1772), Louis XIV of France (1780), Joseph II of Austria (1781) and Leopold of Tuscany (1786). By the end of the nineteenth century, torture was extinct both in Europe and North America. (In Germany, Russia and elsewhere, it was, of course, about to make a terrible comeback.)

Before 9/11, there seems to have been a consensus shared by Western practitioners, both psychologists and intelligence staff, that even when the use of torture and coercive interrogation did provoke testimony, there was no reliable way of telling truth from fiction. Britain learnt these lessons the hardest way possible, with the international condemnation heaped on the Castlereagh interrogation centre in Belfast in the 1970s, the failure of internment and, above all, the collapse of terrorist convictions derived from confessions obtained by coercive questioning in 1989–92. Similar insights lay behind the Israeli Supreme Court's 1999 rejection of what had been the licensed coercion of Palestinian suspects in the occupied territories. However, like the inquisitors of pre-Enlightenment Europe, Theodore S. Bybee and his colleagues seem to have believed that confessions produced by torture and coercion would be the 'queen of proofs'.

They also shared a delusion common amongst advocates of torture in order to combat terrorism – the legend of the 'ticking bomb', the hypothetical case where a terrorist has been captured after planting an explosive device, but before its detonation. Alan Dershowitz of Harvard University anticipated even Bybee, advocating torture in such instances in articles in the *Los Angeles Times* and elsewhere as early as November 2001. With estimable respect for the rule of law, Dershowitz's only proviso was that such torture should not be administered in secret, but by judicial warrant.

'Al-Qaeda plans apparently include efforts to develop and deploy chemical, biological and nuclear weapons of mass destruction,' wrote Bybee:

Under these circumstances, a detainee may possess information that could enable the United States to prevent attacks that potentially could equal or surpass the September 11 attacks in their magnitude. Clearly, any harm that might occur during an interrogation would pale into insignificance compared to the harm avoided by preventing such an attack.

Bybee accepted that applying this argument would depend on circumstances: the more certain interrogators were that a suspect did possess such knowledge, the stronger such a defence to claims of torture would be. But like others who have explored this moral swamp, he did not pause to examine the case which corresponds more closely with reality: the captive who *might* know something about terrorism, even a deadly and imminent attack – but equally, might not.

As the administration's lawyers developed their thinking in 2002–3, the effects of their approach were rapidly apparent on the ground. The full truth may not emerge for years to come. But it is evident that physical and psychological coercion in varying degrees became the norm in numerous locations. As the Taliban collapsed in Afghanistan in the autumn of 2002, interrogators began to use coercive techniques at the US bases at Bagram and Kandahar. Human Rights Watch has reported:[3]

> Many of those arrested by US forces are detained for indefinite periods at US military bases or outposts. While held, these detainees have no contact with relatives or others…Detainees have no opportunity to challenge the basis for their detention, and are sometimes subjected to mistreatment or torture.

According to Human Rights Watch, methods included being forced to stand in painful positions, being doused with cold water, prolonged exposure to heat and cold, and sleep deprivation. Its report quoted a US military spokesman in Afghanistan, Roger King. Denying detainees had been abused, he admitted:

> We do force people to stand for an extended period of time…Disruption of sleep has been reported as an effective way of reducing people's inhibition about talking or their resistance to questioning…They are not allowed to speak to each other. If they do, they can plan together or rely on the comfort of one another. If they're caught speaking out of turn, they can be forced to do things, like stand for a period of time – as payment for speaking out.

King added that a 'common technique' for disrupting sleep was to keep the lights on constantly or to wake detainees every 15 minutes (Rose 2004).

Two homicides of suspects under interrogation in Afghanistan have been recorded by the US military coroner, both caused by 'blunt force trauma'. Freed Guantánamo detainees who passed through these bases have described to me a regime of casual beatings, sleep deprivation and sexual humiliation through the use of repeated body-cavity searches, which, they said, were photographed.

In the spring of 2004, the treatment of prisoners at Abu Ghraib, the US-managed jail in Iraq, became an international scandal, with the publication of photographs depicting forced sex acts, the attachment of electrodes to a hooded prisoner and a grinning American looming over a distressingly youthful corpse. (The overall number of deaths in US custody in Iraq is as yet unknown. In May 2004 the Pentagon confirmed there had been at least 25, 10 of which were being investigated as criminal homicides.)

Finally, there is the secret network of CIA facilities which is said to run across the globe, in places thought to include Jordan, Thailand and, possibly, the British Indian Ocean base of Diego Garcia. It is inside this network that the alleged senior terrorist 'players' captured since 9/11, such as the attacks' planners Ramzi Binalshibh and Khalid Shaikh Mohammed, have always been held and, according to media leaks, tortured (Bowden 2003; Rehl and Johnstone 2004).

However, it is from Guantánamo that the most detailed information about American interrogation methods in the war on terror comes. About 200 Guantánamo prisoners have to date been released, whilst increasing numbers of former guards and interrogators have felt able to 'go public' with their concerns (Lewis 2004). The evidence suggests that at Gitmo, as it is often termed, America has managed a human rights disaster of historic proportions.

According to the freed British detainees Shafiq Rasul, Asif Iqbal, Rhuhel Ahmed and Tarek Dergoul, for most of their first year at Gitmo during 2002, their interrogations remained both relatively infrequent and low key. In January 2003, following the appointment of Major General Miller, there was a distinct change. The frequency and length of interrogations increased beyond recognition: in the following 15 months, Asif Iqbal and Shafiq Rasul estimated that they were questioned almost 200 times. Meanwhile, the methods the interrogators were prepared to use had been transformed.

From the moment Miller was assigned to Guantánamo in November 2002, increasing the camp's intelligence yield became his highest priority. His predecessor, Brigadier General Rick Baccus, was accused on departure by Pentagon officials of 'coddling' the detainees; certainly the evidence from the minutes of his meetings with the Red Cross suggests that he took their welfare seriously. (It was Baccus, for example, who ordered Camp Delta's first books.) Under Baccus's command, the intelligence from Guantánamo was no more than a trickle. Of course, there were two possible reasons for this: either the prisoners may have known very little about terrorism and al-Qaeda, or they were not being questioned with sufficient skill. But Baccus told the task force's interrogators not to scream at detainees, and in other ways did his best to prevent abuse.

By the time of my visit in October 2003, Major General Miller had been in post for almost a year. For him, intelligence was a matter of volume, of productivity, much like the work of the artillery corps where he had spent most of his career: 'Since the beginning of 2003, the amount of intelligence extracted from detainees each month has increased by 600 per cent,' he told me. Nor did this consist of mere tidbits:

> We're talking about high-value intelligence, distributed around the world...We are developing information of enormous value to the nation, enormously valuable intelligence. We have an enormously thorough process that has very high resolution and clarity. We think we're fighting not only to save and protect our families, but your families also. I think of Guantánamo as the interrogation battle lab in the war against terror.

Miller had managed to impress the Pentagon with his self-assured, can-do approach. Unbeknown to me at the time of my visit, he was newly returned from Iraq, where he and a team from Guantánamo had been asked by Donald Rumsfeld to review intelligence operations at the main terrorist detention facility there – Abu Ghraib. According to Major General Janis Karpinski, who was running Abu Ghraib at the time, he was sent to 'Gitmo-ize' it; in the dryer language of Major General Antonio Taguba's report on prisoner abuse there, Miller's mission in the summer of 2003 was 'to review current Iraqi theater ability to rapidly exploit internees for actionable intelligence'.[4] In other words: to make them talk. As of December 2004, Miller is at Abu Ghraib once again, having been reassigned from Gitmo to take charge of military prisons throughout Iraq, despite the occupying coalition's handover to a transitional Iraqi government.

The key to this achievement, Miller told me, was a graduated system of incentives and rewards which he had introduced in early 2003. The detainee who co-operated with his interrogators would be given an accumulating number of up to 29 extra 'comfort items', from 'something as small as an added water cup, to an increased number of letters from home and books to keep in his cell, to added exercise periods and showers, up to a maximum of seven each week'.

Sometimes, Miller averred, interrogators might have to become 'aggressive' with a non-co-operative subject. But his descriptions of his innovations were all about the judicious use of carrots; about exploiting the incentives 'to establish a rapport'. He was, it now seems evident, telling only part of the story. Behind the carrot lurked a menacing and painful stick.

Lieutenant-Commander Charles Swift, a frequent visitor to Gitmo as one of the military defence attorneys assigned to act in the planned tribunals there, told me something of what Miller's system meant for unco-operative prisoners:

> The interrogators were now to be in effective control of the camp, and they would have the final word. You can be a model prisoner, your behaviour can be impeccable, but if you're not co-operating with the interrogators, you're going to be treated like the very worst inmate – the guy who ends up in a stripped down cell for spitting at the guards or throwing excrement. The interrogators decide whether you're the first to eat or the last, and whether your laundry gets done, and who watches you in the shower. Or they might ask for a cell search, and confiscate everything. Then it'll be the interrogator who brings it all back.

General Antonio Taguba's report on abuse at Abu Ghraib sheds further light on Miller's approach. During his visit in 2003, Miller had demanded a 'unified strategy', in which guards would 'set the conditions for the successful interrogation and exploitation of internees/detainees'.[5] Taguba related what the consequences were in Iraq: beatings of prisoners and sexual abuse. Sergeant Javal Davies told Taguba that interrogators had asked him: 'Loosen this guy up for us. Make sure he has a bad night. Make sure he gets the treatment.' The interrogators had thanked him and his colleague Corporal Charles Granier afterwards, saying: 'Good job, they're breaking down real fast. They answer every question. They're giving out good information.' It was Granier who had forced prisoners to strip naked and simulate sex with each other, sometimes arranged in grotesque piles. Taguba asked specialist Sabrina Harman how it was that a detainee came to be photographed whilst placed on a box with wires attached to his fingers, toes and penis. She stated that 'her job was to keep detainees awake. She stated that M[ilitary] I[ntelligence] was talking to Corporal Grainer. She stated: "MI wanted to get them to talk. It is Grainer's job to do things for MI…to get these people to talk."'

There is as yet no evidence that the brutally sexualized abuse which stained America's reputation at Abu Ghraib also took place at Guantánamo. Nevertheless, the system instituted there on Miller's watch was also harshly coercive.

As the pace of interrogations intensified in early 2003, Tarek Dergoul told me, the guards who came to fetch the prisoners began to use a new phrase: 'You have a reservation.' This did not always mean a prisoner would actually be questioned. For one period of about a month in 2003, he said, every day guards would take him to an interrogation booth in chains, seat him, chain him to the ring in the floor and then leave him alone, for eight hours at a time:

> The air conditioning would really be blowing, it was freezing, which was incredibly painful on my amputation stumps. Eventually I'd need to urinate, and in the end I would try to tilt my chair and go on the floor. Inevitably I'd soil myself. It was humiliating. They were watching through a two-way mirror. As soon as I wet myself, a woman MP would come in yelling, 'Look what you've done! You're disgusting'.

Afterwards, he would be taken back to his cell for about three hours. Then, he said, the guards would reappear, and the process begin again.

Sometimes, Dergoul said, the interrogators also used heat: 'The air conditioning control would be turned so it was blowing out air even hotter than what was outside. And sometimes, if you budged from your position, they'd take the chair away, so you'd keel over, tipped in agony on to the floor.' In periods of especially heavy interrogation, he would be given no clean clothes or bedding, or garments which were too small. Another technique was to refuse toilet paper, 'so you can't clean yourself after using the toilet. Or they'd give you like four sheets – not enough to blow your nose'.

Asif Iqbal was also left chained in a booth for many hours, and like Dergoul, was eventually compelled to soil himself. Prisoners were forced to urinate in the booths so often, he said, that it became normal for the interrogators to have their plastic chairs hosed down after each session. Sometimes, music was played at a deafening volume: he remembered having to listen to Eminem, Bruce Springsteen and 'techno' dance music, accompanied by flashing strobe lights. Once, he said, an interrogator showed him explicit pornography, saying: 'Look at that, it's the last time you'll ever see pussy again.' Raised in Britain, he was relatively immune to sexual taunts of this kind: 'I

55

just laughed.' But Arab detainees told him and Dergoul of being left chained in the booths with their underpants around their ankles, a cause of profound humiliation.

Dergoul also described the use of what was known as the 'short shackle,' in which the bonds of the three-piece suit were pulled tight to keep the subject bunched up, whilst chained to the floor. 'After a while, it was agony. You could hear the guards behind the mirror, making jokes, eating and drinking, knocking on the walls. It wasn't about trying to get information. It was just about trying to break you.' Sleep deprivation was also deployed regularly. Rhuhel Ahmed told how the detainees came to speak of 'frequent flyers' – prisoners who were forced to don their chains and move cells, day and night, every two hours. The freed detainees said Gitmo's interrogators also used psychological methods. Amongst the most common was a claim by an interrogator that he had proof of the suspect's 'guilt', a technique which Shafiq Rasul encountered time and again. For example, he was told that photographs of him on an 'al-Qaeda membership form' had been found in a raid on an Afghan cave:

> Actually I'd left my passport in Pakistan. Then the interrogator told me that next to my file they'd found my brother Habib's al-Qaeda file. The interrogator said he wasn't lying, and that next time he'd bring it with him. When it came to next time, he claimed he'd made a mistake.

General Miller's 'carrot,' the incentives available in return for co-operation, sometimes provoked false allegations by one prisoner against another, which would then become the subject of further intensive interrogation. Shafiq Rasul told me:

> They kept taking us and taking us, showing us photos saying: 'This guy says you've done this, this guy says you've done that' – what they meant was that other detainees desperate to get out of there were making allegations, making stuff up that they thought would help them get out of the camp.

His own interrogators told him: '"If you want extra comfort items, get us some info on the people on the block." I refused.' After this session, Rasul said, he was placed on the lowest-level regime as a punishment: 'You only got a thin mat instead of a mattress, and a blanket only between 11 pm and 5 am. During the days in the cell you had just your clothes and the *Koran*.'

Rasul's interrogators repeatedly asked him where they could purchase surface-to-air missiles in his home town of Tipton, apparently because another prisoner had claimed he had made such a purchase. As anyone who has visited the quiet British Midland town of Tipton would know, it was an absurd suggestion.

In June 2003, the situation of the British prisoners Iqbal, Ahmed and Rasul, which had apparently been improving, took a serious turn for the worse. For the previous two weeks, Rasul had been in the relatively comfortable conditions of Camp Four. Now, his interrogators told him, American intelligence had acquired a video of a meeting in 2000 between Osama Bin Laden and Mohammed Atta, the leader of the 9/11 hijackers. Behind Bin Laden were three unidentified men, and someone – presumably another detainee – had alleged they were none other than Iqbal, Rasul and Ahmed.

All three were moved to solitary confinement in Camp Delta's isolation block for three months, where the cell walls are made of solid metal instead of mesh, and the only human contact detainees have is with their interrogators. They were to endure this for the next three months, whilst their interviewers turned on them with a new-found aggression. Rasul said:

> I told them that in 2000, I didn't leave the country, that I was working at the Wednesbury branch of Currys [a British electronic chain store] who would have my employment records, and attending the University of Central England. They told me I could have falsified those records – that I could have had someone working with me at Currys who could have altered the data the company held, and travelled on a false passport.

Finally, as his isolation continued and the interrogators deployed their full range of techniques, Rasul said, he cracked. In a final session, a senior official had come down from Washington:

> My heart is beating, beating, I'm saying it's not me, it's not me, but I'm thinking, 'I'm going to be screwed, I'm on an island in the middle of nowhere, there's nothing I can do'. This woman had come down and she plays me the video. I say, 'Are you blind? That doesn't look anything like me'. But it makes no difference. I'd got to the point where I just couldn't take anymore. 'Do what you have to do,' I told them. I'd been sitting there for three months in isolation so I says 'yes, it's me. Go ahead and put me on trial'.

At around the same time, Ahmed and Iqbal made similar confessions. But the three men from Tipton were lucky. Some time in September 2003, British officials from MI5 came to Guantánamo, armed with the documentary evidence which showed they could not have been in Afghanistan in 2000 after all. Within a few days, they were being held in the ordinary cages again, and being given special privileges, including weekly movies in a building known as the 'love shack' and hamburgers from the Gitmo McDonald's; a few weeks after that, the American government began to talk to their British counterparts about the men's release. 'In the end, we could prove our alibis,' Rasul said. 'But what about other people, especially from countries where travel records may not be available? What if they confess to something they didn't do and then can't prove it wasn't true?'

The fate of Moazzem Begg, one of the British detainees who was not released in March 2004, may well be an example. Intelligence officials have briefed the American media that after being interrogated at Bagram in Afghanistan for a year, he confessed to planning to drop anthrax spores on the House of Commons from a 'drone', an unmanned aerial vehicle. Accurate UAVs are part of the latest generation of American weaponry, and cost millions of dollars each. Yet in previous reporting of his case, the absurdity of Begg's alleged confession – he supposedly claimed to be plotting to launch his deadly flight from Suffolk – has not been addressed. It does not seem implausible to suggest that his 'UAV plot' may have been a fantasy, induced by sheer desperation.

However, according to my interviews with senior US intelligence officials, the manifestly unreliable nature of 'confessions' such as those made by Rasul and Begg is not the only shortcoming of the 'enormously valuable intelligence' supposedly gathered at Guantánamo. Quite separately, four such officials have told me that such claims are misleading and exaggerated, and that the value of information obtained by coercion at Gitmo is relatively low.

The first problem, they have said, is that many of the Guantánamo prisoners should not have been there at all, and knew nothing important about terrorism in the first place. According to Lieutenant-Colonel Christino, who spent much of 2003 as the senior watch officer in the Pentagon's Joint Intelligence Task Force on Terrorism, and previously provided 'intelligence support' for the operation which moved prisoners to Guantánamo, the detainees were victims of a woefully inadequate military intelligence screening process in Afghnanistan. This was 'flawed from the get-go', and conducted mainly by very young and inexperienced reservist soldiers who had undergone only a single 16-week course before being thrust into the intelligence frontline in the war on terror. In large measure, this was the result of the historic over-concentration on electronic intelligence discussed above. But the consequences were serious:

> These kids – as bright and as dedicated to their mission as they may be – lack meaningful life, let alone professional, experiences. Contrast them with their law enforcement counterparts: a police officer will typically have an associates or bachelors degree in criminal justice and spend three to five years doing routine police work before he or she can even apply to become a detective. The army should require a similar degree of seasoning before a Military intelligence soldier becomes a HUMINT specialist responsible for screening or interrogation.

Worse, they were dealing with prisoners from the far side of a deep cultural gulf, and were almost entirely reliant on interpreters, most of them contracted by private corporations. Their quality was often abysmal. A 2003 Pentagon report by Colonel Lawrence H. Saul, director of a military evaluation unit called the Center for Army Lessons Learned, supports that view. In both Iraq and Afghanistan, it states:

> the lack of competent interpreters throughout the theater impeded operations … Bottom line, the US Army does not have a fraction of the linguists required … We have to rely on contract linguists for Dari, Pashtun and the numerous dialects of Arabic … laugh if you will, but many of the linguists with which I conversed were convenience store workers and cab drivers. None had any previous military experience. Most military linguists working in Iraq and Afghanistan only possess, on the average, a 2/2 Forces Command rating – which basically gives them the ability to tell the difference between a burro and a burrito.[6]

Christino said the screeners' inexperience and difficulty in understanding what their prisoners were saying were exacerbated by another factor in Afghanistan. As many freed detainees have claimed:

> initially very few detainees were captured as a result of combat with US troops on the battlefield. Almost all of them were turned over by the Northern Alliance, Pakistani troops or others

who perceived they might get some benefit from doing so. In a generic sense, they were selling their captives to the US Army, and they came with what amounted to a sales pitch – a story to convince our troops that these people were valuable. Their story could be true; it could be fiction, or a combination of the two. The problem was that with inadequate training, little experience and poor translation, our MI soldiers were largely incapable of discerning the difference.

Most military intelligence soldiers were, Christino said, motivated by an honest desire to do the right thing, to 'make a contribution' after 9/11. But for an innocent detainee, this might have disastrous consequences:

> Imagine: A Northern Alliance leader tells you this man is an Arab who was in a terrorist training camp – you want to believe it, and you don't want to take the risk of letting someone dangerous go… Erring on the side of caution you might well write in a report, 'this individual was involved with activities at a mosque known to be connected to al-Qaeda'.

At Guantánamo, Christino and the other officials said, most of the interrogators were equally inexperienced, and equally dependent on poor-quality translators. (In early 2003, a group of Pentagon intelligence staff became so concerned about Gitmo interpreters that they submitted a memorandum to their civilian bosses, recommending that interrogations should be taped and spot-checked as a means of verifying their work. It was rejected.) At the same time, interrogators were highly motivated, whilst they had the freedom to deploy the full menu of incentives and coercion. The result might almost be described as an ideal method of acquiring misleading or false intelligence. Before the arrival of Major General Miller, said Christino:

> Interrogators at Guantánamo obtained information of only minimal to moderate intelligence value. Certainly, they gained useful knowledge about recruitment and training, and perhaps some limited insight concerning financing and logistics, but not much about operations. Then along comes Major General Miller and all of a sudden they are producing 'enormously valuable intelligence'. That phrase could only justifiably be applied to detailed information concerning terrorist capabilities and intentions. I doubt that anyone detained at Guantánamo ever

had access to that type of information; if some claim that they did, they probably did so to either earn the incentives or avoid the maltreatment that General Miller instituted.

Another official, a seasoned former FBI man, said that to prepare an important interrogation would normally take him at least three months. 'I certainly know of no one at Gitmo having the opportunity or the luxury to be able to prepare an interview for three months. Generally, the new hires apprentice in the booths with more experienced guys right from the start. They are rookies.'

'Some good information has come out of Gitmo,' one senior Pentagon analyst said. 'But it doesn't seem much in relation to the various costs of keeping 600-plus detainees.' Christino was more specific. 'Most of the information derived from interrogations at Guantánamo appears to be very general in nature; so general that it is not very useful,' he said:

How much help is it to know that during a class on improvised explosives at a camp in Afghanistan someone discussed bombing apartment complexes or shopping malls in the United States? Chechen terrorists have been bombing apartment complexes in Russia for years and anyone even vaguely familiar with American consumer culture knows that shopping malls would be a good target.

In the time he spent at the Pentagon in 2003, Christino said he had seen 'nothing that indicated a dramatic improvement in the quality of intelligence coming from Guantánamo. What I did observe was a major effort at increasing the quantity of intelligence produced and improving the way it was packaged'. In Christino's view, Guantánamo had not helped to prevent a single terrorist attack.

The broader costs of this aspect of the war on terror may be frighteningly high. Gitmo, Kandahar and Abu Ghraib have absorbed enormous resources which would have been better used elsewhere, whilst producing little valuable intelligence. But using coercion to make detainees talk has not merely been expensive, illegal and ineffective, it has also been counterproductive, inspiring terrorism instead of defeating it. 'The guy with the crewcut, the club and the crucifix, standing over the detainee in goggles and chains symbolizes not only American oppression of the Third World, but also the oppression by governments friendly to America inside Muslim countries,' Dr Tim Winter, lecturer in Islamic studies at Pembroke College, Cambridge, told me. 'People's instinct is to empathize with the guy in the goggles, because that's how they see the world.' According to Winter, a frequent visitor to the Middle East and a fluent Arabic speaker, 'Guantánamo is right up there with the Palestinian conflict as a focal point for anger and political action'.

In the words of one Pentagon intelligence official: 'I'd guess that for every prisoner who goes into Guantánamo, you create ten terrorists or supporters of terrorism.' In Iraq and Saudi Arabia in 2004, we saw the grisly results: Western captives of Islamist groups dressed in orange jumpsuits in simulated Guantánamo cells, caught on video begging for their lives, then beheaded.

In its initial assumptions set out in the memos of Yoo, Bybee and the Pentagon working group cited above, the Bush administration set up a dichotomy: between respect for the law and human rights on the one hand, and practical effectiveness in fighting terrorism. In those barbaric taped executions is the evidence of its falsity.

Notes

1. The documents can be found at www.globalsecurity.org/security/library/news/2004/06/sec-040623-usia04.htm.
2. The term 'enemy combatant' later came to be used widely, and has the same meaning.
3. *Enduring Freedom: Abuses by US Forces in Afghanistan,* Human Rights Watch, New York, March 2004, available at www.hrw.org/reports/2004/afghanistan0304/index.htm.
4. General Antonio Taguba, Article 15-6 Investigation of the 800th Military Police Brigade (www.agonist.org/annex/taguba.htm).
5. Taguba, see note 4.
6. CALL Newsletter: Operation Outreach, Center for Army Lessons Learned Oct 03, No. 03-27, available at www.globalsecurity.org/military/ops/oif-lessons-learned.htm

References

Beccaria, C. (1764) *Of Crimes and Punishments.* Padua, Italy. (online at http://www.crimetheory.com/Archive/Beccaria/Beccaria16.htm).

Bowden, M. (2003) 'Unbound, the truth about torture', *The Atlantic,* September.

Gerecht, R.M. (2001) 'The counterterrorist myth', *The Atlantic,* August.

Jehl, D. and Johnstone, D. (2004) 'CIA expands its inquiry into interrogation tactics', *The New York Times,* 29 August.

Lewis, N.A. (2004) 'Broad use of harsh tactics is described at Cuba base', *The New York Times*, 17 October.

National Commission on Terrorist Attacks upon the United States (2004) *The 9/11 Commission Report*. New York, NY: W.W. Norton.

Rose, D. (2004) *Guantánamo: America's War on Human Rights*. London: Faber & Faber.

Spee, F. von Lagenfield (trans. Hellyer, M.) (2003) *Cautio Criminalis: A Book on Witch Trials*. Charlottesville, VA: University of Virginia Press.

Chapter 4

The interrogation of terrorist suspects: the banality of torture

John J. Pearse

Introduction

It would be difficult to discuss the interrogation of terrorist suspects at this period in time without reference to the allegations of torture at the Abu Ghraib prison in Iraq and at the American detention centre in Guantánamo Bay that have made headline news across the world. These revelations dominate the field and deserve particular attention and comment. In this chapter, therefore, I propose to explore a number of key areas of interest to psychologists and practitioners working in law enforcement that I believe are relevant to the events unfolding across the world. To start with, and in an attempt to provide a credible baseline to develop matters, I will draw on psychological research to challenge the pervasive myth that all terrorists are crazed psychopaths and that only a psycho-pathological condition can account for their actions.

I then propose to examine what takes place 'on the road' to the interrogation room – that is, what are the psychological and external issues that are relevant to interrogating officers that may influence their subsequent attitude and behaviour within the interrogation arena? This will examine the need for interrogators to adopt the perspective of the person they are about to question, to put themselves in his or her shoes and to ask searching and perhaps challenging questions from this perspective. For the purpose of this chapter I will adopt the use of the term interrogation (rather than interview) given that the area under discussion relates to interaction with suspects and not witnesses or victims, and to remain consistent with other authors.

I will then attempt to explain, with reference to a key psychological study, the reports of violence and abusive behaviour attributed to the guards at Abu Ghraib and Guantánamo Bay. Is it possible to account for the apparent change over time in their behaviour? I then propose to try to make sense of the many sensational claims and accounts of individual tactics that have been published in the international media or released by official and unofficial sources. That is, I will impose some order and reframe the numerous techniques within a more manageable number of categories. Such a compartmentalization process will assist with a more user-friendly assessment of their component parts and psychological impact.

Finally, as the subtitle to this chapter suggests, I will attempt to place this whole amazing series of events within a different context. Is it possible to make sense of the moral and ethical decline into the wide-scale use of torture within the interrogation environment?

Terrorists: psychopaths and crazed fanatics?

The first plane loads of detainees started to arrive at Guantánamo Bay (or Gitmo, its more popular US military term) at the beginning of 2002, only a few months after the 11 September terrorist attacks in New York. Indeed, there is an enduring media image of the prisoners arriving dressed in orange jump suits, wearing blacked-out goggles, surgical masks, headphones and shackled hand and foot. This was, according to the chairman of the Joint Chiefs of Staff, General Richard E. Myers, because they were considered so dangerous and bent on destruction that they were crazy enough to 'gnaw through hydraulic lines in the back of a C-17 to bring it down' (Rose 2004: 2). Further insight into relevant psychological characteristics of the detainees was provided by another authoritative source, Donald Rumsfeld, the US Defense Secretary, who on an early visit to the detention camp labelled them 'among the most dangerous, best trained, vicious killers on the face of the earth' (Rose 2004: 8). The result, according to Carol Rosenberg of the *Miami Herald*, was that the guards were concerned that 'they were rabid terrorists, who could rip their throats out' (Rose 2004: 50). In this particular instance therefore the question of their mental state and level of dangerousness appears not to be an issue – the assessment has already been made, very publicly, as extreme.

Let us examine the suggestion that terrorists are crazed fanatics. It is clear that very senior US personnel are content for this message to be publicized and, according to Rosenberg (above), the guards believe this state of affairs, but it is also one of the most widely travelled myths in the terrorist arena. Since the early 1970s a number of academics and scientists have also promoted such a view despite the absence of credible evidence to support this claim and in contradiction to four decades of research and clinical studies that refutes a psycho-pathological hypothesis (Silke 1998, 2003). A penchant that continued to be fuelled in the aftermath of the New York terrorist attacks in September 2001.

An examination of some of the early research in this field is very illuminating and reveals a disturbing trend of analysis and diagnosis, by some authors, solely from media and secondary sources. A classic example is the research undertaken on the infamous Baader–Mainhoff Gang that was responsible for a number of terrorist acts in West Germany in the 1970s. The leader, Andreas Baader, was according to one psychologist a 'sociopath' and 'extremely manipulative...A pathological liar...Baader displays characteristics of a marked psychopathic order' (Cooper 1977: 31). A subsequent psychiatric report, however, states 'nothing was found which could justify their classification as psychotics, neurotics or psychopaths' (Rasch 1979). The important distinction was that Rasch, a professor of psychiatry, had met with and assessed the gang members in prison, whilst Cooper had never actually met Andreas Baader, and was content to formulate his diagnosis from the media and other second hand accounts.

Regrettably, this is not an isolated example, and similar evidence of 'normality' from actual studies of terrorist groups (e.g. the IRA, Italian Red Brigade or the Front de Liberation du Quebec) is often sacrificed to appease the demand for sensational headlines (for a review, see Silke 1998, 2003). The relevance of the need to understand the normalization debate takes on a rather sad and ironic hue in the light of reports that began to emerge in November 2003 that US personnel had arrested many people whose identity was not known to them and who turned out to be civilians unconnected with any terrorist activity. Rose (2004) reports a guard who estimated that at least 200 of those held in the maximum-security cell blocks were harmless, and a senior Pentagon official is quoted as saying that 'at least two thirds of the 600 detainees held as of May 2004 could, he said, be released without hesitation immediately' (Rose 2004: 42). This now leads us to question the impact of the messages emanating from senior US politicians on the guards and interrogators at Gitmo.

Adopting the perspective of the 'other'

One of the core requirements for an effective interrogator is the ability to understand the perspective of the other, that core psychological process inherent in, but not practised by, all humans (Farr 1982; Pearse 1997). I will utilize this technique, the ability to empathize with another, as the single thread that permeates through so many of the key issues in interrogation. It is, I will argue, the critical component that separates successful interactions capable of providing a rich yield of credible information from those that can, as we shall see, only be measured in meaningless quantitative terms. Those who regularly engage in this cognitive process, within law enforcement and the legal profession, for example, will appreciate that under some circumstances it may bring with it a heavy moral and legal responsibility. What would happen, for example, if the guards or interrogators challenged the view of the detainees as crazed psychopaths? Such a cognitive imbalance, thought processes at odds with external information or a previously held belief system, places the individual under stress and the immediate desire is to recreate a sense of cognitive balance, perhaps by 'convincing' oneself that such senior politicians or military officers must be right. The opposite and more confrontational view is likely to lead to the heavy moral or legal standpoint that I referred to above (for information, Heider's balance theory (1958; Hewstone 1988) and Festinger's concept of dissonance (1957) provide the relevant psychological theories and research in this area). In philosophical terms this is how Arendt (1970) characterized the concept of thinking, which for her was the intense and inescapable experience of plurality, an inner dialogue between two internal thinking partners.

Maintaining an open mind and being able to move seamlessly amongst different perspectives represent a valuable and ubiquitous skill that is so important for interrogation personnel. A simple example of the value of shifting perspectives may help to reinforce this view. Whenever I am asked to address an audience, I take every opportunity to sample their views on this subject by prompting them with a simple 'sentence-completion task' (Oppenheim 1968). So, for example, whether I am speaking to the business community in the City of London in relation to counterterrorist measures and prevention advice, to police officers on a terrorist senior investigators' course or addressing a crosssection of delegates at law enforcement or legal conferences I ask them to complete the sentence: 'To me, terrorism means…?' It would prove helpful if the reader could briefly reflect on this question.

The answers from the law enforcement and legal groups tend to reflect their knowledge of the legal definitions, and references are often made to acts demonstrating extreme levels of violence, loss of life and attempts to influence the political debate by violent means. A more personal dimension is apparent from members of the public who consider their own safety (or lack of it) and the levels of fear engendered by terrorist acts and terrorist groups. The notion of the mad terrorist or suicide bomber sometimes permeates the debate. It is not long before the audience reaches some consensus and that is the time to ask them to change their perspective: to that of a terrorist. Again, I would encourage the reader to reflect on this momentarily. As a terrorist, what does 'terrorism' mean?

Interestingly, there is much less variability determined by the identity of each group. Often the thorny issue of the dual (or bidirectional) nature of violence perpetrated by a soldier and that perpetrated by a 'freedom fighter' emerges (for a lively and provocative oversight of this general debate, see 'Truisms and terror', Chomsky 2003: 188ff.). Terrorist acts are now seen (by the same audience) as a form of communication, albeit communication *in extremis* and the layers of emotion that previously accompanied terrorist issues tend to dissipate. The removal of these emotional shrouds is so very important as it provides a less cluttered thinking (and therefore decision-making) environment. A shift towards normalization is beginning to emerge and, from the group of men and women in the City of London, the discussion focused on the concept of terrorist activity as a business. Such perspectives are revealing, informative and often so very practical. I can think of a number of highly successful sting operations mounted against terrorist groups launched and driven on business principles. A recent example would be the downfall of the leaders of the Real IRA sentenced in London and Dublin to 30 years and 20 years imprisonment, respectively (Tendler (London) 2002; Walsh (Dublin) 2003).

The central point is that when faced with the prospect of interrogating a suspected terrorist, in the pre-interrogation planning stage, those responsible must not allow emotions or extreme views to cloud their thought processes or to affect adversely their own behaviour and attitudes. The business model, generated from within the audience, is a particularly valuable contribution as it focuses on the terrorist groups' need for supplies, finance, technical equipment, and training and organizational details. It is in effect a sterile (emotion free) template that can be used to improve understanding and, for interrogators, to direct questioning in a manner that reduces the likelihood that the interaction will degenerate into a highly charged, poorly focused and possibly violent exchange.

Cultural considerations

In the special environment of interrogation, other benefits will accrue by thinking about issues from more than one perspective. One area relates to understanding as much as possible about exactly 'who' it is that is to be interviewed: their strengths, weaknesses and cultural needs and expectations. A second area concerns the need to think about exactly what it is that the interrogator brings into the interaction: his or her preconceptions, biases, beliefs, etc. If we examine the former, understanding as much as possible about the 'who' is paramount in the peculiar circumstances of Gitmo where the detainees have allegedly been removed from a war zone and represent numerous nationalities and diverse cultures.

Michael Gelles and his colleagues (Chapter 2, this volume) reinforce exactly this point in providing a whole chapter dedicated to the very different beliefs, ideologies and life experiences of persons subject to al-Qaeda investigations, such as the Gitmo detainees. This includes the likelihood that such operatives may well have suspended critical thinking and may tend to engage in associative thinking patterns rather than the Western preference for linear construction. For practitioners this translates into the likelihood that, in answer to a simple question – 'where does your brother live? – a detainee may not be able to provide the address in a straightforward manner. In Western culture most people are able to make reference to a road name, number, code, etc., but this may not be the case for Middle-Eastern males who would indulge in less specific linkages that may never achieve the original goal of identifying the actual location. Failure to understand such fundamental differences can lead to an increase in tension and anxiety within the interrogation environment and raise the frustration levels of those concerned.

Interrogator bias

Just as it is important to understand as much as possible about the person to be interviewed, it is also crucial that the interrogator understands some of the internal psychological processes that may be influencing his or her own thought patterns. Research has shown that interrogators bring with them attitudes and beliefs that are likely to influence their behaviour and interrogation techniques. For example, they may have antecedent information and knowledge of any previous convictions; such information is likely to affect their impressions, attitudes and behaviour (Moston *et al.* 1992). There are many reports of prisoners handed over to US forces in Afghanistan with accompanying (unsupported) stories of the prisoners' alleged association with al-Qaeda, or their attendance at terrorist training camps (Rose 2004). Such information secured the $5,000 reward for the mercenary group disposing of the prisoner, but what impact did this information have on the receiving US forces and during the interrogation process?

For law enforcement personnel it is important to appreciate that a person's previous convictions may actually increase an interrogator's belief in the suspect's guilt, which is reflected in a longer and more rigorous interrogation (Firth 1975), and Trankel (1972) has identified a particular bias in interrogation when compared with ordinary conversation. The latter is often a mutual exchange of information whilst the former can be seen as generally one-way, with the suspect answering the interrogator's questions. Such a bias can exert a strong influence on the outcome of the interview. For example, other American research has identified that interrogators 'too frequently become so zealously committed to a preconceived belief in a suspect's guilt or so reliant on their interrogation methods that they mistakenly extract an uncorroborated, inconsistent, and manifestly untrue confession' (Ofshe and Leo 1997: 193).

Whilst it is not possible, within the constraints of this one chapter, to do justice to all the powerful psychological forces inherent in the concepts of bias, peer pressure and group conflict, especially when exacerbated during an armed conflict, I am sure the reader will appreciate how such universal processes can be manipulated with malevolent and dire consequences. In the next section I will attempt to identify some of the psychological factors that might begin to account for the aggressive activity carried out by the guards at both camps and now the subject of internal US military investigation.

The Stamford University prison experiment

Any discussion of the allegations that have surfaced in relation to the two detention centres needs to contain the caveat that what has taken place has done so within the confines of an armed conflict or war zone; circumstances and an environment of survival that tend to deviate considerably from, shall we say, the law enforcement norm. Nevertheless such engagements in the twenty-first century remain subject to international rules and regulations (see Chapter 8, this volume, for a more detailed review of this area). The purpose of the caveat in this chapter is to emphasize the fact that such powerful situational forces tend not to be at play in the normal law enforcement environment but, despite this, it is interesting to note that many of the psychological issues under discussion remain wholly relevant and can be stimulated in an artificial environment far removed from the conflict zone.

Perhaps the most relevant psychological research that addressed the drastic change in human behaviour in a prison environment was that carried out by Philip Zimbardo, at Stamford University in 1971. Zimbardo created a mock prison in the basement of his psychology building and selected 24 mature, emotionally stable, intelligent young men (out of 70) for the study. With the flip of a coin some were designated as 'prisoners' and the rest served as 'guards'. The prisoners were stripped, given a uniform and number, and placed in a cell with two other inmates. They were told the cell would be their home for the next two weeks. The guards were informed that they had the authority to make up their own rules for maintaining law and order and respect in the prison, and were free to improvise new rules at any time during their eight-hour shifts on duty.

The experiment was supposed to last for two weeks but had to be stopped after only six days because, according to Zimbardo:

> it was no longer apparent to most of the subjects where reality ended and their roles began. The majority had indeed become prisoners or guards, no longer able to clearly differentiate between role playing and self...In less than a week the experience of imprisonment undid (temporarily) a lifetime of learning; human values were suspended, self-concepts were challenged and the ugliest...side of human nature surfaced. We were horrified because we saw some guards treat others as if they were despicable animals, taking pleasure in cruelty, while the prisoners became...dehumanized robots who thought

71

only of escape, of their own individual survival and of their mounting hatred for the guards (1971: 4).

Some of the prisoners became severely depressed, confused or hysterical and had to be released after only a few days. Many of the guards became tyrants, arbitrarily using their power and enjoying the control they had over others. Other guards were not as brutal, but they never intervened on behalf of the prisoners and never told the other guards to 'ease off'. This landmark research unequivocally demonstrated that individual behaviour can be controlled by social forces and that, given specific environmental circumstances, individuals can create the very social forces that come to shape their behaviour. It was the subjects themselves who created the reality of their roles and therefore defined the power that the prison structure exerted over them (Zimbardo 1971; Haney et al. 1973). Whilst the study had a number of limitations (it could be argued that the guards were role playing what they thought was typical prison officers' behaviour – given the declared influence of the then recent Paul Newman film *Cool Hand Luke*), these findings do not appear out of place when set against the circumstances currently under discussion.

Psychological research on the impact of the physical environment

The power of the situation and the ability to create their own social forces were clearly evident in relation to the behaviour of the subjects in the Stamford experiment, and the psychological literature also provides some insight into the debilitating impact of oppressive prison regimes such as those believed to be practised at Gitmo and Abu Ghraib. Gudjonsson (1992, 2003), for example, discusses the ways in which the physical environment can affect the psychological state and well-being of detainees. It is recognized that all forms of sensory deprivation, fatigue, social isolation, hunger, sleep deprivation and physical and emotional pain or the threat of such pain can exert a very powerful influence on the decision-making of detainees. According to Forrest (1999), confessions can be extracted very effectively, without any special equipment, by using sleep deprivation, prolonged wall standing, solitary confinement in cold or cramped conditions, and such practices tend to leave no physical after-effects (see also Hinkle 1961; Shallice 1974). It is also known that there is considerable evidence that lack of sleep impairs mental functioning, especially if it is maintained for more than two or three days. The symptoms include lack of motivation, attention problems, cognitive confusion and slowness of thought. Research in this area concluded that between 4 am and 8 am is recognized as the optimum period for these problems to occur (Mikulincer *et al.* 1989).

Up to now I have discussed some of the psychological influences that may impact on an interrogating officer as he or she prepares to engage with a detainee, and I have briefly outlined the powerful situational influences that can dictate and change the behaviour of prison 'guards'. In normal circumstances there is a clear demarcation between the role and responsibilities of these two groups. However, this distinction disappeared at both Guantánamo and Abu Ghraib.

Combining the roles of guard and interrogator

This link is embodied in one man, Major General Geoffrey D. Miller, who assumed command at Gitmo in November 2002 with the express objective of increasing the allegedly poor intelligence yield produced by the previous regime (Rose 2004). According to Miller, a former artillery officer, by July of the following year the amount of intelligence extracted from detainees each month had increased by 600 per cent (Rose 2004: 84) – in quantitative terms.

His efforts were recognized by his superiors who sent him, in the summer of 2003, to the Abu Ghraib prison to review operations there with a view to producing the same rapid increase in intelligence reports. He recommended adopting the system that was working so well for him at Gitmo, where he had merged the functions of two previously distinct sections, the guards and the interrogators, allowing the guards to 'prepare' the detainee for the interrogation process. In effect the guards became subordinate to the interrogation officers. The powerful environmental forces had now been set; it was just that this was not an experiment and it could not be stopped after a few days.

As the attention and voracious appetite of the world's press descended on Abu Ghraib and Gitmo the product of this unification strategy became all too clear. To a number of commentators the revelations, although deeply shocking, bore all the hallmarks of familiar and well reported techniques that had been practised by oppressive regimes for centuries. Those charged with caring for torture victims, such as the Medical Foundation for the Care of Victims of Torture (London), confirm that 'Whilst torturers have been refining torture techniques throughout human history...some methods have survived for millennia' (Forrest 1999: 5).

So whilst the emerging allegations of assault and personal abuse shocked many around the world, they were clearly not new techniques, so the next issues to address are what, if any, is the relationship to the conventional law enforcement environment? And is it possible to improve our understanding of the psychological impact of this considerable repertoire of interrogation tactics?

Interrogation tactics at Abu Ghraib and Guantánamo Bay: the bridge to law enforcement

As I see it there are at least two relevant factors linking interrogation in the police environment and that taking place at Gitmo or Abu Ghraib. The first is the shared objectives of attempting to elicit a confession, obtain evidence or intelligence, or just getting a reluctant detainee to talk. But, secondly, and perhaps more importantly, it is the psychological principles underpinning this elicitation process that I would say represent the strongest connection. Gisli Gudjonsson has discussed the interrogation techniques recommended by Inbau et al. (2001) involving the 'nine steps' approach to a successful interrogation. This quite extensive package has also been broken down into a more manageable dual format by Kassin and McNall (1991), who characterized this approach in terms of 'maximization' and 'minimization' (dealt with in Chapter 7, this volume). I would wish to cover the underlying psychological principles, because if one understands the psychological dynamics inherent in the Reid Technique then the impact and consequences of the activity in Abu Ghraib and Gitmo are more apparent and meaningful. The Reid techniques are in common use in the USA and have been resorted to by officers in the UK in serious criminal cases (Pearse and Gudjonsson 1999).

The psychological characteristics associated with the Inbau–Reid model have been articulated by Bryan Jayne (1986), a director at Reid Associates. He starts with the premise that people will want to avoid the consequences of their actions. They will be motivated to deceive, in order to avoid consequences that are 'real' or 'personal'. The former involves loss of freedom, the latter reduced self-esteem or loss of integrity. Therefore, interrogation can be thought of as the undoing of deception by psychological means. Lying increases a person's internal anxiety and, as this level of anxiety increases, so the individual invokes two main defence mechanisms: 'rationalization' (the offender justifies his or her actions) or 'projection' (where he or she attributes blame elsewhere). The optimum scenario to achieve a confession or to get someone to talk, therefore, would be to decrease a person's perception of the (real or personal) consequences of confession – 'minimization' and, at the same time, increase the (internal) anxiety associated with continued deception – 'maximization'. In layperson's terms, therefore, it is important to consider the psychological impact of brute force, flagrant examples of abuse and the debilitating effect of a coercive physical environment on what the detainee is thinking. To take it a step further it is necessary to consider the psychological impact of individual tactics and the cumulative effect of different groups of tactics that have been employed against a detainee. For the purpose of this chapter I would seek to explain the many reported interrogation techniques within a five-category typology – namely, delivery, maximization, deprivation, manipulation and degradation.

Understanding and categorizing interrogation techniques at Abu Ghraib and Guantánamo Bay

Interrogation techniques practised in a war zone or armed conflict tend to involve techniques carried out at the extremes of human behaviour, such as the extreme levels of coercion and fear that are applied (Forrest 1999; Mackey and Miller 2004), and this distinction is accepted as we seek to compartmentalize these techniques. The five categories are not intended to be mutually exclusive; it will quickly become evident that recurring themes of religious and sexual abuse, for example, underpin a number of techniques in a number of the categories. There are a number of reasons to extend Kassin and McNall's (1991) earlier work. The first is to emphasize the role and importance of the context within which an interrogation takes place – we are, after all, heavily influenced by the situation we are in, as Zimbardo clearly showed. Another reason is that it will provide a more appropriate vehicle to understand the power and influence of psychologically manipulative techniques.

Delivery

This is very much an overarching category, present throughout the remaining four groups, and it is intended to capture the wider influences at play in an interrogation environment beyond the dual-categorization model of Kassin and McNall. In the narrow sense this category concerns the type of questions asked and 'how' the questions are put (i.e. the manner in which they are delivered). For example, for open, closed and leading questions, dialogue may take place in hushed or lowered tones or, at the other end of the spectrum, questioning may take place in a hostile and intimidating environment (Mackey and Miller 2004; Rose 2004). For law enforcement personnel this might extend to officers using raised or aggressive tones, continually interrupting the suspect and refusing to listen to his or her answers, and perhaps shouting and swearing at the suspect. In the broader sense this category also includes 'where' such questioning make take place. Here, one is reminded once more of the early press coverage of detainees at Gitmo who, shackled and clad in orange jump-suits, were bound to small carts and wheeled to the interrogation centre. And at Abu Ghraib where detainees have allegedly been subjected to a range of unacceptable regimes including the use of ferocious dogs as part of the 'warming up' process by the guards on behalf of the interrogation team.

Maximization

According to Kassin and McNall (1991: 234), maximization represents 'a hard sell technique in which the interrogator tries to scare and intimidate the suspect into confessing by making false claims about evidence and exaggerating the seriousness and the magnitude of the charges'. This term has been extended to include any technique which would tend to increase a suspect's internal anxiety and any form of intimidation or challenge directed at the suspect. This will include assault and the threat of assault or continued detention (Pearse 1997; Pearse and Gudjonsson 1999). In purely descriptive terms, during a period of war or armed conflict we would expect to see an increase in the intensity of this physical and psychological regime that would effectively replace Kassin and McNall's scaring and intimidation of the suspect, with an extensive panoply of tactics designed to terrorize and place a suspect in fear for his or her life. (Given the earlier discussion on the bidirectional nature of violence, the reader will note the deliberate inclusion of the use of the verb *terror*.) Maximization is therefore the category designed to capture the harshest of physical and psychological activity.

In relation to Gitmo and Abu Ghraib this will include the shackling of detainees in irons, their 'three-piece suits' (Rose 2004), forcing them to undergo interrogation whilst chained to the floor in the foetal position, and being made to stand for hours, hooded, subjected to intense heat and cold, and loud music.

Having said that such violent acts tend to be confined to war zones, it needs to be remembered that such activity can be carried out by law enforcement officers. Graef (2000) reports the incident of a Haitian man who was sodomized with a plunger handle by several officers in a police station in Brooklyn, USA, and Forrest (1999) provides numerous examples of torture techniques regularly applied by Indian police officers.

Deprivation

This category is in effect a subset of maximization and is included because of the prevailing circumstances often peculiar to war zones and armed conflict where denials of basic human needs tend to be more commonplace. Included within this category will therefore be the denial of sufficient food and water, sleep and rest, suitable accommodation and toilet facilities and other basic rights specified within the Geneva Convention (Convention III: Relative to the Treatment of Prisoners of War 1949).

Taken together these two categories are designed to capture the most basic and brutal attempts by one human being to exercise control and suborn the will of another. This may seem far removed from understanding and applying the various psychological techniques recommended by Inbau *et al.* (2001) but the blunt truth is likely to be that in war zones, interrogators will take shortcuts, they will not have time for 'nine steps'. In the next category we will move away from trying to imagine the effect of physical brutality on a detainee to examine more subtle tactics.

Manipulation

The debilitating effect on a detainee's resolve of physical isolation, depravation and confinement may not, on their own, be sufficient to break a person down. In the UK it was recognized by Lord Chief Justice Taylor (the most senior judge in the country), in *R. v. Paris and others* ([1993] 97 Cr. App. R. 99), that despite the presence of aggressive and intimidating interviewing tactics and the inherently coercive nature of police detention, it was the manipulative and 'insidious questioning' (p. 104) that succeed in eliciting a confession. This can include reducing a detainee's perception of the crime or the consequences of his or her actions, but it will also include manipulating significant details, introducing themes and attacking a person's self-esteem, his or her emotional well-being or stature. Other tactics include embellishment, the manipulative use of important third parties, inducements and offers of leniency or favourable terms.

This powerful combination of psychological manoeuvres often occupies a more latent profile and tends not to grab the headlines to the same extent as the manifestly aggressive maximization methods, but there is no doubt that undermining a detainee's perception of reality is a key feature in any interrogation regime designed to break a person down. Perhaps the most effective example of the use of manipulation that I have been exposed to recently was that practised by the Israeli Security Agency (ISA – formerly Shin Bet). In 2004, I interviewed an unsuccessful suicide bomber at an Israeli detention centre, located near the West Bank. The reason that the 19-year-old youth had failed was because he had become detached from his guide, an 'experienced' 15-year-old responsible for taking the bomber to the intended target. Once in the hands of the ISA (having been originally detained by the Israeli army), the bomber entered an environment that was effectively a complete deception. So, for example, according to his interrogating officer, there was no need to apply any maximization techniques; instead he was befriended and made welcome in the traditional Arab custom.

The interrogating officer spoke excellent Arabic, immediately alleviating the problem of truncated and distorted dialogue through any third party. In his interaction with the youth he was able to draw heavily on the fact that he understood the perspective of the youngster. In this instance, the detainee was a recent recruit plucked from the 'production line' of willing and available candidates in that area of the West Bank. His training amounted to little more than being shown the completed explosive device in a shoulder bag and instructions how to detonate the switch mechanism (although he did spend a few days in contemplation and spiritual preparation).

Accordingly, the officer went to great lengths to reassure him and to create an informal atmosphere with coffee and fruit. He then went on to manipulate the role of other parties (also detained) and also the role of influential third parties – family, village contemporaries and perhaps most important of all his religious beliefs. Aware that the youth would feel burdened with the shame that he would have brought on his family because he had failed in his task, and that he would perceive that he alone would have to accept the blame for this failure, the officer quickly moved to provide face-saving excuses and other classic manipulation tactics. Essentially, the officer was able to convince the youngster that it 'must have been Allah's will that he had remained alive', not that he had failed, but 'Allah in his mercy had decided that he should be reunited with his family on earth'. These, and similar manipulative tactics, elicited a full confession from this 'terrorist suicide bomber' within an hour.

Degradation

Just as depravation can be seen to represent a subcategory of maximization, so this section could be subsumed within manipulation, except that the unique circumstances associated with a war zone tend to propel this specific category into the limelight. Degradation includes all those tactics that are designed to humiliate and degrade a person's self-belief, a violent assault on his or her self-esteem, and cultural or religious beliefs. What appears to have been prevalent in the Abu Ghraib prison complex is the use of simulated sexual acts, carried out by groups of naked and hooded detainees under the control of male and female guards and sometimes with fearsome guard dogs in the vicinity. Such activity clearly falls within this category.

In his description of the allegations of abuse and torture at Gitmo and Abu Ghraib, Meek (2005) crystallizes the essential components of four categories of this suggested typology. He starts by attributing the upsurge in torture and humiliation at the Abu Ghraib prison to the visit of Major General Geoffrey Miller, and the subsequent implementation of his policy of using the guards to soften up the detainees. He notes that, following this visit:

Prisoners were hooded, threatened with rape, threatened with torture, had pistols held to their heads, made to strip naked, forced to eat pork and drink alcohol, beaten till they bled – sometimes with implements, including a broom and a chair – hung from doors by cuffed hands, deceived into thinking they were to be electrocuted, ducked in toilet buckets, forced to simulate masturbation, forced to lie naked in a pile and be photographed, urinated on, menaced and, in one case, severely bitten by dogs, sodomized with a chemical light, ridden like horses, made to wear women's underwear, raped, deprived of sleep, exposed to the mid-day summer sun, put in stress positions and made to lie naked in empty concrete cells, in complete darkness, for days on end (2005: 4).

79

Such a disturbing summary of the four most overt categories can be seen as a violent precursor for what is likely to follow: the 'insidious' and more latent category – manipulation, carried out by those in control of the interrogation.

It is hoped that, by breaking down the many examples of reported techniques into five main categories, the reader will more easily recognize what it is that is taking place, and be better able to appreciate the psychological consequences of such tactics and the relevance of the interplay between and within all five groups.

The banality of torture

The subtitle to this chapter is a direct reference to the influential political commentary by Hannah Arendt on the Adolf Eichmann trial in Jerusalem in 1960 (Arendt 1970). The subtitle to her work was *A Report on the Banality of Evil*. This highly provocative claim by the German-Jewish political philosopher was widely misunderstood at the time as an attempt to lessen the responsibility that should be attached to Nazi war criminals, such as Eichmann, who was responsible for 'the final solution' (his own phrase). In fact, what Arendt was articulating had more to do with the whole philosophical concept of evil, a challenge she had been struggling to come to terms with as she studied the totalitarian regimes of Hitler and Stalin: what was the root of such evil?

Her attendance at the Eichmann trial, on behalf of *New Yorker Magazine*, provided her with the insight she needed to explain what was taking place. In essence, she concluded that Eichmann was incapable of exercising the kind of judgement that would have made his victims' suffering real or apparent for him. It was not the presence of evil that enabled Eichmann to perpetrate the genocide, but the absence of the imaginative capacities that would have made the human and moral dimensions of his activities tangible for him. She described Eichmann as a buffoon, as he was unable to exercise his capacity to think, of having an internal dialogue with himself, of understanding the perspective of the other; that crucial ingredient that I have sought to promote throughout this chapter as the key psychological process underpinning an effective and acceptable interrogation paradigm. For Arendt, therefore, such acts could not be labelled evil as they had no root in the human consciousness. Given the circumstances under investigation today, can acts of torture ever be labelled banal?

Conclusion

In this chapter a distinction has been made between the extreme levels of behaviour practised by interrogators in war zones and areas of armed conflict compared with the attitude and behaviour of interrogators in the conventional law enforcement role. The unifying psychological thread that links both groups is the ability to adopt the perspective of the other. This innate quality has been championed throughout the chapter as it allows the interrogator to consider the detainee as someone other than a highly dangerous psychopath, and the same process can also increase the awareness of the interrogator's own susceptibility to bias, error and prejudice. Attention has also been paid to the corrosive and highly influential role that the physical environment can play under certain circumstances.

As international media coverage has highlighted an extensive array of interrogation techniques practised at Guantánamo Bay and the Abu Ghraib prison, a more straightforward and user-friendly typology has been outlined that is composed of five categories: delivery, maximization, deprivation, manipulation and degradation. This is designed to assist in promoting a better understanding of the psychological influences at work in these interactions.

A simple measure of the impact of this chapter would be to ask how many different perspectives the reader may have adopted during the course of the work. To what extent were you able to understand the perspective of the interrogator and did your views alter as you oscillated between the concepts and meaning of terrorism and terrorist? At any time did you empathize with the detainees and do you now have a different perspective on the banality of torture?

References

Arendt, H. (1970) *Eichmann in Jerusalem: A Report on the Banality of Evil.* Viking Press.

Chomsky, N. (2003) *Hegemony or Survival. America's Quest for Global Dominance.* Harmondsworth: Penguin Books.

Cooper, H.H.A. (1977) 'What is a terrorist: a psychological perspective', *Legal Medical Quarterly,* 1: 16–32.

Farr, R.M. (1982) 'Interviewing: the social psychology of the interview', in C.L. Cooper and P. Makin (eds) *Psychology for Managers.* Macmillan: London.

Festinger, L. (1957) *A Theory of Cognitive Dissonance.* Evanston, IL: Row, Peterson.

Firth, A. (1975) 'Interrogation', *Police Review*, 4324: 1507.

Forrest, D.M. (1999) 'Examination for the late physical after effects of torture', *Journal of Clinical Forensic Medicine*, 6: 4–13.

Geneva Convention (1949) *Convention III: Relative to the Treatment of Prisoners of War*. Geneva, 12 August.

Graef, R. (2000) 'An effective police officer must still be a fair cop', *The Times*, 20 January.

Gudjonsson, G.H. (1992) *The Psychology of Interrogations, Confessions and Testimony*. Chichester: Wiley.

Gudjonsson, G.H. (2003) *The Psychology of Interrogations and Confessions: A Handbook*. Chichester: Wiley.

Haney, C., Banks, C. and Zimbardo, P. (1973) 'Interpersonal dynamics in a simulated prison', *International Journal of Criminology and Penology*, 1: 69–97.

Heider, F. (1958) *The Psychology of Interpersonal Relations*. New York, NY: Wiley.

Hewstone, M. (1988) 'Causal attribution: from cognitive processes to collective beliefs', *The Psychologist: Bulletin of the British Psychological Society*, 8: 323–7.

Hinkle, L.E. (1961) 'The physiological state of the interrogation subject as it affects brain function', in A.D. Biderman and H. Zimmer (eds) *The Manipulation of Human Behaviour*. New York, NY: Wiley.

Inbau, F.E., Reid, J.E., Buckley, J.P. and Jayne, B.C. (2001) *Criminal Interrogation and Confessions* (4th edn). Gaithersberg, MD: Aspen.

Jayne, B.C. (1986) 'The psychological principles of criminal interrogation. An appendix', in F.E. Inbau *et al.* (eds) *Criminal Interrogations and Confessions* (3rd edn). Baltimore, MD: Williams & Wilkins.

Kassin, S.M. and McNall, K. (1991) 'Police interrogation and confessions', *Law Human Behaviour*, 15: 233–351.

Mackey, C. with Miller, G. (2004) *The Interrogator's War: Inside the Secret War against Al Qaeda*. London: John Murray.

Meek, J. (2005) 'Nobody is talking', *Guardian*, 18 February.

Mikulincer, M., Babkoff, H. and Caspy, T. (1989) 'The effects of 72 hours sleep loss on psychological variables', *British Journal of Psychology*, 80: 145–62.

Moston, S., Stephenson, G.M. and Williamson, T.M. (1992) 'The effects of case characteristics on suspect behaviour during police questioning', *British Journal of Criminology*, 32: 23–40.

Ofshe, R.J. and Leo, R.A. (1997) 'The social psychology of police interrogation: the theory and classification of true and false confessions', *Studies in Law, Politics and Society*, 16: 189–251.

Oppenheim, A. (1968) *Questionnaire Design and Attitude Management*. London: Heinemann.

Pearse, J. (1997) 'Police interviewing: an examination of some of the psychological, interrogative and background factors that are associated with a suspect's confession.' Unpublished PhD thesis, University of London.

Pearse, J. and Gudjonsson, G.H. (1999) 'Measuring influential police interviewing tactics: a factor analytic approach', *Legal and Criminological Psychology*, 4: 221–38.

Rasch, W. (1979) 'Psychological dimensions of political terrorism in the Federal Republic of Germany', *International Journal of Law and Psychiatry*, 2: 79–85.

Rose, D. (2004) *Guantanamo. America's War on Human Rights*. London: Faber & Faber.

Shallice, T. (1974) 'The Ulster depth interrogation techniques and their relation to sensory depravation research', *Cognition*, 1: 385–406.

Silke, A. (1998) 'Cheshire Cat logic: the recurring theme of terrorist abnormality in psychological research', *Psychology, Crime and Law*, 4: 51–69.

Silke, A. (2003) 'Becoming a terrorist', in A. Silke (ed.) *Terrorists, Victims and Society: Psychological Perspectives on Terrorism and its Consequences*. Chichester: Wiley.

Tendler, S. (2002) *The Times*, 7 and 8 May (online at www.timesonline. co.uk).

Trankel, A. (1972) *Reliability of Evidence*. Stockholm: Beckmans.

Walsh, I. (2003) *Irish Independent*, 7 August (online at www.independent.ie).

Zimbardo, P. (1971) 'The pathology of imprisonment', *Society*, 9: 4–8.

Part 2

Developments in Research

Chapter 5

The psychology of rapport: five basic rules[1]

Michel St-Yves

Introduction

This chapter considers the crucial importance of communication skills for effective interviewing. It examines a model for establishing and maintaining rapport developed as a result of research for the Sûreté du Québec,[2] Québec, Canada. It concludes by raising questions which indicate the need for further research in this area and by identifying possible areas for fruitful research.

Research into the conduct of investigative interviews has led to a better understanding of the human factors involved in questioning in a criminal justice context and, as a result, to the development of new interview techniques that are much more reliable and effective in eliciting information from witnesses, victims or suspects than standard techniques. Examples include the processes for non-suggestive interviews with children (Yuille 1989) and cognitive interviewing (Fisher and Geiselman 1992). The knowledge gained from research has resulted in these new techniques contributing to a more thoroughly conducted investigation and, at the same time, to reducing the risk of judicial errors. However, one of the most important factors in a successful interview is the relationship created between interviewer(s) and interviewee, yet if it is often neglected and sometimes completely ignored in training programmes. Even the best interview techniques depend on the quality of the relationship established between the two parties.

In this chapter, we concern ourselves with the most basic of all human rapports: that of establishing and maintaining a relationship.

From the first contact to the last, we examine the importance of communication skills and emphasize five basic rules derived from our research which we consider to be essential to conducting an investigative interview successfully:

1. Keeping an open mind and remaining objective.
2. Building up a rapport.
3. Paying attention.
4. Keeping a professional attitude.
5. Knowing how to conclude.

Communication skills are rarely taught in police academies and in some it is still a taboo topic, which is unfortunate given that it has such a central place in improving investigative interviewing practices.

To enter a relationship one has to make contact and exchange information in a way designed to create mutual rapport. It is important to be able to keep an open mind, to pay attention and to have an empathetic attitude that promotes good communication. For rapport to develop, and especially when building up a relationship with a witness, victim or suspect, the ideal is for the relationship to be genuine. We believe that a genuine relationship is more likely to lead to creating trust and confidence in the interviewer and to truthful accounts being provided. Rapport is defined as 'developing an understanding relationship or communication between people' (*Oxford Reference Dictionary*). It is the invisible wave along which information can flow from the one to the other. If there is a problem with rapport the information received may be distorted or not received at all.

Keeping an open mind and remaining objective

We now consider the five basic rules that we have identified that contribute to good rapport in the context of the psychological research from which they have been developed. The first contact with the person being interviewed is often decisive. It is on this first contact that the two parties will form their opinion of one another. This perception will then guide their behaviour. First impressions will be created on the initial information received by the investigator regarding the person to be interviewed (e.g. a written statement, a testimony from a neighbour, a forensic report, a judicial file or even just a picture). Therefore, it is possible, if not probable, that the interviewer will already have formed an impression of the person to be interviewed even before the first meeting. This subjective perception, which is often false, will have a strong influence on the unfolding of the interview. The perceived biases are traps to watch out for. The two most common perception errors identified in psychological research are impression formation and the Rosenthal effect.

Impression formation

Solomon E. Asch (1907–96), a pioneer of social psychology, was the precursor of research on the shaping of impressions. He demonstrated that we form impressions of others based on the first elements perceived. Asch maintained that the first information would be more likely to determine our impression of others than the last information. For example, if we describe a person as intelligent, hard-working, impulsive, critical, hard-headed and envious, the impression of that person is rather positive. If we reverse the description (envious, hard-headed, critical, impulsive, hard-working and intelligent), the impression is negative (Asch 1987). Asch's research demonstrated that the shaping of impressions occurs quickly and leads to a lasting impression. He discovered that it is very hard to get rid of a first impression, especially when it is a false one. The natural tendency is, rather, to try to validate our perception instead of staying receptive and keeping an open mind regarding the other person. This is why it is so important for interviewers to be trained to keep an open mind and to remain objective, as this should increase the likelihood of obtaining the truth.

The Rosenthal effect

The initial impression can have a strong effect on the perception of others and can become a 'Pygmalion' effect that can transform a subjective reality into an objective reality. In the 1960s, Robert Rosenthal, an American psychologist, carried out a study that would become one of the most revolutionary of modern psychology. Rosenthal and Jacobson (1968) gave primary school teachers a list of potentially talented students supposedly chosen after taking psychometrics tests. In reality, these students had been chosen at random. The real goal of the research was not to predict talented students but to condition the teachers without their knowledge. The results observed by Rosenthal exceed all expectations. At the end of the year, the students initially identified at random as potentially talented had progressed a great deal more than the others. Rosenthal and Jacobson (1968) explain this phenomenon in the following way: the prediction of an event (or the belief in its arrival) by individual A regarding individual B will be fulfilled whether it is only in the mind of A or – by a subtle and unforeseen process – by a modification of the real behaviour of B under pressure from the expectations of A.

The perceived biases induced by these preconceived notions therefore condition our behaviour and can have such influence on others that the answers observed are none other than the results of this perceived bias. In the investigative interviewing field, our preconceived notions can also influence our perception and therefore influence the result. In their study of interrogation of suspects, Moston and Stephenson (1993) have observed that investigators were less inclined to give suspects the benefit of the doubt if they had criminal records. Investigators were more inclined to put the emphasis on getting a confession rather than getting to the truth, and may have been acting in a prejudiced and stereotypical way as predicted by Rosenthal. Mortimer (1994) states that investigators who take for granted the fact that their suspect is guilty, even before their meeting, have a tendency to focus more on obtaining a confession and thus use an accusatory interviewing style.

Presumption of innocence or of guilt?

From the outset, the attitude of the investigator towards the suspect will have a major impact on the unfolding of the interrogation. The interviewer can enter into a relationship with the suspect by presuming his or her guilt, his or her innocence or by keeping a neutral position. All these attitudes have advantages and disadvantages.

According to Inbau et al. (2001: 68–70), the presumption of guilt has the advantage of provoking a reaction of resentment from the innocent person, whereas a guilty person has a tendency not to demonstrate any resentment and to show certain non-verbal reactions. Nevertheless, when there is little evidence, a guilty suspect who does not confess swiftly could form the impression that the interviewer is bluffing and therefore becomes psychologically stronger whilst continuing to resist and deceive. If the interviewer is convinced the suspect is guilty, he or she may be biased and may steer his or her questions and interpret the suspect's answers in a biased way, as in the Rosenthal effect. A problem with this approach is that an innocent suspect can also become destabilized, disturbed and confused. There is a risk that the interpretation of these suspicious behaviours may strengthen the bias towards the suspect with potentially serious consequences for the investigation. As for the presumption of innocence, Inbau and his colleagues (2001) consider that this attitude clearly favours innocent suspects and allows the investigator more easily to prove their innocence.

We regard the neutral position as being the best approach because it is more objective and tries to minimize the risk of bias. However, this technique is the most difficult because it is necessary to put aside our personal prejudices, and often those of our colleagues.

Developing rapport requires one to be flexible and to demonstrate a great deal of personal openness (Bull and Cherryman 1995; Shaw 1998; Cherryman and Bull 2001). The quality that we describe as open-mindedness is intended to promote disclosure, notably by bringing down the reservations associated with the fear of being judged negatively.

To initiate a relationship with a witness, victim or suspect the right way, it is first necessary to avoid or reduce all forms of negative contamination. One must break the scripts constructed from our personal and professional experiences, erase the stereotypes and put aside our preconceived notions. We need to protect our perceptions just as much as our forensic colleagues do with crime scenes because, once contaminated, it is often too late.

Building up rapport

To build rapport is to find a balance between what we desire and what the other agrees to. The investigator will increase rapport by being attentive both to the speech (what's said and not said) and to the behaviour (non-verbal indicators, emotions) of his or her interlocutor. The investigator should observe the slightest verbal and non-verbal behaviours and interpret them correctly. The reliability of the interpretation is a hotly disputed subject within psychology because we are prone to make the wrong attributions (for a scientific basis for detecting deception, see Ekman 1992; Vrij 2000). This form of analysis allows the interviewer to judge when and how to ask a question or to make a comment; when to say 'I see' or 'hmm, hmm'; and when and how to confront the subject with his or her remarks or with new evidence. It is because of the complexity of this interrelationship of behavioural dynamics that good interviewing is an art. It is the capacity for cognitive analysis, together with a synchronizing of appropriate behaviours, that usually determines a very good interviewer. Rapport lies at the heart of a good interview. Whereas other techniques can be helpful, rapport can do without these techniques, and techniques without rapport are unlikely to be effective.

All that an interviewer is and does can also have a substantial impact on the person being interviewed. A gesture, a word, an attitude, a posture and even one's personality can generate thoughts and emotions in the other. For example, the interviewer's attitude can remind the subject of, for example, his or her father with whom he or she is or was on bad terms. Or, either by your features or tone of voice, you can remind the interviewee of someone who is dear to him or her. This information may be processed subconsciously, but the impact (which is impossible to predict) is called in psychology 'transference' and 'counter-transference' (Freud 1910: 1912). This phenomenon can sometimes explain why one has more success interviewing certain people than others.

Transference and counter-transference

Certain people, either by their attitude, their personality or even by the nature of the crime itself, generate thoughts – positive or negative emotions – that emanate from their past and that concern important people in their lives. This transference can be positive or negative. When the transference is positive, the person seems to be more likeable and rapport is much easier to establish. When the transference is negative, not only is there no affinity but hostility (although sometimes subtle) may also be present. This hostility can be expressed by cutting remarks, impatience or an attitude which is too authoritative. This happens frequently in regard to people suspected of committing serious crimes. It can also happen when we feel antipathy towards victims or witnesses.

Counter-transference is the sum of the emotions (positive or hostile) the interviewer feels towards the person being interviewed. Thus a suspect can, either by his or her behaviour, looks or the nature of his or her crime, instigate in the interviewer reactions (internal at first) that are expressed in a manner that is more or less perceivable and that may have consequences for the suspect. These reactions are totally human and normal. The interviewer, however, has to be aware of them and take them into account so as to minimize the impact of negative transference during the interview.

Being aware of these phenomena can help investigators understand why they are more or less comfortable with certain people, whether they are victims, witnesses or suspects. This realization allows them to minimize the harmful effects of negative counter-transference. Negative transference may explain numerous situations when rapport is difficult to establish with another person. The phenomenon of 'kindred spirits' may be the result of a positive transferential dynamic on both the interviewer and the person being interviewed. Colloquially, this is sometimes known as being 'on the same wavelength'.

Initiating good contact

First contact is often visual and may be followed by a warm welcome and a hand shake. In a few seconds, a link will have been created, but it will have to be fed if it is to grow. Rapport creates trust and builds a psychological bridge between the interviewer and the interviewee (Collins and Miller 1994; Lieberman 2000; Schafer and Navarro, 2003). According to Shepherd and Kite (1988), a warm welcome is an essential ingredient of a successful interview. Shepherd (1988) identifies two types of abilities needed to develop constructive rapport: 1) interpersonal skills, notably the capacity to communicate and to listen; and 2) the skills needed for cognitive analysis, including an understanding of human psychology. It is mostly the latter that is emphasized during police training. However, without interpersonal skills, rapport may not be possible. As Schafer and Navarro (2003: 39) say: 'A person reveals no secret without rapport.'

When an introduction is completed, the investigator has to explain to the person being interviewed the goals of their meeting. He or she has to satisfy their immediate needs for information and allay any concerns so as to eliminate as much distraction as possible that could be prejudicial to the creation of good rapport. The objective is to create a mood that will encourage the person to talk. Contrary to popular belief, good interviewing is more about listening than about talking. There is nothing more effective than paying attention to someone to encourage him or her to talk.

Paying attention

Hearing does not necessarily mean listening. To listen means to be attentive to what someone is saying. In psychology, this is called 'active listening', a communication technique developed by the American psychologist, Carl Rogers (1902–87). Although at first this may appear simple, this technique is difficult to master because it goes against basic human behaviour. It is, however, indispensable to establishing a trusting link with the others. Rogers' approach (1942) is based upon the unconditional acceptation and valorization of the other, and on empathy and authenticity.

Many investigators do not know how to listen: they do not acknowledge the suspect's concerns. Often, they are only interested in the crime and not in the person being interrogated. They are often preoccupied by their strategies, which makes them less receptive to the other person. Furthermore, investigators are often uncomfortable with silences, particularly when interviews are being filmed. They feel obliged to fill idle periods with useless questions or irrelevant remarks they may have to rectify later (St-Yves and Lavallée 2001).

Active listening is a reading of what the other expresses. It takes into account the words and behaviour of the person being interviewed (the transmitter), and seeks to stimulate the expression of the transmitter's message without interruption, and especially without the transmitter contaminating the message with his or her own scripts.

The major ingredients of active listening are as follows:

- *Minimal encouragement*: encouragements are signs given out to the transmitter that you are really listening to what the interviewee is expressing and without interruption. These signs can be visual (for example, facial expressions, head nodding, posture) or auditory ('OK', 'I see', 'yes', 'Uh hum'). An absence of encouragement can indicate a lack of interest and attention. Encouragements can increase the amount of speech uttered by the transmitter by up to three or four times (Wainwright 1993).

- *Paraphrases*: paraphrases come in many shapes. For example, there is reformulation (reform in your own words what the transmitter said) and reflection, commonly called the 'echo' (repeating the subject's last words or viewpoint). Paraphrases reassure the transmitter that his or her message has been listened to and understood. This will facilitate discussion and rapport.

- *Identification of emotions*: putting into words the emotions expressed by the transmitter shows the depth of your empathy. It also facilitates the awakening of insight.

- *Open questions*: avoid questions that only require a 'yes' or 'no' answer. Avoid the 'why' and 'yes, but' because these questions are pejorative and imply defeat. Open questions reduce the risk of perceptual biases.

- *The 'I'*: using 'I' shows you are concerned about the transmitter's remarks. It humanizes rapport.

- *Silence*: if you cannot find the words to stimulate or reassure the transmitter, it is preferable to say nothing. Silences have their place and have often proved to be beneficial. Silences also allow time to think.

Keeping a professional attitude: interviewing styles

The style of interview adopted by the investigator can have a great influence on the unfolding of the interrogation. Cassell and Hayman (1998) observed that investigators are more likely to obtain a confession than patrol officers. This could be explained by the fact that investigators have more experience than patrol officers and are more capable and self-confident in interrogation (Gudjonsson 2003). Investigators may also have received more advanced training to conduct investigative interviews.

Williamson (1990, 1993) identified four styles of questioning preferred by different types of interviewers based on how friendly or unfriendly they were towards the interviewee and whether they saw the purpose of the interview as obtaining a confession or securing evidence. The interviewers' responses to an extensive range of questions designed to elicit their preferred interviewing strategies and attitudes were then examined in a factor analysis. This analysis revealed four distinct factors:

Factor 1 ('perceived success') indicated a positive attitude towards the questioning of suspects. It was seen as an important task, taken seriously and practised frequently with a significant degree of success as measured by the number of confessions obtained; friendly styles of questioning were preferred.

Factor 2 ('dominance') indicated a preference for unfriendly questioning styles with the use of rapid questioning intended to keep up the pressure on suspects. Trickery was considered necessary, and there was evidence of a lack of sympathy for, and adaptation to, a new legal framework for regulating custodial questioning.

Factor 3 ('perceived difficulty') indicated that, although there was a preference for friendly styles of questioning, this was an area of activity that was found to be difficult and that was not associated with success (if success is taken as obtaining confessions). The legal regulation of custodial questioning meant this style of questioning was more difficult for the police, that they had much less leverage and that their position was therefore weaker than in the past. A clue to the underlying causes of this factor may lie in responses that indicated a need for training.

Factor 4 ('persuasion') indicated an approach where interviewing was seen as a process of bargaining aimed at securing a confession, and this was best achieved through the manipulation of friendly questioning styles. This approach was quite successful and was particularly appropriate in cases where the evidence in the case was weak and where an untruthful denial was expected.

It is important to note that the dominant interviewing style was not associated with success, yet this remains the preferred style of many law enforcement officials. It is also interesting to note that the group of responses indicating that interviewing is an activity that some detectives found difficult suggested need for training. None of the detectives in this study had received any formal interview training because no training courses had been developed in the UK at the time. These responses accord with the finding by Sear and Stephenson (1997) that, at the time of this research, investigators were more at ease with an approach aimed at obtaining a confession rather than an approach designed to collect new information.

Moston and his colleagues (Moston and Engelberg 1993; Moston and Stephenson 1993) have observed that the two styles most frequently used by police officers are the confrontation and the persuasive approach. Often, investigators accused the suspect of committing the crime, informed the suspect of the evidence they had against him or her and then asked the suspect to confirm their allegations. When the interviewers were faced with a denial or silence, they had a tendency to repeat the question in a stronger and more aggressive tone of voice (see the 'dominance' factor above) or simply to respond by silence or by inferring that the suspect was lying (see the 'perceived difficulty' factor above). Faced with opposition, investigators do not always possess the communication abilities to negotiate with the suspect, and so the interview ends with the persistent denial of responsibility (Moston and Engelberg 1993; Moston and Stephenson 1993). Baldwin (1992), in his research into videotaped interviews, puts the emphasis on the need for professionalism and open-mindedness from interviewers, which will allow more time for the suspect to think and to give him or her the opportunity to express his or her point of view.

According to Baldwin (1992), the worst type of interviewer is the one who uses a 'macho' style and who is unable to recognize how this attitude is counterproductive. A humane attitude (including active listening, empathy, openness, respect and a willingness to discover the truth instead of trying desperately to obtain a confession) is a quality that plays an essential role in the unfolding of a good investigative interview (Shepherd 1991; Williamson 1993). A study by Crépault and Boisvenue (2003) into the victims of major crimes demonstrated that, after attentiveness, empathy (sensibility and warmth) is the factor most associated with the satisfaction of the victims concerning police investigations.

In Sweden, Holmberg (2004) analyzed the responses to a questionnaire completed by 83 men convicted of murder or sexual offences. The results showed that, when the police interviewed murderers and sex offenders, suspects perceive attitudes characterized by dominance or humanity. Logistic regression indicated that police interviews marked by dominance are mainly associated with a higher proportion of denials, whereas an approach marked by humanity is associated with admissions. Holmberg argued that, when suspects feel they are respected and acknowledged, they possibly gain more confidence and mental space that allow them to admit to criminal behaviour. In a related study, a group of rape or aggravated assault victims (consisting of 178 women and men) answered a questionnaire concerning police behaviour in interviews. The results from a factor analysis showed that these victims perceived police attitudes to be characterized by dominance or humanity. Interviews characterized by dominance and feelings of anxiety were shown to be significantly associated with victims who omitted to supply important information. Interviews characterized by humanity and with feelings of respect and co-operation were significantly associated with victims who did provide all the relevant information (Holmberg 2004: 26). Given that the use of a domineering style appears to be less effective, it is important to understand why investigators have a tendency to adopt such authoritarian interviewing styles.

The concept of authority

Stanley Milgram made an outstanding contribution to the history of social psychology in his famous and controversial study of the submission to authority. Milgram (1974) recruited a number of volunteers to participate in research he described as concerning training. The people recruited were allocated teacher roles and they were instructed to institute sanctions against a person who was playing the role of a student. This person was, in fact, a member of the research team. The sanctions meted out by the 'teachers' were in the form of electric charges of increasing force, ranging from 0 (not severe) to 10 (extremely severe). The teachers could not see the student but could hear the student's screams when he was receiving the electric shocks. The electric discharges were, of course, fictitious but, from the moment the student expressed pain, the 'teacher' turned towards the researcher who reminded the teacher that he or she had committed him or herself to this course of action. On a scale of severity of sanctions ranging from 0 to 10, psychiatrists previously consulted by Milgram had predicted that the subjects would not exceed 3.5. In the event, more than 65 per cent of subjects delivered sanctions equivalent to 450 volts, which corresponds to a lethal electrical charge.

Milgram's research demonstrates that people in a situation of authority have a great deal of influence on others. His work shows that people have an automatic tendency to respond obediently to the symbols of authority, whether these be a title or a uniform. It is thus necessary to bear in mind that some people subject themselves more readily to police authority (Gudjonsson 1992; Clare and Gudjonsson 1993). People with less than average intellectual ability may feel intimidated when they are being interrogated by people in authority (Gudjonsson and MacKeith 1994; Gudjonsson 1995), and are often more willing and open to suggestion (Clare and Gudjonsson 1995). People who easily subject themselves to authority may also be more inclined to comply with police questioning and, therefore, to make false confessions (Kassin 1997).

In 1971, Zimbardo undertook a study aimed to explore the behaviour of 'normal' people in a prison environment (see Zimbardo et al. 1973; Zimbardo 1975; Chapter 4, this volume). The people recruited for this experiment (which was to last two weeks) comprised male students. On the second day of the experiment, the 'prisoners' rebelled against the exercise of authority, and the desperate 'wardens' responded by humiliating, bullying and even physically abusing the prisoners. After only a few days, the wardens began to behave like sadists and the prisoners became stressed and depressed. Zimbardo prematurely ended this experiment after six days. Zimbardo came to two conclusions. First, when a normal person is submitted to extreme conditions of humiliation and violence, he or she can crumble psychologically, can lose all self-esteem and can become depressed. On the other hand, when an individual is given power, he or she may reveal him or herself as a monster. According to Zimbardo, violence is not something innate but, rather, is closely related to power. The recent allegations of humiliating and sadist behaviour from American soldiers towards Iraqi prisoners detained at Abu Ghraib prison is perhaps a good example of the type of behaviour the Milgram and Zimbardo experiments would have predicted if guards and prisoners are not properly managed.

Because of their duties, police officers have the power to arrest or to detain people. During an interview with a suspect, police officers, in spite of themselves, will exercise the power of their authority. They are in a situation of authority and, therefore, must be conscious of the impact this power has on others and must not abuse it. This should prevent serious injustices occurring. The expression of anger or hostility during an investigative interview can lead to serious consequences. For example, an angry or hostile investigator may react impulsively or even aggressively when faced with a stubborn suspect. This may be manifested in impatience or unkind comments. The interview may then become oppressive which, as we have seen, will destroy rapport and may jeopardize the admission of guilt in court.

Cialdini (1993) suggests that authority can also be defined by competency. Research has shown that people take it for granted that experts know what they're talking about. People have a tendency to accept information on the grounds of the person who proffered it rather than on the grounds of its content (Maddux and Rogers 1983). This is the aura (or halo) effect. For an investigator to be considered a specialist or an authority figure in a suspect's eyes, the investigator must be perceived as competent.

Competency is associated with self-esteem and, by extension, with self-confidence. Interviewers, however, often lack self-confidence (Baldwin 1992). To perform well during an interrogation, investigators must appear self-confident. A lack of confidence can be expressed not only by nervousness but also by hesitations and other verbal hints (tone of voice, the excessive use of euphemisms, etc.). If the investigator is undecided, the evidence may also look uncertain

(St-Yves *et al.* 2004: 147). This can have a considerable influence on the result because the interviewee's perception of the weight of the evidence is the most important factor in deciding whether to admit to or to deny guilt during a police investigative interview (Moston *et al.* 1992).

Knowing how to conclude

The end of an interrogation often creates strong emotions. This can be the result of weariness or the suspect may have been angered by the investigator's questions and the interviewer may feel powerless in the presence of a persistent denial. The investigator who has a tendency to rise easily to anger is the most susceptible to compromising his or her professionalism. The interviewer may also feel a sense of failure which he or she attributes to the suspect. This may explain the tendency to vent frustrations through cutting remarks directed at the suspect. This approach has never been successful and puts an end to any future attempts to obtain information from the subject through questioning. In losing control, the investigator risks hindering the whole investigative process. A better and more strategic response would be to pause so that the interview can be resumed later.

According to Webster's dictionary (1983), to conclude is 'to form a final judgment'. Knowing how to conclude means ensuring that all the legal arguments have been covered, that the suspect has nothing to add and that he or she has been informed of what is going to happen next. Above all, the interviewer must remain professional, whether a confession has been obtained or not. Even in the absence of a confession, information obtained through questioning can be very valuable. Interviewers should always try to leave the door open for the possibility that the interviewee may make a confession in the next hour, the next day or even later, to the interviewer or to someone else. It is important to keep open the channels of communication.

This situation is analogous with crisis negotiations. First, like interviewers, good negotiators possess communication skills and are self-confident, energetic, creative and imaginative in their problem resolution, and they are sensitive to others (Getty and Elam 1988; Allen *et al.* 1990). These qualities are found in the profile of a typical, good investigative interviewer. The philosophy of the Sûreté du Québec reflects this: *Pax per conloquium* – resolution through dialogue (St-Yves *et al.* 2001). In a crisis situation, a good negotiator will first listen carefully and then assist the communication process by asking open questions that allow the other person to say what he or she wants and to express his or her emotions. To understand the individual and to decode all the messages he or she is sending out, the negotiator has to be attentive to a multitude of details: tone of voice, emotions and changes in attitude (Wargo 1990; Divasto 1996). This is another example of having to be on the same wavelength, and it is exactly the same thing with investigative interviews. However, the interviewer is in a better position than the negotiator because the interviewer can assess the suspect's non-verbal behaviour.

The negotiator will build rapport which, consequently, will serve as a bridge to allow the person with whom the negotiation is being conducted to resolve the crisis. Then, according to the pace at which the crisis unfolds (and according to the model developed at the Sûreté du Québec and known as SINCRO[3]), the negotiator will accompany the person throughout the various phases of the crisis until he or she surrenders, preferably voluntarily. The negotiator will do everything in his or her power to permit the person to preserve or to restore his or her dignity, often flattering him or her and then meeting the person again once he or she has given him or herself up to the police. Some negotiators will even accompany the person to hospital to demonstrate the authenticity of the rapport established between them. During an investigative interview, the interviewer who acts in this manner leaves not only a lasting, favourable impression of the rapport in the interviewee's memory but also actively contributes to the reintegrative possibilities for that person through the process of restorative justice (Braithwaite 1998).

Areas for further research

This chapter has examined the importance of communication skills for effective interviewing, and it is the author's opinion that this is an area that has been under-researched. It has been argued that communication skills and rapport can be taught. This assertion, however, raises some interesting questions. For example, can everyone be taught communication skills? It seems some people have better communication skills than others. Is this difference the result of something that has been learnt or are there innate differences in skills between individuals? Perhaps what is needed is a rigorous study that draws on the methodologies of the subdiscipline of the psychology of personality to ascertain whether such individual differences do indeed exist. A battery of selected psychometric tests, or subsets of these tests, could prove fruitful here. It may even be possible to develop a scale that could be used to select people who have an aptitude for interviewing. The anecdotal evidence from experienced interviewers and interview trainers is that successful interviewers seem to have the ability to establish rapport in what appears to be an effortless way. They seem able to create a situation where people trust them, feel relaxed and are happy to talk to them. Our experience is that good interviewers constantly practise and hone their skills wherever they go. In studies of interviewers, we have found that those who are good interviewers do the most interviewing, whereas those who do the most interviewing are generally good, but how far this applies the other way round is uncertain. Do good interviewers do a lot of interviewing because they have an innate ability, or does exposure to a great deal of interviewing mean that people become more skilled? More research is needed if we are to answer such questions as these.

Conclusion

This chapter has described different interviewing styles and compared their effectiveness. Psychological research suggests that a style which contributes to creating rapport is to be preferred, and from this five basic communication rules considered essential for conducting an effective investigative interview can be proposed:

1. *Keep an open mind and remain objective.* There are many traps in the field of interviewing. For example, a lack of objectivity can skew the investigation and can lead investigators to a fabricated outcome. This is called tunnel vision. On the other hand, objectivity aims to find out the truth and does not focus solely on convicting a suspect.

2. *Build rapport.* First and foremost, welcome the person warmly and then create an atmosphere that will encourage him or her to talk freely. This will find the balance between what the interviewer desires to know and what the suspect will agree to disclose. It is necessary to observe and to understand if good rapport is to grow.

3. *Pay attention.* Not paying attention inevitably leads to a fruitless interview. Listening, on the other hand, promotes an understanding of what really happened and not what the interviewer thinks happened.

4. *From start to finish keep a professional attitude.* An unprofessional attitude can be extremely prejudicial to the person being interviewed, especially if he or she is not guilty. An attitude of respect, empathy and open-mindedness favours the disclosure of information and, if appropriate, a confession. It also makes it easier for the courts to accept any disclosure or admission as evidence.

5. *Know how to conclude.* This ensures that everything that has been said has been addressed. The suspect should be allowed to preserve his or her dignity, and the conclusion should consolidate the rapport that has been established. One day this person may need to be interviewed again, so it is important to leave a positive impression. This particular interview may be the beginning, not the end, of a long series of events and relationships. To reach a satisfactory conclusion, interviewers should apply these five rules and should understand that they are the same for everyone.

Notes

1. This chapter is an English adaptation of 'La psychologie de la relation: cinq règles de base' (St. Yves, Tanguay and Crépault, 2004).
2. The Sûreté du Québec is a national police force which is responsible throughout Québec for keeping the peace and maintaining public order, safeguarding individuals' lives, security and basic rights, and protecting their property. The Sûreté du Québec co-ordinates large-scale police operations, participates in the integrity of state institutions and provides security for the Québec transport networks (Mission statement, Sûreté du Québec, www.surete.qc.ca).
3. The acronym SINCRO stands for **S**tratégie d'**I**ntervention et de **N**égociation par **C**ouleurs selon le **R**ythme **O**bservé or, translated loosely, 'response and negotiation strategy using colours and based on the rhythm of the crisis' (St-Yves *et al.* 2001).

References

Asch, S.E. (1987) *Social Psychology.* Oxford: Oxford University Press.
Baldwin, J. (1992) *Video Taping Police Interviews with Suspects – An Evaluation. Police Research Group. Police Research Series* Paper 1. London: Home Office.
Braithwaite, J. (1998) *Crime, Shame and Reintegration.* Cambridge: Cambridge University Press.

Bull, P. (2002) *Communication under the Microscope. The Theory and Practice of Microanalysis*. Hove: Routledge.

Bull, R. and Cherryman, J. (1995) *Helping to Identify Skills Gaps in Specialist Investigative Interviewing: Enhancement of Professional Skills*. (Report to the Home Office Police Research Group.)

Cassell, P.G. and Hayman, B.S. (1998) 'Police interrogation in the 1990s : an empirical study on the effect of Miranda', in R.A. Leo and G.C. Thomas III (eds) *The Miranda Debate, Justice and Policing*. Boston, MA: Northeastern University Press.

Cherryman, J. and Bull, R. (2001) 'Police officers' perception of specialist investigative interviewing skills', *International Journal of Police Science and Management*, 3: 199–212.

Cialdini, R.B. (1993) *Influence: Science and Practice* (3rd edn). Glenview, IL: Scott, Foresman.

Clare, I.C.H. and Gudjonsson, G.H. (1993) 'Interrogative suggestibility, confabulations and acquiescence in people with mild learning disabilities (mental handicap): implications for reliability during police interrogations', *British Journal of Clinical Psychology*, 32: 295–301.

Clare, I.C.H. and Gudjonsson, G.H. (1995) 'The vulnerability of suspects with intellectual disabilities during police interviews: a review and experimental study of decision-making', *Mental Handicap Research*, 8: 110–28.

Collins, N.L. and Miller, L.C. (1994) *Self-disclosure and liking: A meta-analytic review*. Psychological Bulletin, 116, 457–475.

Crépault, D. and Boisvenue, J. (2003) 'Attentes et niveau de satisfaction des victimes de crimes majeurs face à l'intervention des enquêteurs. Direction conseil et développement en enquêtes criminelles', unpublished study, Sûreté du Québec.

Divasto, P.V. (1996) *Negotiating with Foreign Language-Speaking Subjects*. FBI Law Enforcement Bulletin, June 1992, 11–15.

Ekman, P. (1992) *Telling Lies. Clues to deceit in the Market Place, Politics, and Marriage*. New York, NY: Norton.

Fisher, R.P. and Geiselman, R.E. (1992) *Memory-enhancing Techniques for Investigative Interviewing*. Springfield, IL: Charles Thomas.

Freud, S. (1910) 'La technique psychanalytique', in *Perspective d'avenir de la psychologie analytique* (1953). Paris: Presse Universitaire de France.

Freud, S. (1912) 'La dynamique du transfert', in *Perspective d'avenir de la psychologie analytique* (1953). Paris: Presse Universitaire de France.

Getty, V.S. and Elam, J.D. (1988) "Identifying characteristics of hostage negotiators, and using personality data to develop a selection model". In J. Reese and J. Horn (eds.), *Police Psychology: Operational Assistance*, pp. 159–171. Washington, DC: US Government Press.

Gudjonnsson, G.H. (1992) *The Psychology of Interrogations, Confessions and Testimony*. Chichester: Wiley.

Gudjonnsson, G.H. (1995) '"I'll help you boys as I can" – how eagerness to please can result in a false confession', *Journal of Forensic Psychiatry*, 6: 333–42.

Gudjonnsson, G.H. (2003) *The Psychology of Interrogations and Confessions. A Handbook*. Chichester: Wiley.

Gudjonnsson, G.H. and MacKeith, J.A.C. (1994) 'Learning disability and the Police and Criminal Evidence Act 1984. Protection during investigative interviewing: a video-recorded false confession to double murder', *Journal of Forensic Psychiatry*, 5: 35–49.

Holmberg, U. (2004) 'Police Interviews with victims and suspects of violent and sexual crimes; interviewees' experiences and interview outcomes.' Unpublished PhD thesis, Stockholm University.

Inbau, F.E., Reid, J.E., Buckley, J.P. and Jayne, B.C. (2001) *Criminal Interrogation and Confessions* (4th edn). Gaithersburg, MA: Aspen.

Kassin, S.M. (1997) 'The psychology of confession evidence', *American Psychologist*, 52: 221–33.

Lieberman, P. (2000) *Human Language and our reptilian brain: The subcortical bases of speech, syntax, and thought*. Cambridge, MA: Harvard University Press.

Maddux, J.E. and Rogers, R.W. (1983) 'Protection motivation and self-efficacy: a revised theory of fear appeals and attitude change', *Journal of Experimental Social Psychology*, 19: 469–79.

Milgram, S. (1974) *Obedience to Authority*. New York, NY: Harper & Row.

Mortimer, A. (1994) 'Asking the right questions', *Policing*, 10: 111–24.

Moston, S. and Engelberg, T. (1993) 'Police questioning techniques in tape-recorded interviews with criminal suspects', *Policing and Society*, 6: 61–75.

Moston, S. and Stephenson, G. (1993) 'The changing face of police interrogation', *Journal of Community and Social Psychology*, 3: 101–15.

Moston, S., Stephenson, G.M. and Williamson, T.M. (1992) 'The effects of case characteristics on suspect behaviour during police questioning', *British Journal of Criminology*, 32: 23–40.

Rogers, C.R. (1942) *Counselling and Psychotherapy: Newer Concepts in Practice*. Boston, MA: Houghton-Mifflin.

Rosenthal, R. and Jacobson, L. (1968) *Pygmalion in the Classroom*. New York, NY: Holt, Rinehart & Winston.

Schafer, J.R. and Navarro, J. (2003) *Advanced Interviewing Techniques*. Springfield, IL: Charles C. Thomas.

Sear, L. and Stephenson, G.M. (1997) 'Interviewing skills and individual characteristics of police interrogators', in G.M. Stephenson and N.K. Clark (ed.) *Procedures in Criminal Justice: Comtemporary Psychological Issues*. Leicester: British Psychological Society.

Shaw, G. (1998) 'Developing interview skills', in P. Southgate (ed.) *New Directions in Police Training*. London: HMSO.

Shepherd, E. (1988) 'Developing interview skills', in P. Southgate (ed.) *New Directions in Police Training*. London: HMSO.

Shepherd, E. (1991) 'Ethical interviewing', *Policing*, 7: 42–60.

Shepherd, E. and Kite, F. (1988) 'Training to interview', *Policing*, 4: 264–80.

St-Yves, M. (2004) 'L'aveu chez les auteurs de crimes sexuels', in M. St-Yves and J. Landry (eds) *Psychologie des entrevues d'enquête. De la recherche à la practique*. Éditions Yvon Blais.

St-Yves, M. and Lavallée, P.R. (2001) 'Interrogatoire vidéo: état de la situation à la Sûreté du Québec. Étude comparative et évolutive des techniques d'interrogatoires utilisées par la Sûreté du Québec. Direction conseil et développement en enquêtes criminelles.' Unpublished study.

St-Yves, M., Tanguay, M. and Crépault, D. (2004) 'La psychologie de la relation: cinq règles de base', in M. St-Yves and J. Landry (eds) *Psychologie des entrevues d'enquête: de la recherche à la pratique*. Éditions Yvon Blais.

St-Yves, M., Tanguay, M. and St-Pierre, J. (2001) 'Following the rhythm of a crisis', *International Criminal Police Review*, 491: 4–9.

Vrij, A. (2000) *Detecting Lies and Deceit. The Psychology of Lying and the Implications for Professional Practice*. Chichester: Wiley.

Wainwright, G.R. (1993) *Teach Yourself Body Language*. London: Hodder Headlines.

Wargo, M.G. (1990) *Communication Skills for Hostage Negotiators*. Police Marksman, March/April 1990, 52.

Williamson, T.M. (1990) 'Strategic changes in police interrogation: an examination of police and suspect behaviour in the Metropolitan Police in order to determine the effects of new legislation, technology and organizational policies.' Unpublished PhD thesis, University of Kent.

Williamson, T.M. (1993) 'From interrogation to investigative interviewing: strategic trends in police questioning', *Journal of Community and Social Psychology*, 3: 89–99.

Yuille, J.C. (1989) *Credibility Assesment*. Dordrecht: Kluwer Academic.

Zimbardo, P.G. (1975) 'On transforming experimental research into advocacy for social change', in M. Deutsch and H.A. Hornstein (eds) *Applying Social Psychology: Implications for Research, Practice, and Training*. Hillsdale, NJ: Erlbaum.

Zimbardo, P.G., Haney, C., Banks, C. and Jaffe, D. (1973) 'The mind is a formidable jailer: a Piretellian prison', *The New York Times Magazine*, 8 April.

Chapter 6

Confessions by sex offenders[1]

Michel St-Yves

Introduction

Research into police questioning has shown that several factors influence the outcome of an interview with a suspect, one of the most important of which is the attitude of the investigator (Shepherd 1991; Moston and Engelberg, 1993; Williamson 1993; Stephenson and Moston 1994; Holmberg and Christianson 2002). The interview techniques used also have a bearing on the interview (Leo 1996; Inbau *et al.* 2001). Some of the subject's characteristics – such as his or her age and sex (Phillips and Brown 1998), ethnic group (Pearse *et al.* 1998; St-Yves 2002), prior experiences with the judicial system (Neubauer 1974; Softley 1980; Evans 1993; Leo 1996) and personality (Gudjonnsson and Petursson 1991; Gudjonnsson and Sigurdsson 1999; St-Yves 2002) – can also influence whether a subject makes a confession or not. The nature and severity of the crime are also factors that play an important role (Neubauer 1974; Moston *et al.* 1992). This is particularly true when the crime is of a sexual crime nature (Gudjonnsson and Sigurdsson 2000; Holmberg and Christianson 2002; St-Yves 2002, 2004b).

Until now, there have not been many studies of the factors associated with the confessions made by sex offenders. Even the confession rates are disputed. Some have suggested that sex offenders confess more frequently than other types of criminal (Mitchell 1983; Gudjonnsson and Sigurdsson 2000), whereas others have observed the contrary (Holmberg and Christianson 2002; St-Yves 2002).

This chapter analyzes the major factors associated with confessions and denials with regard to sex offenders. It presents a detailed portrait of sex offenders who confess or deny their crimes and suggests some strategies that may encourage confessions. It should be borne in mind that confessions by sex offenders are important because confessions are often the major, if not the only, evidence of guilt (St-Yves 2002, 2004b).

The frequency of confessions made by sex offenders

In a study of 394 subjects who were not exclusively sex offenders, Mitchell (1983) found that sex offenders confessed much more often to the police (89.3 per cent) than all other categories of suspect (52.5 per cent). Gudjonnsson (1992) explains this finding by the fact that sex offenders may be less inclined to live with a strong sense of guilt, which thus stimulates their need to confess.

More recently, in a study in Iceland of 89 convicted subjects (of which 59 were sex offenders), Gudjonnsson and Sigurdsson (2000) observed higher confession rates for child molesters (83 per cent) in comparison with rapists (61 per cent), but the rates were not significantly higher than rates observed with other types of violent offender. In an earlier study, Nugent and Kroner (1996) also observed that child molesters confess more frequently to the police. Gudjonnsson and Sigurdsson (2000) explained their results by suggesting that child molesters feel a stronger urge to confess than rapists or other types of violent offender.

These British and Icelandic results seem to contradict those found in Canadian research. In a recent study of 496 sex offenders sentenced to a term of imprisonment of two years and more, St-Yves (2002) found that the majority of the subjects (66.5 per cent) had not co-operated with police officers at the time of their arrest, either by refusing to answer questions (41.2 per cent) or by denying the offence entirely (22 per cent). Of those who made a self-incriminating statement, 15.2 per cent made a partial confession and 18.3 per cent a statement comparable with the one given by the victim. The confession rate observed in this study (33.5 per cent) is much smaller than those rates observed by Mitchell (1983) and Gudjonnsson and Sigurdsson (2000), as well as the rates found in recent studies that do not focus exclusively on sex offenders, where the rate varies between 42 and 65 per cent (Moston et al. 1992; Leo 1996; Cassell and Hayman 1998;

Pearse *et al.* 1998; Phillips and Brown 1998; Clarke and Milne 2001; St-Yves and Lavallée 2002).

Nevertheless, in line with the Gudjonnsson and Sigurdsson study (2000), we found that child molesters, particularly homosexual paedophiles, collaborated more frequently with the police than rapists. Child molesters, who may have an underlying sense of guilt and an introverted personality profile, had a confession rate of 71.8 per cent which comes close to percentages obtained by Gudjonnsson and Sigurdsson (2000).

The low rates of confession obtained in the St-Yves (2002) study may be explained in several ways. First and foremost, the social significance of the crime may be sufficient to inhibit a confession: the subjects in the study had committed a crime serious enough to be sentenced to a term of imprisonment. The seriousness of the offence may also be a significant factor. In general, sexual crimes are judged more severely by the public than other types of crimes, even when the latter are, objectively, more serious. Finally, proof of such a crime is often difficult to establish, especially crimes involving young children. These factors could explain why the number of confessions increases dramatically once an offender is sentenced. Indeed, the confession rate for sentenced offenders varies between 70 per cent (for rapists) and 98.7 per cent (for child molesters) (St-Yves 2002).

A factor in a study carried out by Holmberg and Christianson (2002) could explain the reason why confession rates by sex offenders are sometimes lower than all other types of criminal, including those who have committed more serious crimes. In an exploratory study aimed at comparing the perception of 43 murderers and 40 sex offenders regarding their interrogation by the police and their tendency to confess or deny their crimes, Holmberg and Christianson (2002) observed that the sex offenders were less likely than the murderers to confess their crimes to the police. The percentages obtained were 28 per cent for the sex offenders and 49 per cent for the murderers. To explain these results, the authors suggest that murderers often regard their treatment by the police as being humane, whereas sex offenders find this a humiliating experience that inhibits them from confessing.

Whilst it may be impossible to explain why these results are so different, some factors may account for the disparities in the results. For example, the Mitchell study was undertaken more than 20 years ago when the judicial and cultural framework was different from the four recent studies and the methodology employed also differed.

Factors associated with confessions

Certain characteristics of the suspect, the type of crime and the context of the interview should allow us to predict whether the suspect will confess or not (Moston *et al.* 1992). To evaluate the impact of the chracteristics, this section examines such factors as modus operandi, the sex of the victim, the link between the offender and victim, the offender's marital status, his or her sense of guilt and IQ, and the investigator's attitude towards the offender.

Characteristics of the crime

Sex offenders who used physical violence are less likely to confess than those who did not use violence (St-Yves 2002). This finding agrees with the work of Neubauer (1974) and Mitchell (1983), who established that suspects interrogated for violent crimes were less likely to confess than those interrogated for crimes against property. The significance of the crime, therefore, seems to influence considerably the decision whether or not to confess. It seems reasonable to conclude that, the more violent the crime, the more suspects are afraid of the harshness of the sentence and, therefore, the more they are likely to deny their guilt. Studies by Moston and his colleagues, for example, have shown that, the more serious the crime, the more suspects tend to use their right to remain silent and to demand the help of an attorney (Moston *et al.* 1992; Stephenson and Moston 1994). Eysenck and Gudjonnsson (1989) also suggest that, the more serious the crime, the more harsh will be the sentence and, therefore, the probability of obtaining a confession is slim (an exception to this finding is the study by Holmberg and Christianson 2002). Holmberg and Christianson found that the confession rate of murderers was twice that of sex offenders. This shows, therefore, that the severity of the crime does not solely account for differences in confession rates.

In a recent study, Beauregard *et al.* (2005) observed that angry sexual murderers confess more frequently to the police than sadistic sexual murderers (61.6 per cent as against 33.3 per cent, respectively). Once sentenced, at the time of their induction to prison, all anger murderers (100 per cent) had admitted their crime, compared with 81.3 per cent of sadistic murderers. Beauregard and his colleagues believe these differences are due in part to the offenders' personalities and to the severity of the crime. Having realized the seriousness of their action, angry murderers might be burdened by remorse and would therefore be more likely to confess their crimes to the police.

This was not the case with sadistic murderers. Furthermore, subjects motivated by anger might have acted impulsively, often under the influence of intoxicating substances (minimizing factors), whereas the sadistic murderers often premeditate their crimes (aggravating factors).

Modus operandi

In our study of police interviews with sex offenders, we explored certain aspects of the offenders' modus operandi to ascertain if these could predict confession or denial. Even with an aggravating factor that will increase the harshness of the sanction, we did not find any significant link between the level of the premeditation of the crime and the fact that a suspect confesses or not to the police. This was also the case for the use of a weapon and the type of sexual act (coital versus non-coital) committed. Finally, believing that this could have been used by the offender to minimize his criminal responsibility, we explored, in vain, alcohol or drug consumption in the hours prior to the offence (St-Yves 2002).

The sex of the victim

The vast majority of victims of sexual crimes are female (Hanson 1991; Hilton 1993; St-Yves and Pellerin 2002) – about three out of four victims, according to Correctional Services of Canada statistics (St-Yves et al. 1999). In the study we conducted on the interrogation of sex offenders, offenders against male victims confessed more often to police officers than offenders against female victims (St-Yves 2002). This could be explained by the fact that heterosexual offenders use coercive violent means more often than homosexual paedophiles (Proulx et al. 1999) and that, as mentioned before, the more violent the crime, the less likely the suspect will confess. This link between the sex of the victim and the confession rate could also be explained by the victim's age. In this study, all the male victims were minors. As many have observed, child molesters confess more readily to the police than rapists (Nugent and Kroner 1996; Gudjonnsson and Sigurdsson 2000; St-Yves 2002).

Links between the offender and victim

Gudjonnsson and Sigurdsson (2000) observed that child molesters offend most frequently in their immediate surroundings, whereas rapists' targets are usually acquaintances. In a study conducted at the Correctional Services of Canada, we observed that, above all, the heterosexual paedophiles tended to offend in their immediate surroundings (St-Yves *et al.* 1999).

In this study we wanted to ascertain if the link between the offender and the victim had an impact on rates of confession. In other words, do sex offenders who have an intimate link with their victims confess at the same rate as those who have no link with their victims? We did not know whether this link would facilitate (i.e. more emotions are involved if the victim is close to the offender), or inhibit (i.e. emotional detachment if the victim is a stranger) a confession. Contrary to expectations, sex offenders who have an intimate link with their victims do not confess to the police more than those who have sexually assaulted a stranger (St-Yves 2002).

Characteristics of the suspect

Age

Most authors agree that the older the offender is, the less likely he is to confess his crime to the police (Leiken 1970; Neubauer 1974; Baldwin and McConville 1980; Softley 1980; Mitchell 1983; Richardson *et al.* 1995; Pearse *et al.* 1998; Phillips and Brown 1998). However, we did not observe this with sex offenders (St-Yves 2002). It should be added, however, that the subjects in our study were on average 40 years old, which is much older than the prison population as a whole (average age 32 years old) (St-Yves *et al.* 1999; Correctional Service of Canada 2001).

Ethnic group

Many authors have observed that white people confess more frequently than people of other races. Confession rates for white subjects vary between 58 and 62 per cent, compared with 44–49 per cent for other races (Pearse *et al.* 1998; Phillips and Brown 1998). This variation seems even more pronounced for sex crimes. St-Yves (2002) observed that white subjects were five times more likely (35 per cent compared with 7 per cent) to confess their crimes to the police authorities than sex offenders from other ethnic backgrounds. Could this be related to the fact that the vast majority of police officers in Quebec are white? It is also possible that some non-white sex offenders are, by culture or religion, less inclined to confess to a sex crime.

Marital status

St-Yves (2002) found that single men are more likely to confess than married men (38 per cent compared with 24 per cent, respectively). A partner seems to be an inhibiting factor, possibly because crimes of a sexual nature can jeopardize a relationship. As noted by Gudjonnsson (1992), amongst the factors that inhibit a confession are concerns regarding hurting the family and relatives or the fear of being rejected. Single men would obviously be less concerned by this.

Criminal background

Unlike many authors, St-Yves (2002) did not observe any link between previous offending and confession rates. This was also observed by Leiken (1970), Zander (1979) and Phillips and Brown (1998), who found that previous offending had no influence on the incidence of confession, even when a distinction is made between sex crimes and non-sex crimes.

Intelligence

St-Yves et al. (1999) found that sex offenders tended not to be very well educated and that, in 55.7 per cent of cases, the offenders were considered to be of below-average intelligence. Using the same sample of sex offenders, Guay (2001) observed that the intellectual level of sex offenders sentenced to a term of imprisonment is largely below that of the general population. In a more recent study, St-Yves (2002) found that, the higher the IQ of sex offenders, the more likely they are to confess during a police interrogation. The global average IQ[2] for people who confessed is 85.2 per cent compared with 80.6 per cent (the difference is marginally significant) for those who did not confess. This difference becomes significant when we compare the two groups for their verbal IQ (86.4 per cent compared with 79.6 per cent, respectively). This difference may be explained by the fact that, the more intelligent or educated the subject, the more he understands that collaboration can help to explain or justify his actions. They perhaps also know that a co-operative attitude may be beneficial when sentenced (Cusson 1998). Subjects who have a lower IQ may prefer to remain quiet and to be represented by an attorney.

Sense of guilt

Subjects who report a sense of guilt (including remorse) about their offences are more inclined to confess than those who do not report such feelings (Gudjonnsson and Petursson 1991). St-Yves (2002) observed that almost half the sex offenders studied (47.8 per cent) who confessed their crime during the police interrogation mention a sense of guilt, compared with 32.5 per cent of those who did not confess. As mentioned by many authors, a sense of guilt seems to stimulate the need to confess (Horowitz 1956; Reik 1959; Gudjonnsson 1992, 1999). However, Gudjonnsson (1992) mentions that the shame associated with a crime can be sufficient to inhibit a confession, even though remorse is present. This could explain the results of the study by Holmberg and Christianson (2002), who found that sex offenders confessed less frequently than murderers because they felt humiliated during the police interrogation.

The attitudes of the investigator

It is important to establish at the outset an empathetic relationship with the sex offender to encourage him to talk about his vulnerability, suffering and powerlessness (Langfeldt 1993). Holmberg (1996) noted that sex offenders who confessed describe the conversation they had with the police as being a very humane experience, full of empathy. However, those who denied their crime described the police interview as being oppressive and confrontational.

Holmberg and Christianson (2002) observed that sex offenders were almost twice as likely to deny their crime than were murderers. Almost half the sex offenders (43 per cent) considered the interviewer as being impatient, compared with one out of four murderers. One out of three sex offenders were aggressive during the interrogation, compared with 12 per cent of murderers. The authors, to a great part, attributed this to the attitude of the interviewers. Subjects who found the police officer's attitude humane are more inclined to confess, compared with those who found the police officer's attitude domineering. Confession rates are three times higher for those who found the investigator's approach humane.

The conclusions of Holmberg and Christianson (2002) are compatible with those of many other researchers and confirm that the interviewer's attitude is a key factor when interviewing suspects (Shepherd 1991; Williamson 1993; Gudjonnsson and Sigurdsson 1999; Milne and Bull 1999; St-Yves et al. 2004).

The personality profile of the offender who confesses

The study we conducted at the Correctional Services of Canada allowed us to identify three sex-offender profiles that may have a bearing on their attitude towards confession (St-Yves 2002). The first group, described as 'submissive collaborators', confessed the most readily during police interrogations. The second group, called 'reluctant collaborators', rarely confessed their crimes during the interrogation, even after being sentenced. The third group, the 'dormant collaborators', almost never co-operated with the police authorities but, once convicted, they admitted their crimes in the same proportion as the submissive collaborators.

The submissive collaborator

Within this group most sex offenders, for the major part (71.8 per cent) (complete disclosure in 39.7 per cent of cases), confessed during police interrogations. Only one subject out of five (20.5 per cent) refused to talk and/or to ask to speak to an attorney. These subjects sexually assaulted a minor (93.6 per cent) and demonstrated a sense of guilt after committing their crimes (78.2 per cent). Submissive collaborators have a dependency personality profile, as measured by the Millon Clinical Multiaxial Inventory (MCMI). They also rated highly on this personality scale as being dependent, avoidant, schizoid and schizotypic. Once convicted, almost all (98.7 per cent) submissive collaborators admitted having committed the crimes for which they were found guilty. The majority of these subjects (61.5 per cent) made complete confessions. They are also the ones who recognize most often the negative consequences of their crimes for the victim (60.3 per cent) and their responsibility for their crimes (94.9 per cent). Two thirds (64.1 per cent) of submissive collaborators recognized that they had a sexual disorder.

The reluctant collaborator

These individuals almost never co-operated with the police authorities (17.8 per cent). Most refused to talk and/or to ask to speak to an attorney (47.8 per cent) or they denied everything (27.8 per cent). When these subjects co-operated, only 6.7 per cent made a complete confession. These reluctant collaborators are almost all rapists (91.1 per cent) who rarely demonstrated a sense of guilt (30 per cent). Compared with the submissive collaborators, they tend to have a narcissistic personality disorder. Reluctant collaborators also score more highly on personality scales as being histrionic and anti-social than submissive collaborators. Once convicted, reluctant collaborators often made a confession (70 per cent), but not many recognized the negative consequences of their actions (31.1 per cent), and their responsibility for their crimes (63.3 per cent). Few recognized they had a sexual disorder (25.6 per cent).

The dormant collaborator

These offenders rarely confess on their arrest (13.3 per cent). Only 10 per cent of those who co-operate made a complete confession. Most refused to talk (70 per cent) or denied everything (15 per cent). Dormant collaborators have offended against a minor (100 per cent) but, unlike the submissive collaborators, few demonstrated a sense of guilt for their crimes (20 per cent). Their personality profile is similar to that of reluctant collaborators. It was in this group that we found the most narcissistic personalities, according to MCMI. They are also the subjects who scored most highly as being histrionic and anti-social. Once convicted, dormant collaborators admitted their crimes in a proportion comparable (93.3 per cent) with submissive collaborators. Most recognized their responsibility for their crimes (88.3 per cent), one out of two (48.3 per cent) recognized the negative consequences of their actions for their victims and a little more than a half (56.7 per cent) admitted having a sexual disorder. These percentages lie in-between the ones we found for submissive collaborators and reluctant collaborators.

The grouping analysis (cluster K-means) we conducted in this study allowed us to identify three sex-offender profiles, each reacting differently during police interviews. The two groups of non-co-operative subjects (reluctant collaborators and dormant collaborators) differed mostly by the age of their victims. One was a paedophile, the other a rapist. These non-co-operative subjects scored the most highly on personality scales as being extroverted, narcissistic, histrionic and anti-social. This supports the observations of Gudjonnsson and Petursson (1991), who established that extroverted individuals are stronger during police interrogations. The co-operative subjects (the submissive collaborators) differed from the non-co-operative subjects by their sense of guilt and by their personality profile, which is more inclined to be introverted, dependent, avoidant, schizoid and schizotypic. Once convicted, dormant collaborators confessed their crimes in proportions comparable with submissive collaborators, whereas reluctant collaborators tended to continue to deny their guilt.

Promoting confessions

Even though some factors related to the crime seem to be associated with confession rates, especially the level of violence and the age of the victim (paedophile versus rapist), it seems that it is the subject's personal characteristics that most have the most influence on whether a subject confesses.

As shown in many studies, sex offenders who have an introverted personality profile are more likely to confess than the extroverted offenders because they are more inclined to have remorse and to feel the need to confess. They also have a greater tendency to be anxious and give up easily when pressurized during an interrogation (Gudjonnsson and Petursson 1991; Gudjonnsson and Sigurdsson 1999; St-Yves 2002). Eysenck and Gudjonnsson (1989) also noted that introverted subjects are more inclined than extroverted subjects to live with a sense of guilt. This could explain why they experience so much anxiety when they deny or lie, and why they often feel relieved after confessing. Even if a subject is likely to confess, Gudjonnsson (1992) suggests that the shame linked to the crime, especially if it is a sexual crime, can be enough to inhibit a confession. Holmberg and Christianson (2002) observed exactly the same phenomenon. A sense of shame could explain why many offenders have a tendency to be reluctant to give a version of the events that conforms to the one given by the victim (Salter 1988; Birgisson 1996). They probably compromise by making a partial and limited confession, which satisfies their need to confess whilst, at the same time, minimizing their feelings of shame when they describe the offence (Gudjonnsson 2003: 154).

To prevent these inhibitors (shame and humiliation) from hindering the confession process, we must first alleviate internal pressures (culpability, the need to confess) so that an offender is able to confess in full. Sex offenders who do not confess differ from co-operative subjects by an absence of guilt and by their extroverted personality profile (Gudjonnsson and Petursson 1991; Gudjonnsson and Sigurdsson 1999; St-Yves 2002). Even though anti-social personality types are generally not co-operative during police interrogations (Gudjonnsson and Petursson 1991), it is the narcissistic who resist the most. It is also the rapists who are the most resistant, and it is the rapists who are most often diagnosed as being psychopaths, above all if they are polymorphic (paedophiles and rapists) sex offenders (Porter *et al.* 2000).

Since extroverted sex offenders experience few emotions concerning their crimes, they have a greater tendency to give in to external pressures (persuasive police interrogation techniques, the attitudes of the investigator, fear of confinement). Since these individuals do not usually live with remorse and do not feel the need to confess, the investigator has to rely on the quality of the evidence and on interrogation techniques to obtain a confession. According to Gudjonnsson and Sigurdsson (2000), rapists are more sensitive to the strength of the evidence than child molesters.

In short, the major obstacle to a confession is the offender's personality profile. For sex offenders who have an introverted profile, it seems that loss of self-esteem, shame and humiliation are the most pronounced inhibiting factors, whereas for extroverted offenders it is the personal consequences regarding their image and reputation. For introverts, confession is a private matter whereas, for extroverts, it is more of a public affair.

Conclusion

Until now, the research has encouraged us to believe that sex offenders confess less often to the police than most other types of criminals. One out of three sex offenders confess their crimes to the police during the interrogation, at least in the Province of Quebec. The typical portrait of the sex offender who confesses is a single white male with a minor victim, who used no or almost no, violence towards his victim, who expressed remorse and who has an introverted personality profile (St-Yves 2002).

The rare incidence of confessions by sex offenders seems to be closely linked to two major factors: 1) the personal consequences (shame, humiliation) and 2) the attitude of the investigator. The perpetrators of sexual crimes seem to be more sensitive to the personal consequences than other types of criminal. For those sex offenders who have an introverted personality profile, confession seems to be a personal affair (self-esteem, integrity) whereas, for extroverts, confession seems to be a public affair (image, reputation). We have to remove these inhibiting factors if we are to obtain a confession.

The investigator's attitude is very important because it is closely linked to the personal consequences. Even if it is true that sexual crimes are, without doubt, the crimes that raise the most public outrage, the investigator has to adopt a facilitating attitude towards the offenders. He or she has to do everything he or she can to prevent the personal consequences from hindering the confession process. The personal consequences must not become an inhibiting factor. The best strategy, therefore, remains a humane approach.

Notes

1. This chapter is an English adaptation of 'L'aveu chez les auteurs de crimes sexuels' (St-Yves 2004a).
2. IQ was meseared via a computerized aptitude test called TAI (Test d'Aptitude Informatisée), an intelligence test validated on a French Canadian population. The IQ test was given at the Regional reception centre (RRC) via computer. The RRC's main function is to evaluate federal inmates so that they can be directed, according to their needs in matters of security and institutional programmes, to the most appropriate prisons.

References

Baldwin, J. and McConville, M. (1980) *Confessions in Crown Court Trials: Royal Commission on Criminal Procedure. Research Study 5.* London: HMSO.

Beauregard, É., Proulx, J., Brien, T. and St-Yves, M. (2005) 'Deux profils de meurtriers sexuels: la colérique et le sadique.' In J. Proulx *et al.* (eds) *Les meurtriers sexuels: Analyse comparative et nouvelles perspectives.* Montreal: Presses Université de Montréal.

Birgisson, G.H. (1996) 'Differences of personality, defensiveness, and compliance between admitting and denying male sex offenders', *Journal of Interpersonal Violence*, 11: 118–25.

Cassell, P.G. and Hayman, B.S. (1998) 'Police interrogation in the 1990s : an empirical study of the effects of Miranda', in R.A. Leo and G.C. Thomas III (eds) *The Miranda Debate, Justice and Policing.* Boston, MA: Northeastern University Press.

Clarke, C. and Milne, R. (2001) *National Evaluation of the PEACE Investigative Interviewing Course. Police Research Award Scheme. Report* PRAS/149. Portsmouth: Institute of Criminal Justice Studies, University of Portsmouth.

Correctional Service of Canada (2001) *Basic Facts about Federal Corrections.* Ottawa: Public Works and Government Services Canada.

Cusson, M. (1998) *Criminologie actuelle*. Paris: Presse Universitaire de France.

Evans, R. (1993) *The Conduct of Police Interviews with Juveniles. Royal Commission on Criminal Justice Research. Report 8*. London: HMSO.

Eysenck, H.J. and Gudjonnsson, G.H. (1989) *The Causes and Cures of Criminality*. New York, NY and London: Plenum Press.

Guay, J.-P. (2001) 'La relation intelligence-crime: le cas de délinquants sexuels sous juridiction fédérale.' Thèse de doctorat inédite, Université de Montréal.

Gudjonnsson, G.H. (1992) *The Psychology of Interrogations, Confessions and Testimony*. Chichester: Wiley.

Gudjonnsson, G.H. (1999) 'Feelings of guilt and reparation for criminal acts', in M. Cox (ed.) *Remorse and Reparation*. London: Kingsley.

Gudjonnsson, G.H. (2003) *The Psychology of Interrogations and Confessions. A Handbook*. Chichester: Wiley.

Gudjonnsson, G.H. and Petursson, H. (1991) 'Custodial interrogation: why do suspects confess and how does it relate to their crime, attitude and personality?', *Personality and Individual Differences*, 12: 295–306.

Gudjonnsson, G.H. and Sigurdsson, J.F. (1999) 'The Gudjonnsson Confession Questionnaire-Revised (GCQ-R): factor structure and its relationship with personality', *Personality and Individual Differences*, 27: 953–68.

Gudjonnsson, G.H. and Sigurdsson, J.F. (2000) 'Differences and similarities between violent and sex offenders', *Child Abuse snd Neglect*, 24: 363–72.

Hanson, R.K. (1991) 'Characteristics of sex offenders who were sexually abused as children', in R. Langevin (ed.) *Sex Offenders and their Victims: New Research Findings*. Toronto: Juniper.

Hilton, N.Z. (1993) 'Childhood sexual victimization and lack of empathy in child molesters: explanation or excuse?', *International Journal of Offender Therapy and Comparative Criminology*, 37: 287–96.

Holmberg, U. (1996) *Sexualbroottsförövares upplevelser av polisförhör*. Kristianstad: Högskolan Kristianstad.

Holmberg, U. and Christianson, S.A. (2002) 'Murderers' and sexual offenders' experiences of police interviews and their inclination to admit or deny crimes', *Behavioral Sciences and the Law*, 20: 31–45.

Horowitz, M.W. (1956) 'The psychology of confession', *Journal of Criminal Law, Criminology and Police Science*, 47: 197–204.

Inbau, F.E., Reid, J.E., Buckley, J.P. and Jayne, B.C. (2001) *Criminal Interrogation and Confessions* (4th edn). Gaithersberg, MD: Aspen.

Jayne, B.C. (1986) 'The psychological principles of criminal interrogation', in F.E. Inbau *et al.* (eds) *Criminal Interrogation and Confession* (3rd edn). Baltimore, MD: Williams & Wilkins.

Langfeldt, T. (1993) *Sexologi*. Oslo: Ad Notam Gyldendal.

Leiken, L.S. (1970) 'Police interrogation in Colorado: the implementation of Miranda', *Denver Law Journal*, 47: 1–53.

Leo, R.A. (1996) 'Inside the interrogation room', *Journal of Criminal Law and Criminology*, 86: 266–303.

Milne, R. and Bull, R. (1999) *Investigative Interviewing. Psychology and practice.* Chichester: Wiley.

Mitchell, B. (1983) 'Confessions and police interrogation of suspects', *Criminal Law Review*, 596–604.

Moston, S. and Engelberg, T. (1993) 'Police questioning techniques in tape recorded interviews with criminal suspects', *Policing and Society*, 3: 223–37.

Moston, S., Stephenson, G.M. and Williamson, T.M. (1992) 'The effects of case characteristics on suspect behaviour during police questioning', *British Journal of Criminology*, 32: 23–40.

Moston, S., Stephenson, G.M. and Williamson, T.M. (1993) 'The incidence, antecedents, and consequences of the use of the right to silence during police questioning', *Criminal Behavior and Mental Health*, 3: 30–47.

Neubauer, D.W. (1974) 'Confessions in Prairie City: some causes and effects', *Journal of Criminal Law and Criminology*, 65: 103–12.

Nugent, P.M. and Kroner, D.G. (1996) 'Denial, response styles, and admittance of offenses among child molesters and rapists', *Journal of Interpersonal Violence*, 11: 475–86.

Pearse, J., Gudjonnsson, G.H., Clare, I.C.H. and Rutter, S. (1998) 'Police interviewing psychological vulnerabilities: predicting the likelihood of a confession', *Journal of Community and Applied Social Psychology*, 8: 1–21.

Phillips, C. and Brown, D. (1998) *Entry into the Criminal Justice System: A Survey of Police Arrests and their Outcomes.* London: Home Office.

Porter, S., Fairweather, D., Drugge, J., Hervé, H., Birt, A. and Boer, D.P. (2000) 'Profiles of psychopathy in incarcerated sexual offenders', *Criminal Justice and Behavior*, 27: 216–33.

Proulx, J., Perreault, C., Ouimet, M. and Guay, J.-P. (1999) 'Les agresseurs sexuels d'enfants: Scénarios délictuels et troubles de la personnalité', in J. Proulx *et al.* (eds) *Les violence criminelles*, Éd. Les Presses de l'Université Laval, 187–216.

Reik, T. (1959) *The Compulsion to Confess: On the Psychoanalysis of Crime and Punishment.* New York, NY: Farrar, Straus & Cudahy.

Richardson, G., Gudjonnsson, G.H. and Kelly, T.P. (1995) 'Interrogative suggestibility in an adolescent forensic population', *Journal of Adolescence*, 18: 211–16.

Salter, A. (1988) *Treating Child Sex Offenders and Victims. A Practical Guide.* London: Sage.

Shepherd, E. (1991) 'Ethical interviewing', *Policing*, 7: 42–60.

Softley, P. (1980) *Police Interrogation: An Observational Study in Four Police Stations. Research Study 4.* London: HMSO.

Stephenson, G.M. and Moston, S. (1994) 'Police interrogation', *Psychology, Crime and Law*, 1: 151–7.

St-Yves, M. (2002) 'Interrogatoire de police et crime sexuel: profil du suspect collaborateur', *Revue Internationale de Criminologie et de Police Technique et Scientifique*, 1: 81–96.

St-Yves, M. (2004a) 'L'aveu chez les auteurs de crimes sexuels', in M. St-Yves and J. Landry (eds) *Psychologie des entrevues d'enquête. De la recherche à la pratique.* Éditions Yvon Blais.

St-Yves, M. (2004b) 'Factors associated with confessions by sexual offenders.' Poster session presented at the first International Conference on Police Interviewing, École nationale de Police du Québec (Nicolet), 9–11 February.

St-Yves, M., Brien, T., Guay, J.-P., Granger, L., McKibben, A., Ouimet, M., Pellerin, B., Perreault, C. and Proulx, J. (1999) 'A descriptive profile of incarcerated sex offenders', *Correctional Service of Canada, Forum on Corrections Research*, 11: 11–14.

St-Yves, M. and Landry, J. (2004) 'When the attitude of the investigators tells more than the suspect.' Paper presented at the first International Conference on Police Interviewing, École nationale de Police du Québec (Nicolet), 9–11 February.

St-Yves, M. and Lavallée, P.R. (2002) 'L'interrogatoire vidéo: état de la situation à la Sûreté du Québec. Direction conseil et développement en enquêtes criminelles.' Sûreté du Québec, document inédit.

St-Yves, M. and Pellerin, B. (2002) 'Sexual victimization and sexual delinquency: vampire or Pinocchio syndrome?', *Correctional Service of Canada, Forum on Corrections Research*, 14: 55–6.

St-Yves, M., Tanguay, M. and Crépault, D. (2004) 'La psychologie de la relation: cinq règles de base', in M. St-Yves and J. Landry (eds) *Psychologie des entrevues d'enquête. De la recherche à la practique.* Éditions Yvon Blais.

Williamson, T.M. (1993) 'From interrogation to investigative interviewing. Strategic trends in police questioning', *Journal of Community and Applied Social Psychology*, 3: 89–99.

Zander, M. (1979) 'The investigation of crime: a study of cases tried at the Old Bailey', *Criminal Law Review*, 203–19.

Chapter 7

The psychology of interrogations and confessions

Gisli H. Gudjonsson

Introduction

'Investigative interviews' are an important form of evidence gathering. The main objective is to obtain information that is detailed, complete, comprehensible, valid (in legal settings the words 'safe' and 'reliable' are commonly used to describe validity) and relevant to the legal issues in the case that need to be established and proved. There are a number of governmental and local agencies that are involved in conducting investigative interviews, including the police, customs and excise, the military, and the security services. The focus in this chapter is on investigative interviews in relation to suspects for the purpose of potential prosecution. Here confessions are often crucial in securing a conviction. It is therefore not surprising that police interviewers have traditionally focused on obtaining confessions rather than merely gathering information. In this chapter I discuss the nature of confessions in the area of criminal justice, review the relevant theories and empirical evidence, and show how interrogation can go wrong in terms of producing false confessions.

Interrogation

The term 'interrogation' is principally used in the literature and in police practice to refer to the questioning of criminal suspects, typically involving a confrontation, whereas the term 'interviewing' is more commonly used in cases of witnesses and victims. The term 'investigative interviewing' has been proposed to cover both the interviewing of witnesses and suspects (Williamson 1993). However, for the purpose of this chapter we shall use the term 'interrogation' as we are specifically discussing the questioning of suspects.

Traditionally, interrogation has focused primarily on obtaining a confession, whereas during the early 1990s, particularly in England, the focus shifted somewhat towards general evidence gathering of 'reliable' information with less emphasis on obtaining confessions *per se* (Williamson 1993).

Police training manuals

The purpose of this section is to discuss briefly the tactics and techniques advocated by practical interrogation manuals. Nearly all published interrogation manuals originate in the USA (Leo 1992, 1994). However, in 1992 a new approach to interrogation was developed and implemented in England, which was developed through the collaboration between police officers, psychologists and lawyers (Williamson 1994; see also Chapter 8, this volume). The mnemonic 'PEACE' was used to describe the five distinct parts of the new interview approach ('Preparation and Planning', 'Engage and Explain', 'Account', 'Closure' and 'Evaluate'). An important theory behind this new interview approach, particularly in cases of witnesses, victims and co-operative suspects, is the work of Fisher and Geiselman (1992) into the 'cognitive interview.' There is some evidence for the validity of this new approach to interviewing (Clarke and Milne 2001).

However, traditionally, practical interrogation manuals are based on the experience of interrogators and offer techniques aimed at breaking down suspects' resistance. The main assumptions made in police training manuals are that many criminal cases can only be solved by obtaining a confession and unless offenders are caught in the commission of a crime they will be reluctant to confess and need to be interrogated using persuasive techniques comprising trickery, deceit and psychological manipulation. The main process involved is breaking down denials and resistance, whilst increasing the suspect's desire to confess (e.g. Inbau *et al.* 2001).

Persuasion in the context of interrogation is the process of convincing suspects that their best interests are served by their making a confession (Leo 1994). In order to achieve this objective the police may engage in a range of deception strategies (e.g. exaggerating the evidence against the suspect or presenting the suspect with false evidence of guilt, misrepresenting the nature or seriousness of the offence, presenting suspects with scenarios that make them unwittingly incriminate themselves).

The authors of most police interrogation manuals ignore the possibility that their recommended techniques could, in certain instances, make a suspect confess to a crime that he or she had not committed. Zimbardo (1967) argued, on the basis of his early review of American police training manuals, that the techniques recommended were psychologically 'coercive' and an infringement of the suspect's dignity and fundamental rights. This was an important recognition that psychological manipulation and deceptive interrogation techniques have the potential to cause false confessions to occur. Gudjonnsson (1992) illustrated by research evidence and case studies the risk of false confessions occurring during custodial interrogation. Subsequently American scientists have written extensively about the potential dangers of coercive interrogation techniques.[1]

Inbau et al. (2001) recommend that prior to the interrogation proper suspects should be interviewed informally, preferably in a non-custodial setting where they do not have to be informed of their rights. This is a non-accusatory interview the purpose of which is for the investigator to establish rapport and trust, trick the suspect into a false sense of security, gather detailed information about the suspect and his or her background, ascertaining by observations of verbal and non-verbal signs whether or not the suspect is guilty, and offering the suspect the opportunity of telling the truth without confrontation. If after this interview the investigator is 'definite or reasonably certain' about the suspect's guilt then the interrogation proper commences, using the 'Reid Technique'. This is a highly confrontational and accusatory process of interrogation and consists of a nine-step approach aimed at breaking down resistance (Kassin and Gudjonnsson, 2004).

There is a serious problem with interrogators relying on behavioural indicators and other similarly weak indictors of deception (e.g. hunches, impressions) during the non-accusatory interview, because police officers often make mistakes when they try to distinguish between lies and truths in police interviews (Vrij 2004b).

The Reid Technique, which is extensively used by interrogators in the USA (Inbau et al. 2001), involves the following nine steps:

Step 1: 'direct positive confrontation' involves the suspect being told with 'absolute certainty' that he or she committed the alleged offence.

In cases where the interrogator has no evidence against the suspect this should not be revealed and, if necessary, the interrogator should pretend that there is evidence. The interrogator then tries to persuade the suspect of the advantages of telling the truth (i.e. the truth as assumed by the interrogator). After a while, with denials persisting, the interrogator then proceeds to step 2.

Step 2: 'theme development.' Here the interrogator suggests various 'themes' to the suspect that are aimed either to minimize the moral implications of the alleged crime or to give the suspect the opportunity of accepting 'moral excuses' for the commission of the crime (i.e. face-saving excuses). This allows the suspect to accept physical responsibility for the crime whilst at the same time minimizing either the seriousness of it or the internal blame for it. The themes selected will depend on the case, but may include the following:

• Tell the suspect that anyone else in his or her position or circumstance might have committed the same type of offence, attempting to reduce the suspect's feelings of guilt for the offence by minimizing its moral seriousness.

• Suggest to the suspect a morally acceptable reason for the offence, using praise and flattery as a way of manipulating the suspect.

• Catch the suspect telling some incidental lie.

• Get the suspect somehow to associate him or herself with the crime.

• Suggest there was a non-criminal intent behind the act (e.g. the criminal act may have been accidental or committed in self-defence rather than intentionally).

Step 3: 'handling denials.' Repeated denials are seen as placing the suspects at a psychological advantage. The interrogator is advised to stop them by persistently interrupting the suspects and telling them to listen to what he or she has got to say. Inbau *et al.* (2001) recommend the use of the 'friendly-unfriendly' technique when the attempts at sympathy and understanding have failed. This technique involves two interrogators working together, one of whom is friendly and sympathetic and the other being unfriendly and critical.

Step 4: 'overcoming objections' requires the interrogator to overcome the objections that the suspect may give as an explanation or reason for his or her innocence. It is argued that once the suspect feels that the objections are not getting him or her anywhere he or she begins to show signs of withdrawal from active participation in the interrogation. The suspect is now thought to be at his or her lowest point and the interrogator needs to act quickly in order not to lose the psychological advantage he or she has gained.

Step 5: 'procurement and retention of suspect's attention.' When the interrogator notices the suspect's passive signs of withdrawal he or she should try to reduce the psychological distance between him or herself and the suspect and to regain the suspect's full attention. This is achieved by moving physically closer to the suspect, leaning forward towards the suspect, touching the suspect gently, mentioning the suspect's first name and maintaining good eye contact with the suspect. As a result of this ploy, a guilty suspect becomes more attentive to the interrogator's suggestions.

Step 6: 'handling suspect's passive mood' is a direct continuation of step 5. When it looks like the suspect's resistance is about to break down, the interrogator focuses the suspect's mind on a specific and central theme concerning the reason for the offence. The interrogator displays signs of understanding and sympathy and urges the suspect to tell the truth. The suspect is then placed in a more remorseful mood by having him or her become aware of the stress he or she is placing upon the victim by not confessing. The interrogator appeals to the suspect's sense of decency and honour, and religion if appropriate.

The main emphasis seems to be to play upon the suspect's potential weaknesses in order to break down his or her remaining resistance. A blank stare and complete silence are an indication that the suspect is ready for the alternatives in step 7.

Step 7: 'presenting an alternative question.' The suspect is presented with two possible alternatives for the commission of the crime. Both alternatives are highly incriminating, but they are worded in such a way that one alternative acts as a face-saving device whilst the other implies some repulsive or callous motivation. It represents the culmination of theme development and, in addition to face-saving, it provides an incentive to confess (i.e. if the suspect does not accept the lesser alternative others may believe the worst-case scenario). This is the most important part of the Reid model and one commonly seen in cases where suspects' resistance has been broken down during interrogation. It is a coercive procedure where suspects are pressured to choose between two incriminating alternatives when neither may be applicable. This is a dangerous technique to apply, particularly amongst suspects who are of below-average intelligence (Gudjonnsson 2003a).

The psychological reasoning behind the alternative question is as follows:

'A person is more likely to make a decision once he had committed himself, in a small way, toward that decision. This is precisely what the alternative question accomplishes during an interrogation. It offers the guilty suspect the opportunity to start telling the truth by making a single admission' (Inbau *et al.* 2001: 353).

Step 8: 'having suspect orally relate various details of offence' operates once the suspect has accepted one of the alternatives given to him or her in step 7 and consequently providing a first self-incriminating admission. In step 8 the initial admission is developed into a detailed confession which provides details of the circumstances, motive and nature of the criminal act.

Inbau *et al.* (2001) state that it is important at this point in the interview for the interrogator to be alone with the suspect, because the presence of another person may discourage the suspect from talking openly about the offence. Once a full confession has been obtained the interrogator asks somebody to witness the confession.

Step 9: 'converting an oral confession into a written confession' is important because a signed confession is much stronger legally than an oral one. Suspects can subsequently deny that they ever made an oral confession, but it is much more difficult to challenge a written confession that has the suspect's signature on it. Inbau and his co-authors warn that delaying taking a written statement may result in the confessor having been able to reflect upon the legal consequences of the confession and retracting it.

Kassin and McNall (1991) argue that the interrogation techniques in the above nine-steps approach consist of two main strategies: 'maximization' and 'minimization'. The former strategy involves the interrogator frightening the suspect into a confession by exaggerating the strength of evidence against him or her and the seriousness of the offence. The 'minimization' strategy, by contrast, involves the interrogator tricking the suspect into a false sense of security and confession by offering sympathy, providing face-saving excuses, partly blaming the victim or circumstances for the alleged offence and minimizing the seriousness of the charges. Kassin and McNall (1991) provide convincing experimental evidence to show some of the inherent dangers of these so-called 'subtle' interrogation approaches on the perceptions of potential judges and jurors. These interrogation approaches contain implicit ('hidden') messages that have important conviction and sentencing implications, generally against the interest of the defendant. Kassin and McNall's experiments are important because they show that the techniques advocated by Inbau and his colleagues are inherently coercive in that they communicate implicit threats and promises to suspects. These experiments raise serious concerns about the use of 'maximization' and 'minimization' as methods of interrogation and the confessions they produce should be used cautiously as evidence in court.

Gudjonnsson (2003a) has raised a number of ethical issues with the Reid Technique, including the use of trickery, deceit and dishonesty as a way of breaking down resistance. These measures do on occasions result in a false confession, either because suspects are made to believe that they have committed a crime of which they have no previous recollection, or merely because they are escaping the pressure of the custodial environment.

The frequencies with which different methods of interrogation are used or what effects they have on guilty and innocent suspects are unknown (Kassin and Gudjonnsson, 2004). A number of researchers have conducted naturalistic studies of real-life police interrogations (e.g. Irving 1980; Moston *et al.* 1992; Leo 1996, Pearse and Gudjonnsson 1996; Medford *et al.* 2003). There is no research evidence about the effectiveness and risks of a false confession involving the Reid Technique but in the USA the techniques based on the Reid approach to interrogation are particularly common (Leo 1996). In England most run-of-the-mill interrogations are very short (80 per cent of interviews are completed in less than half an hour) and there is not much confrontation or pressure taking place (Pearse and Gudjonnsson 1996). However, in the more serious cases the dynamics change considerably and Reid-like approaches are used to break down resistance, often rendering confession evidence inadmissible at trial (Pearse and Gudjonnsson 1999).

The interrogation of terrorist suspects

Terrorist suspects in England who are detained under the Terrorism

Act 2000 are subject to special provisions (Home Office 2004), which means that their detention can be extended to up to 14 days.

Following the terrorist attacks on the USA on 11 September 2001, interrogation for the purpose of intelligence gathering has become much more prominent (Mackey and Miller 2004; Rose 2004). Great concerns have been raised about the treatment of prisoners by the military and security service in Afghanistan and Guantánamo Bay (Rose 2004). In the words of one experienced American military interrogator: 'But one of the most crucial weapons in the war on terrorism may be the abilities of a relative handful of soldiers and spies trained in the dark art of getting enemy prisoners to talk' (Mackey and Miller 2004: xxii). The same authors claim that 'Fear is often an interrogator's best ally' (p. 8) and 'By the time of our departure from the baking, arid plains of Bagram, we could boast that virtually no prisoner went unbroken' (p. xxv). The rest of Mackey and Miller's book describes in detail how psychological manipulation and coercive techniques are used to break down the resistance of terrorist suspects.

The techniques described in detail by Mackey and Miller of current practice by the military are clearly highly coercive and oppressive in nature and questions must be asked about the real value of these techniques for obtaining reliable information for intelligence gathering. It is likely that the occasional elicitation of apparently useful information for intelligence gathering reinforces this approach and serves as a justification for its use, irrespective of the amount of irrelevant and unreliable information obtained.

Confessions

A major difficulty in comparing the confession rate amongst different studies is that confessions are defined in different ways. In addition, a distinction is not always drawn in the studies between 'admissions' and 'confessions'. In its broadest sense a confession may be construed as 'any statements which tend to incriminate a suspect or a defendant in a crime' (Drizin and Leo 2004: 892), including denials, which causes great confusion among researchers (Gudjonnsson 2003a). A better operational definition, and a more correct legal definition, is to use *Black's Law Dictionary* to distinguish between a 'confession' and 'admission'. It defines a confession as 'a statement admitting or acknowledging all facts necessary for conviction of a crime' and an 'admission' as 'an acknowledgement of a fact or facts tending to prove guilt which falls short of an acknowledgement of all essential elements of the crime' (cited in Drizin and Leo 2004: 892).

Self-incriminating admissions, not amounting to the suspect accepting responsibility for the crime and giving a detailed narrative account of his or her actions, are not proper confessions. For example, a suspect may admit to having been in the vicinity of the crime or even claim to have witnessed it. Such admissions may be highly incriminating, but they must be distinguished from confessions. Even the comment 'I did it' without a detailed explanation should be treated as an admission and not as a confession.

Theoretical models of confessions

Confessing to a crime during custodial interrogation has potentially serious consequences for the individual concerned. Generally, the more serious the crime the more severe the consequences are going to be. Offenders' self-esteem and integrity are often adversely affected, their freedom and liberty are at risk, and there may be other penalties (e.g. a financial penalty, a community service). In extreme cases the death penalty may be imposed (Ofshe and Leo 1997a). In view of this it is perhaps remarkable to find that a substantial proportion of all suspects confess during custodial interrogation (i.e. in England the confession rate has remained about 60 per cent for the past 25 years or more; see Gudjonnsson 2003a for a review). Why should this be the case? A number of theoretical models are available to explain why suspects confess to crimes that they have committed. Theoretical models of confessions are important because they assist in understanding why suspects confess to crimes they have committed and because they generate hypotheses that can be tested empirically by direct research.

Gudjonnsson (2003a) reviewed six models of confessions: the 'Reid model' (Jayne 1986); 'a decision-making model' (Hilgendorf and Irving 1981); 'psychoanalytic models' (e.g. Reik 1959); 'an interactional model' (Moston et al. 1992); 'a cognitive-behavioural model' (Gudjonnsson 2003a); and the 'Ofshe–Leo model' (Ofshe and Leo 1997a).

Each model looks at confessions from a different perspective and, taken together, the models provide an important insight into the reasons why suspects tend to confess during custodial interrogation.

The Reid model of confession

Jayne (1986) provides a model for understanding the process whereby suspects' resistance and denial break down during interrogation. The model builds upon the 'nine steps' of interrogation proposed by Inbau *et al.* (1986).

Interrogation is conceptualized within the model as the psychological undoing of deception. The focus is exclusively on police-induced confessions where a confession follows a denial. It is inherent in this model that most people are reluctant to confess, because of the perceived deleterious consequences of making a confession. This makes them motivated to deceive the interrogator. According to the model, a suspect confesses when the perceived consequences of a confession are more desirable than the anxiety generated by the deception. The interrogator can manipulate the perceived consequences and perceived anxiety associated with denial. There are four essential criteria for changing the suspect's expectancies and beliefs:

1. The credibility and perceived sincerity of the interrogator (i.e. the building up of rapport and trust).

2. Understanding of the suspect's attitudes and identifying weaknesses so that these can be used through subtle psychological manipulation to break down resistance.

3. The suspect needs to accept the interrogator's suggestions, which means that the more suggestible the suspect, the easier it is to obtain a confession from him or her.

4. The interrogator must be vigilant as to whether or not the suspect is accepting the theme suggested, whether the suspect needs more anxiety enhancement, and if the timing of the presentation of an alternative is right.

Persuasion is essential to this process and is viewed as a dynamic process that needs to be regulated according to the strengths and weaknesses of the suspect. According to Jayne (1986), it is particularly difficult to elicit a confession from suspects with high tolerance for anxiety and guilt manipulation. There are a number of manipulative ploys that can be used by interrogators to reduce the perceived consequences of confessing during interrogation. This is mainly achieved by presenting the suspect with themes that increase self-deception, cognitive distortion and self-justification ('minimization'), whilst increasing perceived anxiety about persisting with denials, for example by emphasizing or exaggerating the evidence against the suspect ('maximization').

The model predicts that the effectiveness of the interrogation will depend on the extent to which the interrogator is able to identify the suspect's vulnerabilities, exploiting them to alter the suspect's belief system and perceptions of the consequences of making admissions, and persuading him or her to accept the interrogator's version of the 'truth'. This is a potentially powerful way of breaking down resistance during interrogation. According to Inbau *et al.* (2001), it results in an 80 per cent success rate, although the authors provide no objective evidence for this claim.

A decision-making model of confession

The focus of this model is on the decision-making of suspects during custodial interrogation (Hilgendorf and Irving 1981). The model was developed by Hilgendorf and Irving after they had been commissioned by the Royal Commission on Criminal Procedure to provide a comprehensive review of the interrogation process (Hilgendorf and Irving, 1981). Hilgendorf and Irving argue that one of the main advantages of their model is that it is 'closely linked to the legal concepts of voluntariness and oppression' (p. 81).

The basic premise of the model is that, during interrogation, suspects become engaged in a demanding decision-making process. Some of the basic decisions that the suspect has to make include:

- whether to speak or remain silent;
- whether to make self-incriminating admissions or not;
- whether to tell the truth or not;
- whether to tell the whole truth or only part of the truth; and
- how to answer the questions asked by the police interrogator.

Hilgendorf and Irving argue that decisions are determined by the following:

- Perceptions of the courses of action available to the suspect.
- Perceptions of the 'subjective' probabilities of the likely occurrence of various consequences attached to these courses of action.
- The utility values or gains attached to these courses of action.

Suspects have to consider the kind of different options there are available to them and then evaluate the likely consequences attached to these various options. For example, if they confess are they likely to be charged with the offence? If they insist on their innocence is the interrogation likely to continue and their detention prolonged?

The decision-making of the suspect is determined by the subjective probabilities of occurrence of the perceived consequences. In other words, it is what the suspect *believes* at the time to be the likely consequences that influence his or her behaviour rather than the objective reality of the situation. For example, an innocent suspect may confess under the misguided belief that since he or she is innocent no court will bring in a guilty verdict and that the truth will eventually come out (Gudjonnsson 2003a).

The suspect has to balance the potential consequences against the perceived value ('utilities') of choosing a particular course of action. For example, would a confession inevitably lead to cessation of interrogation and would the suspect be allowed to go home? Hilgendorf and Irving argue that threats and inducements can markedly influence the decision of the suspect to confess because of the perceived power the police have over the situation and the apparent credibility of their words.

Hilgendorf and Irving postulate that there are a number of *social, psychological* and *environmental* factors that can influence the suspect's decision-making during police interrogation. On occasions these factors can undermine the reliability of the suspect's confession when police interrogators:

- manipulate the social and self-approval utilities during interrogation in order to influence the decision-making of the suspect;

- manipulate the suspect's perceptions of the likely outcome concerning a given course of action (e.g. by minimizing the seriousness of the alleged offence and by altering perceptions of the 'cost' associated with denial, resistance and deception); or

- impair the suspect's ability to cope with effective decision-making by increasing anxiety, fear and compliance.

Psychoanalytic models of confession

Psychoanalytic models (e.g. Reik 1959; Berggren 1975; Rogge 1975) rest upon the assumption that the feelings of remorse and the need to elevate it are the fundamental causes of confessions. Reik (1959) provides a detailed formulation and argues that the unconscious compulsion to confess plays an important part in religion, myths, art, language and other social activities, including crime. Reik relies heavily on Freud's concepts of the id, ego and superego where a confession is seen as 'an attempt at reconciliation that the superego undertakes in order to settle the quarrel between the ego and the id' (p. 216). The superego is seen to play an important role in the need of the individual to confess. A punitive superego may result in the development of a strong feeling of guilt and need for self-punishment. This may result in a 'compulsion' to confess, and on occasion false confession.

Within this model, the development of the feeling of guilt after transgression and the unconscious need for self-punishment are seen as universal. It is only after the person has confessed that the ego begins to accept the emotional significance of the deed. A confession serves the function of relieving the person from the feeling of guilt and is therefore inherently therapeutic. A similar argument is put forward by Berggren (1975) who argues that a confession produces a sense of relief with cathartic effects. For a satisfactory cathartic effect to occur the confession has to be to a person in authority, such as a priest or police officer.

Rogge (1975), like Reik and Berggren, argues that confessions are based on feelings of guilt. He suggests that feelings of guilt are made up of two components, fear of losing love and fear of retaliation.

An interaction process model of confession

Moston et al. (1992) developed a model that helps us explain how the background of a suspect and case characteristics influence the interrogator's style of questioning, which in turn affects the suspect's behaviour and the outcome of the interview. The model postulates that the suspect's initial response to an allegation, irrespective of his or her involvement in the crime under investigation, is influenced by the interaction of three main groups of factors:

1. The background characteristics of the suspect and the offence (e.g. type of offence, the severity of the offence, age and sex of suspect and the suspect's personality).

2. The contextual characteristics of the case (e.g. legal advice, the strength of the police evidence). A distinction is drawn between the suspect's initial reaction to the accusation and his or her subsequent responses.

3. The interviewer's questioning technique.

The main strength of the model is its emphasis on looking at the interaction of variables, rather than viewing each of them in isolation. The outcome of the interview is dependent upon an interaction process of a number of factors. One important implication of the model is that background characteristics of the suspect and the case, in conjunction with contextual factors, influence the interrogator's beliefs, attitudes and style of questioning, which in turn influences the suspect's behaviour. In recent years there has been a growing interest in the influence of the personality and attitude of the interrogator and how these impact on the interview process and outcome (Gudjonnsson 2002). In addition, case characteristics may strongly influence the behaviour of *both* the suspect and the interrogator. The main limitation of the model is that it does not focus on the mental state and cognitive processes of the suspect.

A cognitive-behavioural model of confession

This model was first described by Gudjonnsson (1989) and expanded in *The Psychology of Interrogations, Confessions and Testimony* (Gudjonnsson 1992). It incorporates the essential components of the other models. Within this model confessions are best construed as arising through the existence of a particular relationship between the suspect, the environment and significant others within that environment. In order to understand that relationship it is important to look closely at the *antecedents* and the *consequences* of confessing behaviour within the framework of behavioural analysis:

- *Antecedents* refers to events that occur prior to interrogation. These are the factors that may trigger or facilitate a confession. A large number of different factors may be relevant, such as state of shock, fatigue, illness, deprivation of food and sleep, stress, social isolation, feelings of guilt and bereavement.

- There are two main types of *consequence*, 'immediate' (or 'short term') and 'long-term' consequences. The immediate or short-term consequences occur within minutes or hours of the suspect confessing to the alleged crime. The long-term consequences take place within days, weeks or years of the suspect confessing. The types of consequence, whether immediate or delayed, depend on the nature and circumstances of the case and the psychological characteristics of the individual concerned.

Antecedents and consequences are construed in terms of *social* (e.g. isolation from one's family and friends, the nature of the interrogation), *emotional* (e.g. uncertainty and distress associated with the arrest and confinement, feelings of guilt and shame), *cognitive* (i.e. the suspect's thoughts, interpretations, assumptions and perceived strategies of responding to a given situation), *situational* (e.g. the circumstances of arrest, length and nature of the confinement) and *physiological* (e.g. physical pain, headaches, increased heart rate, blood pressure, rate and irregularity of respiration, and perspiration) events.

The Ofshe–Leo model

Based on their work into disputed and false confessions, Ofshe and Leo (1997a, 1997b) developed a classification of confessions, which they believe apply equally to true and false confessions. There are five levels of confession (voluntary, stress-compliant, coerced-compliant, non-coerced-persuaded and coerced-persuaded), categorized into two groups (true or false). Each type of confession can be either true or false, depending on the circumstances of the individual case, which means that there are 10 possible outcome scenarios. The focus of this model is very much on the interrogation process itself (i.e. what the police say and do) and a psychological description of the type of confession elicited. The model postulates that confessions are chiefly elicited due to police pressure or legally defined coercion and individual differences and interactive processes are of relatively minor importance. This model appears to be particularly relevant to coerced confessions (i.e. where the police have made threats or offered inducements) irrespective of the guilt or innocence of the suspect.

Comments on the models

There are some overlaps between the different models, although each makes different assumptions about why suspects confess to the police during questioning. For example:

- The undoing of deception.
- The outcome of a decision-making process.
- Feelings of remorse.
- Interactions between the background and the characteristics of the suspect, the nature of the case and contextual factors.

- The nature of the relationship between the suspect, the environment and significant others within that environment.
- Interrogative pressure and coercion.

Taken as a whole, the models suggest that suspects confess when they perceive that the evidence against them is strong (irrespective of whether this is real or distorted), when they need to relieve feelings of guilt, when they have difficulties coping with the custodial pressure (i.e. interrogation and confinement) and when they focus primarily on the immediate consequences of their actions rather than the long-term ones. Although the suspect's personality and psychological strengths and weaknesses are considered important in some of the models (i.e. the Reid model, the cognitive-behavioural model) in producing confessions and denials, the nature of the specific vulnerabilities and traits is not well articulated, except in relation to suggestibility and compliance (Gudjonnsson 2003a).

A model of the interrogative process

Gudjonnsson (2003b), influenced by the work he was doing in the 1980s and 1990s with Dr James MacKeith on high-profile British cases of miscarriages of justice (Gudjonnsson and MacKeith 1988,

Police factors
- Custodial pressures

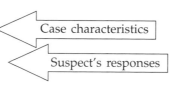

- Interrogative pressures

- Personality of interviewers

Vulnerabilities
- Physical health

- Mental health

- Psychological vulnerabilities

Support
- Solicitor

- Appropriate adult

Figure 7.1 An interactional model of the interrogative process

1997), developed a model to describe the interrogation process that would help the expert witness and researcher in evaluating cases of disputed confessions. The interaction model (Figure 7.1) shows the kind of factors that need to be considered when evaluating cases of disputed confessions.

First, there are factors associated with the custody itself (i.e. the nature and duration of the confinement), the interrogation (i.e. the techniques and ploys used by the interrogator, the intensity of the interrogation, duration and number of interviews) and the personality, attitudes and behaviour of the interrogator (e.g. for a review see Gudjonnsson 2002). In relation to attitudes and demeanour, Holmberg and Christianson (2002) found that interview styles rated as 'dominant' were associated with denials, whereas interview styles marked by 'humanity' were associated with admissions. There are a number of methodological weaknesses in this study (e.g. it was a pilot survey, some of the respondents appear not to have understood the questionnaire and there was a very poor response rate).

Case characteristics (i.e. the seriousness and notoriety of the crime) and the responses of the suspect to the detention and interrogation also need to be considered. These closely interact with the custodial and interrogative factors. For example, the behaviour of the police will generally be influenced by the nature of the crime they are investigating and how the suspect reacts initially to the detention and interrogation. If a suspect gives a full and apparently frank confession to the police at the beginning of an interview then there is usually no need for confrontational interaction and challenges. However, if the police do not believe the account given by the suspect then there may be confrontation, robust challenges and psychological manipulation aimed at overcoming the resistance and denials (Pearse and Gudjonnsson 1999; Inbau et al. 2001).

Whether or not suspects confess or deny the offence is significantly related to the strength of the evidence against them at the time of the interrogation. For example, Moston et al. (1992) found that where the evidence against suspects was rated as 'weak', 76.6 per cent denied the offence, in contrast to 66.7 per cent who made self-incriminating admissions where the evidence was rated as 'strong'. This finding is consistent with research among criminals (Gudjonnsson and Sigurdsson 1999), which consistently shows that there are three main reasons why suspects confess to crimes they have committed: 1) perception of the evidence against the suspect; 2) an internal need to confess, particularly in violent and sex crimes; and 3) custodial and interrogative pressures. In general, suspects confess to a combination of these three factors, but the single most important reason is the suspect's perception of the evidence against him or her (Gudjonsson 2003a).

There is evidence that the duration of detention, nature of the interrogation techniques used and dynamics in the police interview are related to the severity of the crime being investigated and it is here that custodial and interrogative factors tap more into psychological vulnerabilities (Gudjonsson 2003a). Pearse and Gudjonsson (1999, 2003) used a special coding frame, the 'Police Interviewing Analysis Framework' (PIAF), to analyze the social interaction between the interviewer and suspect from the tape recordings of real-life interrogation and to identify the techniques that were associated with moving suspects from a position of denial to a confession. Each five-minute segment of interrogation was carefully scrutinized and the results were subjected to a factor analysis. The three most salient factors that were associated with the breaking down of resistance were all 'overbearing' in character and were labelled as 'intimidation' (e.g. maximizing the seriousness of the offence and the anxiety of the suspect when denying the offence), 'robust challenge' (i.e. repeatedly challenging lies and inconsistencies) and 'manipulation' (i.e. minimizing seriousness of the offence, inducements, theme development). These techniques, which are similar to those recommended by Inbau *et al.* (2001), were effective in breaking down resistance and securing a confession. However, this was achieved at a high level of risk of the confession being rendered inadmissible by a court due to coercion and the defendant consequently being acquitted. In contrast, there were two further more 'sensitive' styles employed, albeit to a lesser degree, referred to as 'appeal' and 'soft challenge', which proved particularly effective with sex offenders and did not undermine the admissibility of the confession as they were not construed as being coercive.

The PIAF has not only succeeded in analyzing, measuring and displaying the nature and type of tactics employed, but it has also discriminated between overbearing and sensitive tactics, as determined by legal judgments (Pearse and Gudjonsson 2003).

In a unique real-life observational study of run-of-the-mill cases at two English police stations, over 170 suspects were psychologically assessed by clinical psychologists prior to their being interviewed by the police (Gudjonsson *et al.* 1993). Subsequently, all tapes of interviews with the suspects were analyzed to find out what factors were associated with denial and confessions (Pearse *et al.* 1998). The great majority of the interviews were very short (i.e. 80 per cent lasted less than 30 minutes and 95 per cent were completed within one hour), the confession rate was 58 per cent, there was little interrogative pressure in the tactics used and very few suspects moved from a denial to a confession (see Gudjonnsson 2003a for a detailed review of the findings). Logistic regression analysis was performed on the data. The dependent (outcome) variable was confession versus denial. The independent variables included the suspect's age, ethnicity, mental state, intelligence, suggestibility, illicit drug taking, criminal history, police interview tactics and presence or absence of a legal adviser. The strength of the evidence against the suspect was not measured in this study.

Two factors were highly predictive of a denial (i.e. the presence of a legal adviser and a previous history of imprisonment), whereas only one variable predicted a confession (i.e. whether the suspect had told the researcher that he or she had taken illicit drugs within 24 hours of arrest). The main implications of the findings are that in the run-of-the-mill English cases where there is little interrogative pressure or persuasion taking place and the great majority of suspects who confess do so right at the beginning of the interview. Psychological vulnerabilities, apart from illicit drug taking, which probably makes suspects eager to be released from custody as quickly as possible and therefore more willing to confess, are of little relevance, and having a legal representative and previous experience of imprisonment are strongly associated with a denial. However, in the more serious cases, psychological vulnerabilities and police pressure become much more important (Gudjonnsson 2003a).

The second important set of factors are the specific vulnerabilities of the detainee, which are associated with his or her physical and mental health, as well as more specific psychological vulnerabilities, such as suggestibility, compliance, acquiescence and anti-social personality traits (Gudjonnsson 2003a). In addition, children and juveniles (Drizin and Colgan 2004; Redlich et al. 2004) and persons with learning disabilities (Fulero and Everington 2004) are particularly at risk of giving unreliable accounts of events when not carefully interviewed. Sleep deprivation increases the person's susceptibility to suggestions (Blagrove 1996).

Thirdly, the impact of the presence or absence of a solicitor and appropriate adult during the interrogation needs to be evaluated as a part of the overall custodial environment. The impact of the presence of a solicitor on suspects' behaviour during interrogation is well established (Gudjonnsson 2003a). There is evidence emerging from our current work at police stations that the mere presence of an appropriate adult in an interview, even if he or she does not contribute directly in the interview process (i.e. he or she tends to remain silent), influences positively the behaviour of the police and solicitors (Medford *et al.* 2003). Medford *et al.* (2003) found that the presence of an appropriate adult increased the likelihood that a solicitor would also be present in an interview, there was overall less interrogative pressure in the interview and the solicitor took a more active role in the interview.

How interrogation can go wrong

Gudjonnsson (2003a) argues that police interrogation can go 'wrong' in the sense that it results in 'undesirable consequences' for the criminal justice system or the suspect. There are a number of ways in which this can happen:

- A confession, even if true, being ruled inadmissible during a suppression hearing due to the coercive nature of the interrogation.

- Causing a suspect to give a false confession, coerced confessions resulting in resentment and resulting in the suspect retracting it and failing to co-operate with the police in the future.

- Coercion resulting in the suspect developing a post-traumatic stress disorder, and undermining public confidence in the police.

- Poor interviewing resulting in suspects failing to give a confession when they would otherwise do so (e.g. suspects who would have confessed in their own time refuse to confess when they feel they arc being rushed or unfairly treated by the police).

- Suspects who have already confessed may retract their confession when they feel they are pressured too much to provide further information. This phenomenon is known as 'the boomerang effect' (Gudjonnsson 2003a).

- Coersive interviewing results in suspects becoming resentful of the police, which may result in their retracting their confession and being reluctant to confess during further interviews (Gudjonnsson 2003a).

Conclusions

Interrogations remain an important investigative tool. There are immense differences between the current investigative interviewing techniques and conditions of custodial confinement, as practised in England, and those legally allowed and practised in the USA. In spite of the greater restrictions in England imposed on interrogators with the implementation of PACE, the confession rate has not been reduced and it remains considerably higher than the confession rates reported in the USA (Gudjonnsson 2003a; Kassin and Gudjonnsson, 2004). The evidence suggests that suspects confess for three main reasons – perceptions of the strength of the evidence against them, internal pressure, and custodial and interrogative pressure (including techniques using deceit, trickery and psychological manipulation). Unusually, suspects confess for a combination of reasons, but perception of the strength of evidence is the single most important reason. This has important implications for investigators. Where the evidence against the suspect is weak or flawed, interrogative and custodial pressures increase the risk of false confessions. Investigators should be aware that false confessions do occur on occasions, for a variety of reasons, including suspects wanting to protect somebody else, not being able to cope with the interrogative and custodial pressures, and psychological vulnerabilities (Gudjonnsson 2003a).

Note

1. These include Wrightsman and Kassin (1993); Ofshe and Leo (1997a, 1997b); Kassin (1998); Leo and Ofshe (1998); McCann (1998); Leo (1998, 2001a); and, more recently, Kassin and Gudjonnsson (2004).

References

Berggren, E. (1975) *The Psychology of Confessions*. Leiden: E.J. Brill.
Blagrove, M. (1996) 'Effects of length of sleep deprivation on interrogative suggestibility', *Journal of Experimental Psychology: Applied*, 2: 48–59.
Clarke, C. and Milne, R. (2001) *National Evaluation of the PEACE Investigative Interviewing Course. Police Research Award Scheme. Report* PRAS/149. Portsmouth: Institute of Criminal Justice Studies, University of Portsmouth.

Drizin, S.A. and Colgan, B.A. (2004) 'Tales from the juvenile confessions front', in G.D. Lassiter (ed.) *Interrogations, Confessions, and Entrapment.* New York, NY: Kluwer Academic.

Drizin, S.A. and Leo, R.A. (2004) 'The problem of false confessions in the post-DNA world', *North Carolina Law Review*, 82: 891–1007.

Fisher, R.P. and Geiselman, R.E. (1992) *Memory Enhancing Techniques for Investigative Interviewing: The Cognitive Interview.* Springfield, IL: Charles C. Thomas.

Fulero, S.M. and Everington, C. (2004) 'Mental retardation, competency to waive *Miranda* rights, and false confessions', in G.D. Lassiter (ed.) *Interrogations, Confessions, and Entrapment.* New York, NY: Kluwer Academic.

Gudjonnsson, G.H. (1989) 'The psychology of false confessions', *Medico-Legal Journal*, 57: 93–110.

Gudjonnsson, G.H. (1992) *The Psychology of Interrogations, Confessions and Testimony.* London: Wiley.

Gudjonnsson, G. (2002) 'Who makes a good interviewer? Police interviewing and confessions', in M. Bockstaele (ed.) *Politieverhoor en Personality-Profiling.* Brussels: Uitgeverij Politeia nv.

Gudjonnsson, G.H. (2003a) *The Psychology of Interrogations and Confessions. A Handbook.* Chichester: Wiley.

Gudjonnsson, G.H. (2003b) 'Psychology brings justice: the science of forensic psychology', *Criminal Behaviour and Mental Health*, 13: 159–67.

Gudjonnsson, G.H., Clare, I.C.H., Rutter, S. and Pearse, J. (1993) *Persons at Risk During Interviews in Police Custody: The Identification of Vulnerabilities. Royal Commission on Criminal Justice.* London: HMSO.

Gudjonnsson, G.H. and MacKeith, J.A.C. (1988) 'Retracted confessions: legal, psychological and psychiatric aspects', *Medicine, Science and the Law*, 28: 187–94.

Gudjonnsson, G.H. and MacKeith, J. (1997) *Disputed Confessions and the Criminal Justice System. Maudsley Discussion Paper* 2. London: Institute of Psychiatry.

Gudjonnsson, G.H. and Sigurdsson, J.F. (1999) 'The Gudjonnsson Confession Questionnaire-Revised (GCQ-R): factor structure and its relationship with personality', *Personality and Individual Differences*, 27: 953–68.

Hilgendorf, E.L. and Irving, M. (1981) 'A decision-making model of confessions', in M. Lloyd-Bostock (ed.) *Psychology in Legal Contexts: Applications and Limitations.* London: Macmillan.

Holmberg, U. and Christianson, S.A. (2002) 'Murderers' and sexual offenders' experiences of police interviews and their inclination to admit and deny crimes', *Behavioral Sciences and the Law*, 20: 31–45.

Home Office (1985) *Police and Criminal Evidence Act 1984.* London: HMSO.

Home Office (2004) *Police and Criminal Evidence Act 1984 (s. 66), Codes of Practice A–F.* London: HMSO.

Inbau, F.E., Reid, J.E. and Buckley, J.P. (1986) *Criminal Interrogation and Confessions* (3rd edn). Baltimore, MD: Williams & Wilkins.

Inbau, F.E., Reid, J.E., Buckley, J.P. and Jayne, B.C. (2001) *Criminal Interrogation and Confessions* (4th edn). Gaithersberg, MD: Aspen.

Irving, B. (1980) *Police Interrogation. A Case Study of Current Practice. Research Studies* 2. London: HMSO.

Jayne, B.C. (1986) 'The psychological principles of criminal interrogation', in F. Inbau *et al.* (eds) *Criminal Interrogation and Confessions* (3rd edn). Baltimore, MD: Williams & Wilkins.

Kassin, S.M. (1998) 'More on the psychology of false confessions', *American Psychologist*, 53: 320–1.

Kassin, S.M. and Gudjonnsson, G.H. (2004) 'The psychology of confessions: a review of the literature and issues', *Psychological Science in the Public Interest*, 5, 33–67.

Kassin, S.M. and McNall, K. (1991) 'Police interrogations and confessions: communicating promises and threats by pragmatic implication', *Law and Human Behavior*, 15: 233–51.

Leo, R.A. (1992) 'From coercion to deception: the changing nature of police interrogation in America', *Crime, Law and Social Change: An International Journal*, 18: 35–59.

Leo, R.A. (1994) 'Police interrogation in America: a study of violence, civility and social change.' Unpublished PhD thesis, University of California at Berkeley.

Leo, R.A. (1996) 'Inside the interrogation room', *Journal of Criminal Law and Criminology*, 86: 266–303.

Leo, R.A. (1998) 'Miranda and the problem of false confessions', in R.A. Leo and G.C. Thomas III (eds) *The Miranda Debate, Justice and Policing*. Boston, MA: Northeastern University Press.

Leo, R.A. (2001a) 'False confessions. Causes, consequences and solutions', in S.A. Westervelt and J.A. Humphrey (eds) *Wrongly Convicted. Perspectives on Failed Justice*. London: Rutgers University Press.

Leo, R.A. (2001) 'Questioning the relevance of Miranda in the twenty-first century', *Michigan Law Review*, 99: 1000–28.

Leo, R.A. and Ofshe, R.J. (1998) 'The consequences of false confessions: deprivations of liberty and miscarriages of justice in the age of psychological interrogation', *Journal of Criminal Law and Criminology*, 88: 429–96.

Mackey, C. and Miller, G. (2004) *The Interrogator's War. Inside the Secret War against Al Qaeda*. London: John Murray.

McCann, J.T. (1998) 'A conceptual framework for identifying various types of confessions', *Behavioral Sciences and the Law*, 16: 441–53.

Medford, S., Gudjonnsson, G.H. and Pearse, J. (2003) 'The efficacy of the appropriate adult safeguard during police interviewing', *Legal and Criminological Psychology*, 8: 253–66.

Moston, S., Stephenson, G.M. and Williamson, T.M. (1992) 'The effects of case characteristics on suspect behaviour during questioning', *British Journal of Criminology*, 32: 23–40.

Ofshe, R.J. and Leo, R.A. (1997a) 'The decision to confess falsely: rational choice and irrational action', *Denver University Law Review*, 74: 979–1122.

145

Ofshe, R.J. and Leo, R.A. (1997b) 'The social psychology of police interrogation: the theory and classification of true and false confessions', *Studies in Law, Politics and Society*, 16: 189–251.

Pearse, J. and Gudjonnsson, G.H. (1996) 'Police interviewing techniques at two south London Police Stations', *Psychology, Crime and Law*, 3: 63–74.

Pearse, J. and Gudjonnsson, G.H. (1999) 'Measuring influential police interviewing tactics: a factor analytic approach', *Legal and Criminological Psychology*, 4: 221–38.

Pearse, J. and Gudjonnsson, G.H. (2003) 'The identification and measurement of "oppressive" police interviewing tactics in Britain', in G.H. Gudjonnsson (ed.) *The Psychology of Interrogations and Confessions. A Handbook*. Chichester: Wiley.

Pearse, J., Gudjonnsson, G.H., Clare, I.C.H. and Rutter, S. (1998) 'Police interviewing and psychological vulnerabilities: predicting the likelihood of a confession', *Journal of Community and Applied Social Psychology*, 8: 1–21.

Redlich, A.D., Silverman, M., Chen, J. and Steiner, H. (2004) 'The police interrogation of children and adolescents', in G.D. Lassiter (ed.) *Interrogations, Confessions, and Entrapment*. New York, NY: Kluwer Academic.

Reik, T. (1959) *The Compulsion to Confess: On the Psychoanalysis of Crime and Punishment*. New York, NY: Farrar, Straus & Cudahy.

Rogge, O.J. (1975) *Why Men Confess*. New York, NY: Da Capo Press.

Rose, D. (2004) *Guantánamo. America's War on Human Rights*. London: Faber & Faber.

Vrij, A. (2004a) 'Guidelines to catch a liar', in P.A. Granhag and L.A. Strömwall (eds) *The Detection of Deception in Forensic Contexts*. Cambridge: Cambridge University Press.

Vrij, A. (2004b) 'Why professionals fail to catch liars and how they can improve', *Legal and Criminal Psychology*, 9: 159–81.

Williamson, T.M. (1993) 'From interrogation to investigative interviewing. Strategic trends in the police questioning', *Journal of Community and Applied Social Psychology*, 3: 89–99.

Williamson, T.M. (1994) 'Reflections on current police practice', in D. Morgan and G. Stephenson (eds) *Suspicion and Silence. The Rights of Silence in Criminal Investigations*. London: Blackstone Press.

Wrightsman, L.S. and Kassin, S.M. (1993) *Confessions in the Courtroom*. Newbury Park, CA: Sage.

Zimbardo, P.G. (1967) 'The psychology of police confessions', *Psychology Today*, 1: 17–20, 25–7.

Chapter 8

Towards greater professionalism: minimizing miscarriages of justice

Tom Williamson

Introduction

Experience has shown that trust and confidence in justice can be damaged where there is an over-reliance on confession evidence that ignores the importance of evidence available from questioning witnesses and victims. Confession-focused questioning can, and almost certainly does, lead to miscarriages of justice. This applies in both adversarial and inquisitorial jurisdictions but the legal framework can minimize or exacerbate the degree of reliance on confession evidence.

Confession-oriented approaches to investigative interviews not only encourage human rights abuses but may also mask low levels of interviewing skills. In jurisdictions where interviews are fully or partly tape recorded, analysis of the tapes frequently reveals low levels of questioning skill. Attention will be drawn to an alternative approach based on research that shows that the outcome of an interview with a suspect correlates highly with the strength of the evidence in any particular case. Based on these insights an ethical and principled approach to investigative interviewing is advocated which elevates the importance of interviews with witnesses and victims, and treats the investigation as a 'search for the truth', as opposed to a process of persuasion to obtain a confession.

Analysis of miscarriage of justice cases in England, Canada and the USA reveals that there are many commonly recurring contributing factors. One factor has been called 'tunnel vision' which occurs where the investigator becomes so focused upon an individual or incident that no other person or incident registers in his or her thinking. Legislative responses to miscarriages of justice often require greater accountability and transparency in the conduct of investigations and the use of recording technology is an example of this trend. Based on experience of these developments in many different countries it is now feasible to describe a framework for investigative interviewing that would be effective in minimizing the risk of miscarriages of justice.

In particular, sound, scientifically based training programmes are urgently needed to assist investigators acquire the necessary interviewing skills to function at the higher professional standards that will be required in the twenty-first century. In addition, by providing accreditation for investigative skills training and pathways into higher education programmes, investigators and interviewers can develop a deeper knowledge and understanding of the current scientific research and social context of their work. These approaches can provide the basis for 'licence to practise' arrangements as well as leading to academic qualifications.

There is sufficient common ground in the academic and practitioner communities for reaching broad agreement on evidence-based best practice statements that not only reinforce ethical values and respect for human rights but also investigative effectiveness.

The local criminal justice context and a search for the truth

Even if al-Qaeda had not attacked the USA on 9 September 2001, investigators and interviewers within liberal democracies were facing challenges regarding the reliability of evidence obtained through questioning during an investigation. Police questioning of suspects, victims and witnesses occurs within the context of the type of criminal justice system that obtains within a particular jurisdiction. In Europe, systems of justice are either derived from the 'Anglo-Saxon' or 'common law' tradition, categorized as 'adversarial' or, alternatively, from an 'inquisitorial' tradition which applies in continental Europe and is based on a 'Roman' or 'civil law' tradition. The Royal Commission on Criminal Justice (Runciman 1993: 3) in England examined both approaches and pointed out that: 'It is important not to overstate the difference between the two systems: all adversarial systems contain inquisitorial elements, and vice versa.' They considered whether a change in the direction of more inquisitorial procedures might not reduce the risks of mistaken verdicts and conceded:

But we do recognise the force of the criticisms which can be directed at a thoroughgoing adversarial system which seems to turn a search for the truth into a contest played between opposing lawyers according to a set of rules which the jury does not necessarily accept or even understand (p. 3).

The commission also acknowledged that the greater use of forensic evidence in the criminal courts was a move towards a more inquisitorial approach. The commission identified the impetus for change as 'mistaken verdicts'. When miscarriages of justice are identified and become public knowledge in industrialized countries they invariably draw attention to police incompetence and sometimes to police corruption and lead to calls for politicians to act to reform the system (Macpherson 1999). Media criticism of recent examples of police investigative incompetence in Japan have led to a far-reaching reform programme (Ellis *et al.* in press). The Japanese system lays heavy emphasis on confessions (*ji haku hencho*) (Bayley 1991; Finch 1999), with the police concentrating on obtaining confessions at the expense of interviewing witnesses and gathering physical or forensic evidence (Watson 1995).

It is important that a political response should go beyond making the police the 'fall guys' for weaknesses in the criminal justice system (McBarnet 1979). Stephenson (1992: 243) reviewed the psychology of criminal justice and concluded that: 'at each stage of criminal processing findings have been accumulated that seriously challenge conventional views and assumptions about the propriety of the system. This knowledge should be used to fuel critical evaluation of the law's activities.' What is apparent is that the publicity that such cases attract undermines public trust and confidence in the police and the justice system and erodes the reciprocity necessary for the police successfully to discharge their responsibilities in a way that respects human rights and is supported by the 'will of the people' (Wright 2002: 44–6). No system of policing is sustainable unless it enjoys the support of the people. For this reason it is important to identify and address police action that erodes trust and confidence.

There has been a continuous stream of officially recognized miscarriage of justice cases in the UK. Gudjonsson identifies 22 landmark British Court of Appeal cases.[1] These were mainly cases that involved disputed confessions. In many of these cases psychological evidence relating to suggestibility and compliance was considered seriously by the court (Gudjonsson 2003[2]). There is an increasing willingness for the courts to accept expert evidence from forensic psychologists (Gudjonsson and Haward 1998).

The role of the police in criminal investigations

In England, the Royal Commission on Criminal Procedure (1981) was appointed amid growing concern about the police role in the investigation of offences. The *Police and People in London* series of public surveys discovered that seven types of serious misconduct by the police were believed to occur but abuse of custodial questioning was the most worrying. The PSI Report found:

> The use of threats and unfair pressure in questioning is the kind of misconduct that is thought to be most widespread. About half of informants think it happens at least occasionally, but perhaps more important, one-quarter think that it often happens – that it is a usual pattern of behaviour by police officers. The other kinds of misconduct are thought to happen at least occasionally by a substantial proportion of Londoners, while about one in ten Londoners think police officers fabricate evidence, and use violence unjustifiably on people held at police stations (Smith 1983: 325).

Another survey found that the public were more critical of the police where they have a high degree of contact with the police and are subject to a high level of victimization (Jones *et al.* 1986).

The primacy of interrogation in detecting offences

One of the reasons for these concerns is the importance that confession evidence plays in court proceedings. Bottomley and Coleman (1980) found that only 10 per cent of cases were detected as a result of intelligence or forensic evidence. The interrogation of suspects was the most important means of detecting offences. In 1977 approximately 25 per cent of all detections were offences 'taken into consideration' by the courts for sentencing purposes that resulted from the questioning of someone arrested for another offence.[3]

In an observational study for the royal commission of how police interrogations were conducted in four police stations Softley found that about 60 per cent of suspects made a full confession or a damaging admission (Softley 1981). In a similar study Irving (1981) found that obtaining a confession was the main purpose of a police interrogation. An examination of cases heard in the Crown Court (McConville *et al.* 1991; Baldwin 1992) found that 13 per cent would have failed to reach a *prima facie* level without confession evidence and another 4 per cent would probably have been acquitted. Where suspects had made statements to the police, half of them amounted to a full confession.

At this point in the history of criminal investigation in England and Wales it would appear that the police role in detecting offences was primarily one of interrogation and less that of inquiry. To understand why a confession was so important it is necessary to consider the way in which adversarial systems of justice operate.

The adversarial system is not a search for the truth (Zander 1994). Zander (1994a) argues that:

> the common law system has never made the search for the truth, as such, its highest aim. It is not that there is any objection to the truth emerging. But centuries ago it was appreciated that the truth is many-sided, complex, and difficult to ascertain. Even when all the relevant evidence is admissible, we commonly do not know for sure whether the defendant was, or, was not, innocent or guilty The common law system does not ask whether the defendant is guilty or innocent but rather the more manageable question – can it be proved beyond a reasonable doubt that he is guilty?

The way in which a prosecution case is prepared was examined by McConville *et al.* (1991) who argued that the investigation was not remotely like a search for the truth conducted subject to due process rules of law, but rather investigators motivated by crime control concerns manipulated the paperwork in ways that supported a conviction. Inconvenient information was filtered out, witness statements were shaped by police questioning aimed at developing and then supporting a prosecution account.

The investigative process turned on the central role of interrogation and detention placed the suspect in a hostile environment where custodial questioning takes place on police terms. This issue was considered by the US Supreme Court in the case of *Miranda* v. *Arizona*, which addressed the vulnerability of suspects facing custodial questioning. The Supreme Court considered custodial questioning to be inherently coercive and ensured that no statement made during police questioning and no evidence discovered as a result of that statement can be admitted in evidence at trial unless the suspect is first warned of, amongst other things, his or her right to consult with and to have counsel present during questioning. If unable to afford a lawyer, one will be provided at public expense, although this relates to a very restricted category of indigent defendants (Cole 1999). Any waiver to the right has to be made explicitly by the suspect. The members of the Royal Commission on Criminal Procedure (1981) were clearly influenced by the *Miranda* rules and this was reflected in the proposals that they made for regulating custodial interviews in England and Wales. Their recommendations were included in the Police and Criminal Evidence Act 1984 (PACE) and the codes of practice issued under s. 66 (revised in 2004).

The Police and Criminal Evidence Act 1984

When the Police and Criminal Evidence Act 1984 was implemented it provided a legislative framework for the regulation of custodial questioning. Under s. 76 of PACE it is no longer up to the defence to show that something had happened in the interrogation that would render the statement unreliable, it is up to the prosecution to show that nothing had happened to make the statement unreliable. Furthermore, under s. 78 of the Act the trial judge can exclude anything that is considered to be 'unfair' such as deception by the interviewing officers or providing misleading information. In *R.* v. *Heron* the judge acquitted the defendant when, *inter alia*, the interviewing officers misled the accused regarding identification evidence in a homicide case.[4]

Section C of the codes of practice cover the detention, treatment and questioning of persons by police officers. The Act entitled suspects to free legal advice and also provided for the tape recording of interviews with suspects. It is now almost unheard of that an interview will be conducted which is not either audio or videotape recorded and this has made a very important contribution to the regulation of custodial questions and also in identifying skills deficits.

The important contribution of technology to regulating custodial questioning

Early research into the quality of the police interviews, which was possible through the analysis of video and audio tape recordings, revealed that interviewing skills were generally poor. The interviewers appeared inept, nervous, ill at ease and lacking in confidence. Questioning was conducted on the basis of assumption of the suspect's guilt. Suspects were given very little opportunity to speak and when they did so the interviewing officer(s) constantly interrupted them. The officers had a fragile grasp of the legal points needed to prove the offence. The interviewing style was harrying and aggressive. There were examples of unfair inducements (Baldwin 1992). This reflected a continuing over-reliance on confession evidence under the new legislation. The reliance on confession evidence also meant that witnesses and victims were frequently not interviewed thoroughly and so were unable to provide all the information they were capable of giving as evidence. The role of the police in the investigation of offences was still one of persuading suspects to confess rather than engaging in a process of inquiry, which was a search for the truth.

In an analysis of over 1,000 tape recorded interviews in London, Williamson (1990) found that there was a very strong statistical correlation between the strength of the evidence and the outcome of the interview. Where the evidence was weak, 77 per cent of suspects denied the allegation and where the evidence was strong, 67 per cent of suspects made admissions (see Table 8.1).

Developing a principled approach to investigative interviewing

Clearly there was a need for a change of culture to meet the aspirations of the new legislation and to prevent challenges to the evidence obtained through questioning. This resulted in the creation of a national committee on investigative interviewing that involved police officers, lawyers and psychologists. The committee produced the seven *Principles for Investigative Interviewing* which were circulated

Table 8.1 Strength of evidence and outcome of interview

Strength of evidence	No. of cases	% of admissions	% of denials	% neither admit nor deny
Weak	274	9.9	76.6	13.5
Moderate	363	36.4	45.2	18.5
Strong	430	66.7	16.3	17.0
Total cases	1,067	–	–	–

Source: Williamson (1990).

to all police forces in Home Office circular 22/1992 which encouraged officers to see their role as searching for the truth:

- The role of investigative interviewing is to obtain accurate and reliable information from suspects, witnesses or victims in order to discover the truth about matters under police investigation.

- Investigative interviewing should be approached with an open mind. Information obtained from the person who is being interviewed should always be tested against what the interviewing officer already knows or what can reasonably be established.

- When questioning anyone a police officer must act fairly in the circumstances of each individual case.

- The police interviewer is not bound to accept the first answer given. Questioning is not unfair merely because it is persistent.

- Even when the right of silence is exercised by a suspect, the police still have a right to put questions.

- When conducting an interview, police officers are free to ask questions in order to establish the truth, except for interviews with child victims of sexual or violent abuse which are to be used in criminal proceedings. They are not constrained by the rules applied to lawyers in court.

- Vulnerable people, whether victims, witnesses or suspects, must be treated with particular consideration at all times.

The circular marked the start of a very successful investigative interviewing training programme, called PEACE, which led to changing interviewer behaviour in the UK (see also Chapter 9, this volume). PEACE is a mnemonic describing the stages in an interview:

P   Preparation and planning.
E   Engage and explain.
A   Allow interviewee to provide an account.
C   Clarify, challenge and conclude.
E   Evaluate evidence obtained through questioning.

The national training programme has now become a mandatory part of the curriculum for the training of all police officers. The

Youth Justice and Criminal Evidence Act 1999 allows videotaping of interviews with vulnerable witnesses, which can then be used as evidence-in-chief. The Association of Chief Police Officers has conducted a national review of investigative interview training that will recommend further training to take place at five levels or tiers:

1. Recruit (or probationary officer) training.

2. Investigators volume crime.

3. Investigators of serious crime or specialist interviews with children or vulnerable interviewees.

4. Supervisors who would be line managers trained to supervise the interview process.

5. Interview co-ordinators who would form a national cadre of highly trained and experienced investigators who have made a study of interviewing and can provide consultancy advice in investigations.

Effective representation for suspects at public expense has also contributed to a growth in professionalism for police and lawyers. The recording technology also demonstrated that suspects were not being adequately represented. The Law Society has created training courses and an accreditation system for legal advisers has ensured that legal representation is of a good quality (Bridges and Choongh 1998).

The Police and Criminal Evidence Act provided various rights for detainees. They have the right to inform someone of their arrest (s. 5) and to consult privately with a legal representative (s. 6), which can only be waived with the authority of a superintendent. This waiver only applies where there is fear of immediate harm and so in practice is rarely exercised; detainees have a right of access to the codes of practice. Custody officers dealing with their detention must provide a written notice of their rights. They must be informed of the grounds for their detention.

The codes also contain provision for special groups of detainees. Interpreters must be provided for those who only speak a foreign language or are deaf. Juvenile detainees must have a parent or guardian informed of their detention. Detainees with a mental handicap have the right to have someone who is experienced in dealing with learning difficulties (called an 'appropriate adult') attend the interview in addition to the person providing legal advice.

The duration for which the police can detain a person is strictly regulated. A review of detention must be conducted within 6 hours of arrival at the police station by an inspector and then a further review within 15 hours. Detention beyond 24 hours requires a review and authorization by a police superintendent for detention for up to 36 hours. On application to a magistrates court detention in very serious cases can be authorized for up to 96 hours. Detainees must be charged as soon as the police have sufficient evidence to prosecute. There must be no further questioning after charge.

Disclosure of prosecution evidence

The government has introduced legislation covering disclosure by the prosecution of all material collected during the course of the inquiry. This has provided a new level of openness and accountability subjecting the investigation process to new levels of scrutiny strongly reinforcing the notion of an investigation as a search for the truth and curtailing selective disclosure of information by investigators or prosecution. The Criminal Procedure and Investigations Act 1996 (s. 23) provides the basis for the disclosure of material gathered during the course of an investigation. Primary prosecution disclosure involves material in the possession of the prosecution, which might undermine the case against the accused. Secondary prosecution disclosure involves material, which might assist in a defence disclosed in a statement. The prosecution can make application to the court for the agreement not to disclose sensitive material, such as the identity of an informant. The disclosure process works by separating the roles of the senior investigating officer from that of the disclosure officer. The investigating officer is required to follow all lines of inquiry whether they point to or away from the suspect.

All information obtained during an investigation must be recorded. This includes negative information – for example, the number of people in a particular place at a particular time who said that they saw nothing. There is a duty to retain all material including material casting doubt on the reliability of a confession and material casting doubt on the reliability of a witness. All material is to be listed in a schedule of non-sensitive material.

Criminal Cases Review Commission

The Criminal Appeal Act 1995 created the Criminal Cases Review Commission whose function is to review all allegations of miscarriages of justice. So far over 100 cases have been referred to the Court of Appeal. The commission has reviewed over 4,000 cases and currently has 450 cases under review.[1] A similar review commission has been established in Scotland but with wider terms of reference making intervention easier whenever they suspect a miscarriage of justice. A Home Affairs Select Committee of the House of Commons has investigated cases of historical child abuse and has drawn attention to what it believes to be widescale miscarriages of justice (HAC 2002). Cases of this type represent a significant proportion of the applications to the Criminal Cases Review Commission.

Miscarriages of justice in the USA and Canada

A similar trajectory of change can be discerned from miscarriage of justice cases in the USA and Canada. A symptom of what can go wrong in custodial questioning has been described in Canadian inquiries into miscarriages of justice as 'tunnel vision'. According to the Right Honourable Peter de C.C. Cory (2001):

Tunnel Vision is insidious. It can affect an officer or, indeed, anyone involved in the administration of justice with sometimes tragic results. It results in the officer becoming so focussed upon an individual or incident that no other person or incident registers in the officer's thoughts. Thus, tunnel vision can result in the elimination of other suspects who should be investigated. Equally, events which could lead to other suspects are eliminated from the officer's thinking. Anyone, police officer, counsel or judge can become infected by this virus.

I recommend that attendance annually at a lecture or a course on this subject be mandatory for all officers. The lecture or course should be updated annually and an officer should be required to attend before or during the first year that the officer works as a detective.

Courses or lectures that illustrate with examples and discuss this problem should be compulsory for police officers and they would undoubtedly be helpful for counsel and judges as well.[6]

Tunnel vision is an enduring feature of 'cop culture' and the response by practitioners to miscarriages of justice is frequently to go into denial and assume that defendants somehow managed to get off on a technicality.

Concerns in Canada regarding the vice of tunnel vision had previously been expressed by the Honourable Fred Kaufman QC a former judge of the Quebec Court of Appeal who was appointed in 1996 to conduct the inquiry designated the 'Commission on Proceedings Involving Guy Paul Morin' which relates to a miscarriage of justice case in the Province of Ontario, Canada. The commissioners found staggering the fact that certain parties at the inquiry continue to suffer from tunnel vision. It was all the more concerning since the parties referred to are a prosecution barrister (McGuigan), and a detective investigating in the case (Fitzpatrick). The commission reported:

> Mr. McGuigan still believes that the informants were telling the truth and that Guy Paul Morin lied about his 'confession'. Detective Fitzpatrick holds similar views. Indeed, though Mr. McGuigan believes that Mr. Morin is innocent, he also believes that he and his family deliberately concocted a false alibi. An innocent person has been known to tender a false confession — though mostly in the context of a police investigation. An innocent person has been known to tender a false, concocted alibi. I have found that Mr. Morin did not confess to May; I also have no doubt that Mr. Morin and his family (however imperfectly conveyed) did not concoct his alibi. The fact that Mr. McGuigan still accepts Mr. May's evidence, in the fact of Mr. Morin's proven innocence, May's recantations, May's non-rehabilitation, and most importantly, in the face of May falsely alleging that McGuigan himself was a conspirator in framing Morin, is 'tunnel vision' in the most staggering proportions. The fact that Detective Fitzpatrick still accepts Mr. May's evidence, in the face of these facts and May's false claims that Fitzpatrick had threatened to kill May, etc. demonstrates an equally persistent 'tunnel vision'. These findings of 'tunnel vision' also explain the need for the recommendations which later follow (Commission on Proceedings Involving Guy Paul Morin, Executive Summary: 11).

The USA has a federal constitution and so there is no equivalent of England's Police and Criminal Evidence Act 1984 covering the whole of the USA. Laws relating to investigation, where they exist, are passed at the local or state level. The American constitution guarantees its citizens certain rights. The US Supreme Court set out in *Miranda* v. *Arizona* the rights of citizens who were being questioned by the police. This includes the right to legal representation. However, since *Miranda*, the US Supreme Court has consistently watered down the rights articulated in *Miranda*. In *Gideon* v. *Wainwright*, under the Sixth Amendment to the Constitution, indigent defendants have a right to a lawyer to provide 'effective assistance' in trials for serious offences. Effective assistance has been considered by the courts to include lawyers who are drunk, asleep, on drugs, or who in capital cases were unable to name a single Supreme Court decision on the death penalty (Cole 1999: 88–96; Scheck *et al.* 2000: 183–92).

In 2000 the US government spent $97.56 billion on their criminal justice system of which 50 per cent was spent on the police and prosecution and only 1.3 per cent on indigent defence. Eighty per cent of all defendants are indigent. However the right to indigent defence now only applies after formal proceedings have begun and the encounter is at a critical stage. It does not relate to pre-charge questioning. There is no provision for indigent representation in post-conviction proceedings even in death penalty cases (*Pennsylvania* v. *Finlay* (1987) 481. US 51). There has until recently been no provision for defendants with learning difficulties although this may have changed as a result of a Supreme Court decision in June 2002.

There is a rising tide of exonerations of prisoners in North America, many based upon DNA testing, which is revealing how frequently miscarriages of justice can occur. Many of the exonerations have involved death penalty cases in states such as Illinois, Florida, Oklahoma and Texas. Non-death penalty states such as Massachusetts have exonerated prisoners and face a steady stream of new claimants. A recent review of the convictions of 33 innocent persons in Massachusetts revealed that mistaken eyewitness identifications occurred in over half the identified miscarriages and misconduct by police or prosecutors in over one third, and both are features of 'tunnel vision' (Fisher 2002).

In April 2002 Governor Ryan of the State of Illinois published the report of a committee which he established to review the death penalty in Illinois. It found that almost half the defendants should not have been convicted. The commission made a total of 80 recommendations including the creation of a state-wide panel to review prosecutors' requests for the death penalty; banning death sentences on the mentally retarded (*sic*); significantly reducing the number of death eligibility factors; and the videotaping of interrogations with homicide suspects.

Analysis of miscarriages of justice cases reveals that the contributory factors are depressingly similar. The list includes:

- 'junk' forensic science;
- abuse or misuse of informants, including jailhouse snitches;
- manipulating witnesses to refute alibi evidence;
- misuse of offender profiling techniques;
- poor skills for interviewing witnesses and suspects;
- fabrication of evidence (perjury) or 'gilding the lilly';
- misconduct by lawyers; and
- the psychological vulnerability of many suspects.

Another important factor in miscarriages of justice has been 'cop' and 'prosecution' cultures:

- The unprofessional relationship between corrupt cops and bad lawyers.
- 'Cop culture' where loss of objectivity and bad judgement manifest themselves in either 'tunnel vision' or what some have called 'noble cause corruption', which is simply an attempt to control criminal activity by criminal or unconstitutional methods.

Most members of the public take police competence in the investigation of serious offences for granted. However there is mounting evidence from many jurisdictions that this confidence is frequently misplaced.

Public inquiries: similar recommendations

When miscarriages of justice have been identified and august figures have conducted their official reviews we find that there is a great similarity in the recommendations. These include the following:

- Improved protocols for eyewitness identification.
- The requirement for audio or videotaped records of the witness statements and the custodial questioning of suspects.
- Ensuring prosecutors have full access to records of police investigations.

- Legislation to require disclosure of any material evidence held by the prosecution to the defence.
- The creation of some form of tribunal to investigate miscarriages of justice.
- The appointment of civilian oversight bodies.

When the miscarriage of justice cases where the defendants in 74 cases who are actually innocent are examined to identify the causes leading to wrongful convictions, junk forensic science was a factor in 69 per cent of cases, police misconduct in 50 per cent of cases and false confessions in 20 per cent of cases (Scheck *et al.* 2000: 361). Although 'junk' science was a factor in the Court of Appeal decision in the case of the 'Birmingham Six', there has been much less criticism of forensic science in Britain than in the USA. In England the forensic science laboratories have been removed from the control of the police and are now a stand-alone government agency.

The response in Britain to miscarriages of justice has been through legislation to put in place a rigorous regulatory regime, which has been strictly enforced by the judges. Technology has been adopted to ensure that custodial questioning is open and transparent, and that what is said during questioning is said freely and recorded accurately. On their own these approaches will have only a limited effect, without a concomitant investment in the training and education of investigators and interviewers to change an investigative culture which is over-reliant on confession evidence.

Investing to develop investigative professionalism

In the UK the government has established a Police Standards and Skills Organization (now amalgamated as part of a larger Justice Sector Skills Council) and a National Centre for Police Excellence which is charged under the Police Reform Act 2003 with developing investigative doctrine and training products that will professionalize the investigative process.[7] The lack of detective skills is one of the major challenges facing the police service. The new programme to help professionalize investigative practice will produce clear job descriptions for each investigative role. A competency framework for each role has also been developed. This will lead to a very large change in the way detective resources are trained and managed. A national register will be created for particular skills, including investigative interviewing. The training will have to be approved by a national board and the training deliverers will have to be licensed. Each officer will be required to maintain a professional development portfolio to record the evidence of his or her continuous professional development. This will involve supervision by line mangers, support from mentors and assessment by trained and qualified assessors against the defined competencies and standards. These developments will inevitably lead over time to a form of 'licence to practise'. Accreditation of the training by universities will provide pathways into higher education.[8] They should lead to British investigators in the twenty-first century being skilled, educated and licensed.

Conclusion

Recent research has led to serious questions being raised about the reliability of evidence obtained by investigators through questioning. This can be affected by the way investigators adapt to the requirements of the system of justice in which they operate. There would appear to be a number of steps that societies can take in order to minimize miscarriages of justice that result from 'tunnel vision' and over-reliance on confession evidence.

Good pre-trial investigation and custodial questioning processes will provide better evidence and reduce the over-reliance on confession evidence and encourage a search for the truth. Making better use of forensic evidence and more thorough questioning of victims and witnesses to enable them to give their best evidence will be more likely to enable courts to reach the truth. Greater sensitivity in interviewing might help the guilty to provide a truthful account and for those who are vulnerable it would prevent many future miscarriages of justice. Quality legal representation for accused at public expense and disclosure of prosecution evidence are important safeguards. Formal systems for reviewing alleged miscarriages of justice and robust civilian oversight arrangements are an important investment. Independent status for forensic science laboratories should prevent some of the 'junk' science that has been a feature in miscarriage of justice cases.

There needs to be greater recognition that truth and justice suffer when criminal justice systems become too adversarial. As Stephenson (1992) identified, many of the current systems are fundamentally flawed. New approaches to professionalizing investigative competence are being developed which should lead to twenty-first century investigators being skilled, qualified and licensed to practise in their disciplines, including investigative interviewing. Sound scientific research should be the foundation upon which this new professionalism is built. There is sufficient common ground in the academic and practitioner communities for evidence-based best practice statements to be agreed which not only reinforce ethical values and respect for human rights but also investigative effectiveness, minimizing the risk of false confessions and miscarriages of justice.

In conclusion, it is possible to minimize the risk of miscarriages of justice if we do four things:

1. Make some changes to our systems of criminal justice for better regulating custodial questioning.
2. Make better use of audio and video technology for recording investigative interviews.
3. Train investigators to search for the truth and teach them more effective questioning skills.
4. Above all, we should teach everyone involved in criminal justice the dangers of 'tunnel vision' and ways to avoid it.

Improving trust and confidence in the criminal justice system will occur when there is a greater level of professionalism in the core competency of investigative interviewing.

Notes

1. Presentation to the 'wrongful convictions' conference, the Criminal Justice Institute, Harvard Law School, 19 April 2002.
2. Gudjonsson (2003) provides a comprehensive analysis of the cases referred to above (see Table 16.1: 439). See also Mullin (1990) and Victory (2002).
3. See Simmons (2002), Table 8.02, showing the current level to be 13 per cent.
4. Unreported, Leeds Crown Court, 18 October 1993.
5. For a review of the work of the CCRC from its inception in 1997 to 2000, see James et al. (2000).
6. This description of 'tunnel vision' in police investigations and criminal justice, together with his recommendations to address the problem are taken from the Inquiry Regarding Thomas Sophonow, a miscarriage of justice case in the Province of Manitoba, Canada.
7. See the PSSO website (www.psso.co.uk) and www.centrex.police.uk for the National Centre for Policing Excellence.

8. A Foundation Degree in Investigation and Evidence is being developed by the Institute of Criminal Justice Studies, University of Portsmouth, which was due to commence in 2004.

References

Baldwin, J. (1992) *Video Taping Police Interviews with Suspects – an Evaluation. Police Research Series Paper* 1. London: Home Office.

Baldwin, J. and McConville, M. (1981) *Confessions in Crown Court Trials. Research Study* 5. *Royal Commission on Criminal Procedure (1981)* (Cmnd 8092). London: HMSO.

Bayley, D. (1991) *Forces of Order: Policing Modern Japan*. Berkeley, CA: University of California Press.

Beck, U. (1992) *Risk Society*. London: Sage.

Bottomley, A.K. and Coleman, C.A. (1980) 'Police Effectiveness and the public: the limitations of official crime rates', in R.V.G. Clarke and J.M. Hough (eds) *The effectiveness of Policing*. Farnborough: Gower.

Bridges, L. and Choongh, S. (1998) *Improving Police Station Legal Advice*. London: Legal Aid Board and Law Society.

Cole, D. (1999) *No Equal Justice. Race and Class in the American Criminal Justice System*. New York, NY: The New Press.

Ellis, T., Hamai, K., Lewis, C. and Williamson, T. (in press) 'Rising crime in Japan?', *Myth, Reality, Media Representation and the Role of the Police*.

Finch, A.J. (1999) 'The Japanese police's claim to efficiency: a critical view', *Modern Asia Studies*, 33: 483–511.

Fisher, S.Z. (2002) 'Convictions of innocent persons in Massachusetts: an overview', *Boston University Public Interest Law Journal*, 12: 63.

Gudjonsson, G.H. (2003) *The Psychology of Interrogations and Confessions. A Handbook*. Chichester: Wiley.

Gudjonsson, G.H. and Haward, L.R.C. (1998) *Forensic Psychology. A Guide to Practice*. London: Routledge.

Home Affairs Select Committee (2002) *The Conduct of Investigations into Past Cases of Abuse in Children's Homes* (HC 836-1). London: House of Commons.

Irving, B. (1981) *Police Interrogation. A Case Study of Current Practice. Research Study* 2. *Royal Commission on Criminal Procedure (1981)* (Cmnd 8092). London: HMSO.

James, A., Taylor, N. and Walker, C. (2000) 'The Criminal Cases Review Commission: economy, effectiveness and justice', *Criminal Law Review*, March: 125–208.

Jones, T., MacLean, B. and Young, J. (1986) *The Islington Crime Survey: Crime Victimization and Policing in Inner-city London*. London: Gower.

Macpherson of Cluny, Sir W. (1999) *The Stephen Lawrence Inquiry* (Cm 4262-1). London: HMSO.

McBarnet, D.J. (1979) 'Arrest: the legal context of policing', in S. Holdaway (ed.) *The British Police*. London: Arnold.

McConville, M., Sanders, A. and Leng, R. (1991) *The Case for the Prosecution: Police Suspects and the Construction of Criminality*. London: Routledge.

Moston, S., Stephenson, G.M. and Williamson Thomas, M. (1992) 'The effects of case characteristics on suspect behaviour during police questioning', *British Journal of Criminology*, 32: 23–40.

Mullin, C. (1990) *Error of Judgement. The Truth about the Birmingham Bombings*. Dublin: Poolbeg.

Neyroud, P. and Beckley, A. (2001) *Policing, Ethics and Human Rights*. Cullompton: Willan Publishing.

Ofshe, R. J. and Leo, R.A. (1997) 'The social psychology of police interrogation. The theory and classification of true and false confessions', *Studies in Law, Politics and Society*, 16: 189–251.

Runciman, Viscount of Doxford (1993) *The Royal Commission on Criminal Justice* (Cm 2263). London. HMSO.

Ryan, G.H. (2002) *The Governor's Commission on Capital Punishment*. Office of the Governor, State of Illinois (online at www.idoc.state.il.us/ccp).

Scheck, B., Neufeld, P. and Dwyer, J. (2000) *Actual Innocence. Five days to Execution, and other Dispatches from the Wrongly Convicted*. New York, NY: Doubleday.

Simmons, J. (2002) *Crime in England and Wales 2001/2002. Home Office Statistical Bulletin*. London: Home Office.

Smith, D.J. (1983) *Police and People in London. I. A survey of Londoners*. London: Policy Studies Institute.

Smith, D.J. and Gray, J. (1983) *Police and People in London. IV. The Police in Action*. London: Policy Studies Institute.

Softley, P. (1981) *Police Interrogation: an observational study in four police stations. Research Study No 4 Royal Commission on Criminal Procedure (1981)* (Cmnd 8092). London: HMSO.

Steer, D. (1981) *Uncovering Crime: The Police Role. Research Study 7. Royal Commission on Criminal Procedure (1981)* (Cmnd 8092). London: HMSO.

Stephenson, G.M. (1992) *The Psychology of Criminal Justice*. Oxford: Blackwell.

Victory, P. (2002) *Justice and Truth. The Guildford Four and Maguire Seven*. London: Sinclair-Stevenson.

Watson, A. (1995) 'The dark cloud over Japanese criminal justice: abuse of suspects and forced confessions', *Justice of the Peace and Local Government Law*, 5 August: 516–19.

Williamson, T.M. (1990) 'Strategic changes in police interrogation: an examination of police and suspect behaviour in the Metropolitan Police in order to determine the effects of new legislation, technology and organisational policies.' Unpublished PhD thesis, University of Kent at Canterbury.

Wright, A. (2002) *Policing. An Introduction to Concepts and Practice.* Cullompton: Willan Publishing.

Young, J. (1999) *The Exclusive Society: Social Exclusion, Crime and Difference in Late Modernity.* London: Sage.

Zander, M. (1994a) 'Ethics and crime investigation by the police', *Policing*, 10: 39–48.

Chapter 9

Will it all end in tiers? Police interviews with suspects in Britain[1]

Andy Griffiths and Becky Milne

Introduction

The interviewing of witnesses and suspects is a core function of policing across the world. In Britain, historically there was no formal interview training for police officers and officers learnt from watching others (Moston and Engleberg 1993; Norfolk 1997). The concept of training officers to interview witnesses was unheard of, confessions obtained from interviews with suspects were seen as the best evidence of guilt and 'good' interviewers were those who could persuade suspects to confess to crimes. In 1992, the Association of Chief Police Officers for England and Wales published the first national training programme for interviewing. This was designed to train police officers to interview both witnesses and suspects (Central Planning and Training Unit, 1992). It was known as the PEACE interview model (see p. 172). A decade later an updated five-tier interview strategy is in the process of being implemented as the latest step in the evolution of police interviewing within the UK. The strategy has built upon the foundation laid down by the PEACE model. It has developed the original single model into a more comprehensive approach drawn from academic research in the subject and fresh developments in the criminal justice system. The new approach is designed to cater for officers at different stages of their careers and for dealing with different types of crimes. Tier one is an introduction to interviewing for new police officers, probationers or police recruits. Tier two is a development of this and is aimed at more experienced officers engaged in dealing with everyday crime such as theft and assault (similar to the original PEACE course). Tier three is designed to equip officers to deal with complex and serious crime and is an umbrella term encompassing separate courses for interviewing 1) suspects (see later for a full description); 2) witnesses (the enhanced cognitive interview: see Milne and Bull 1999 for a full description); and 3) witnesses who may be vulnerable or intimidated (Youth Justice and Criminal Evidence Act 1999; Home Office and Department of Health 2001). Tier four deals with monitoring and supervision of the quality of interviews and tier five introduces the role of the interview co-ordinator for complex and serious crime. This chapter is concerned with what is now known as tier three suspect interviewing but what was previously described as 'advanced' interviewing.

Most of the identified problems with police interviews prior to PEACE were due to miscarriages of justice linked to false confessions. Although subsequent legislative changes (for example, the mandatory audio tape recording of all interviews with suspects and the right for a suspect to have a legal representative present) should prevent a repetition of these cases, they caused significant damage to the reputation of the police. The modern transparency of the suspect interview process has seen attention switched more recently to the evidence of key *witnesses* in major criminal trials and how the police conduct these interviews and present the evidence from them. Witness interviewing had not received this level of public scrutiny previously because it had not resulted in dramatic acquittals but the steady growth of research targeted at this area and certain key cases such as the murder of a young boy in London where the evidence of a key witness was discredited (Laville 2002; Tendler 2002) have raised the awareness of problems in this area in much the same way as interviewing of suspects prior to 1992 (see Bull and Milne 2004 for a review).

The history of interviewing in England and Wales shows that interviewing needs to be both effective and ethical. This is especially true in the investigation of serious crime because of the implications of wrongdoing. This chapter concentrates on interviews with suspects and initially provides a brief summary of that recent history. It then traces the birth of advanced interviewing from the original PEACE model and outlines the key differences between the two. Finally, the chapter describes a study undertaken to evaluate the effectiveness of advanced interviewing and presents the preliminary results from this empirical research. The chapter culminates with a discussion on how interviewing will progress.

A recent history of police interviews with suspects

Prior to 1984 police interviews in England and Wales were governed by Judges' Rules. These 'rules' were merely administrative guidance that originated in the early part of the twentieth century. Officers were permitted to conduct interviews unrecorded and then to write an account of the interview from memory. The officer's recollection of the interview was then presented in court from the notes. Disquiet over this approach began to grow in the late 1970s.

A small research study conducted as part of the Royal Commission on Criminal Procedure (1981) observed sixty interviews with suspects at one police station in England. The observers reported a large number of persuasive and manipulative tactics used by interviewers to obtain confessions (Irving and Hilgendorf 1980). The full commission report resulted in the government passing the Police and Criminal Evidence Act 1984 (PACE). This Act made significant changes to the detention and treatment of those suspected of criminal offences in England and Wales. It introduced the right to have a legal adviser present throughout the interview process and phased in the mandatory audio recording of interviews with suspects held in police stations. The existence of a permanent and accurate record of an interview exposed frequent failings in police interviews. The changes brought about by PACE also allowed researchers a window into the interview room. As a result a plethora of work examining police interviewing practices began. For the first time people other than the police officer and the suspect could hear an accurate record of the interview. The resultant research confirmed that police interviews were in need of revision but not just in the areas identified by the Royal commission (Moston *et al.* 1992; Baldwin 1993; Mortimer 1994a, 1994b; Pearse and Gudjonsson 1996). Baldwin's study of 400 interviews found interviewers who were 'nervous and ill at ease'. Officers were also found to have an accusatory mindset when interviewing. For example, one study examined 1,000 interviews and found the overwhelming aim of the interviewers to be securing a confession (Moston *et al.* 1992). Officers were also seen to be using coercive techniques that were consistent with unethical American interview styles (e.g. *Criminal Interrogation and Confessions*, Inbau *et al.* 1986; see Mortimer 1994a for a summary of this approach). The later case of *Heron* (see below) highlighted the fact that confessions elicited through this style of interviewing would not be admitted in a court of law in England and Wales. Yet, where confessions did occur other research found this had little to do with the skill of the officer but rather factors such as the strength of the evidence (Moston *et al.* 1992; Baldwin 1993; Stephenson and Moston 1994; Pearse and Gudjonsson 1996).

Around the same time as this research was being conducted a series of miscarriages of justice attributable to false confessions began to appear. In October 1989 a group of terrorist suspects, known as the 'Guildford Four' who had been convicted of some of the worst bombings committed on mainland Britain in modern times, were acquitted on appeal. The confessions that had been central pillars of their convictions in 1975 were shown to be unreliable and, in some cases, fabricated. The group had spent years in jail as a result. In 1991, in a separate case, six suspects convicted of other terrorist bombings (the Birmingham Six) were released when confession evidence that had secured their convictions in 1974 was also discredited (Gudjonsson 2003). In 1993, Thomas Heron, who was on trial for the murder of a young girl, was acquitted when the interviews which led to his confession were dismissed by the trial judge as 'oppressive'. Unlike the Guildford Four and Birmingham Six where the interviews were not tape recorded (having taken place before this was a legislative requirement), the *Heron* interviews *were* tape recorded. Also, whereas the terrorist suspects alleged that threats and violence were used to extract their confessions, Heron's confession was obtained by tactics such as overstating evidence and emphasizing the benefits of admitting the offence. The judgment extended the definition of oppression to include these manipulative tactics as well as overt violence. The *Heron* case has been described as a watershed in police interviewing which marked the end of persuasive interview techniques in England and Wales (Clarke 1994). The successful appeals of the Guildford Four and Birmingham Six and the acquittal of Heron received widespread publicity and brought heavy criticism of the police and affected public opinion. A contemporary survey of the general public reported that 73 per cent of the participants believed that the police broke the rules to obtain convictions (Williamson 1991). By 1993 police interviews were described as a grave concern (Shepherd 1993). More recent statistics show acquittal rates at trial rising to an all time high of 43 per cent by 2001 (Robbins 2001). One of the reasons put forward for this poor interviewing was the absence of officially approved interview techniques and a lack of standardized training.

As a consequence of this situation, the Association of Chief Police Officers acted. The result was the development of the seven principles of investigative interviewing (see Milne and Bull 1999 and Chapter 8, this volume) and a national model for investigative interviewing known as PEACE (also Chapter 8, this volume, and below). The intention was to train every officer in England and Wales of inspector rank and below. In accordance a huge training operation was initiated over the next five years. The most recent evaluation of PEACE found that interviews with suspects had improved since its inception but that further development was still necessary (Clarke and Milne 2001). Nevertheless, PEACE was a significant step forward and an attempt to end miscarriages of justice. It was devised as a 'one size fits all' training course for officers regardless of skill, experience or the offence under investigation.

Tier 3: advanced suspect interview training

In the period before the implementation of PEACE individual police forces in Britain had responded to the criticism of the judiciary and academics by seeking to develop their own interview techniques in the absence of national guidance. The development of advanced interviewing has replicated that pattern. In the years following the implementation of PEACE certain forces recognized that the 'one size fits all' model was not sufficient to cater for all needs. In particular, serious crime demanded a higher level of interview technique that was both ethical and effective if convictions were to be obtained. PEACE fulfilled an important role in limiting oppressive interviews but there was still a need to develop further effective interview techniques.

This led, specifically, to the development of the concept of 'advanced interview' training for detectives investigating serious crime in certain forces. During the same period defence legal advisers improved their own training that in turn created a further need for increased professionalism by investigating officers. Added to this, legislative changes encompassed within the Criminal Justice and Public Order Act 1995 also made the subject of interviewing more complex for both officers and legal advisers. For example, this act introduced a change to the right of silence in that if a suspect failed to account for certain evidence at the time of interview a court may be allowed to draw an inference of guilt from this silence.

After this period of unilateral development of advanced interviewing by some police forces and in the light of the research examining the 'effectiveness' of PEACE training (Clarke and Milne 2001), the National Investigative Interview Strategic Steering Group representing ACPO decided to review the level of police interview training. After national consultation the original PEACE model was further developed into the current five-tier strategy outlined previously. As a result what started as 'advanced interviewing' is now more accurately referred to as 'specialist interviewing'.

Comparison of course content: PEACE and advanced training

The original PEACE interview course lasted one week. It was designed to teach officers to interview both witnesses and suspects. The content was a combination of theoretical input and practical application achieved through role-play interviews between students. The PEACE model of interviewing puts forward a five-stage approach to all interviews. A summary of each stage as applied to suspect interviews appears below:

- *Planning and preparation* deals with both the legal and logistical issues of interview preparation. Under 'legal' an officer would prepare an interview plan encompassing the points to prove and defences to an offence plus the subject areas to be covered in the interview. Logistical considerations would include preparing the interview room, assembling equipment and arranging the attendance of other professionals.

- *Engage and explain* covers the opening phase of an interview. It ensures that legal requirements, such as reiterating the detainee's right to legal advice, are covered and also deals with explaining the interview process to the suspect.

- *Account and clarification* covers the obtaining of a suspect's account of the incident. This includes an initial or first account followed by more in-depth probing of areas from that account plus areas identified by the interviewer's preparation as relevant. If the account obtained identifies discrepancies with other evidence this culminates in 'clarification' or 'challenge' using that evidence.

- *Closure* deals with the end phase of the interview. There are legal requirements in the closing of an interview as there are at the start. It also includes explanations to the suspect of what may happen after the interview.

- *Evaluation* is a post-interview phase defined as assessing the information obtained in the interview *and* the interviewer's own performance within the interview. This is with a view to future development.

The advanced interview course is three weeks long and aims to train students to interview suspects for the most serious of offences, including murder. The advanced interview course combines theory and practice but the amount of each completed over a three-week period is naturally much higher than the one-week course. There is a higher balance of theoretical input in the early part of the course but this alters as the course progresses and the students focus heavily on interview practicals where peer feedback is used to assist development. The skills taught build upon those underpinning the PEACE course. Therefore, there is no conflict between this type of course and the PEACE model which remains the bedrock of British police interviewing. Rather, the advanced course is a development of the PEACE model and aims to further students' knowledge of questioning, interview planning and legal matters associated with interviewing. A major difference is that instead of focusing on crimes such as theft and minor assault which were the basis of the PEACE course, the students concentrate on interviews for crimes such as murder, rape and serious assault.

One major difference between the PEACE course and the advanced course is assessment. The PEACE course has no access test to gain entry to the course. Neither does it conclude with a formal assessed interview. The 'advanced' course has both. Prior to attending the course candidates will conduct an assessed role-play interview on a case such as theft or minor assault. If successful they attend the course where, at the end, they have to plan, prepare and conduct a role-play interview for an offence such as rape or serious assault. This interview is assessed against set criteria. Only when successful are officers permitted to interview suspects for the most serious of cases.

Each part of the PEACE model is dealt with in more detail. During sessions concerning 'preparation and planning', methods of analyzing information are discussed and practised. Officers are trained to focus on setting objectives for each interview and ensuring they are achieved. Interview planning has been significantly affected by the most important legal changes of recent years mentioned previously. This is the amendment to a suspect's right to silence. This is where suspects still have the right to refuse to answer questions but if they then give an explanation at court the honesty of this may be questioned. This has had the effect of making the amount of information made available to the suspect prior to interview critical. Legal advisers in England and Wales are entitled to certain information prior to interview but officers have discretion as to what information to disclose beyond this. The decision over which information to disclose and what to withhold has become pivotal to a successful interview.

'Engage and explain' as taught on the one-week course is a functional process. Officers read from a prompt card to ensure they cover all legal requirements. On the advanced course building rapport with suspects within the legal constraints is deemed crucial to conducting an effective interview. A significant amount of time is spent within the first week of the course explaining the importance of rapport and encouraging officers to develop their own style. The students are also taught to cover all necessary legal issues without the use of cue or prompt cards. Students are encouraged to dispel cultural assumptions of guilt as such assumptions produce biased questioning designed to establish guilt as opposed to an account (Moston *et al.* 1992; Mortimer 1994a). Having dealt with the preparatory and introductory phases in the first few days of the course the students move on to the 'account' phase of the interview. Training in the 'account' stage encompasses the need to structure the obtaining of information from a suspect and the use of appropriate questioning techniques in order that the information obtained is reliable and accurate. A large amount of time is spent on this phase developing the officers' ability to obtain and probe a suspect's account using productive questioning techniques. This skill forms a key area of development for most officers. This extends to the clarification or challenge phase. Students are taught not to be judgemental or inappropriate when putting evidence that contradicts a suspect's account even where it seems obvious that the suspect is lying. The 'evaluation' of the interview is addressed by introducing students to models of feedback and assessing their ability both to assess themselves and to deliver objective feedback to their peers. The assessment of the post interview product is also addressed in great detail. Students analyze the answers given to their detailed questions in order to identify inconsistencies in a suspect's account.

Does advanced training work?

The advanced interview course represents an intensive investment in individual officers and so the key question is 'does it work?' Over the last three years Griffiths and Milne have been conducting research examining this very question. Fifty students who have successfully completed the course have agreed to participate in the study. Data collection for the study is complete but what follows is a discussion of preliminary findings based on a sample of 15 of the advanced interviewers (60 interviews). The purpose of the research is to establish:

- whether students who complete the course improve as interviewers;
- if they do improve in what ways they demonstrate this improvement; and
- whether these improvements transfer to the workplace and persist over time.

Audio tapes of four interviews by each of the officers have been collected. These have been marked against a set of criteria that was developed from a scale used by Clarke and Milne (2001). Individual elements of the interview process are broken down into 120 criteria. Examples include compliance with legal requirements at the start and finish of the interview plus behaviours such as rapport building and summarizing the interviewee's account at periodic points within the interview. The use of questions by the interviewers is the subject of a specific range of criteria. Eight different categories of question (open, probing, appropriate closed, inappropriate closed, leading, multiple, forced choice and opinion/statement) are evaluated in each interview by the use of the Griffiths Question Map (GQM). This tracks the chronology of question usage to identify the most productive strategies. Improved ability in this area is critical in establishing whether advanced interviewers have succeeded in moving away from the 'confession'-based approach criticized by both courts and psychologists to a more open-minded approach based upon obtaining an account from a suspect. The criteria are either scored on a yes/no basis for simple criteria such as 'gave time and date' or a five-point Likert scale for more complex criteria such as 'development of rapport'. In this scale '1' represents very poor and '5' excellent. The first two interviews collected are the role-play interviews conducted by the student to gain access to the course (interview A) and the assessed interview at the end of the course (interview B). The third interview is an interview conducted with a real suspect shortly after the student's graduation from the course (interview C). The fourth and final interview is another real-life interview conducted up to one year later (interview D). Interviews C and D (real life) concern interviews for crimes such as rape and murder. Offences carrying life imprisonment as a maximum penalty make up 75 per cent of this part of the sample. (A separate control of 30 interviews conducted by PEACE-trained officers has also been collected and scored against identical criteria.) The discussion below concerns the sample of advanced trained interviewers.

Figure 9.1 shows the comparative results across the sample of 15 detective officers in terms of their overall performance in four assessed interviews (60 interviews). Interview A is the role-play interview that officers conduct to gain access to the course. The average performance of the sample in this interview is assessed as 2.25. The marking guide for the scale suggests '3' as PEACE standard and so this result indicates a poor overall standard. This is especially true when one considers that the figure represents only successful applicants for the course. This result is significant because officers have time to prepare for the assessment and attend as volunteers seeking access to the course. Interview B, the final assessed interview undertaken at the conclusion of the training course, shows there is a significant improvement in the overall standard of interviews conducted across this group. The mean score of the group is 4.1. This is classified as 'skilful' within the marking guide. This score is achieved under similar test pressure as the first interview in that the officers have

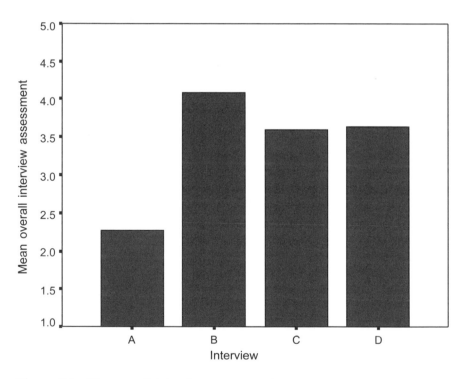

Figure 9.1 The overall interview assessment

to pass the interview to graduate from the course. However, the interview concerns a more complex offence than the entry test and so the level of performance achieved clearly shows that the officers' skills have developed as a result of the intensive training. As before the figure only shows officers who successfully complete the course. The interviews conducted after return to the workplace C and D show some erosion in overall skill but still demonstrate a higher level of skill than *prior* to training. This erosion could be accounted for by the fact that the interviews assessed are 'real' and not simulated or the fact that they take place under 'real' conditions. For example, some of the interviews collected take place late at night when officers have been on duty for an extended period. The most telling comparison is the difference between the last interview (D) and the first interview (A). This indicates that even after some time has elapsed there is an appreciable improvement in the overall level of skills displayed by the sample since they were assessed before the course.

Figure 9.2 shows mean scores for the same sample but focuses on one criterion; the ability to deliver the caution or right to silence. This is the conditional caution referred to earlier. The wording of this caution is: 'You are not obliged to say anything. But it may harm your defence if you do not mention when questioned something you later rely on in court. Anything you do say may be given in evidence.'

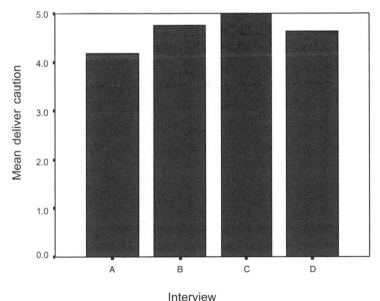

Interview

Figure 9.2 Assessment of the delivery of the caution

Whilst many officers read the words from a card advanced interviewers are expected to deliver the caution without prompts. The cue cards are removed from the interview room for the assessment interviews (A and B). The criterion is assessed on the officer's ability to deliver the caution word perfect at an appropriate pace. The results from the sample show that even prior to training, competence in this area was high with an average score of 4.2. The level of performance for this criterion is preserved over time with a mean score of 4.6 for the last interview (D). The ability to quote the caution verbatim is important because the wording is a legal requirement and could result in a case being lost if given incorrectly. It is also a simple area to assess because it is easy for an assessor to spot errors in the words used. Other criteria (for example, structure of topics) present greater problems because there is a greater subjective element to evaluating this skill. The delivery of the caution improves to a high standard after training and remains at this level in the first workplace interview. However, it is worthy of note that the overall difference between the mean performance of the sample prior to training and after is less than one point on the scale.

Figure 9.3 represents a more complex skill. This is the explanation of the caution or right to silence. When this caution was introduced in 1995 it was more complicated than the previous version. The law (PACE 1984) also required that officers ensured that a suspect understood this fundamental human right. Guidance was issued to officers and the first interview (A) scores indicate that officers explained the right to an acceptable standard prior to extra training. However, it should be noted that any of the criteria within the introductory phase of the interview can be practised as an officer knows they will arise during every interview. Therefore the respectable mean score of 3.8 might not be a realistic portrayal of officers' practical ability but rather their preparation for the test. When assessing the performance of the sample against this criteria it can be seen that there appears to be a greater improvement after training than in the simpler 'delivery of the caution criterion' but also a more marked decline in the skill level displayed after return to the workplace (C and D). The ability to explain this important legal point in clear, concise language is seen as important in building trust and rapport with a suspect. Whereas the caution itself has one form of words the explanation of it can be approached in several ways and it may be this factor which produces the difference in performance over time. Listening to the audio tapes shows certain officers cutting down the explanation in interview D. This may be the result of them making their own decisions as to the importance of the explanation or experimenting with different ways to explain it but omitting key elements.

Figure 9.4 shows one of the most complex criteria. This concerns an officer's ability to structure the areas of the interview. This is critical in conducting skilful interviews. The topics, or subjects, discussed are different in every interview and impossible to rehearse like the introductions or legal elements. Therefore the officer's ability to cover the relevant subjects in the appropriate sequence is tested on every occasion. The aim is to produce an interview that closely examines the key evidence and does not waste time probing irrelevancies. The ability to do this becomes more difficult the longer an interview lasts and the more complicated the subject matter. The interviews assessed in the study vary in length from 32 minutes to over 4 hours. Interview A lasts no longer than 45 minutes and concerns simple crimes. However, officers' ability to structure these interviews is poor on average, the mean score being 2.1. Very few officers

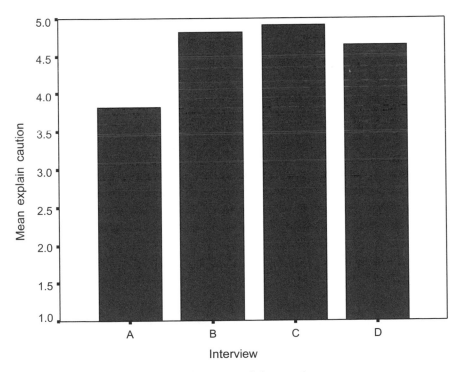

Figure 9.3 Assessment of explanation of the caution

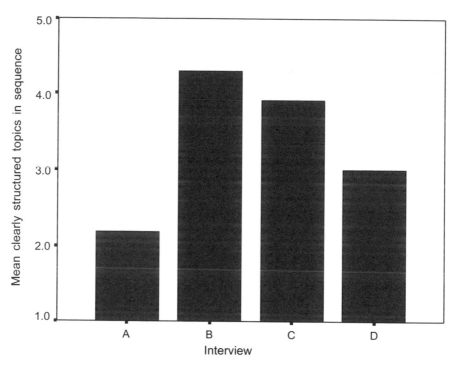

Figure 9.4 Assessment of the structure of topics in sequence

scored higher than 3. Interview B concerns a serious crime with a significant amount of information to question the suspect about. Despite this the sample display a skilled performance in this area, the mean score being 4.4, which shows a significant improvement over interview A. In the discussion regarding Figure 9.3 the point was made about officers practising their introductions in order to improve their scores. This is not possible with the criterion subject of Figure 9.4 because the information available for every interview is unique and presents previously unseen issues. The skills loss found in the workplace interviews (C and D) concerning this criterion is significant. In particular, interview D shows a significant decrease since training. This illustrates the difference between maintaining improvement within simple or complex criteria. As a final point it should be noted that even with the skills loss officers show a higher level of skill in more complex interviews one year after training than before training.

The ability to question a suspect using appropriate question types is fundamental to advanced interviewing. The course spends extensive time raising awareness of different question types and the damaging effect certain types of questions can have. Figure 9.5 shows the skills of the sample across all four interviews within this area. The initial interview (A) records a mean score of 3.3 for the sample. This equates to a PEACE standard in the marking guide. As in the earlier discussion the sample shown in this figure were all successful in this interview in that they gained access to the course. The level of skill displayed in this complex area is comparatively high in interview B, being 4.2. The workplace interviews (C and D) show a small skill loss even when examining the last interview assessed (D). Further, the performance at that point is significantly better than before training despite the interviews being for more serious offences. Comparing the results of this criterion and that of topic structure suggests that officers find the latter easier to learn (interview B mean 4.4 compared with 4.2 for use of questions) but more difficult to maintain over time; (interview D mean of 3.0 compared with 3.9 for use of questions).

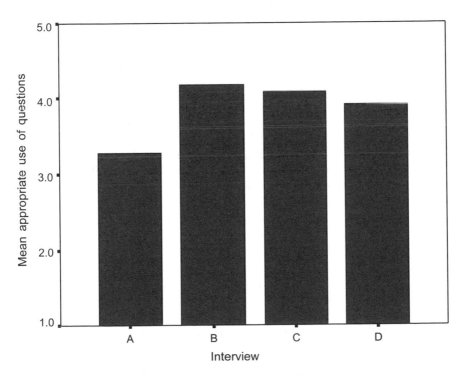

Figure 9.5 Assessment of the appropriate use of questions

The Griffiths Question Map (GQM)

The initial criteria developed to assess the employment of question types within an interview used a Likert scale to evaluate appropriate and inappropriate questions. However, it was soon apparent that, although this was a useful indicator which allowed comparison with other criteria in the scale (as above), there was a need for a more in-depth analysis of question usage which went beyond simply counting the number of each type of question used in an interview. The result was the Griffiths Question Map (GQM). The following is a brief description of the GQM (for a fuller description, see Griffiths and Milne in preparation). The GQM divides questions into eight types, split into productive and non-productive categories:

1. Open questions defined as those allowing a full range of response (e.g. 'Describe everything that happened in the shop?' or 'Tell me about the argument with your wife?'). These questions encourage longer and more accurate answers from interviewees.

2. Probing questions defined as more intrusive and requiring a more specific answer, usually commencing with the active words 'who', 'what, 'why', 'where', 'when' 'which' or 'how' (e.g. 'You said you pushed your wife over, *which* part of her body hit the ground first?'). These are appropriate when obtaining further detail following an initial account.

3. Appropriate closed yes/no questions which are used at the conclusion of a topic where open and probing questions have been exhausted. They are typically used to establish legal points (e.g. 'Did you strike the other man more than the one time you have described?').

These are all defined as productive questions and appropriate to obtaining an account from the interviewee. The remaining question types are defined as unproductive and associated with poor questioning:

4. Inappropriate closed yes/no questions which could appear identical in wording to an 'appropriate closed' question but are used at the wrong point in the interview and therefore become unproductive because they either allow an evasive interviewee the easy option in giving less detailed answers or close down the range of responses

available to an interviewee (e.g. 'Could you describe the man who pushed you ?').

5. Leading questions which suggest an answer in formal content to an interviewee (e.g. 'Are you normally that aggressive after drinking?').

6. Multiple questions which constitute a number of sub-questions asked at once. This makes it difficult to ascertain which one the interviewee is meant to answer (e.g. 'How did you get there, what did you do inside and when did you first decide to steal the car?'). Multiple questions also include multiple concept questions. This is where an interviewer asks about two concepts at once (e.g. What did *they* look like?').

7. Forced choice questions which only offer the interviewee a limited number of possible responses (e.g. 'Did you kick or punch the other woman?').

8. Opinion or statement defined as posing an opinion or putting statements to an interviewee as opposed to asking a question (e.g. 'I think you did assault the other person').

The GQM allots an individual line to each question type as shown below. In addition other information can be entered on the map (e.g. time). The map is used when observing an interview live or listening to a recording after the event. Each question is plotted on to the appropriate line as it is posed in the interview forming a 'map' of the way in which the interviewer uses different types of questions across the timeline of the interview. Context is an essential component in assessing question usage and the 'map' illustrates the way in which questions are used far better than simply scoring of the frequency of a particular question type. The same question construction can have different classifications depending where in time and space it comes in the interview. The following are examples of the use of the GQM in the research examining the effectiveness of advanced interview training.

Figure 9.6 is a map of an assessed interview conducted by an officer prior to attending the training course (interview A). The interview lasted 45 minutes and concerned an offence of assault where the suspect gave an account denying the offence. As can be seen the officer has made extensive use of probing questions ($n = 56$) compared with open questions ($n = 20$). There are a number of closed yes/no questions that have been assessed as appropriate

Time

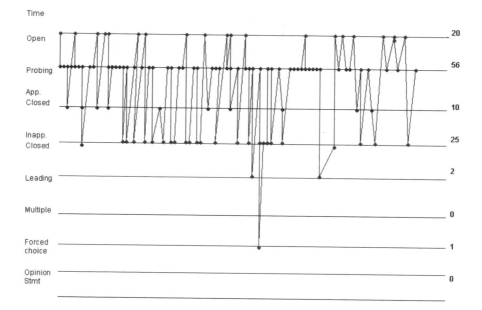

Figure 9.6 The GQM of an interview for assault

($n = 10$); however, a high number of inappropriate closed yes/no questions were deemed inappropriate ($n = 25$). There are hardly any leading questions ($n = 2$) and only one forced choice question. Overall the chronology of question use reveals recurring patterns of sequences of probing questions with less use of any other question type. The majority of questions used were productive. As a result the officer was successful in gaining access to the course but needs developmental training in the appropriate use of closed yes/no questions.

Figure 9.7 is a map of part of a real-life interview with a murder suspect conducted by the same officer after training (interview C). The map depicts a 43-minute period in the early part the interview, spread across two audio tapes (note that audio tapes last a maximum of 45 minutes and the timescale reverts to 2 halfway across the map). Looking across the whole map the officer has still made a greater use of probing questions ($n = 51$) compared with open questions ($n = 17$). The officer has also used a number of appropriate closed yes/no questions ($n = 20$) but has only used two ($n = 2$) unproductive questions in the whole interview. This is a significant improvement to the previous interview. However, a detailed look at the map

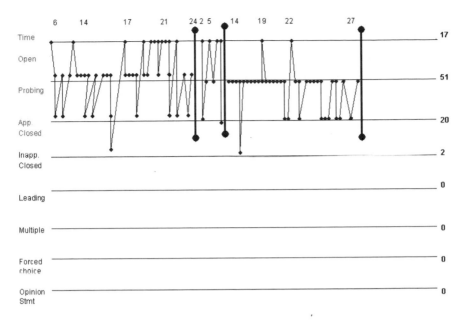

Figure 9.7   The GQM for an interview with a murder suspect

reveals more interesting information. This map depicts two different phases of the interview. The period from 6 to 24 minutes in the first interview represents the first account phase of the interview and shows the use of both open and probing questions. The second tape (from 2 to 27 minutes) on the map shows more detailed questioning about two topics where the interviewer required more detail. In particular the second topic, which ran from 14 to 27 minutes, shows a string of probing questions and a definite change in style from the more varied use of open and probing questions in the first account. The interviewer also employs a number of appropriate closed yes/no questions towards the end of the topic to close down the topic area having obtained the information required. It can be seen that there is a clear difference between the use of question types in the interviews depicted in Figures 9.6 and 9.7. The latter interview conducted after training is more organized and logical in its structure whereas the former interview, which took place prior to training appears to show a random and unstructured approach. In addition, the use of questions by this officer has altered in that the questions in Figure 9.7 are exclusively productive and confined to the top-three question types.

Figure 9.8 is a map of a real interview with a suspect accused of sexually assaulting a child. The interview was not conducted by an officer who had received advanced interview training and was collected as part of the control sample. Initial examination of the map reveals a completely different profile from either of the previous two interview maps. This interview lasted 42 minutes. Although the interviewer commences with an open question he quickly descends into a predominate use of inappropriate closed yes/no and leading questions with the majority of questions being unproductive. Of particular note is the use of opinion and statement. The first example of this occurred at 30 minutes and consisted of a comment 'I have interviewed this girl and I know she is not lying'. Nine similar comments followed in the last 12 minutes of the interview. The GQM of the interview shows that the officer became increasingly frustrated with his inability to gain an admission from the interviewee and resorted to unsupported accusations. The interview terminates with the officer expressing his view that the suspect was guilty of the alleged offence. Further research into this particular interview revealed that the judge excluded the interview from the subsequent trial and the defendant was acquitted.

This brief description of the GQM and preliminary findings shows that the use of questions is a critical factor in evaluating the legality

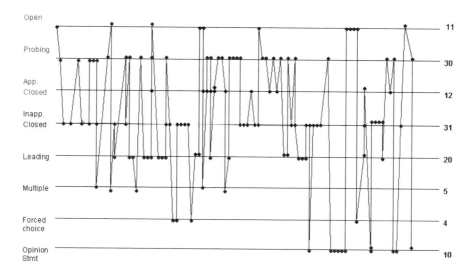

Figure 9.8 The GQM for an interview with a child abuse suspect

and effectiveness of interviews. The development of the GQM has continued and it has now been incorporated into police training courses where officers are using it to evaluate their own use of questions in order to identify strengths and weaknesses (see Griffiths and Milne in preparation).

Conclusions

All officers attempting to gain access to the advanced course have been PEACE trained. Nevertheless, the level of skill demonstrated by the research sample in interview A overall is below that expected from PEACE-trained officers, similar to the findings of Clarke and Milne (2001). Detailed examination of individual criteria suggests that the officers score higher in areas associated with legal requirements that can be defined as simple criteria. The more complex areas associated with more difficult skills such as topic structure and questioning show a low level of skill across the sample before training (interview A). This lends support to the hypothesis that the original PEACE course was effective at preventing illegal and oppressive interviews but less effective at improving the ability of officers to obtain and probe accounts. After training (interview B) the sample show an improvement in every criterion examined. The level of improvement varies dependent on the criterion and ability prior to training but the complex criteria demonstrate appreciable improvements. This is despite the fact the final course interview (B) is more complex than the first interview (A). Overall these improvements transfer to the workplace. However, there is a marked decline in the performance of the sample in some of the more complex criteria in the last interview assessed (D). This suggests a need for refresher training in these complex areas. This finding has resource implications for any organization deciding to initiate such a programme.

The development of advanced training, therefore, can be judged to have improved the skills of the interviewers in this sample. If such results are replicated across all police interviewers trained using this method then the implementation of the tiered approach can be judged to have improved police interviews with suspects immediately after training. However, the importance of monitoring and ongoing refresher training can be evidenced from the skills loss apparent within the complex criteria as time elapses after training. GQMs assessed from interviews some time after the course (interview D) show a wide variation of profile, further evidencing that need.

Tier four is solely concerned with the monitoring and evaluation of interviews in order to provide regular objective feedback. This area should be the subject of further research to evaluate its effect. These preliminary findings demonstrate that, with the appropriate training, officers can improve their skills and conduct effective and professional interviews. This is essential in securing safe convictions in the most serious of cases if the confidence of the public is to be maintained.

Note

1. The term 'Britain' or 'British' has been used throughout the chapter for ease of reading. However, it should be noted that England and Wales have different laws from Scotland and Northern Ireland. Comments about historical cases relate to England and Wales only. However, police forces within Scotland and Northern Ireland are adopting the five-tier strategy and so comments regarding the development of interviewing are relevant to all four countries.

References

Baldwin, J. (1993) 'Police interview techniques: establishing truth or proof', *British Journal of Criminology*, 33: 325–52.

Bull, R. and Milne, R. (2004) 'Attempts to improve the police interviewing of suspects', in G.D. Lassiter (ed.) *Interrogations, Confessions and Entrapment*. New York, NY: Kluwer Academic.

Central Planning and Training Unit (1992) *A Guide to Interviewing*. Harrogate: Home Office.

Clarke, C. and Milne, R. (2001) *National Evaluation of the PEACE Investigative Interviewing Course*. Police Research Award Scheme (PRAS/149).

Clarke, M. (1994) 'The end of an era', *Police Review*, 102: 22–5.

Griffiths, A. and Milne, R. (in prep.) *The Griffiths Question Map (GQM). A Training Manual*.

Gudjonsson, G.H. (2003) *The Psychology of Interrogations and Confessions*. Chichester: Wiley.

Home Office and Department of Health (2001) *Achieving Best Evidence*. London: HMSO.

Inbau, F.E., Reid, J.E. and Buckley, J.P. (1986) *Criminal Interrogation and Confessions* (3rd edn). Baltimore, MD: Wilkins & Wilkins.

Irving, B.L. and Hilgendorf, L. (1980) *Police Interrogation: The Psychological Approach – a Case Study of Current Practice*. London: HMSO.

Laville, S. (2002) 'The Damilola trial', *Daily Telegraph*, 26 April.

McGurk, B.J, Carr, M.J. and McGurk, D. (1993) *Investigative Interviewing Courses for Police Officers: An Evaluation. Police Research Series Paper* 4. London: Home Office.

Milne, R. and Bull, R. (1999) *Investigative Interviewing: Principles and Practice.* Chichester: Wiley.

Mortimer, A. (1994a) 'Cognitive processes underlying police investigative interviewing behaviour.' PhD thesis, University of Portsmouth.

Mortimer, A. (1994b) 'Asking the right questions', *Policing*, 10: 111–23.

Moston , S. and Engleberg, T. (1993) 'Questioning techniques in tape recorded interviews with criminal suspects', *Policing and Society*, 3: 223–37.

Moston, S., Stephenson, G.M. and Williamson, T.M. (1992) 'The effects of case characteristics on suspect behaviour during police questioning', *British Journal of Criminology*, 32: 23–40.

Norfolk, G.A. (1997) *Fit to Be Interviewed by the Police.* Harrogate: Association of Police Surgeons.

Pearse, J. and Gudjonsson, G.H. (1996) 'Police interviewing techniques at two south London police stations', *Psychology, Crime and Law*, 3: 63–74.

Robbins, T. (2001) 'Acquittals by juries reach record levels', *The Sunday Times*, 28 January.

Shepherd, E. (1993) 'Ethical interviewing', in E. Shepherd (ed.) *Aspects of Police Interviewing. Issues in Criminology and Legal Psychology* 18. Leicester: British Psychological Society.

Stephenson, G.M. and Moston, S.J. (1994) 'Police interrogation', *Psychology, Crime and Law*, 1: 151–7.

Tendler, S. (2002) 'Damilola police "created witness to avert failure"', *The Times*, 15 May.

Williamson, T (1991) *Police Investigations – Interview Techniques.* London: Seminar Paper Reprints.

Williamson, T. (1993) 'From interrogation to investigative interviewing: strategic trends in police questioning', *Journal of Community and Applied Social Psychology*, 3: 89–99.

Chapter 10

The Reid Technique of interviewing and interrogation

Joseph P. Buckley

Introduction

A process of interviewing and interrogation, which has come to be known as the Reid Technique, was initially developed in the 1940s and 50s and described in the first edition of the book, *Criminal Interrogation and Confessions*, by Fred E. Inbau and John E. Reid, published in 1962. During the next 43 years the Reid Technique continued to evolve and several new editions of the book were published, with the fourth edition published in 2001 (co-authored by Inbau, Reid, Joseph Buckley and Brian Jayne).

The technique is taught in seminars across the USA, Canada, Europe and Asia by John E. Reid and Associates, Inc.[1] Hundreds of thousands of investigators have received this training. As a process that scrupulously honours the rights of the individual and the guidelines established by the courts, the Reid Technique is widely considered to be the most effective interrogation technique in use today. In fact, Wayne State University Law School Professor Joseph Grano said in his review of the third edition of *Criminal Interrogation and Confessions*: 'This is the only technique a modern civilized society should use' (1984).

In June, 2004 the US Supreme Court, in the case *Missouri* v. *Seibert*, recognized John E. Reid and Associates as a law-enforcement training resource that properly teaches the advisement of *Miranda* rights. This chapter will outline the essential elements of the Reid Technique.

Distinctions between interviews and interrogations

The Reid Technique includes both an interview and interrogation process. The terms 'interview' and 'interrogation' are often used interchangeably by investigators, depending on the audience being addressed. At the outset of this chapter I would like to describe some of the essential differences between an interview and interrogation so that the reader will have a clear understanding of what we mean by these terms as they appear in text.

Characteristics of an interview

An interview is non-accusatory
This should be the case even when the investigator has clear reason to believe that the suspect is involved in the offence or has lied to him or her. By maintaining a non-accusatory tone, the investigator is able to establish a much better rapport with the suspect which will assist in any interrogation that might follow the interview. A guilty subject is more likely to volunteer useful information about his or her access, opportunity, propensity and motives if the questions are asked in a non-accusatory fashion. In addition, the suspect's behavioural responses to interview questions can be more reliably interpreted when the questions are asked in a conversational, rather than challenging manner. The investigator should remain neutral and objective during the interview process.

The purpose for an interview is to gather information
During an interview the investigator should be eliciting investigative and behavioural information. Examples of investigative information include the relationship between the suspect and the victim, to establish the suspect's alibi or access to the crime scene. During an interview the investigator should closely evaluate the suspect's behavioural responses to interview questions. The suspect's posture, eye contact, facial expression and word choice as well as response delivery may each reveal symptoms of truthfulness or deception. Ultimately, the investigator must make an assessment of the suspect's credibility when responding to investigative questions. This is primarily done through evaluating the suspect's behavioural responses during the interview, along with independent assessment of factual information.

An interview may be conducted early during an investigation
Because the purpose for an interview is to collect information, it may be conducted before evidence is analyzed or all the factual information about an investigation is known. Obviously, the more information the investigator knows about the crime and the suspect, the more meaningful will be the subsequent interview of the suspect. However, on a practical level, the investigator should take advantage of any opportunity to conduct an interview regardless of sketchy facts or the absence of specific evidence.

An interview may be conducted in a variety of environments
The ideal environment for an interview is a room designed specifically for that purpose. Frequently, however, interviews are conducted wherever it is convenient to ask questions – in a person's home, or office, in the back seat of a squad car or on a street corner.

Interviews are free flowing and relatively unstructured
Whilst the investigator will have specific topics to cover during the interview, the responses a suspect offers may cause the investigator to explore unanticipated areas. The investigator must be prepared to follow up on these areas because the significance of the information may not be known until later during the investigation.

The investigator should take written notes during a formal interview
Note taking during a formal interview (one conducted in a controlled environment) serves several important functions. Not only will the notes record the subject's responses to interview questions but, by taking notes, the investigator will be more aware of the subject's behaviour. Note taking also slows down the pace of the questioning. It is much easier to lie to questions that are asked in a rapid-fire manner. By creating silence between each question, the deceptive subject experiences greater anxiety when given time to think about his or her deceptive response, and is more likely to display behaviour symptoms of deception. Furthermore, an innocent suspect may become confused or flustered when a rapid-fire approach to questioning is used.

Characteristics of an interrogation

An interrogation is accusatory
A deceptive suspect is not likely to offer admissions against self-interest unless he or she is convinced that the investigator is certain

of his or her guilt. Therefore, an accusatory statement, such as 'Joe, there is absolutely no doubt that you were the person who started this fire', is necessary to display this level of confidence. On the other hand, if the investigator merely states 'Joe, I think you may have had something to do with starting this fire', the suspect immediately recognizes the uncertainty in the investigator's confidence which reinforces his or her determination to deny any involvement in committing the crime.

An interrogation involves active persuasion

The fact that an interrogation is conducted means that the investigator believes that the suspect has not told the truth during non-accusatory questioning. Further questioning of the suspect is unlikely to elicit the presumed truth. In an effort to persuade the suspect to tell the truth the investigator will use tactics which make statements rather than ask questions. These tactics will also dominate the conversation; for someone to be persuaded to tell the truth that person must first be willing to listen to the investigator's statements.

The purpose of an interrogation is to learn the truth

A common misperception exists in believing that the purpose of an interrogation is to elicit a confession. Unfortunately, there are occasions when an innocent suspect is interrogated and only after the suspect has been accused of committing the crime will the suspect's innocence become apparent. If the suspect can be eliminated based on his or her behaviour or explanations offered during an interrogation, it must be considered successful because the truth was learnt. Often, of course, an interrogation will result in a corroborated confession, which again accomplishes the goal of learning the truth.

An interrogation is conducted in a controlled environment

Because of the persuasive tactics utilized during an interrogation, the environment needs to be private and free from distractions.

An interrogation is conducted only when the investigator is reasonably certain of the suspect's guilt

The investigator should have some basis for believing a suspect has not told the truth before confronting the suspect. The basis for this belief may be the suspect's behaviour during an interview, inconsistencies within the suspect's account, physical evidence or circumstantial evidence coupled with behavioural observations.

Interrogation should not be used as a primary means to evaluate a suspect's truthfulness – in most cases, that can be accomplished during a non-accusatory interview.

The investigator should not take any notes until after the suspect has told the truth and is fully committed to that position
Premature note-taking during an interrogation serves as a reminder to the suspect of the incriminating nature of his or her statements and can therefore inhibit further admissions against self-interest. Only after the suspect has fully confessed, and perhaps after the confession has been witnessed by another investigator, should written notes be made documenting the details of the confession.

Benefits of conducting an interview before an interrogation

The majority of interrogations are conducted under circumstances in which the investigator does not have overwhelming evidence that implicates the suspect – indeed, the decision to conduct an interrogation is an effort possibly to obtain such evidence. Frequently, prior to an interrogation, the only evidence supporting a suspect's guilt is circumstantial or behavioural in nature. Under this condition conducting a non-accusatory interview of the suspect is indispensable with respect to identifying whether or not the suspect is, in fact, likely to be guilty. Furthermore, the information learnt during the interview of a guilty suspect, when there is sparse incriminating evidence linking him or her to the crime, is necessary to conduct a proper interrogation.

In those instances where there is clear and convincing evidence of a suspect's guilt, it may be tempting for an investigator to engage directly in an interrogation, bypassing the interview process. This is generally not advisable for the following reasons:

1. The non-accusatory nature of the interview affords the investigator an opportunity to establish a level of rapport and trust with the suspect that cannot be accomplished during an accusatory interrogation.

2. During an interview the investigator often learns important information about the suspect that will be beneficial during an interrogation.

3. There is no guarantee that a guilty suspect will confess during an interrogation. However, if that same guilty suspect is interviewed he may lie about his alibi, possessing a particular weapon, knowing the victim or having access to a certain type of vehicle. During a subsequent trial the investigator may be able to demonstrate that the statements made during the interview were false, and thus provide evidence contributing to the finding of the suspect's guilt.

4. There is a psychological advantage for the investigator to conduct a non-accusatory interview before the accusatory interrogation. For the interrogation to be successful, the suspect must trust the investigator's objectivity and sincerity. This is much more easily accomplished when the investigator first offers the suspect an opportunity to tell the truth through conversational questioning.

An exception to the foregoing suggestion may be the situation when the suspect is caught in an incriminating circumstance or clearly evidences a desire to tell the truth during initial questioning. Under this circumstance, an immediate interrogation may be warranted. As an example, a car that was recently reported stolen may be pulled over after a brief chase. In this circumstance, conducting a non-accusatory preliminary interview of the driver makes little sense. If the suspect waives his or her *Miranda* rights, the arresting officer would certainly be wise to confront the suspect immediately, perhaps with a statement similar to 'We know you took this car. Did you take it just for a joy ride or were you going to use it as a get-away car for a robbery?'

Summary

Traditionally, investigators have made little or no distinction between interviewing and interrogation. However, advancements in these specialized techniques suggest that clear differences exist and ought to be recognized. As will later be presented, some investigators are inherently good interviewers but lack the same intrinsic skills during an interrogation – and vice versa. An effective investigator will have gained skills in both these related, but distinctly different, procedures.

Suggestions for setting up the interview/interrogation room

Establish a sense of privacy

The room should be quiet, with none of the usual 'police' surroundings and with no distractions within the suspect's view. (If existing facilities permit, a special room or rooms should be set aside for this purpose.) The room should be as free as possible from outside noises and should also be a room into which no one will have occasion to enter or pass through during an interview. This will not only instil a sense of privacy, but also the less the surroundings suggest a police detention facility, the less difficult it will be for the suspect or arrestee who is really guilty to implicate him or herself. The same surroundings will also be reassuring to the innocent suspect. Therefore, there should be no bars on the windows. (There should be an alternative means of protection against any attempts to escape.) In a windowless room that has no air-conditioning system, a mechanical blower or exhaust system may be installed without much difficulty to improve ventilation and to eliminate, or at least minimize, noises. (The room should have its own thermostatic controls.)

Remove locks and other physical impediments

For non-custodial police or private security interviews, there should be no lock on the door of the interviewing room, nor should there be any other physical impediment to an exit by the suspect if he or she desires to leave the building itself. This will help minimize claims of false 'imprisonment'. The room should also be devoid of any large objects or drapes that might cause the suspect to believe that a concealed third person can overhear his or her conversation with the investigator.

Remove all distractions

Interview rooms should be of plain colour, should have smooth walls and should not contain ornaments, pictures or other objects that would in any way distract the attention of the person being interviewed. Even small, loose objects, such as paper clips or pencils, should be out of the suspect's reach so that he or she cannot pick up and fumble with anything during the course of the interview. Tension-relieving activities of this sort can detract from the effectiveness of an interrogation, especially during the critical phase when a guilty person may be trying desperately to suppress an urge to confess. If pictures or ornaments are used at all, they should only be on the wall behind the suspect. If there is a window in the room, it, too, should be to the rear.

Minimize noise

No telephone should be present in the interview room because, amongst other disadvantages, its ringing or use constitutes a serious distraction. Also, if the investigator wears a beeper, it should either be put in the vibrator mode or turned off during the interrogation. In addition, any noise emanating from the heat or ventilating system should be minimized to reduce the distraction.

Arrange chairs properly

The chairs for the investigator and suspect should be separated by about four feet and should directly face each other, without a desk, table, or any other object between them. The chairs should be the type normally used as office equipment without rollers.

Straight-back chairs should be used for the suspect as well as the investigator. Other types of chairs induce slouching or leaning back, and such positions are psychologically undesirable. A suspect who is too relaxed whilst being questioned may not give his or her full attention to the investigator, and this will create an unnecessary hurdle. Similarly, this is no occasion for the investigator to relax. His or her full attention and alertness are highly essential. Whenever possible, the seating arrangement should be such that both the investigator and the suspect are on the same eye level. Most certainly, to be scrupulously avoided are chairs with lowered front legs or other deviations that place the suspect in an 'inferior' posture or prevent him or her from making normal changes in his or her posture.

The Reid nine steps of interrogation

To be clear, the word 'guilt' as used in this text only signifies the investigator's opinion. In no way does it connote legal guilt based upon proof beyond a reasonable doubt. Accordingly, it is in that context this part of the text presents the tactics and techniques for the interrogation of suspects whose guilt, in the *opinion* of the investigator, seems definite or reasonably certain. Amongst them are the nine steps of interrogation.

The investigator's goal during an interrogation is to persuade a suspect to tell the truth. Largely because of movie and television portrayals of interrogation, the average citizen has little appreciation for the persuasive efforts required to convince a guilty suspect to offer admissions against self-interest.

As a result of many years' experience, primarily on the part of the staff of John E. Reid and Associates under the guidance of the late John E. Reid, the interrogation process has been formulated into nine structural components – the nine steps of criminal interrogation. These nine steps are presented in the context of the interrogation of suspects whose guilt seems definite or reasonably certain. It must be remembered that none of the steps is apt to make an innocent person confess and that all the steps are legally as well as morally justifiable.

Step 1: the positive confrontation

This involves a direct, positively presented confrontation of the suspect with a statement that he or she is considered to be the person who committed the offence. At this stage, the investigator should pause to evaluate the suspect's verbal and non-verbal response. A suspect who says nothing and looks down to the floor will be approached somewhat differently from the suspect who crosses his or her arms and leans back in the chair whilst stating, 'You're crazy. I swear, I didn't do it'. Regardless of the suspect's initial response to the direct positive confrontation, the investigator will proceed to offer a reason as to why it is important for the suspect to tell the truth. This *transition statement* introduces the interrogation theme.

Step 2: theme development

In step 2, the investigator expresses a supposition about the reason for the crime's commission, whereby the suspect should be offered a possible moral excuse for having committed the offence. To accomplish this, the investigator should generally attempt to affix moral blame for the offence upon some other person (e.g. an accomplice, the victim) or some particular circumstance such as an urgent need by the suspect of money in order for the suspect to support him or herself or family. If a suspect seems to listen attentively to the suggested 'theme', or seems to be deliberating about it, even for a short period of time, that reaction is strongly suggestive of guilt. On the other hand, if the suspect expresses resentment over the mere submission of such a suggestion, this reaction may be indicative of innocence.

Step 3: handling denials

During development of the interrogation theme, a guilty person, as well as an innocent one, can be expected to offer denials of involvement in the offence. The investigator should then embark upon step 3, which consists of suggested procedures for handling the initial denials of guilt. Basically, this step involves discouraging the suspect's repetition or elaboration of the denial and returning to the moral excuse theme that comprises step 2. An innocent person will not allow such denials to be cut off; furthermore, he or she will attempt more or less to 'take over' the situation rather than to submit passively to continued interrogation. On the other hand, a guilty person will usually cease to voice a denial, or else the denials will become weaker, and he or she will submit to the investigator's return to a theme.

Step 4: overcoming objections

This involves the task of overcoming the suspect's secondary line of defence following the denial – offering reasons as to why he or she would not, or could not, commit the crime. These excuses will consist of what may be viewed as 'objections' from the suspect, presented in the form of explanations oriented around economic, religious, or moral reasons for not committing the crime. These excuses are normally offered only by the guilty suspect, particularly when they come after the denial phase of the interrogation. They are significant in that they constitute evasions of a bold denial by the substitution of the less courageous statement as to why the suspect did not or could not commit the offence under investigation. Such an objection causes less internal anxiety than the utterance of an outright denial.

Step 5: procurement and retention of a suspect's attention

When a guilty suspect's verbal efforts (denials and objections) are ineffective in dissuading the investigator's confidence, the suspect is likely mentally to withdraw and 'tune out' the investigator's theme. Step 5 consists of the procurement and retention of the suspect's full attention, without which the interrogation may amount to no more than an exercise in futility. During step 5, the investigator will clearly display a sincerity in what he or she says. Helpful in achieving this is an increase in the closeness of the previously described seating arrangement between investigator and suspect and physical efforts by the investigator to maintain eye contact with the suspect.

Step 6: handling the suspect's passive mood

This involves recognizing the suspect's passive mood. During this stage the suspect is weighing the possible benefits of telling the truth, and this is generally reflected in changes within the suspect's non-verbal behaviour (tears, a collapsed posture, eyes drawn to the floor).

Step 7: presenting an alternative question

This step is the utilization of an alternative question – a suggestion of a choice to be made by the suspect concerning some aspect of the crime. Generally one choice is presented as more 'acceptable' or 'understandable' than the other. This choice will be in the form of a question such as 'Was this the first time, or has it happened many times before?' Whichever alternative is chosen by the suspect, the net effect of an expressed choice will be the functional equivalent of an incriminating admission.

Step 8: developing the details of the offence

Following the selection of an alternative, step 8 involves having the suspect orally relate the various details about the offence that will serve ultimately to establish legal guilt. These details can include where the fatal weapon was discarded or where the stolen money was hidden and the motive for the crime's commission.

Step 9: the written confession

Finally, step 9 relates to the confession itself. This step involves the recommended procedure for converting an oral confession into a written one.

Before proceeding to apply any of the nine steps, the *Miranda* warnings must be given to a custodial suspect and a waiver must be obtained. In custodial cases, this must occur before the interview. Unless the investigator knows that this has already been done by the person who presented the suspect for the interview, or by someone else in authority prior to the interview, the investigator should give the warnings and obtain the waiver.

False confessions: the issues

In the past several years a number of false confession cases have received extensive publicity. In several of these cases the convicted individual has been exonerated by DNA testing and the actual perpetrator, in turn, has been identified. In these cases it is important to examine in detail exactly what happened; what went wrong; what are the lessons to be learnt; and what are potential safeguards that can be put into place to prevent future mistakes.

To be sure, in the experience of most professional interrogators the frequency of false confessions is rare. When we do learn of them, however, the interrogation tactics and techniques should be scrupulously examined, as well as the circumstances surrounding the interrogation. When this has been done, there are four factors that appear with some regularity in false confession cases:

1. The suspect is a juvenile.
2. The suspect suffers some mental or psychological impairment.
3. The interrogation took place over an inordinate amount of time.
4. The interrogators engaged in illegal tactics and techniques.

Juveniles/mental impairment

Every interrogator must exercise extreme caution and care when interviewing or interrogating a juvenile or a person who is mentally or psychologically impaired. Certainly these individuals can and do commit very serious crimes. But when a juvenile or person who is mentally or psychologically impaired confesses, the investigator should exercise extreme diligence in establishing the accuracy of such a statement through subsequent corroboration. In these situations it is imperative that interrogators do not reveal details of the crime so that they can use the disclosure of such information by the suspect as verification of the confession's authenticity.

When a juvenile younger than 15, who has not had any prior experience with the police, is advised of his or her *Miranda* rights, the investigator should carefully discuss and talk about those rights with the subject (not just recite them) to make sure that he or she understands them. If it is apparent that the suspect does not understand his or her rights, no interrogation should be conducted at that time. The same is true for a person who is mentally or psychologically impaired.

Threats/promises

A review of the available information in false confession cases has revealed that in many of the interrogations the investigators engaged in the use of impermissible threats and promises. Interrogators in these cases have made such statements as the following:

- You're not leaving this room until you confess.

- If you tell me you did this you can go home and sleep in your own bed tonight (when such is not the case).

- You will be sentenced to the maximum term unless you confess.

- With the evidence that we have, there's no doubt that you will be convicted of this. The only question is how long you are going to sit in jail.

- If you don't tell the truth I will get your children turned over to protective services and you'll never see them again.

- The other guys want to charge you with first-degree murder but if you tell me it was just manslaughter nothing bad will happen to you.

It goes without saying that in the questioning of a criminal suspect no professional interrogator should engage in any illegal interrogation practices, including any threats, promises of leniency or the exercise of any physically abusive tactics. Furthermore, the rights of the suspect should be scrupulously respected.

Theme development

It has been suggested by some that the interrogator's effort to develop a theme during the interrogation is not just offering the suspect a moral excuse for his or her criminal behaviour, but is actually offering the suspect a promise of reduced punishment. The following are several quotations from *Criminal Interrogation and Confessions* (Inbau, Reid, Buckley and Hayne 4th edn 2001) that clarify this issue:

> During the presentation of any theme based upon the morality factor, caution must be taken to avoid any indication that the minimization of the moral blame will relieve the suspect of criminal responsibility (p. 235).

As earlier stated, the interrogator must avoid any expressed or intentionally implied statement to the effect that because of the minimized seriousness of the offense, the suspect is to receive a lighter punishment (p. 246).

In applying this technique of condemning the accomplice, the interrogator must proceed cautiously and must refrain from making any comments to the effect that the blame cast on an accomplice thereby relieves the suspect of legal responsibility for his part in the commission of the offense (p. 263).

The Investigator Anthology From Jayne and Buckley (2000: 414):

During theme development, caution must be exercised, however, not to tell the suspect that if the crime was committed for a morally acceptable reason that the suspect will be accorded leniency.

Alternative questions

In the Reid Technique the alternative question should never threaten consequences or offer promises of leniency. The following are *improper* alternative question:

- Do you want to co-operate with me and tell me what happened, or spend the next five to seven years behind bars?
- Do you want to be charged with first-degree murder, which will mean life in prison, or was this just manslaughter?
- Are you going to get this straightened out today, or do you want to spend a few days in jail to think about it?

There has been the suggestion by some critics of police interrogation techniques that the alternative question 'Was this your idea or did your buddies talk you into it?' is potentially dangerous because it offers a suspect (including an innocent one) only two choices, both of which amount to an admission of guilt. Obviously the third choice is for the suspect to deny any participation in the commission of the crime that is under investigation.

However, there is an additional issue raised by some critics about the alternative question – namely, that saying 'Was this your idea or did your buddies talk you into it' is essentially the same as saying 'If this was your idea you are going to spend time in jail, but if your buddies came up with the idea you won't have any problems'. This theory is called 'pragmatic implication' and was developed from a research study in which college students read various transcripts of interrogations and then speculated on the type of punishment the suspects would receive based on the interrogation process used. Specifically, the students theorized that when the interrogator suggested in a murder case interrogation that the victim may have done or said something to have provoked the suspect, that he or she would receive the same punishment as in those interrogations in which the suspect was directly offered a promise of leniency that if he or she confessed he or she would receive less punishment.

The courts have rejected the idea that a confession is inadmissible if a suspect confesses because he or she harbours some internal hope that his or her confession may lead to a lesser sentence:

- *State v. Nunn*: 'even if a suspect ... influenced perhaps by wishful thinking ... assumed that he would get more lenient treatment ... [this] would not, as a matter of law, make the confession inadmissible.'

- *R. v. Rennie*: 'Very few confessions are inspired solely by remorse. Often the motives of the accused are mixed and include a hope that an early admission may lead to an early release or a lighter sentence.'

- *R v. Oickle*: The Supreme Court of Canada indicated that the type of alternative question we suggest does not create an inadmissible confession, and offered a clear test of whether or not an implied threat or promise crosses the legal line: 'The most important decision in all cases is to look for a *quid pro quo* offer by interrogators, regardless of whether it comes in the form of a threat or a promise.'

Confession corroboration

As we have stated earlier, it is imperative that interrogators do not reveal details of the crime so that they can use the disclosure of such information by the suspect as verification of the confession's authenticity. In each case there should be documented 'hold back' information about the details of how the crime was committed; details from the crime scene; details about specific activities perpetrated by the offender; etc. The goal is to match the suspect's confession against these details to establish the veracity of the statement. It should be remembered, however, that suspects do not always tell us everything that they did and they do not always remember all the details themselves:

> It is also a fact that most confessors to crimes of a serious nature will lie about some aspect of the occurrence, even though they may have disclosed the full truth regarding the main event. They will lie about some detail of the crime for which they have a greater feeling of shame than that which they experienced with respect to the main event itself (Inbau *et al*. 2001: 106).

> Lies of justification and omission are commonplace in written confessions. Many of these lies represent the suspect's attempt to present his crime in the most favorable light, others have a more direct bearing, such as protecting the name of an accomplice or concealing involvement in another crime (Jayne and Buckley 2000: 472).

> Some confessions contain misinformation because of the suspect's perceptual distortions. During a kidnapping and murder of a child, the suspect may have vivid recollections of committing the crime, but have no specific recollections of the clothes the child was wearing (Jayne and Buckley 2000: 472).

Many crimes are committed when the suspect is experiencing intense emotions (fear, anger, frustration). Just as victims tend to focus on the robber's weapon during a robbery, the emotions a guilty suspect experiences can bias attention and memory retrieval of specific details. As cognitive psychologist Daniel Schacter writes (1996: 473): 'When a person has actually experienced trauma, the central core of the experience is almost always well remembered; if distortion does occur, it is most likely to involve specific details.'

Nevertheless, when significant and substantial contradictions exist between the known facts about the crime and what the suspect describes in his or her confession, extreme care must be exercised in the assessment of the confession's validity.

Factors to consider

With the above discussion in mind, the following represents some factors to consider in the assessment of the credibility of a suspect's confession. These issues are certainly not all inclusive, and each case must be evaluated on the 'totality of circumstances' surrounding the interrogation and confession but, nevertheless, these are elements that should be given careful consideration:[2]

1. The suspect's condition at the time of the interrogation:
   - physical condition (including drug and/or alcohol intoxication);
   - mental capacity; and
   - psychological condition.
2. The suspect's age.
3. The suspect's prior experience with law enforcement.
4. The suspect's understanding of the language.
5. The length of the interrogation.
6. The degree of detail provided by the suspect in his or her confession.
7. The extent of corroboration between the confession and the crime.
8. The presence of witnesses to the interrogation and confession.
9. The suspect's behaviour during the interrogation.
10. The effort to address the suspect's physical needs.
11. The presence of any improper interrogation techniques.

Notes

1. Visit www.reid.com for details.
2. For more information on these issues go to 'Education Information' at www.reid.com and click on the 'Critics Corner'.

References

Grano, J. (1984) 'Selling the idea to tell the truth: the professional interrogator and modern confession law', *Michigan Law Review*, 84: 662.

Inbau, F.E., Reid, J.E., Buckley, J. and Jayne, B. (2001) *Criminal Interrogation and Confessions* (4th edn). Gaithersburg, MD: Aspen.

Jayne, B. and Buckley, J. (2000) *The Investigator Anthology*. Chicago, IL: John E. Reid & Associates.

Schacter, D. (1996) *Searching for Memory: The Brain, the Mind and the Past*. New York, NY: HarperCollins.

Chapter 11

A critical appraisal of modern police interrogations

Saul M. Kassin

Introduction

Let me begin with a story that already has historic value in the annals of wrongful convictions. This was an infamous case that took place in 1989 in New York City. Known as the 'Central Park jogger case', it involved a young woman, an investment banker, who was beaten senseless, raped and left for dead. It was a heinous crime that horrified the city. The victim's skull had multiple fractures, her eye socket was crushed and she lost three quarters of her blood. Defying the odds, she survived; but to this day, she is completely amnesic for the incident. Soon thereafter, solely on the basis of police-induced confessions taken within 72 hours of the crime, five African- and Hispanic-American boys, 14–16 years old, were convicted of the attack and sentenced to prison. There were no physical traces of the defendants at the crime scene and no traces of the scene on them. At the time, however, it was easy to understand why detectives aggressively interrogated the boys, some of whom were 'wilding' in the park that night.

Four of the five jogger confessions were videotaped and presented to the juries at trial. The tapes (which showed only the confessions, not the precipitating 14½–30 hours of interrogation) were compelling, as the boys described in vivid detail how the jogger was attacked, when, where and by whom, and the role that they played in the process. One boy physically re-enacted the way he allegedly pulled off the jogger's running pants. A second boy said he felt peer-pressured to join in his 'first rape' and he expressed remorse. These confessions, portions of which were aired on television, fooled not only two trial juries but an entire city and nation – including myself, a native New Yorker who followed the case closely when it broke. Thirteen years later, Matias Reyes, in prison for three rapes and a murder committed after the jogger attack, stepped forward with a voluntary, accurate, independently corroborated confession supported by DNA evidence (semen found on the victim's body and socks excluded the boys as donors in 1989; the district attorney prosecuted the boys solely on the basis of the confessions and argued to the jury that just because police did not capture *all* the perpetrators does not mean they did not get *some* of them). As the result of a painstaking and thorough re-examination of the case, including an analysis of the original confessions, the Manhattan District Attorney's Office joined a defence motion to vacate the boys' convictions, which was granted in 2002 (*New York* v. *Wise et al.* 2002).

The assault on the Central Park jogger was a horrific, violent act. Yet the case also now stands as a shocking tale of five false confessions resulting from a single investigation. Despite its notoriety, this case illustrates a phenomenon that is not new or unique. The pages of history reveal many tragic miscarriages of justice involving innocent men and women who were prosecuted and wrongfully convicted solely on the basis of false confessions. I would not hazard an estimate as to the prevalence of the problem, which is unknown. Within the recent population of post-conviction DNA exonerations, 20–25 per cent had confessions in evidence (Scheck *et al.* 2000; http://www.innocenceproject.org).[1]

Notably, these tragic outcomes occurred because innocent people were interrogated, because they confessed, and because prosecutors, judges and trial juries believed their false confessions. Indeed, when false confessors plead not guilty and proceed to trial, the jury conviction rate is 81 per cent, a figure that led Drizin and Leo (2004: 959) to lament that confession evidence is 'inherently prejudicial and highly damaging to a defendant, even if it is the product of coercive interrogation, even if it is supported by no other evidence, and even if it is ultimately proven false beyond any reasonable doubt'. This sobering result suggests that there are not adequate safeguards in the criminal justice system to catch the mistakes – which increases the pressure on police to ensure that their practices elicit accurate outcomes.

The jogger case also points to a sequence of three potential problems to watch for in a police investigation: 1) that innocent people are often targeted for interrogation, despite a lack of evidence of their involvement, based solely on an interview-based judgement; 2) certain interrogation techniques can cause innocent people to confess to crimes they did not commit; and 3), afterwards, it is difficult for investigators, attorneys, judges and juries to distinguish between true and false confessions. I will argue that there are risks of error inherent in each link of this three-step chain of events – from the pre-interrogation interview, to the interrogation that elicits an admission, to the full confession that is so difficult for trial judges, juries and others to assess.

Before launching into a critique of current interrogation practices, let me put my predispositions on the table. First, I know that most police investigators are well intended, well trained and competent, so it is not my intent to paint an unflattering portrait of the profession. But performance can be improved at every step in the process. Secondly, I am not an ideological zealot looking to handcuff cops in their pursuit of criminals. I think everyone would agree that the surgical objective of interrogation is to secure confessions from suspects who are guilty but not from those, misjudged, who are innocent. Hence, I think everyone would also agree that the process itself should be structured to produce outcomes that are diagnostic, as measured by the observed ratio of true to false confessions. Adopting this strictly pragmatic position has two implications. The first is that I recognize that society's relative tolerance for false-positive and false-negative errors may well shift as a function of contextual factors (e.g. one could reasonably argue that the fundamental value, rooted in Blackstone's *Commentaries on the Laws of England*, that it is better to acquit ten guilty people than to convict one who is innocent, may have to be 'tweaked' in extreme conditions, as in the questioning of terrorism suspects who pose an imminent threat). Secondly, whilst the exclusion from evidence of involuntary confessions serves a number of important values – such as the desire to ensure that these statements are reliable, to protect a defendant's due process rights and to deter repugnant police conduct that undermines the public's trust in government – the research I will talk about is driven by cold, pragmatic concerns for reliability.

The pre-interrogation interview: a platform for bias and error

The first problem is that innocent people are often targeted for interrogation, despite the absence of any evidence of their involvement, based solely on an investigator's hunch. Consider, for example, the military trial of *U.S.* v. *Bickel* (1999), in which I testified as an expert witness. In this case, the defendant confessed to rape as a result of interrogations by five agents. There was no independent evidence against the defendant. So, when asked why they interrogated him so forcefully, one investigator said that Bickel behaved in a deceptive manner:

> His body language and the way he reacted to our questions told us that he was not telling the whole truth. Some examples of body language is that he tried to remain calm but you could tell he was nervous and every time we asked him a question his eyes would roam and he would not make direct contact, and at times he would act pretty sporadic and he started to cry at one time.

Correctly, I think, this defendant was acquitted by a jury of military officers.

Numerous other examples illustrate the problem. In Florida, Thomas Sawyer was interrogated for 16 hours for sexual assault and murder because his face flushed red and he appeared embarrassed during an initial interview, a reaction seen as a sign of deception. What the investigators did not know at the time was that Sawyer was a recovering alcoholic and also had a social anxiety disorder that caused him to sweat profusely and blush in public situations. Ultimately, the charges were dropped. Then there was the California case of 14-year-old Michael Crowe, falsely accused in the murder of his sister Stephanie. Michael confessed after intense interrogations, but the charges were dropped when a drifter in the area was found with the victim's blood on his clothing. According to the detectives in this case, Crowe became a prime suspect in part because they felt that he had reacted to his sister's death with inappropriately little emotion.

The first problem can be traced to the pre-interrogation interview. As per the Reid Technique, the police do not commence interrogation until and unless they have made an initial, interview-based judgment that the suspect is lying. Sometimes that judgment is reasonably based on reports from witnesses or informants, or on other forms of extrinsic evidence. At other times, however, that judgment is based on nothing more than a hunch, a clinical impression that detectives form during a non-confrontational interview. In *Criminal Interrogation and Confessions*, for example, Inbau *et al.* (2001) advise investigators to look for behavioural symptoms or indicators of truth and deception in the form of verbal cues (e.g. long pauses, qualified or rehearsed responses), non-verbal cues (e.g. gaze aversion, frozen posture, slouching) and behavioural attitudes (e.g. unconcerned, anxious, guarded). They also recommend the use of various 'behaviour provoking questions' designed to elicit responses that are presumed diagnostic of guilt and innocence (e.g. 'What do you think should happen to the person who did this crime?' 'Under any circumstances, do you think the person who committed this crime should be given a second chance?'). In these ways, they claim, investigators can be trained to judge truth and deception at an 85 per cent level of accuracy – an average that substantially exceeds human lie-detection performance obtained in any of the world's laboratories.

As this initial judgment becomes a pivotal choice-point in a case, determining whether a suspect is interrogated or sent home, it is important to determine scientifically how – and how well – that judgment is made. As an empirical matter, there are reasons to be sceptical. Over the years, large numbers of psychological studies involving thousands of subjects from all over the world have consistently failed to support the claim that groups of individuals can attain such high average levels of accuracy at judging truth and deception. Rather, this research has shown that people perform at no better than chance level; that training produces, at best, small and inconsistent improvements compared with control groups; and that police, judges, customs inspectors, psychiatrists, polygraph examiners and other experts perform only slightly better than chance, if at all. In general, professional lie catchers exhibit accuracy rates in the range from 45 to 60 per cent, with a mean of 54 per cent (for reviews, see Vrij 2000; Memon *et al.* 2003; Granhag and Strömwall 2004).

One might argue that performance in these laboratory experiments is poor because participants are asked to detect truths and lies uttered in relatively low involvement situations, which can weaken deception cues. But forensic research on the detection of high-stakes lies has thus far produced mixed results. One might also argue that professionals would be more accurate when they personally conduct the interviews than when they observe sessions conducted by others. But research clearly does not support this notion either. In short, there is no scientific evidence to support the claim that professionals, trained or not, can distinguish truths and lies simply by observing a person's interview behaviour. This result is not particularly surprising in light of the kinds of deception cues that form the basis for training. For example, Inbau *et al.* (2001) focus on several visual cues – such as gaze aversion, non-frontal posture, slouching and grooming gestures

– that are not empirically predictive of truth and deception (for a comprehensive meta-analysis of deception cues, see DePaulo *et al.* 2003).

In studies that illustrate the point, my colleagues and I have examined the extent to which special training in deception detection increases judgment accuracy in a specifically forensic context. In one study, Kassin and Fong (1999) randomly assigned some college students but not others to receive training in the Reid Technique using videotapes and written materials on the behavioural symptom analysis. Next they created a set of videotapes that depicted brief interviews and denials by individuals who were truly guilty or innocent of committing one of four mock crimes. As in past studies in non-forensic settings, observers were not proficient at differentiating between truthful and deceptive suspects better than would be expected by chance. In fact, those who underwent training were less accurate than naïve controls – but more confident. Closer inspection of the data revealed that the training procedure itself produced a response bias towards guilt.

From a practical standpoint, this study was limited by the fact that the observers were college students, not police detectives, and their training was condensed, not offered as part of professional development to those with prior experience. To address these issues, Meissner and Kassin (2002) conducted a meta-analysis and a follow-up study to test the performance of experienced investigators. Looking at past research, they found that police investigators and trained participants, relative to naïve controls, exhibited a proclivity to judge targets in general as deceptive rather than truthful. Next, they used Kassin and Fong's videotapes to compare police and college student samples and found that the police exhibited lower, chance-level accuracy, a response bias towards judgments of deception and significantly more confidence. Within our sample of investigators, both years of experience and special training correlated significantly with the response bias – but not with accuracy. It appears that special training in deception detection may lead investigators to make pre-judgments of guilt, with high confidence, that are biased and frequently in error.

Let me be clear that I am not prepared to claim that it is impossible to increase the accuracy of judgments made in this domain. High average levels of lie-detection accuracy may be rare, but some individuals are intuitively and consistently better than others (Ekman *et al.* 1999). It is also clear that lying leaves behavioural traces that may provide clues as to how to improve performance (DePaulo *et al.* 2003). Hence, it may be necessary to reconceptualize the current approach. Following traditional models of polygraphic lie detection, professionals tend to search for behavioural cues that betray stress (e.g. gaze aversion), a presumed symptom of deception. But this approach may be misguided. Indeed, after shadowing homicide detectives for a year in Baltimore, Simon (1991: 219) may have captured the essence of the problem:

> Nervousness, fear, confusion, hostility, a story that changes or contradicts itself – all are signs that the man in an interrogation room is lying, particularly in the eyes of someone as naturally suspicious as a detective. Unfortunately, these are also signs of a human being in a state of high stress.

Recent research suggests the possibility of an alternative approach that focuses on the fact that lying is an effortful cognitive activity. In one study, Newman *et al.* (2003) asked subjects to lie or tell the truth about various topics (including, in one study, the commission of a mock crime) and found that when people lie, they use fewer first-person pronouns and fewer 'exclusive' words such as *except, but* and *without*, words that indicate cognitive complexity, which requires effort. In a second study, Walczyk *et al.* (2003) instructed subjects to answer various personal questions truthfully or deceptively and found, both within and between subjects, that constructing spontaneous lies – which requires more cognitive effort than telling the truth – increases response time. Perhaps because lying is effortful, observers would be more accurate if asked to make judgments that are indirect but diagnostic. In a third study, Vrij *et al.* (2001) found that subjects made more accurate discriminations of truths and lies when asked 'How hard is the person thinking?' than when asked 'Is the person lying?'

As an empirical matter, it is also possible that certain 'behaviour-provoking questions' suggested by the Reid Technique, and others of a similar nature, will enhance an investigator's ability to discriminate between truthful and deceptive suspects. For example, Inbau *et al.* (2001) suggest that police ask suspects for an opinion of what should happen to the person who committed the crime, whether that person should get a second chance and what the results of forensic tests will show about their own involvement – the assumption being that innocents will not hesitate in their responses to be punitive, uncompromising and self-confident. Of potential relevance in this regard is recent research indicating that innocent people are more likely than perpetrators to waive their rights to silence, to counsel and to a line-up – co-operative acts, like a willingness to undergo a polygraph, physical examination, or house search, that may betray a naïve phenomenology of innocence (Kassin 2005).

In short, when it comes to making accurate discriminations, it remains a reasonable goal to seek future improvements in training as a way to make police more effective interviewers and lie detectors (Bull and Milne 2004; Granhag and Stromwall 2004; Vrij 2004). For now, however, it is vital that police be mindful of their own limitations and stay vigilant whilst they interrogate to the possibility that their first impressions were mistaken.

Interrogation: a guilt-presumptive process of influence

In the past, the police often practised 'third degree' methods of custodial interrogation – inflicting physical or mental pain and suffering to extract confessions and other types of information from crime suspects. Amongst the methods used were prolonged confinement and isolation; explicit threats of harm or punishment; deprivation of sleep, food and other needs; extreme sensory discomfort (e.g. shining a bright, blinding strobe light on the suspect's face); and assorted forms of physical torture (e.g. suspects were tied to a chair and smacked to the side of the head or beaten with a rubber hose, which seldom left visible marks). The use of such methods declined precipitously from the 1930s to the 1960s and was replaced by a more professional approach to policing and by interrogations that are more psychological in nature, as in the Reid Technique (for a review, see Leo 2004).

Despite this historic and seismic paradigm shift, modern interrogations continue to put innocent people at risk to confess to crimes they did not commit. To begin with, the two-step approach – in which an interview generates a judgment of deception, which, in turn, sets into motion an interrogation – is inherently flawed. Inbau *et al.* (2001: 78) advise that 'The successful interrogator must possess a great deal of inner confidence in his ability to detect truth or deception, elicit confessions from the guilty, and stand behind decisions of truthfulness'. Thus, interrogation is by definition a guilt-presumptive process, a theory-driven social interaction led by an authority figure who has formed a strong belief about the suspect and who measures success by the ability to extract an admission from that suspect. For innocent people who are initially misjudged, one would hope that police would remain open-minded and re-evaluate their beliefs over the course of the interrogation. But the two-step approach makes this an unreasonable expectation. Over the years, research has shown that once people form a belief, they selectively seek and interpret new information in ways that verify that belief even in the face of contradictory evidence. This problem contributes to the errors committed by forensic examiners, whose assessments of handwriting samples, ballistics, and other 'scientific' evidence are often corrupted by prior beliefs, a problem uncovered in many DNA exoneration cases (Risinger *et al.* 2002). To complicate matters further, people unwittingly create behavioural support for their beliefs, producing a self-fulfilling prophecy. This effect was first demonstrated by Rosenthal and Jacobson (1968) in their classic report on the effects of teachers' expectancies on students' performance. Similar results have been obtained in military, business and other organizational settings (McNatt 2000).

In a story that illustrates how investigators can be blinded by the guilt-presumptive lens they wear, a man confessed to his wife's murder after 19 hours of interrogation when police 'bluffed' him into thinking they had DNA evidence to be tested (*Missouri* v. *Johnson* 2001). During interrogation, it is common for police to bluff in this manner about having independent evidence on the assumption that the suspect, whom they presume guilty, will realize the futility of denial and capitulate. What they cannot see, however, is that to an innocent but beleaguered person, who is naïve about the use of this tactic, the 'threat' of DNA may be construed as a promise of future exoneration – ironically making it easier to confess. In this case, the defendant – who was instantly acquitted by a jury – explained afterwards that he confessed because he was exhausted and knew that the test results would show his innocence.

The process of interrogation is not only guilt presumptive but powerful in its impact. Inbau *et al.* (2001) advise interrogators to remove the suspect from familiar surroundings and place him or her in a small, barely furnished, soundproof room housed within the police station. Against this physical backdrop, a nine-step process begins with the positive confrontation and the development of alternative themes – and ends with a full written or oral confession. Conceptually, this approach is designed to get suspects to incriminate themselves by increasing the anxiety associated with denial, plunging them into a state of despair and minimizing the perceived consequences of confession. Glossing over the specifics, interrogation is reducible to an interplay of three processes: *isolation* for some indefinite period of time, which increases stress and the incentive to relieve that stress; *confrontation*, in which the interrogator accuses the suspect of the crime, expresses certainty in that opinion and blocks all denials, sometimes citing real or manufactured evidence to support the charge; and *minimization*, in which the sympathetic interrogator morally justifies the crime in the form of an alternative version of events (e.g. that it was spontaneous, accidental, provoked or peer pressured), which can lead a suspect to infer that he or she will be treated with leniency. The net effect is to trap the suspect so that he or she sees confession as the most effective means of 'escape'.

In the interrogation room, as in other settings, some individuals are more vulnerable to manipulation than others, particularly if they are characteristically prone to exhibit social compliance or interrogative suggestibility. Youth, naïvete, a lack of intelligence, cultural upbringing, and social anxiety and various psychological disorders that impair cognitive and affective functions, present unique sources of vulnerability to watch for (see Gudjonnsson 1992, 2003). Certain situational factors can also increase the risk of a false confession, even amongst suspects who are not by nature vulnerable. One such risk factor is time: as a tactical matter, interrogators isolate suspects in custody – but for how long? Prolonged isolation is likely to be accompanied by fatigue, feelings of helplessness, and a deprivation of sleep, food and other biological needs, mental states that impair complex decision-making. Yet whereas most interrogations last 1–2 hours (Leo 1996), and whilst 3–4 hours is generally sufficient (Inbau *et al.* 2001), a study of documented false-confession cases in which interrogation time was recorded showed that 34 per cent lasted 6–12 hours, 39 per cent lasted 12–24 hours, and the mean was 16.3 hours (Drizin and Leo 2004). Following the Police and Criminal Evidence Act 1984 in Great Britain, police should be trained to set time limits on the process, or at least flexible guidelines, as well as periodic breaks from questioning for rest and meals.

A second problem concerns the presentation of false evidence. This tactic often takes the form of outright lying to suspects – for example, about an alibi that allegedly failed to corroborate the suspect's story; an eyewitness identification that was not actually made; fingerprints, hair or blood that was not found; or polygraph tests they did not really fail. The presentation of false evidence is implicated in the vast majority of false confession cases that have been documented for analysis. In addition, laboratory research shows that it increases the risk that innocent people would confess to acts they did not commit and, at times, internalize guilt for outcomes they did not produce (e.g. Meyer and Youngjohn 1991; Kassin and Kiechel 1996). Especially disconcerting in this regard is the role that the polygraph has played. The polygraph is best known for its use as a lie-detector test but, because it is not admissible in most courts, police use it primarily to induce suspects to confess. Far too often, however, false confessions have been extracted by police examiners who told suspects they had failed a lie-detector test. This tactic is so common that Lykken (1998: 235) coined the term 'fourth degree' to describe it. This problem recently led the National Research Council Committee to Review the Scientific Evidence on the Polygraph to warn of the risk of polygraph-induced false confessions (National Research Council 2003).

A third potential problem concerns the use of minimization, the process by which the police suggest to a suspect that the crime in question was provoked, an accident or otherwise morally justified. By design, minimization tactics lead people to infer that they will be treated with leniency if they confess – even when no explicit promises are made (Kassin and McNall 1991). In the laboratory, this tactic led 18 per cent of innocent college students to confess that they cheated on a problem that they were supposed to solve without assistance (Russano et al. 2005). Although more work is needed to compare the different alternative themes and the conditions under which this tactic puts innocent people at risk, it appears that minimization – by communicating leniency 'under the radar' – may at times induce confessions in suspects who are beleaguered and feeling trapped, even if innocent.

Taking stock of what psychological science has, and has not, achieved when it comes to police interrogations, it is clear that researchers have thus far sought to identify the risks, with an eye towards reducing the number of false confessions and wrongful convictions. To develop fully a science of interrogation, however, researchers must also help the police to build a better mousetrap. The surgical objective is simple: develop interrogation techniques that are 'diagnostic' to the extent that they increase the observed ratio of true to false confessions.

This objective brings with it some important implications. First, because the decision to confess is largely influenced by a person's expectations of the consequences, both guilty and innocent people are most likely to capitulate when they believe that there is strong evidence against them (Moston et al. 1992). As the police are more likely in nature to have direct and circumstantial proof of guilt against perpetrators than against innocent suspects who are falsely accused, the practice of confronting suspects with real evidence should increase the diagnosticity of the confessions that are ultimately elicited. To the extent that the police are permitted to misrepresent the evidence, however, and lie to suspects, the guilty and innocent become equally trapped and similarly treated, reducing diagnosticity. On the question of how to confront suspects with real evidence for maximum impact, recent research suggests that it may be easier to 'trap' those who are guilty into betraying their culpability by strategically delaying the disclosure of crime details rather than disclosing details early, as part of a positive confrontation. In a study involving a mock crime and investigation, Hartwig *et al.* (2005) found that when they disclosed facts at the outset, both guilty and innocent suspects managed to shape their responses in ways that were consistent. When the disclosures were delayed, however, guilty suspects seeking to evade detection held back in describing what they knew but were more likely than innocents to contradict the facts that were withheld – inconsistencies that betrayed attempted deception. More work is needed, but this initial study suggests that the timing of disclosures can be used to differentiate between guilty and innocent suspects.

Narrative confessions as Hollywood productions

Confession evidence is powerful in court and hard to overcome. To safeguard against the wrongful convictions they elicit and their consequences, therefore, it is vitally important that confessions be accurately assessed prior to the onset of court proceedings. We have seen that people are poor lie detectors and cannot readily distinguish between true and false *denials*. But can people in general, and law enforcement officers in particular, distinguish between true and false *confessions*?

One could argue that even if the process of interrogation is psychologically coercive, and even if innocent people sometimes confess, there is no problem to solve to the extent that the errors are ultimately detected by authorities and corrected. Essential to this presumed safety net is a commonsense assumption, built on blind faith, that 'I'd know a false confession if I saw one'. There are three reasons for concern about whether people can detect as false the confessions of innocent suspects. The first is that generalized common sense leads us to trust confessions the way we trust other behaviours that are not tainted by self-interest. Reasonably, most people believe they would never confess to a crime they did not commit and they cannot imagine the circumstances under which anyone else would do so.

A second reason for concern is that people are typically not adept at deception detection. We saw earlier that neither lay people nor professionals can accurately separate truths from lies. The question remains as to whether they can distinguish true and false confessions. Kassin *et al.* (2005) examined this question in a study on the performance of police investigators and lay people. First, we recruited male prison inmates in a state correctional facility to take part in a pair of videotaped interviews. Each inmate was asked to give a full confession to the crime for which he was in prison. Each free narrative was then followed by a standardized list of questions concerning who, what, when, where, how and other details. In a second interview, each inmate was instructed to concoct a false confession on the basis of a one- or two-sentence description of a crime committed by a different inmate. Using this procedure, we created a videotape that depicted ten different inmates, each giving a single true or false confession to one of five crimes: aggravated assault, armed robbery, burglary, breaking and entering, and automobile theft. The tape was shown to college students and police investigators (two thirds of whom had received training in interviewing and interrogation). The result: neither group was significantly more accurate than would be expected by chance, but the investigators were more confident in their judgments and more likely to commit false-positive errors, trusting the false confessions.

There are two possible explanations for why the investigators were unable to distinguish the true and false confessions and why they were less accurate on average than college students. One is that training and experience introduce a bias that systematically reduces judgment accuracy. This is not terribly surprising in the light of the kinds of behavioural deception cues that form part of the basis for training (e.g. such visual cues as gaze aversion, non-frontal posture, slouching and grooming gestures are not correlated with truthtelling or deception; see DePaulo *et al.* 2003). A second possible explanation is that the police in our sample were impaired by our use of a paradigm in which half the observed confessions were false – a percentage that is likely far higher than the real-world base rate for false confessions. To the extent that law enforcement work leads investigators to presume most confessions true, then the response bias imported from the police station to the laboratory may have proved misleading for a study in which half the confessions were false. To test this latter hypothesis, we conducted a second study in which we neutralized the response bias by instructing all subjects prior to the task that half the confessions were true and half were false. This manipulation did reduce the overall number of 'true' judgments amongst investigators, but they were still not more accurate than students or chance performance, only more confident.

When it comes to the assumption that 'I'd know a false confession if I saw one', there is a third reason for concern: real-life false confessions, when elicited through a process of interrogation, contain content cues that people associate with truth-telling. In most documented false confessions, the statements ultimately presented in court are compelling, as they often contain vivid and accurate details about the crime, the scene and the victim – details that can become known to an innocent suspect through the assistance of leading interview questions, overheard conversations, photographs, visits to the crime scene and other second-hand sources of information invisible to the naïve observer. To further obfuscate matters, many confessions are textured with what I call 'elective' statements. Often innocent suspects describe not just what they allegedly did, and how they did it, but *why* – as they self-report on revenge, jealousy, desperation, capitulation to peer pressure and other prototypical motives for crime. Sometimes they add apologies and expressions of remorse. In some cases, innocent suspects will correct minor errors that appear in the written statements that are derived from them, suggesting that they read, understood and verified the contents. To the naïve spectator, such statements appear to be voluntary, textured with detail and the product of personal experience. Uninformed, however, this spectator mistakes illusion for reality, not realizing that the taped confession is much like a Hollywood drama – scripted by the police theory of the case, rehearsed during hours of unrecorded questioning, directed by the questioner and ultimately enacted on paper, tape or camera by the suspect.

The Reid Technique offers advice on how to create these illusions of credibility. Inbau *et al.* (2001) recommend that interrogators insert minor errors (such as a wrong name, date or street address) into written confessions so that the suspect will spot them, correct them and initial the changes. The goal is to increase the perceived credibility of the statement and make it difficult for the defendant later to distance him or herself from it. Because only perpetrators should be in a position to spot these errors, this technique appears to have great potential. However, Inbau *et al.* advise that, to play it safe, 'the investigator should keep the errors in mind and raise a question about them in the event the suspect neglects to do so' (p. 384). Similarly, they advise detectives to insert into written confessions irrelevant personal history items known only to the 'offender'. 'For instance, the suspect may be asked to give the name of the grade school he attended, the place or hospital in which he was born, or other similar information' (p. 383). Of course, for the suspect who is not the offender but an innocent person, the insertion of neutral, crime-irrelevant biographical details from his or her own life has no diagnostic value. Like the error correction trick, however it merely creates a false illusion of credibility.

The *post hoc* assessment of confessions

In theory, the police, prosecutors and others can assess suspects' statements with some degree of accuracy through a genuine effort at corroboration. A full confession contains both an admission of guilt and a post-admission narrative in which suspects recount not just what they did but how, when, where and with whom. Evaluating such a statement should involve a three-step process. The first step requires a consideration of the conditions under which the statement was made and the extent to which coercive techniques were used. As in the 'totality of circumstances' approach that American courts use to determine voluntariness, relevant factors in this inquiry include a consideration of suspect characteristics such as age, intelligence and mental state; the physical conditions of detention; and the use of stated or implied promises, threats and other social influence tactics used during interrogation. Still, whilst the presence of personal and situational risk factors cast doubts on a confession, they do not invalidate it. Coerced confessions may well be true; innocent people sometimes confess voluntarily, without prompting. The second step requires a consideration of whether the confession contains details that are accurate, not erroneous, in relation to the verifiable facts of the crime. A confession can prove guilt or at least guilty knowledge (or it may fail to do so) to the extent that it is 'generative', furnishing the police with crime facts that were not already known or leading to evidence that was not already available. An often overlooked but necessary third step concerns a requirement of *attribution* for the source of the details contained in the narrative confession. A confession has diagnostic value if the accurate details it contains were knowable only to a perpetrator and were not derivable from such second-hand sources as news accounts, overheard conversations, leading interview questions, photographs or visits to the crime scene (see Ofshe and Leo 1997; Hill 2003).

This three-step analysis can be illustrated in the videotaped false confessions in the Central Park jogger case described earlier. On tape, these defendants confessed to a gang rape in statements that seemed vividly detailed, voluntary and the product of personal experience. But examination of the conditions under which the statements were made reveals the presence of troubling risk factors. The boys were 14–16 years old, and at the time of their videotaped statements, they had been in custody and interrogation by multiple detectives for a range of 14–30 hours. The passage of time may not be visible to the naïve consumer of the final product, but it brings heightened pressure, a dogged refusal to accept denials, fatigue, despair and often a deprivation of sleep and other needs. As to other aspects of the situation, the detectives and suspects disagreed in significant ways about what went on during the many unrecorded hours of questioning. They disagreed, for example, over whether the parents had access to their boys, whether threats and physical force was used and whether promises to go home were made.

The conditions of interrogation contained classic elements of coercion, but that does not absolve the guilty or invalidate their confessions. The Central Park jogger confessions were compelling precisely because the narratives contained highly vivid details, including an on-camera physical re-enactment. From start to finish, however, the narratives were riddled with inconsistencies and factual errors of omission and commission. When asked about the jogger's head injury, one boy said she was punched with fists; then when prompted to recall a blunt object, he said they used a rock; moments later, the rock turned to bricks. Across the defendants, the statements diverged. Each and every defendant minimized his own role in the assault, placing 'them' at centre stage. When two of the suspects were taken to the crime scene and asked to point to the site of the attack, they pointed in different directions. Factual errors were also numerous. One suspect said the jogger wore blue shorts and a T-shirt; she wore long black tights and a long-sleeve jersey. Another said the jogger and clothes were cut with a knife; there were no knife cuts. A third suspect did not seem to know the victim bled; she bled profusely. A fourth said that one of the boys he was with ejaculated; yet no traces of that boy's semen were found. None of the defendants knew the location of the attack, that the jogger was left at the bottom of a ravine, that her hands were tied or that she was gagged with her own shirt.

Pointing to the presence of accurate details in these statements, the naïve spectator will see the confessional glasses as half full, not half empty. In the light of all that is known about the problems with eyewitness memory, it is not reasonable to expect perfection in the accounts of crime suspects. This assertion, however, invites a third analytical step, an attribution as to the source of the accurate details. A confession can prove guilt if it contains details knowable only to the perpetrator, details not derivable by second-hand sources. Yet in the jogger case, after dozens of collective hours of unrecorded questioning, and amidst disputes as to what transpired, there is no way to know whether crime facts were furnished to the defendants, wittingly or unwittingly, through the process. Indeed, one need not stray from the videotaped confessions to hear the prosecutor ask leading questions that functioned not only to elicit information *from* the suspects but to communicate information *to* the suspects. Without apparent regard for the ownership of the facts being extracted, she steered one boy's story through a broken but persistent sequence of leading questions: 'Medical evidence says something other than a hand was used... what?' and 'Don't you remember someone using a brick or a stone?' In a move that grossly undermined all opportunity to get a confession indicative of guilty knowledge, the detectives inexplicably took one suspect on a supervised visit to the crime scene *before* taking his videotaped confession. The district attorney then showed him graphic photographs of the victim. For diagnostic purposes, it makes no sense to contaminate a suspect's confession by spoon feeding him information in these ways, rendering the source of his subsequent knowledge ambiguous. Whether he was there or not, the visit and photographs endowed him with key visual facts about the victim, crime and place – facts fit for a full confession. Importantly, Inbau *et al.* (2001) advise police to withhold key crime details so that they can ask suspects to corroborate their admissions.

Crime perpetrators have the unique capacity to reveal information about their actions that the police did not already know and produce evidence that police did not already have. Yet the statements of the Central Park jogger defendants – individually and collectively – were not generative in these ways. Lacking such corroboration, the case against the five defendants was like a house of cards, with each boy's confession built squarely and solely upon the foundation of the others' confessions. In December 2002, this house of cards collapsed under the weight of an imprisoned serial rapist who voluntarily confessed to the attack, who furnished the police with crime facts that proved accurate and not previously known, and whose semen was present on the jogger.

Towards the videotaping of interrogations

To assess accurately the incriminating value of confessions, the police, prosecutors and fact finders must have access to a videotape recording of the entire interview and interrogation. In Great Britain, the Police and Criminal Evidence Act 1985 mandated that all suspect interviews and interrogations be taped. In the USA, Inbau *et al.* (2001) have long opposed the videotaping of interrogations, only recently changing course. The FBI continues to prohibit the practice. Today, a handful of states require electronic recording in custodial settings and others do so on a voluntary basis (for an excellent historical overview of this practice, see Drizin and Reich 2004).

There are a number of presumed advantages to a policy of videotaping interviews and interrogations in their entirety, all of which should provide for a more effective safety net. First, videotaping will deter the police from using overly guilt-presumptive, duplicitous and forceful interrogation tactics. Secondly, videotaping will deter frivolous defence claims of coercion where none existed. Thirdly, a videotaped record provides an objective and accurate account of all that transpired during interrogation, an all-too-common source of dispute in the courtroom (e.g. about whether rights were administered and waived; whether detectives yelled, intimidated, threatened, made promises or lied to the suspect; and whether the details in a confession came from the police or suspect). All this should increase the fact-finding accuracy of judges and juries. For the tapes to be complete and balanced, however, entire sessions should be recorded and the camera should adopt a 'neutral' or 'equal focus' perspective that shows both the accused and his or her interrogators (Lassiter *et al.* 2001).

In the USA, the videotaping experience has been well received wherever it has been used. Several years ago, a National Institute of Justice study revealed that amongst those police and sheriff's departments that videotaped interrogations, the vast majority found the practice useful (Geller 1993). More recently, Sullivan (2004) interviewed officials from 238 police and sheriff's departments in 38 states who voluntarily recorded custodial interrogations and found that they enthusiastically favoured the practice. Amongst the reasons cited were that recording permits detectives to focus on the suspect rather than take copious notes, increases accountability, provides an instant replay of the suspect's statement that reveals information initially overlooked and reduces the amount of time detectives spend in court defending their interrogation conduct. Contradicting the most common criticisms, respondents in this study reported that videotaping interrogations did not prove too costly or inhibit suspects from talking to police.

The Central Park jogger case revealed a sequence of three problems: innocent people are often targeted for interrogation on the basis of judgments of deception that are frequently in error; certain processes of interrogation can cause people to confess to crimes they did not commit; and it is difficult for the police, attorneys, judges and juries to identify false confessions once they occur. The risks inherent in this chain of events suggests that there are not adequate safeguards in the criminal justice system. One would hope that recent advances in DNA testing and forensic-psychological research will bring together collaborative groups of law enforcement professionals, attorneys, social scientists and policy-makers to scrutinize current practices – the goal being to increase the effectiveness of interviews and interrogations, as measured by the diagnosticity of the outcomes they produce.

Note

1. This percentage is even higher in homicide cases. In fact, as many false confessions are discovered before there is a trial, are not reported by police and are not publicized by the media, it is clear that the known cases represent the tip of a much larger iceberg (Drizin and Leo 2004; Gross et al. 2005).

References

Blackstone, W. *Commentaries on the Laws of England (1765–1769)*, second edition with corrections and all footnotes. http://www.lonang.com/exlibris/blackstone/

Bull, R. and Milne, B. (2004) 'Attempts to improve the police interviewing of suspects', in G.D. Lassiter (ed.) *Interrogations, Confessions and Entrapment*. New York, NY: Kluwer Academic.

DePaulo, B.M., Lindsay, J.J., Malone, B.E., Muhlenbruck, L., Charlton, K. and Cooper, H. (2003) 'Cues to deception', *Psychological Bulletin*, 129: 74–112.

Drizin, S.A. and Leo, R.A. (2004) 'The problem of false confessions in the post-DNA world', *North Carolina Law Review*, 82: 891–1007.

Drizin, S.A. and Reich, M.J. (2004) 'Heeding the lessons of history: the need for mandatory recording of police interrogations to accurately assess the reliability and voluntariness of confessions', *Drake Law Review*, 52: 619–46.

Ekman, P., O'Sullivan, M. and Frank, M.G. (1999) 'A few can catch a liar', *Psychological Science*, 10: 263–6.

Geller, W.A. (1993) *Videotaping Interrogations and Confessions. National Institute of Justice: Research in Brief.* Washington, DC: US Department of Justice.

Gilbert, D.T. and Malone, P.S. (1995) 'The correspondence bias', *Psychological Bulletin*, 117: 21–38.

Granhag, P.A. and Strömwall, L.A. (eds) (2004) *The Detection of Deception in Forensic Contexts.* Cambridge: Cambridge University Press.

Gross, S.R., Jacoby, K., Matheson, D.J., Montgomery, N. and Patel, S. (2005) 'Exonerations in the United States 1989 through 2003.' *Journal of Criminal Law and Criminology*, 95: 523–53.

Gudjonnsson, G.H. (1992) *The Psychology of Interrogations, Confessions, and Testimony.* London: Wiley.

Gudjonnsson, G.H. (2003) *The Psychology of Interrogations and Confessions: A Handbook.* Chichester: Wiley.

Hartwig, M., Granhag, P.A., Strömwall, L.A. and Vrij, A. (2005) 'Deception detection via strategic disclosure of evidence.' *Law and Human Behavior*, 29: 469–84.

Hill, M.D. (2003) 'Identifying the source of critical details in confessions', *Forensic Linguistics*, 10: 23–61.

Inbau, F.E., Reid, J.E., Buckley, J.P. and Jayne, B.C. (2001) *Criminal Interrogation and Confessions* (4th edn). Gaithersberg, MD: Aspen.

Kassin, S.M. (1997) 'The psychology of confession evidence', *American Psychologist*, 52: 221–33.

Kassin, S.M. (2005) 'On the psychology of confessions: does *innocence* put *innocents* at risk?', *American Psychologist*, 60: 215–28.

Kassin, S.M. and Fong, C.T. (1999) 'I'm innocent!' Effects of training on judgments of truth and deception in the interrogation room', *Law and Human Behavior*, 23: 499–516.

Kassin, S.M. and Kiechel, K.L. (1996) 'The social psychology of false confessions: compliance, internalization, and confabulation', *Psychological Science*, 7: 125–8.

Kassin, S.M. and McNall, K. (1991) 'Police interrogations and confessions: communicating promises and threats by pragmatic implication', *Law and Human Behavior*, 15: 233–51.

Kassin, S.M., Meissner, C.A. and Norwick, R.J. (2005) '"I'd know a false confession if I saw one": a comparative study of college students and police investigators', *Law and Human Behavior*, 29: 211–27.

Kassin, S.M. and Sukel, H. (1997) 'Coerced confessions and the jury: an experimental test of the "harmless error" rule', *Law and Human Behavior*, 21: 27–46.

Lassiter, G.D., Geers, A.L., Munhall, P.J., Handley, I.M. and Beers, M.J. (2001) 'Videotaped confessions: is guilt in the eye of the camera?', *Advances in Experimental Social Psychology*, 33: 189–254.

Leo, R.A. (1996) 'Inside the interrogation room', *The Journal of Criminal Law and Criminology*, 86: 266–303.

Leo, R.A. (2004) 'The third degree', in G.D. Lassiter (ed.) *Interrogations, Confessions, and Entrapment*. New York, NY: Kluwer Academic.

Lykken, D.T. (1998) *A Tremor in the Blood: Uses and Abuses of the Lie Detector*. Reading, MA: Perseus Books.

McNatt, D.B. (2000) 'Ancient Pygmalion joins contemporary management: a meta-analysis of the result', *Journal of Applied Psychology*, 85: 314–322.

Meissner, C.A. and Kassin, S.M. (2002) '"He's guilty!" Investigator bias in judgments of truth and deception', *Law and Human Behavior*, 26: 469–80.

Meissner, C.A. and Kassin, S.M. (2004) '"You're guilty, so just confess!" Cognitive and behavioral confirmation biases in the interrogation room', in D. Lassiter (ed.) *Interrogations, Confessions, and Entrapment*. New York, NY: Kluwer Academic/Plenum.

Memon, A., Vrij, A. and Bull, R. (2003) *Psychology and Law: Truthfulness, Accuracy and Credibility*. London: Jossey-Bass.

Meyer, R.G. and Youngjohn, J.R. (1991) 'Effects of feedback and validity expectancy on response in a lie detector interview', *Forensic Reports*, 4: 235–44.

Milne, R. and Bull, R. (1999) *Investigative Interviewing: Psychology and Practice*. New York, NY: John Wiley.

Moston, S., Stephenson, G.M. and Williamson, T.M. (1992) 'The effects of case characteristics on suspect behaviour during questioning', *British Journal of Criminology*, 32: 23–40.

National Research Council, Committee to Review the Scientific Evidence on the Polygraph, Division of Behavioral and Social Sciences and Education (2003) *The Polygraph and Lie Detection*. Washington, DC: National Academies Press.

Newman, M.L., Pennebaker, J.W., Berry, D.S. and Richards, J.M. (2003) 'Lying words: predicting deception from linguistic styles', *Personality and Social Psychology Bulletin*, 29: 665–75.

Nickerson, R.S. (1998) 'Confirmation bias: a ubiquitous phenomenon in many guises', *Review of General Psychology*, 2: 175–220.

Ofshe, R.J. and Leo, R.A. (1997) 'The decision to confess falsely: rational choice and irrational action', *Denver University Law Review*, 74: 979–1122.

Risinger, D.M., Saks, M.J., Thompson, W.C. and Rosenthal, R. (2002) 'The *Daubert/Kumho* implications of observer effects in forensic science: hidden problems of expectation and suggestion', *California Law Review*, 90: 1–56.

Rosenthal, R. and Jacobson, L. (1968) *Pygmalion in the Classroom: Teacher Expectation and Pupils' Intellectual Development*. New York, NY: Holt, Rinehart & Winston.

Russano, M.B., Meissner, C.A., Narchet, F.M. and Kassin, S.M. (2005) 'Investigating true and false confessions within a novel experimental paradigm', *Psychological Science*, 16: 481–86.

Scheck, B., Neufeld, P. and Dwyer, J. (2000) *Actual Innocence*. Garden City, NY: Doubleday.

Simon, D. (1991) *Homicide: A Year on the Killing Streets*. New York, NY: Ivy Books.

Sullivan, T.P. (2004) *Police Experiences with Recording Custodial Interrogations*. Chicago, IL: Northwestern University School of Law, Center on Wrongful Convictions.

Vrij, A. (2000) *Detecting Lies and Deceit: The Psychology of Lying and the Implications for Professional Practice*. London: Wiley.

Vrij, A. (2004) 'Why professionals fail to catch liars and how they can improve', *Legal and Criminal Psychology*, 9: 159–81.

Vrij, A., Edward, K. and Bull, R. (2001) 'Police officers' ability to detect deceit: the benefit of indirect deception detection measures', *Legal and Criminological Psychology*, 6: 185–97.

Walczyk, J.J., Roper, K.S., Seemann, E. and Humphrey, A.M. (2003) 'Cognitive mechanisms underlying lying to questions: response time as a cue to deception', *Applied Cognitive Psychology*, 17: 755–74.

Zuckerman, M., DePaulo, B.M. and Rosenthal, R. (1981) 'Verbal and nonverbal communication of deception', *Advances in Experimental Social Psychology*, 14: 1–59.

Chapter 12

Investigative interviewing and the detection of deception

Mark G. Frank, John D. Yarbrough and Paul Ekman

The Improving Interpersonal Evaluations for Law Enforcement and National Security technique

The Improving Interpersonal Evaluations for Law Enforcement and National Security technique (IIE) is derived from observations of real-life field interviews combined with the latest scientific behavioural analysis. It originated in the dissatisfaction of working police towards their interviewing training. This dissatisfaction caused J.J. Newberry (US Bureau of Alcohol, Tobacco and Firearms, now retired) to observe the techniques of the most successful working police officers (those who when they chose to charge a suspect typically obtained a conviction, and who other officers viewed as being the most effective interviewers). These observations were elaborated and refined, based upon close contact with behavioural scientists with expertise in human memory, emotion and expressive verbal and non-verbal behaviour, including deception (e.g. Yuille 1989; Ekman and Frank 1993, Newberry 1999; Ekman 1985/2001; Frank and Ekman 1997, 2004a, 2004b; O'Sullivan 2005). In summary, this approach noted that good police interviewers were excellent communicators. They listened well, built good rapport with their interviewees and they were sharp observers of verbal and non-verbal behaviours, which included being good detectors of deceit. The techniques of these good interviewers were quantified by the behavioural scientists and then developed into training packages that addressed building the individual skills along with full application of the techniques to live interviews.

We will describe here the development of the interviewing training that was combined into what became known as 'analytic interviewing' initially by J.J. Newberry, with the active participation of the authors above, Professors Paul Ekman and Mark Frank, retired police officers such as John Yarbrough, and other scientists and law enforcement officers. As we explain in the conclusion, not all these individuals are continuing to work together, and now there is a choice between two distinct organizations: the Institute for Analytic Interviewing and Improving Interpersonal Evaluations.

The basic assumptions of the IIE interview

First, the IIE makes a few key assumptions about the purpose of doing any interview, be it a suspect, witness or informant. The first assumption is that the purpose of any interview is to find the truth. It defines the truth as what the interviewee actually believes to be true (Newberry 1999). This assumption applies to suspect, witness, or informant interviews, background investigations or intelligence-gathering interviews, or almost any type of interview. This purpose is in stark contrast to what many beginning police officers believe, and on occasion, are formally taught. The IIE instructors note that when they ask a typical group of police officers 'what is the purpose of doing an interview?' a very high proportion of them indicate 'get a confession' as their primary purpose. This is not too surprising, as many techniques taught in law enforcement stress the confession as the goal of an interrogation (Inbau *et al.* 1986). Although the IIE approach is not opposed to obtaining confessions, it notes that shifting the focus away from the confession and more towards the truth – whatever that might be – would seem to reduce the likelihood of obtaining a false confession (see Dwyer, Neufeld, and Scheck 2000, for a description of false convictions, many involving false confessions). Moreover, the slight shift away from the confession seems to keep the investigator focused on information gathering, rather than rendering a judgment. This is important because it is the information gathered from the suspect or witness that may contradict or be consistent with the physical evidence or other witness accounts, or that will provide clues towards other lines of inquiry and so forth. It is this information that will ultimately convict or exonerate the suspect.

Secondly, the IIE approach assumes that besides knowing *what* a person believes to be true, it is just as important to know *why* he or she believes it. Did he or she read it, hear it, see it or experience it? In order to conduct a proper investigation, one must have the most accurate information possible. Knowing how the individual received and processed the information will tell the interviewer why the person believes it to be true, and in the process unmask clues as to the accuracy of the statement. Take the example of a witness to a traffic accident who claims to have 'seen the whole thing', although he or she had his or her back to the accident at the precise moment of impact. Careful questioning of such a witness as to why he or she believes one driver was at fault, and why he or she says one car crossed the red light and why he or she was at that location – rather than just what happened – will in all likelihood reveal that the witness first heard the impact, and then turned to look at the scene. This would reveal a witness who could not have actually seen the moment of impact, and thus his or her account up to that moment may not be accurate.

Thirdly, the IIE approach also assumes that people do give truthful information that can be inaccurate. For example, information can become inaccurate through two people having an honest difference of opinion, or a person having a mistaken recall, or having a false memory, amongst others (Haugaard and Repucci 1992). However, people also lie. To distinguish a lie from other forms of inaccurate information, the IIE approach uses Ekman's definition of a lie – a deliberate attempt to mislead, without the prior notification of the target of the lie (Ekman 1985/2001). This means that lies are consciously fabricated, distorted or concealed by the liar. Thus a person who provides factually incorrect information is not necessarily lying, unless the person who delivers it knows it will mislead. If a person truly believes he is Napoleon, he is not lying, although he will be incorrect. If the person knows he is not Napoleon but claims to be, then he is lying. This definition also means that people can give their implicit or explicit approval to be misled for some interpersonal situations, and this would not be lies. For example, we give our approval to being misled when viewing a play or movie, and allow the actor to pretend to be a different person without labelling him or her a liar. Likewise, Ekman (1985/2001) describes how in real-estate negotiations, it is implied that the price of the house is not necessarily the only price the seller will take, and the potential buyer knows that because bargaining situations imply this. Thus, the price listed for a house is not considered a lie – although concealing information or fabricating a story about some serious structural damage would be a lie. If the purpose of any interview is to find the truth, and this purpose is clearly stated to the subject of that interview, then any attempt to conceal, distort or fabricate information would be clearly a lie in that interview context as there is really no area in the interview proper where an investigator would give his or her consent to being misled.

The basic processes of the IIE

The IIE describes the processes by which an investigator can maximize the amount of accurate information, whilst minimizing the amount of inaccurate information obtained in an interview. It is best thought of as a series of steps not too dissimilar to the PEACE model (see Chapters 8 and 9, this volume), although the IIE addresses specific techniques. The IIE uses the first six letters of the alphabet as the memnonic for its process:

- Awareness
- Baseline
- Changes
- Discrepancies
- Engagement
- Follow-up.

Awareness

Awareness in the IIE means that an investigator must become aware of the ways in which information may be inaccurate. Knowing this allows the investigator to take steps and apply techniques for reducing the chances that this will happen. For example, two witnesses to a traffic accident who offer contradictory accounts of the accident does not guarantee that one must by lying. Thus an investigator who knows how human memory can be affected – through simple processing limitations or the biasing affects of closed, ended questions and so forth – can reduce the likelihood of his or her own behaviour biasing the quality of the information.

Awareness also means that the investigators must be aware of their own physical and personality traits. For example, if the investigator is a female who is interviewing a male who subscribes to a brand of fundamentalist religious belief that views females as subservient to males, she may receive a hostile reception from this interviewee. Likewise, a physically big male may generate fear in his interviewee by simply shaking the interviewee's hand. There are age, status, ethnic and other factors as well to consider. An interviewer who is aware of these physical traits and their dynamic impact can take steps to reduce their impact on the interview process. In particular, an area that the investigator must become aware of are the cross-cultural dynamics that develop in an interview. For example, many Asian cultures (such as Chinese) demonstrate respect by not looking directly into the eyes of the other. This is in contrast to many western cultures, in which one is expected to look into the eyes of the person one is talking to. Moreover, many of the physical traits described earlier will interact with these cultural dynamics – for example, many cultures apply very strict age, gender and/or generational status rules. Regardless, an interviewer who is aware of these issues will be much less likely to misinterpret the behaviours and accounts presented to him or her.

Similarly, one must be aware of personality traits and particular biases and how they may work against obtaining accurate information. An investigator who is aggressive and high energy may interrupt his or her interviewee too much and thus disrupt his or her account. If an investigator is aware of this trait, he or she can develop techniques to nullify it. For example, investigators may teach themselves to allow for the silence, or to expect it, or they may learn to listen whilst positioning their hand over their mouths and gently grab their lip as a constant reminder not to interrupt. These sorts of skills were observed in the anecdotal study of effective police officers, and laboratory research confirms that more socially competent and sensitive people are more likely not to interrupt others, particularly distressed individuals offering accounts of their problems (Christensen *et al.* 1980). Likewise, an interviewer who is aware of a bias against certain types of people – red-haired people, snobby people or whatever – would be able to take compensatory steps to insure he or she does not treat these individuals in way that may put off the subject and serve as an obstacle to communication.

Baseline

As an investigator becomes aware of these aforementioned factors, he or she should also be observing the normal mode of behaviour for the subject. The normal style of behaviour is referred to as the baseline behaviour. The interviewer should note how expressive the subject was, how much he or she moved his or her hands, feet and head as he or she spoke, what characteristic gestures he or she used, what tone of voice he or she had, what sort of words he or she used, and so forth. This will become the basis for noting the general personality and interaction style of the interviewee, and it provides a clear control sample to compare any behavioural changes in the subject during the interview.

Changes

Ekman (Ekman and Friesen 1969; Ekman 1985/2001) first noted that detecting deceptive behaviours is most effectively done within the subject – i.e. one must compare the subject to the subject (Ekman and Friesen 1972, 1974; Ekman *et al.* 1976). The IIE approach adopted this idea and built in training techniques to help investigators improve their abilities to note not only the baseline behaviours, but also when behaviours deviate from this baseline. These changes are essential to understanding when an individual is convinced of the accuracy of a statement he or she just uttered, uncertain of that statement or even deliberately misleading with that statement. Moreover, the IIE approach instructs investigators to label these changes from the baseline behaviour as 'hotspots', rather than lies, although research has shown that these hotspots can betray deception or concealed emotion at rates greater than chance (Ekman and Frank 1993; Frank and Ekman 1997; Ekman 1985/2001). At its core, a hotspot means that the topic under discussion, or some segment of it, has caused the subject to experience an emotion, or has caused the subject to have to think hard on his or her feet. The IIE approach recognizes that there are a number of reasons why a person would feel an emotion, or be forced to think on his or her feet, besides lying. This is why IIE stresses the phrase 'hotspot' when these behaviours are noted, rather than lie – to force the interviewer to recognize this topic has caused a reaction and, later, when the moment is right, to address that topic to ascertain why the subject showed such a reaction to it. It could be because the subject is lying, but it could be due to the topic generating an emotion for a different reason. Ekman (1985/2001) describes how a high US government official who was under investigation showed a marked demeanour change when questioned about an important lunch meeting with another official who had violated US law. He pointed out that this change in demeanour could be due to lying, but it could also be due to an argument he had with his wife about lunch-related issues. Thus, the most accurate inference when recognizing a hotspot is that it is strong evidence that the subject is thinking on his or her feet, or is experiencing an emotional reaction to the topic (Ekman 1985/2001). But it is still enormously useful to the investigator who spots it because he or she can then ask questions to ascertain the source of the hotspot, which in turn may reveal an important area of inquiry that the interviewee may be trying to avoid or conceal. The scientific basis for this is discussed shortly.

Discrepancies

Discrepancies refer to the discrepancy not only within the verbal and non-verbal communication channels, but also between the verbal and non-verbal communication channels. For example, an investigator observes a person issuing a statement about his or her kidnapped child, stating he or she witnessed the kidnapping whilst exhibiting the emotion of sadness. The IIE-trained interviewer would examine this person's expressive behaviour looking for clear evidence of discrepancies in the person's verbal and non-verbal behaviour, or within the non-verbal elements of sadness such as looking for sadness in the face, voice, and body. In a falsified sadness, not all these channels will be consistent with the emotion of sadness. Likewise across these communicative channels, a subject who shows a shrug when he or she states 'I saw the whole thing', is discrepantly non-verbally communicating 'I am uncertain'. Or a subject who says 'no' in response to a question, yet nods his or her head indicating 'yes', is also showing discrepant behaviour. When these discrepancies are noted, they too are classified as hotspots (Ekman 1985/2001). The scientific basis for discrepancies being informative to the investigator will be discussed shortly.

Engagement

Engagement refers to the process by which the interviewer engages the interviewee. The IIE approach addresses the skill set needed to create an environment that makes it as easy as possible for the subject to be truthful and accurate. The observations of good interviewers suggest that they listen more than they talk, and that they create a more comfortable environment by building rapport with the subject. It also means that an investigator must learn how to ask open-ended questions, to phrase his or her questions in a way to foster recall and detail, and not to ask leading questions.

IIE teaches investigators specific techniques for building rapport. Researchers have defined rapport as consisting of a state of similarity, empathy and liking (Bernieri *et al.* 1996), resulting in a feeling of positivity, attentiveness and co-ordination (Tickle-Degnen and Rosenthal 1990). Knowing these building blocks of rapport enables the investigator to adopt the habits that will facilitate similarity, empathy and liking. For example, one technique for establishing similarity is actively to seek out areas of commonality. An investigator and a subject might both have children, or have grown up in the same town, had the same course of study in school, have followed the same sports or teams and so forth. Thus, in the process of talking with the subject an interviewer would identify areas of commonality as means by which he or she can establish this personal connection with the subject. This then functions as a means to foster conversation between the two. It is astounding how human beings will organize themselves into in and out groups based on even the most trivial characteristics, and that once someone feels he or she has this in-group bond he or she views the other quite differently (e.g. Tajfel 1978). Imagine meeting someone from your home town whilst on holiday in a very remote location. One would typically feel some special bond to this person almost immediately (however, we would not feel this special bond if we met him or her walking down the street of our home town because this similarity would not be salient). Regardless, one can be made to feel some connection to total strangers by finding any thread of commonality. Thus, an investigator who does this creates a more comfortable environment for conversation – and particularly for a truthful person who, odds are, will be nervous if he or she is falsely suspected of a crime.

Another technique to facilitate rapport is mirroring. Mirroring refers to the active effort of the interviewer to match the behaviours of the interviewee. This is based upon the finding that two people in rapport tend to exhibit postural and speech congruence (Charney 1966; LaFrance and Broadbent 1976; Trout and Rosenfeld 1980; Capella 1981; LaFrance 1979, 1985). Some behaviours that an interviewer may mirror include seating posture, resting a hand on the chin or even using the same level of vocabulary. Research shows that when people are mirrored they feel much more comfortable with their interaction partner and like him or her more than when they are not mirrored (Chartrand and Bargh 1999). Moreover, not only do those in rapport show congruent behaviours, but when they are comfortable with the conversation they tend to synchronize their behaviours (Bernieri and Rosenthal 1991). In fact, IIE suggests periodically testing rapport by having the interviewer adjust his or her position deliberately, to see if the subject follows. IIE also warns against being too obvious in doing this, for if a subject thinks an interviewer is simply imitating him or her, he or she may feel mocked, and that will destroy rapport.

Another technique to building rapport – although limited by jurisdiction and local custom – is to touch the subject. This means an occasional gentle touch, in socially appropriate areas like the forearm or upper arm, can facilitate rapport by demonstrating that the interviewer feels empathy and even likes the subject (or at least is not repelled by the subject), as research has shown that people in rapport tend to touch each other more (Moore 1985). As stated earlier, though, one must be aware of the cultural implications for a touch, and in some situations it can work against the interviewer (for example, some fundamentalist forms of religions would consider it harmful for a female investigator to touch a male subject). By listening carefully and courteously to the subject whilst building rapport, the investigator increases the chance that the subject will believe the investigator feels empathy for him or her, and does not reject him or her as disgusting or unworthy. This sort of environment is much more conducive to conversation and increases the willingness of the subject to co-operate. Collins *et al.* (2002) tested this by having subjects view a suicide on videotape, and then one third were interviewed by a person who was brusque, one third by someone who was neutral and one third by someone who had built rapport with the subjects (it was the senior author who conducted all the scripted interviews). They then transcribed these eyewitness accounts of this suicide and scored them on the basis of how many correct and incorrect elements were in the account. They found that those subjects with whom the interviewer built rapport recalled approximately 50 per cent more accurate information than the subjects with whom the interviewer was neutral or was brusque. Moreover, there was no difference in the amount of inaccurate information offered by the subjects across conditions. This study shows for the first time that at least as far as witness interviews go, rapport building is an essential element in maximizing the accuracy of the account.

As part of the engagement process, IIE also describes techniques for phrasing questions that maximize the elicitation of diagnostic information. For example, IIE warns against asking leading questions, multiple-choice questions, compound questions and so forth, as these can either confuse the subject or reveal case information to the subject such that if he or she chooses to lie he or she can create a more effective false alibi that accounts for the case information. Instead, the IIE approach teaches investigators to allow for an initial uninterrupted account – similar to the PEACE model – and then to ask open-ended questions and to choose carefully words that solicit information, words that command and words that connote detail. For example, solicitation words are those used in common politeness ('could you please', 'would you please', etc.), and these appear to be more effective in obtaining an initial narrative from the subject. Command words are more directed (such as 'tell me about', 'describe your relationship') and, when offered in an open-ended fashion, push the subject for more detail on specific issues. Words that connote detail encourage the subject to sharpen the topic further, and include words such as 'specifically' (as in 'tell me specifically about') or 'describe in detail your relationship'. The IIE approach also teaches techniques for reviewing the information with the subject, obtaining sequences of events and so forth, including techniques derived from the cognitive interview (Geiselman *et al.* 1986) which have shown to be effective in generating accurate recall.

Follow-up

The IIE approach acknowledges that a confession without corroborating evidence is worthless. Thus after making themselves aware of context and interpersonal variables, and then engaging the subject, observing baseline behaviour, noting changes and discrepancies, and obtaining as complete an account from the subject as possible, interviewers need to follow up on that information so that they can confirm or disconfirm some, none or all the elements of the subject's account. It also suggests what other information can be brought to bear on this account (e.g. are there surveillance cameras in the locations the subject has claimed to have been at the time of the crime? etc.). Although IIE does spend quite a lot of time discussing the importance of behavioural information, these hotspots are best seen as a means towards helping the investigator gather hard information or to identify an account either consistent or inconsistent with the other evidence in the case – a tool in the toolbox approach. IIE recognizes that evidence trumps behaviour – i.e. that ultimately it is this hard evidence, not the behavioural displays of the subject, that will convict or exonerate him or her.

Research supporting the use of changes and discrepancies as hotspot indicators

The IIE approach to identifying hotspots relies upon the scientific analysis of human behaviour when in emotional situations. In particular, it has been based upon Paul Ekman's seminal work on human emotion and deception, and the research streams generated from it.

Ekman's research suggests that two families of behavioural clues betray deception – clues related to a liar's thinking about what he or she is saying, and clues related to a liar's feelings (including his or her feelings about deception) (Hocking and Leathers 1980; Ekman and Frank 1993; Ekman 1985/2001).

Cognitive clues

For example, in order to mislead someone deliberately, a liar must fabricate, distort or conceal facts, describe events that did not happen or that he or she did not witness or suppress critical information. However, the process of thinking about or creating this misinformation can leave behavioural signs. These signs range from a hesitation in the speech, to a misplaced word or a contradictory statement, to very vague accounts with less logical structure (see DePaulo *et al.* 2003 for a review). These types of clues are particularly evident in situations in which the liar should know exactly what he or she has done without having to think too much about it. A witness who claims to have been present at a crime scene should be able to tell the court, without too much thought, where he or she was standing when he or she witnessed the event. If the witness was not present at that scene, he or she would have to create the details necessary to convince someone that he or she was there. This on-the-spot thinking, research has shown, often manifests itself in many speech hesitations, speech disfluencies and errors, often with fewer of the hand or facial gestures that typically illustrate speech (Ekman and Friesen 1972; Ekman *et al.* 1976; DePaulo *et al.* 1985).

The choice of words can also betray this on-the-spot thinking (e.g. Stiff and Miller 1986). In simple terms, liars are less immediate, use more general, simple words to recall and generate thoughts and use less concrete words (reviewed by DePaulo *et al.* 2003). On top of this, the deceptive witness would have to be very careful not to contradict his or her statements made during his or her initial interviews. In more precise terms, work by Yuille and colleagues on credibility assessment (e.g. Porter and Yuille 1995, 1996; Yuille and Porter 2000) identified a number of characteristics – up to 24 – that distinguished an actual memory of an event from a fabricated memory of an event. One example of a characteristic includes whether a subject spontaneously reproduces dialogue in his or her account – it appears real memories are more likely to feature such elements.

Emotional clues

Not only do witnesses, defendants or victims who are lying have to think out the lie and maintain a consistent story, but often emotions are aroused within them that are associated with these lies. Emotions can enter into the lie process in one of two ways – first, the person testifying could be lying about his or her feelings or emotions, or, secondly, the act of lying may produce feelings or emotions within the liar. The same principles apply regardless of how the emotions are initiated. Research has shown that when emotions are aroused, changes are unbidden and occur automatically (reviewed by Ekman 2003). Subjectively people report that they do not *choose* which emotion to experience, but instead report that emotions *happen* to them in specific situations. We know this through our own experience. For example, during times when we may feel blue, we do things that we hope will make us feel better – we go for a walk, eat some calorie-laden food, rent a comedy video – but whether we actually feel happy afterwards is never guaranteed. Likewise, if we have to give an important presentation to the boss, and find ourselves nervous, it is very hard simply to stop being nervous (despite the suggestions of our well meaning friends). These changes occur within a split second and are considered fundamental features of an emotional response (Frijda 1986; Ekman 2003).

Research has shown that anger, disgust, fear, happiness, sadness, and surprise each have unique physiological profiles (Ekman *et al.* 1983); moreover, when subjects are asked to pose facial expressions of anger, disgust, fear, happiness, sadness and surprise, the same patterns of emotion-specific physiology have been found (Levenson *et al.* 1990). This same link between facial expressions and emotion-specific physiology has also been found in different subject groups, such as the elderly (Levenson *et al.* 1991), and in a matrilineal, Muslim, non-western culture (Levenson *et al.* 1992). Research has also found that specific emotions have specific central nervous system (CNS) patterns of hemispheric brain activation, as measured by the electroencephalogram (EEG).

However, part of this emotional response, besides changes in heart rate, blood pressure, and so forth (Ekman *et al.* 1983; Levenson *et al.* 1992), is a change in voice tone (Scherer 1984) as well as a facial expression of that emotion (Izard 1994; Ekman 1994, 2003). In terms of the voice, researchers note particular patterns in fundamental frequency and amplitude that distinguish anger from fear and these emotions from others, and there is some limited evidence that these vocal profiles for emotions are universal across cultures (Scherer and Walbott 1994). For example, in anger the fundamental frequency gets lower (lower pitch), and the amplitude higher (i.e. louder), whereas in fear the fundamental frequency gets higher (higher pitch) and the amplitude softer (i.e. quieter).

In terms of the face, research has shown that emotions such as anger, contempt, disgust, fear, happiness, sadness and surprise appear on people's faces during an emotional experience, often despite their efforts to hide them (e.g. Ekman *et al.* 1988, 1991; Frank and Ekman 1997). The systematic study of how facial expressions link with emotion originated with the publication of Darwin's book *The Expression of the Emotions in Man and Animals* (1872/1998). In this book, Darwin proposed that humans across all cultures have distinct facial expressions for particular emotions, and that these expressions are produced involuntarily as a result of that emotion (through what he called 'nerve force'). Darwin defined emotions as being behavioural and physiological reactions that have assisted humans and animals survive the various life challenges they faced throughout their evolutionary history. For example, the fear reaction assisted humans and animals to escape danger, the anger reaction assisted humans and animals to fight rivals and so forth. Those who possessed these emotional reactions were more likely to live to reproductive age and therefore pass their genes on to the next generation. What Darwin argued (and elaborated later by others, e.g. Plutchik 1962; Tomkins 1962, 1963; Ekman 1992, Izard 1994) is that social animals, such as humans, must communicate these emotions to others in the group because emotions express imminent behaviour, such as striking out in anger, fleeing in fear, avoiding spoiled food in disgust, approachability in happiness and other action tendencies (e.g. Frijda 1986). The expression of imminent behaviour allows humans to co-ordinate their behaviours in ways to reduce conflict, avoid danger and increase harmony.

The evidence for the universality of the emotions of anger, contempt, disgust, fear, happiness, sadness and surprise is quite compelling, where people from all continents on the planet – including pre-literate and visually isolated societies – agree which emotion belongs to which expression (Ekman and Friesen 1971; Izard 1971, 1994; Ekman 1994, 2003). Parallel evidence for universality came from observations of children who were born blind and deaf. These visually and auditory impaired children experienced spontaneous emotions, and they showed similar expressions of emotion as their sighted counterparts (Eibl-Eibesfeldt 1973).

However, Ekman (2003) and others have stressed that these expressions are not reflexes. In fact, he argued that different cultures and subcultures learn different rules to regulate their expression of emotion – what he called 'display rules' (Ekman 1972). For example, Japanese culture, unlike North American culture, has a display rule that prohibits the expression of emotions such as anger or disgust to higher-status people. When Japanese and Americans were secretly observed whilst watching a gory film, both cultural groups showed facial expressions of disgust. When Japanese and Americans were shown this film in the presence of a high status person, the Japanese smiled whereas the Americans still showed facial expressions of disgust – even though both groups still experienced disgust (Ekman and Friesen 1971). Ekman (1972) proposed that these display rules can apply within cultures as well, as in North America, where boys are typically taught to suppress sadness, and girls are taught to suppress anger.

Based on these and other findings, Ekman (1977) proposed his neuro-cultural theory of emotions. This theory argued that certain basic human emotions had specific physiological patterns, and that these emotions produced particular facial expressions that were universal across all cultures, but that the ultimate facial expression of these emotions was modified, exacerbated, suppressed or masked by social learning processes dependent upon cultural or local customs. However, Ekman argued that if the emotional experience is of sufficient intensity, the facial expression for that emotion would 'leak' through and be visible despite efforts by the person to control or hide them (e.g. Ekman 1985/2001). These leaks can be partial or whole expressions, and can often be micromomentary in duration. He called these 'microexpressions' and they have been shown to be useful in uncovering deceit (Ekman and Friesen 1969; Ekman and O'Sullivan 1991; Ekman et al. 1988, 1991; Frank and Ekman 1997, 2005).

The idea that the face can express deliberate, learned expressions, as well as more involuntary, unbidden facial expressions of emotion is supported by the architectural neuroanatomy of the face. There appear to be two distinct neural pathways that mediate facial expressions, each one originating in a different area of the brain: one pathway for voluntary, willful facial actions, and a second for involuntary, emotional facial actions (Tschaissny 1953; Meihlke 1973; Myers 1976). The voluntary facial movements – along with other voluntary movements – originate in the brain's cortical motor strips. These impulses arrive at the face via the pyramidal motor system. Involuntary facial movements originate in the subcortical areas within the brain. These areas are associated with the production of emotion. These impulses arrive at the face via the extrapyramidal motor system. This dual-pathway hypothesis is supported by clinical reports of patients with lesions on the cortical motor strip, who show paralysis when asked to pose an expression such as a smile, but who show perfect bilateral smiles when told a joke that causes them to feel happy (Brodal 1981). Likewise, patients with lesions of the subcortical areas of the brain (such as the basal ganglia) have difficulty showing spontaneous, emotional facial expressions; however, these patients are able to move their facial muscles on command (Karnosh 1945). These facial action observations are so reliable that in the pre-CAT scan era they served as diagnostic criteria for pyramidal and extrapyramidal lesions (DeMyer 1980). Current research is attempting to isolate further areas of production of various facial expressions (e.g. Anderson and Phelps 2000).

Not only do voluntary and involuntary facial actions differ by neural pathway, but the actions mediated by these pathways manifest themselves differently. In a normal person, voluntary pyramidal motor-system-based movements are limited solely by individual effort. A person can consciously move a facial muscle quickly or slowly and hold that action for a brief or long period of time, depending upon the dictates of the circumstance and individual endurance. However, extrapyramidal motor system based facial actions are characterized by synchronized, smooth, symmetrical, consistent and reflex-like or ballistic-like actions on the part of the component facial muscles (reviewed by Rinn 1984). Relatively speaking, these actions appear to be less under the deliberate control of the individual (e.g. Frank *et al.* 1993; Frank 2003). Moreover, research has shown that facial expressions that are driven by actual felt emotion have different characteristics from those that are mimicked emotions, including subtle differences in the muscles used in the expression (Ekman and Friesen 1982; Frank and Ekman 1993; Frank *et al.* 1993). These subtle differences have been called 'reliable' behavioural signs of emotion (Ekman 1985/2001) because few people can actually mimic them. For example, when people feel the emotion of happiness their facial expression involves the contraction of the large muscles that surround the eyes (producing a 'crows' feet' appearance) along with an upward contraction of the lip corners (Ekman and Friesen 1982). When people are faking happiness or enjoyment, they will contract their lip corners, but do not – or cannot – contract the large muscles that surround the eyes (Frank and Ekman 1993). Although a large-intensity smile will also generate the 'crows' feet' appearance, at lower intensities 'crows' feet' would be a reliable sign of actual felt enjoyment.

These facial expressions of emotion must have some significance for our species, as recent research with functional magnetic resonance imaging (fMRI) has shown that there are specific areas of the brain that respond just to these emotional expressions. When researchers show a photo of a facial expression of emotion (typically the same photos used in the universality studies described earlier), they have found that anger seems to activate the right orbitofrontal cortex and anterior cingulate cortex (Blair *et al.* 1999). Disgust seems to activate the anterior insula and limbic cortico-striatal-thalamic area (Phillips *et al.* 1997). Fear seems to activate the left amygdala (Morris *et al.* 1996; Whalen *et al.* 1998). Happiness seems to activate the left side of the lateral frontal, mid-frontal, anterior temporal and central anterior scalp regions (Davidson *et al.* 1990; Ekman and Davidson 1993). Sadness seems to activate the left amygdala and right temporal lobe (Blair *et al.* 1999). What this means is that humans appear to be biologically wired to perceive these specific emotion facial expressions.

How the expression mechanisms can betray deception

If the situation involves assessing the true feelings of a witness, then the lie catcher should try to observe the presence or absence of as many of these reliable clues to the emotions as possible within the face and voice. In the face, these reliable signs include the narrowing of the red margins of the lips in anger, the upward and inward contraction of the area between the eyebrows in fear, and the upward raise of the inner corners of the eyebrows in sadness (see Ekman 2003 for a more complete list of these behavioural signs of emotions). For example, one of the authors, a retired sheriff's deputy, described how an abusive man claimed he would not harm his wife if she were to return to their apartment to remove her belongings and, as he was making his claims of complete co-operation, the red margins of his lips became more and more narrow. The deputy at the time noted this as a gut feeling. Given that the man said all the co-operative things, the deputy asked the woman to enter the apartment to claim her belongings. When she entered, the man struck her in front of the deputy. In this case, it was the presence of the reliable sign that should have tipped off the deputy that the man was feeling anger but struggling to control it.

However, research has been undertaken into the face and voice when the stakes are high – i.e. where the liar faces benefits for successful lying and punishments for unsuccessful lying (Ekman 1985/2001; DePaulo *et al.* 2003). For example, research has shown that facial expressions of fear, distress and disgust distinguish liars and truth tellers at over 76 per cent accuracy (Frank and Ekman 1997); when voice measures are added, this accuracy rises to 86.5 per cent (Ekman *et al.* 1991). Even more recent work by Frank and Ekman (2005), using a counterterrorism paradigm, has pushed this up to 90 per cent accuracy. These behavioural signs are often obvious but, at other times, occur so fleeting as to be micromomentary. Ekman and Friesen (1969) called these micromomentary expressions of emotion 'microexpressions', and the evidence suggests that they can be as brief as ¼ of a second. It also appears that only expert lie catchers detect these microexpressions with any accuracy, whereas average to poor lie catchers miss them (Ekman and O'Sullivan 1991; Ekman *et al.* 1999; Frank and Ekman 1997; Frank 2005). These expressions are often micro because in a situation where someone is motivated to lie, they will attempt to manage their facial behaviour so as to not look 'guilty'. Thus, a 'tug of war' over control of the face ensues between the subcortical, emotional regions and the cortical motor strip. This attempt to squelch the expressions minimizes their scale and duration. These microexpressions were first discovered using Ekman and Friesen's Facial Action Coding System – a laborious technique for reliably coding all visible muscle movement, not just that presumed to be related to emotion (Ekman and Friesen 1978). It involves careful, back and forth viewing of behaviours that can take up to 3 hours of coding time to code one minute of behaviour. However, this hard work did identify these emotional displays that people with the naked eye did not see. Moreover, with as little as 30 minutes of training, people can be taught to improve significantly their abilities to spot microexpressions in real time (Ekman 2005; Frank and Ekman, 2005).

How emotions can betray deception

There are situations in which lies are betrayed by people who falsely portray an emotion. One of the most argued-about aspects of the *Menendez* case in California – where two brothers killed their well-to-do parents but claimed to have been driven to that act by their parents' relentless physical and sexual abuse – involved whether the displays of sadness by the two brothers when they described their actions were real or feigned; that is, whether their sadness was a genuine display of remorse over being forced, due to the years of abuse, to kill these evil parents before their parents killed them; or whether it was the simulated sadness of two culpable siblings designed to gain sympathy from the judge and jury so they could collect their sizeable inheritance.

Another way in which understanding emotions can help is to identify the current states of mind of subjects. For example, one of the authors viewed a videotape of a walk-through with a subject suspected of murdering his parents. As the subject described finding the bodies of his father and mother, he showed sadness. However, only when describing his mother did he show signs of sadness featuring the reliable facial muscles. This provided an important clue as to how he felt about each parent and his relationship with each, and would be useful information to an interviewer who later interviewed this suspect.

Other lies do not necessarily involve the topic of what one truly feels but, instead, involve how the lie itself generates an emotion within someone. A witness may conceal the fact that his or her friend actually threw the first punch in an assault, or the witness may conceal the fact that he or she never saw the dispute, but was simply parroting the alleged victim's account. However, this witness may feel guilt about making up the account of the assault, or he or she may feel fear of being jailed for perjury or he or she may feel enjoyment at the fact that he or she has outsmarted the police into believing his or her account of the assault. Thus lies can produce emotions independent of the act in which the lie was designed to conceal or falsify. Once these emotions are involved, they must be concealed if the lie is not to be betrayed. There are many emotions which could be involved in deception, but three seem most intertwined with deceit – fear of being caught in the lie, guilt about lying, and delight in having duped someone (Ekman 1985/2001).

Fear of being caught
Low levels of fear may help a liar get away with his or her deceptions by maintaining the liar's alertness. In moderate and high levels, fear can produce behavioural signs that can be noticed by the skilled lie catcher (e.g. Frank and Ekman 1997; Ekman, *et al.* 1999; DePaulo *et al.* 2003). There are a number of factors that can influence fear of being caught – for example, if the lie catcher has a reputation for being tough to fool, the liar may feel more fear. If the liar has not had much practice at telling and getting away with the lie, then his or her fear of being caught would increase. Conversely, a lying witness who has been able to convince police investigators of his or her fictional account of a crime would gain confidence and would not feel as fearful of being caught (after all, he or she hasn't been caught yet). Likewise, this practice enables the liar to anticipate other possible questions, and thus further reduce the fear of getting caught. Finally,

besides the fear of being caught, a lying witness may show fear of punishment – that is, punishment for the act upon which the lie was designed to conceal. In other words, the stronger the punishments for the crime, for perjury or getting caught in general, the more fear a deceptive witness is likely to show (e.g. Frank and Ekman 1997).

Deception guilt
Deception guilt refers to a feeling about lying, and not the legal issue of whether someone is guilty or innocent. Deception guilt refers to the guilt felt when lying; for example, a witness may feel happiness at helping out a friend by claiming that the defendant threw the first punch, but later may feel guilty about lying. This situation can be reversed as well – he or she may feel guilt about helping out the friend, but feel no guilt about lying about it (or some can feel guilt for both, and some for neither). What is important is that it is not necessary to feel guilty about the content of a lie in order to feel guilty about lying. Like fear of being caught, deception guilt can vary in strength. For example, severe guilt can be a tortuous experience, undermining the sufferer's most fundamental feelings of self-worth (Ekman 1985/2001).

There are a number of factors which function to increase the amount of guilt a liar might feel. First, it seems that there are people who are particularly prone to guilt – for example, those who suffer from generalized anxiety disorders. These individuals often have very strict upbringings and have been severely punished for lying, or have been led to believe that lying is one of the most severe sins. Conversely, psychopaths – who have been reported to show no remorse or shame and an incapacity for love – may be much harder to detect than the average person due to their limited capacity to feel guilt (Hare 1970). Secondly, a close relationship between the liar and the target of the lie, such that they share values, respect each other and so forth, also functions to augment guilt feelings. Conversely, a liar who does not share values with the target would feel less guilt; and a witness who despises the legal system may not feel guilty about lying in court, much the same way in which a spy or terrorist feels no guilt about lying to a representative of an enemy government. Finally, if the target of the lie is impersonal or anonymous, then less deception guilt is generally felt. A witness who lies to a videotape camera or in an affidavit may feel less guilt than if he or she lied to an actual person. However, guilt often causes people to rationalize their deceits, so the witness may convince him or herself that the defendant had always been a troublemaker and deserved to be arrested, even though the defendant was not responsible for initiating the current altercation.

Duping delight

Lying can produce positive as well as negative emotions. The lie may be viewed as a proud accomplishment. Peter Sutcliffe, the man convicted of being the Yorkshire Ripper, expressed his delight whilst he was twice interrogated and then dismissed by the police before ultimately being caught. There are a number of factors that may cause an increase in duping delight – if the target is hard to fool, or if there is an audience who is aware of the deception and enjoying the performance. Thus, a lying witness may enjoy the fact that he or she is sitting in centre stage of the courtroom, in front of his or her friends, whilst he or she regales them with his or her bogus account of an assault.

It should be noted that these emotions can occur simultaneously or in any combination. For example, witnesses may feel guilt over producing a bogus account of the assault, or fear being caught perjuring themselves, as well as a certain delight in being able to pull off the lie in front of all these supposedly important legal professionals.

Cautions

It must be noted that these thinking and feeling clues are just that – clues that witnesses, defendants and victims are thinking, or clues that they are feeling or concealing some emotion. To date no one has been able to identify a human equivalent of a 'Pinocchio response' – that is, there is no one behavioural sign or constellation of signs that, across every person, in all situations, indicates that a person is lying. Thus, a lie catcher who identifies the behavioural clues described above must always infer why a witness would show guilt, or fear or delight, or why a witness would mull something over. This is why the concept of calling these incidents of emotional or cognitive leakage 'hotspots' rather than lies is the preferred notation in IIE. Someone who judges leaked emotions or cognitive efforts as a lie may be right, but may be wrong, as there can be other reasons why someone would feel fear or enjoyment besides lying. Someone who judges these same behaviours as hotspots will be much less likely to be wrong, and can use this evidence to gather even more evidence. Moreover, the interviewer who judges hotspot, rather than liar will be more likely to continue to ask questions and gather information, rather than succumb to the human tendency to assume if he or she caught the person lying that person must be guilty – and this premature conclusion can result in more haphazard and incomplete information collection from that point.

Conclusions about detecting deception

The IIE approach suggests the most effective way to detect deception from behaviour is to look for changes in baseline – an expressive person suddenly becomes much less expressive for a particular topic, but then becomes expressive again for different topics – and/or to note when the verbal and non-verbal information do not match – subtle or micro happiness when talking about a murder, or fear when talking about an innocuous topic like lunch, or even micro shrugging, which indicates uncertainty, when talking about something he or she claims he or she definitely did. The IIE approach trains investigators to recognize these changes in baseline – or times when the verbal and non-verbal behaviours are discrepant – and teaches investigators to understand thoroughly why the person is showing these hotspots. However, the IIE approach discourages investigators from making a judgment of 'lie' when he or she sees these changes or discrepant behaviours but, instead to make a judgment of hotspot. Given that there are no universal clues to deceit, an investigator who renders a judgment of 'lie' might be wrong; however, given the years of work on emotion and cognition, an investigator who instead renders a judgment of 'hot spot' will not be wrong. Moreover, a judgment of hotspot encourages the investigator to keep gathering information, whereas we have noted in the past that investigators who make a judgment of liar tend to slack off in their information gathering, because now they assume they have the right person – despite evidence that shows most people, including trained law enforcement officers, should exercise caution about their abilities to spot lies (Kraut and Poe 1980; DePaulo and Pfeifer 1986; Ekman and O'Sullivan 1991; Ekman *et al.* 1999).

The IIE approach recognizes that an oppressive, pressured push towards a confession does not generate the best information or make the strongest cases as they are put forward in a court of law. It recognizes the importance of uninterrupted accounts. It recognizes a careful consideration of the means of putting forth questions to the subjects and also recognizes the use of behavioural indicators to help generate areas of inquiry and to facilitate the vetting of such information. However, as stated earlier, it views these behavioural indicators and techniques to be a means towards helping the investigator gather information, and not as evidence in and of itself. The only way to know with 100 per cent certainty is to have unimpeachable corroborating evidence. That sort of evidence is only gained by a close examination of the physical evidence, and through a comparison of the stated account of the suspect/witness/informant to the physical evidence and other statements.

Epilogue

In 2005 the scientists (deception experts, Ekman, Frank and O'Sullivan, and memory and verbal statement expert, Yuille) and most of the law enforcement officers (Fretter, Harms and Yarbrough) formed a separate organization called 'Improving Interpersonal Evaluations for Law Enforcement and National Security', with the acronym IIE. The primary focus continues to be on interviewing and combining scientific knowledge with law enforcement experience. J.J. Newberry continues to direct the Institute of Analytic Interviewing, but without the participation of the individuals named above.

References

Anderson, A.K. and Phelps, E.A. (2000) 'Expression without recognition: contributions of the human amygdala to emotional communication', *Psychological Science*, 11: 106–11.

Bernieri, F.J., Gillis, J.S., Davis, J.M. and Grahe, J.E. (1996) 'Dyad rapport and the accuracy of its judgment across situations: a lens model analysis', *Journal of Personality and Social Psychology*, 71: 110–29.

Bernieri, F.J. and Rosenthal, R. (1991) 'Interpersonal coordination: behavior matching and interactional synchrony', in R.S. Feldman and B. Rime (eds) *Fundamentals of Nonverbal Behavior*. New York, NY: Cambridge University Press.

Blair, R.J.R., Morris, J.S., Frith, C.C., Perrett, D.I. and Dolan, R.J. (1999) 'Dissociable neural responses to facial expressions of sadness and anger', *Brain*, 122: 883–93.

Brodal, A. (1981) *Neurological Anatomy: In Relation to Clinical Medicine*. New York, NY: Oxford University Press.

Capella, J.N. (1981) 'Mutual influence in expressive behaviour: adult-adult and infant-adult dyadic interaction', *Psychological Bulletin*, 89: 101–32.

Charney, E.J. (1966) 'Postural configurations in psychotherapy', *Psychosomatic Medicine*, 28: 305–15.

Chartrand, T.L. and Bargh, J.A. (1999) 'The chameleon effect: The perception-behavior link and social interaction', *Journal of Personality and Social Psychology*, 76: 893–910.

Christensen, D., Farina, A. and Boudreau, L. (1980) 'Sensitivity to nonverbal cues as a function of social competence', *Journal of Nonverbal Behavior*, 4: 146–56.

Collins, R., Lincoln, R. and Frank, M.G. (2002) 'The effect of rapport in forensic interviewing', *Psychiatry, Psychology, and Law*, 9: 69–78.

Darwin, C. (1872/1998) *The Expression of the Emotions in Man and Animals*. New York, NY: Oxford University Press (3rd edn, with commentaries by Paul Ekman).

Davidson, R.J. (1984) 'Affect, cognition and hemispheric specialization', in C.E. Izard *et al.* (eds) *Emotion, Cognition, and Behavior*. New York, NY: Cambridge University Press.

Davidson, R.J. (1992) 'Emotion and affective style: hemispheric substrates', *Psychological Science*, 3: 39–43.

Davidson, R.J., Ekman, P., Saron, C., Senulius, J. and Friesen, W.V. (1990) 'Approach-withdrawal and cerebral asymmetry: emotional expression and brain physiology I', *Journal of Personality and Social Psychology*, 58: 330–41.

Davidson, R.J. and Tomarken, A.J. (1989) 'Laterality and emotion: an electrophysiological approach', in F. Boller and J. Grafman (eds) *Handbook of Neuropsychology*. Amsterdam: Elsevier.

DeMyer, W. (1980) *Technique of the Neurological Examination*. New York, NY: McGraw-Hill.

DePaulo, B.M., Lindsay, J.J., Malone, B.E., Muhlenbruck, L., Charlton, K. and Cooper, H. (2003) 'Cues to deception', *Psychological Bulletin*, 129: 74–112.

DePaulo, B.M. and Pfeifer, R.L. (1986) 'On-the-job experience and skill at detecting deception', *Journal of Applied Social Psychology*, 16: 249–67.

DePaulo, B.M., Stone, J. and Lassiter, D. (1985) 'Deceiving and detecting deceit', in B.R. Schlenker (ed.) *The Self and Social life*. New York, NY: McGraw-Hill.

Dwyer, J., Neufeld, P. and Scheck, B. (2000) *Actual Innocence: Five Days to Execution and Other Dispatches from the Wrongly Convicted*. New York, NY: Doubleday.

Eibl-Eibesfeldt, I. (1973) 'The expressive behavior of the deaf-and-blind born', in M. von Cranach and I. Vine (eds) *Social Communication and Movement*. San Diego, CA: Academic Press.

Ekman, P. (1972) 'Universal and cultural differences in facial expressions of emotion', in J.K. Cole (ed.) *Nebraska symposium on Motivation 1971*. Lincoln, NE: University of Nebraska Press.

Ekman, P. (1977) 'Biological and cultural contributions to body and facial movement', in J. Blacking (ed.) *Anthropology of the Body*. London: Academic Press.

Ekman, P. (1979) 'About brows: emotional and conversational signals', in M. von Cranach *et al.* (eds) *Human Ethology*. Cambridge: Cambridge University Press.

Ekman, P. (1992) 'Facial expressions of emotion: new findings, new questions', *Psychological Science*, 3: 34–8.

Ekman, P. (1994) 'Strong evidence for universals in facial expressions: a reply to Russell's mistaken critique', *Psychological Bulletin*, 115: 268–87.

Ekman, P. (1985/2001) *Telling Lies*. New York, NY: Norton.

Ekman, P. (2003) *Emotions Revealed*. New York, NY: Henry Holt.

Ekman, P. (2005) 'Enhancing the communication of emotions – the amplifier', *Media Psychology Division of American Psychological Association*, Winter: 11.

Ekman, P. and Davidson, R.J. (1993) 'Voluntary smiling changes regional brain activity', *Psychological Science*, 4: 342–5.

Ekman, P. and Frank, M.G. (1993) 'Lies that fail', in C. Saarni and M. Lewis (eds) *Lying and Deception in Everyday Life*. New York, NY: Guilford.

Ekman, P. and Friesen, W.V. (1969) 'Nonverbal leakage and clues to deception', *Psychiatry*, 32: 88–105.

Ekman, P. and Friesen, W.V. (1971) 'Constants across cultures in the face and emotion', *Journal of Personality and Social Psychology*, 17: 124–9.

Ekman, P. and Friesen W.V. (1972) 'Hand movements', *Journal of Communication*, 22: 353–74.

Ekman, P. and Friesen, W.V. (1974) 'Detecting deception from the body or face', *Journal of Personality and Social Psychology*, 29: 288–98.

Ekman, P. and Friesen, W.V. (1978) *The Facial Action Coding System*. Palo Alto, CA: Consulting Psychologists Press.

Ekman, P. and Friesen, W.V. (1982) 'Felt, false, and miserable smiles', *Journal of Nonverbal Behavior*, 6: 238–52.

Ekman, P., Friesen, W.V. and Ancoli, S. (1980) 'Facial signs of emotional experience', *Journal of Personality and Social Psychology*, 39: 1125–34.

Ekman, P., Friesen, W.V. and O'Sullivan, M. (1988) 'Smiles when lying', *Journal of Personality and Social Psychology*, 54: 414–20.

Ekman, P., Friesen, W.V. and Scherer, K. (1976) 'Body movement and voice pitch in deceptive interaction', *Semiotica*, 16: 23–7.

Ekman, P., Levenson, R.W. and Friesen, W.V. (1983) 'Autonomic nervous system activity distinguishes between emotions', *Science*, 221: 1208–10.

Ekman, P. and O'Sullivan, M. (1991) 'Who can catch a liar?', *American Psychologist*, 46: 913–20.

Ekman, P., O'Sullivan, M. and Frank, M.G. (1999) 'A few can catch a liar', *Psychological Science*, 10: 263–66.

Ekman, P., O'Sullivan, M., Friesen, W.V. and Scherer, K. (1991) 'Invited article: face, voice, and body in detecting deceit', *Journal of Nonverbal Behavior*, 15: 125–35.

Frank, M.G. (2003) 'Getting to know your patient: how facial expression reveals true emotion', in M. Katsikitis (ed.) *The Clinical Application of Facial Measurement: Methods and Meaning*. Dordrecht: Kluwer.

Frank, M.G. (2005) *Decoding Deception and Emotion by Australians and Americans*. Manuscript under review.

Frank, M.G. and Ekman, P. (1993) 'Not all smiles are created equal: the differences between enjoyment and nonenjoyment smiles', *Humor: The International Journal of Research in Humor*, 6: 9–26.

Frank, M.G. and Ekman, P. (1997) 'The ability to detect deceit generalizes across different types of high stake lies', *Journal of Personality and Social Psychology*, 72: 1429–39.

Frank, M.G. and Ekman, P. (2004a) 'Nonverbal detection of deception in forensic contexts', in W. O'Donohue and E. Levensky (eds) *Handbook of Forensic Psychology*. New York, NY: Elsevier.

Frank, M.G. and Ekman, P. (2004b) 'Appearing truthful generalizes across different deception situations', *Journal of Personality and Social Psychology*, 86: 486–95.

Frank, M.G. and Ekman, P. (2005) *Counter-terrorism Paradigm and Deception*. Manuscript in preparation.

Frank, M.G., Ekman, P. and Friesen, W.V. (1993) 'Behavioral markers and recognizability of the smile of enjoyment', *Journal of Personality and Social Psychology*, 64: 83–93.

Frijda, N. (1986) *The Emotions*. Cambridge: Cambridge University Press.

Geiselman, R.E., Fisher, R.P., MacKinnon, D.P. and Holland, H.L. (1986) 'Enhancement of eyewitness memory with the cognitive interview', *American Journal of Psychology*, 99: 385–401.

Hare, R.D. (1970) *Psychopathy: Theory and Research*. New York, NY: Wiley.

Haugaard, J.J. and Repucci, N.D. (1992) 'Children and the truth', in S.J. Ceci *et al.* (eds) *Cognitive and Social Factors in Early Deception*. Hillsdale, NJ: Erlbaum.

Hocking, J.E. and Leathers, D.G. (1980) 'Nonverbal indicators of deception: a new theoretical perspective', *Communication Monographs*, 47: 119–31.

Inbau, F.E., Reid, J.E. and Buckley, J.P. (1986) *Criminal Interrogation and Confessions*. Baltimore, MD: Williams & Wilkins.

Izard, C.E. (1971) *The Face of Emotion*. New York, NY: Appleton-Century Crofts.

Izard, C.E. (1977) *Human Emotions*. New York, NY: Plenum Press.

Izard, C.E. (1994) 'Innate and universal facial expressions: evidence from developmental and cross-cultural research', *Psychological Bulletin*, 115. 288–99.

Karnosh, L.J. (1945) 'Amimia or emotional paralysis of the face', *Diseases of the Nervous System*, 6: 106–8.

Kraut, R.E. and Poe, D. (1980) 'Behavioral roots of person perception: the deception judgments of customs inspectors and laymen', *Journal of Personality and Social Psychology*, 39: 784–98.

LaFrance, M. (1979) 'Non-verbal synchrony and rapport: analysis by the cross-lagged panel technique', *Social Psychology Quarterly*, 42: 66–70.

LaFrance, M. (1985) 'Postural mirroring and intergroup relations', *Personality and Social Psychology Bulletin*, 11: 207–17.

LaFrance, M. and Broadbent, M. (1976) 'Group rapport: posture sharing as a non-verbal indicator', *Group and Organizational Studies*, 1: 328–33.

Levenson, R.W., Carstensen, L.L., Friesen, W.V. and Ekman, P. (1991) 'Emotion, physiology, and expression in old age', *Psychology and Aging*, 6: 28–35.

Levenson, R.W., Ekman, P. and Friesen, W.V. (1990) 'Voluntary facial action generates emotion-specific autonomic nervous system activity', *Psychophysiology*, 27: 363–84.

Levenson, R.W., Ekman, P., Heider, K. and Friesen, W.V. (1992) 'Emotion and autonomic nervous system activity in the Minangkabau of West Sumatra', *Journal of Personality and Social Psychology*, 62: 972–88.

Meihlke, A. (1973) *Surgery of the Facial Nerve.* Philadelphia, PA: Saunders.

Moore, M.M. (1985) 'Nonverbal courtship patterns in women: content and consequences', *Ethology and Sociobiology*, 6: 237–47.

Morris, J.S., Frith, C.D., Perrett, D.I., Rowland, D., Young, A.W., Calder, A.J. and Dolan, R.J. (1996) 'A differential neural response in the human amygdala to fearful and happy facial expressions', *Nature*, 383: 812–15.

Myers, R.E. (1976) 'Comparative neurology of vocalization and speech: proof of a dichotomy', *Annual Review of the New York Academy of Sciences*, 280: 745–57.

Newberry, J.J. (1999) *The Analytic Interview Manual.* Unpublished manual.

O'Sullivan, M. (2005) 'Emotional intelligence and deception detection: why most people can't "read" others, but a few can', in R.E. Riggio and R.S. Feldman (eds) *Applications of Nonverbal Communication.* Mahwah, NJ: Lawrence Erlbaum Associates.

Phillips, M.L., Young, A.W., Senior, C., Brammer, M., Andrew, C., Calder, A.J., Bullmore, E.T., Perrett, D.I., Rowland, D., Williams, S.C.R., Gray, J.A. and David, A.S. (1997) 'A specific neural substrate for perceiving facial expressions of disgust', *Nature*, 389: 495–8.

Plutchik, R. (1962) *The Emotions: Facts, Theories, and a New Model.* New York, NY: Random House.

Porter, S. and Yuille, J.C. (1995) 'Credibility assessment of criminal suspects through statement analysis', *Psychology, Crime and Law*, 1: 319–31.

Porter, S. and Yuille, J.C. (1996) 'The language of deceit: an investigation of the verbal clues in the interrogation context', *Law and Human Behavior*, 20: 443–58.

Rinn, W.E. (1984) 'The neuropsychology of facial expression: a review of the neurological and psychological mechanisms for producing facial expressions', *Psychological Bulletin*, 95: 52–77.

Scherer, K. (1984) 'On the nature and function of emotions: a component process approach', in K. Scherer and P. Ekman (eds) *Approaches to Emotion.* Hillsdale, NJ: Erlbaum.

Scherer, K.R. and Walbott, H.G. (1994) 'Evidence for universality and cultural variation of differential emotion response patterning', *Journal of Personality and Social Psychology*, 66: 310–28.

Stiff, J.B. and Miller, G.R. (1986) '"Come to think of it ...": interrogative probes, deceptive communication, and deception detection', *Human Communication Research*, 12: 339–57.

Tajfel, H. (1978) *Differentiation between Social Groups: Studies in the Social Psychology of Intergroup Relations.* Oxford: Academic Press.

Tickle-Degnen, L. and Rosenthal, R. (1990) 'The nature of rapport and its nonverbal correlates', *Psychological Inquiry*, 1: 285–93.

Tomkins, S.S. (1962) *Affect, Imagery, Consciousness* (Vol. 1, *The Positive Affects*). New York, NY: Springer.

Tomkins, S.S. (1963) *Affect, Imagery, Consciousness* (Vol. 2, *The Negative Affects*). New York, NY: Springer.

Trout, D.L. and Rosenfeld, H.M. (1980) 'The effect of posture lean and body congruence on the judgment of psychotherapeutic rapport', *Journal of Nonverbal Behavior*, 4: 176–90.

Tschiassny, K. (1953) 'Eight syndromes of facial paralysis and their significance in locating the lesion', *Annual Review of Otology, Rhinology, and Laryngology*, 62: 677–91.

Webb, N.C. (1974) 'The use of myoelectric feedback in teaching facial expression to the blind', *American Foundation for the BlindResearch Bulletin*, 27: 231–62.

Whalen, P.J., Rauch, S.L., Etcoff, N.L., McInerney, S.C., Lee, M.B. and Jenike, M.A. (1998) 'Masked presentations of emotional facial expressions modulate amygdala activity without explicit knowledge', *The Journal of Neuroscience*, 18: 411–18.

Yuille, J.C. (1989) *Credibility Assessment.* New York, NY: Kluwer Academic/ Plenum Publishers.

Yuille, J.C. and Porter, S. (2000) 'Deception', in A.E. Kazdin (ed.) *Encyclopedia of Psychology. Vol. 2.* London: American Psychological Association, Oxford University Press.

255

Part 3

Developments in Regulation

Chapter 13

Recovered memories

James Ost

When she was 27, Alice, a successful businesswoman, embarked upon a course of hypnotherapy to help her overcome an eating disorder. The hypnotherapist told her, 'you will start to remember things – things that you won't want to remember but they still come flooding back'. After six or seven sessions of hypnotherapy, Alice indeed began to recover memories of being sexually abused by her uncle sixteen years previously. Whilst Alice claimed to have always been aware that something was not right in her life, she also claimed that, prior to the hypnotherapy, she had had no memory of any episodes of abuse (Ost 2000).

The memory wars

In the last decade and a half psychologists were involved in the 'memory wars', one of the most contentious debates to date – contentious enough that Pezdek and Banks refer to it as close to a 'religious war' (1996: xii; see also Brown *et al.* 2000; Ost 2003). The question that has caused such a divide in professional opinion concerns the extent to which memories, such as those 'recovered' by Alice, reflect events that actually occurred. Partly due to the uncertainties surrounding cases like these, the statutes of limitations, previously barring such cases from being tried in court, were lifted in many states in America (although there are no time restrictions to bringing such charges under UK law). These changes enabled individuals like Alice to sue, or bring criminal charges against, their parents (or other alleged abusers) where the only evidence was previously 'repressed' or 'dissociated' memories of childhood abuse that individual had allegedly 'recovered' in adulthood (Underwager and Wakefield 1998). One problem with allowing such testimony is that there is, in fact, no reliable evidence that individuals 'repress' or 'dissociate' memories of traumatic events (although they may choose not to *report* such events; see McNally 2003; cf. Brown *et al.* 1998). A further problem is that, as we shall see in this chapter, research has shown that it is possible for people to come to report compelling and vivid 'memories' of events that never occurred (Hyman *et al.* 1995; Loftus and Pickrell 1995; Pezdek *et al.* 1997; Porter *et al.* 1999; Ost *et al.* in press). This raises the serious possibility that at least some of these 'recovered memories' might, in fact, be iatrogenic productions of the therapeutic process itself (hence the term 'false memories').

Indeed, there have been a number of high-profile malpractice cases in the USA where patients have taken legal action against their former therapists, accusing them of implanting 'false' memories of abuse, sometimes winning considerable damage settlements (see Loftus 1997). Furthermore, in one case an accused father was allowed, as a third party, to bring malpractice charges against his daughter's former therapist and was awarded $500,000 in damages (see Johnston 1997). In a recent case in the UK, the General Medical Council (GMC) disciplined a general practitioner for using inappropriate questions and suggestions to lead a 13-year-old patient to believe falsely that she had been sexually assaulted (Catchpole 2003). These, and other cases like them, highlight the importance of raising awareness amongst practitioners and policy-makers of the issues surrounding such cases in order that potential miscarriages of justice are avoided and that genuine victims of abuse receive the support they need. However, the issues are far from straightforward.

One concern is that claims of childhood abuse are sometimes made following, or during, an individual's participation in so-called 'recovered memory therapy'. Recovered memory therapy, although a contentious term to some, is a blanket term covering any therapeutic treatment in which the prime goal is to uncover repressed, dissociated or otherwise unavailable 'memories' of trauma, in order to resolve present-day psychological problems (Lindsay and Read 1994, 2001). Professional opinion, however, is sharply divided over the risks associated with such therapy. On the one hand there are researchers who claim that certain traumatic experiences are permanently stored in one form or another, that it is possible to revive 'memories' of these long-forgotten events and that such 'memories' are generally accurate (see Brown *et al.* 1998; Cameron 1996; Freyd 1998; Salter 1998). If this argument is wrong then families can be torn apart, individuals falsely branded as paedophiles and, sometimes, wrongly incarcerated (see Pendergrast 1996) on the basis of such 'recovered memories'. On the other hand are researchers who claim that some of these 'recovered memories' arose as a result of inappropriate and highly suggestive therapeutic techniques (Brandon *et al.* 1997; Hyman and Loftus 1997; Tsai *et al.* 2000; Lindsay and Read 1994, 2001; Lynn *et al.* 2003; see also Hyman 2000). But if this claim is wrong the results are equally as tragic, not only in individual cases, but also at a wider level. As Conway (1997) states, one serious concern is that genuine victims of childhood sexual assault will be less willing to come forward if there is a risk that their testimony may be dismissed as a case of 'false memory'. Despite the polarized nature of the debate there is some evidence that a 'middle ground' is emerging (Read 1999; Shobe and Schooler 2001; Ost 2003) with researchers on both sides acknowledging the possibility that some long-delayed claims of childhood abuse are genuine, whilst some are not. Whilst it is unethical to test the specific claim that participants can be led falsely to report that they were victims of abuse, a number of laboratory methods have been developed to examine how, and under what circumstances, people might come falsely to report other, sometimes traumatic, events from their past. The purpose of this chapter is to review critically 1) laboratory studies that have examined how people can come to report 'memories' of childhood events that did not occur; 2) the effect of certain 'memory recovery' techniques on the accuracy of memory reports; and 3) the possible effects of support groups on remembering. We will see that, although much research is still required, the available evidence clearly shows that it is possible, under certain circumstances, for people to come to report falsely that they remember entire events that did not occur, or that they did not experience.

Three main 'false memory' methods

There are three main methods that psychologists have used to examine the circumstances under which individuals might come to report events, or details of events, that they did not experience: 1) the DRM method; 2) the misinformation method; and 3) the parental misinformation method. As will be seen, there are strengths and weaknesses with each method. For example, whilst the parental misinformation method appears to be directly measuring the likelihood that an individual will report an entire *memory* of an event he or she did not experience, the DRM method examines the likelihood that an individual will falsely recognize a lure as being part of a previously presented list of semantically related items. This means that these methods do not speak equally to the question of whether an individual can come to report that he or she remembers an entirely false, autobiographical, emotionally charged childhood event (see Smeets *et al.* in press). There is also a further problematic distinction concerning whether these methods are tapping into, or changing, *memories* of past events, *beliefs* about past events, *confidence* about whether a past event occurred or not, or simply *reports* about past events (Smeets *et al.* in press; see also Ost 2003; Loftus and Bernstein 2005). Furthermore, whilst it has been argued that a false *belief* is an important (and necessary) precursor to developing a false *memory* (Gudjonnson 2003), it does not follow that a false belief will always *lead* to a false memory (Ost 2003). Therefore some caution is warranted in interpreting these findings as a whole. Nevertheless, all three methods are widely cited in the literature as providing evidence that 'false memories' can occur. With these important caveats in mind, each method will now be critically examined.

The DRM method

Roediger and McDermott (1995) adapted a method previously developed by Deese (1959; referred to as the DRM method). In a typical study, participants are asked to remember a list of words, such as mad, fear, hate, rage, temper, fury, ire, wrath, happy, fight, hatred, mean, calm, emotion, enrage. Some time later, participants are recalled for a 'surprise' memory test and are asked to indicate whether the word 'anger' was contained in the original list. Many of them frequently report remembering the critical non-presented word (e.g. 'anger') as having been present in the original list. Several studies have successfully replicated this effect, with various different experimental manipulations (see, for example Gallo *et al.* 1997; Brainerd and Reyna 1998; Smith and Hunt 1998). Roediger and McDermott (1995: 803) claim that the results of these studies 'reveal a powerful illusion of memory: People remember events that never happened'.

There also appear to be individual differences that leave certain participants more likely to succumb to the DRM effect. For example

Winograd *et al.* (1998) found that participants who scored more highly on measures of dissociation (high scorers on this measure have a tendency to experience problems in the integration of thoughts and feelings) and vividness of mental imagery (high scorers report having more vivid imaginative abilities) were more likely to claim to remember the critical non-presented words. However, as Freyd and Gleaves (1996) note, there are important differences between misremembering words that have not been presented in a list and misremembering an otherwise happy childhood as being abusive. Similarly, Wilkinson and Hyman (1998) demonstrated that, in laboratory experiments, there are important differences between participants' performance on word-list tasks and their performance on autobiographical memory tasks. They found that self-reported dissociative tendencies were related to errors on both the word list and autobiographical memory, but that self-reported vividness of mental imagery was only related to errors on the word-list (DRM) task. Wilkinson and Hyman (1998) argue that this is because remembering words and remembering autobiographical events rely on different underlying psychological processes. They argue that it is therefore unwise to assume that participants who are susceptible to the DRM are also more vulnerable to developing false autobiographical memories.

The misinformation method

The second method that psychologists have used examines whether subtle changes in the way in which questions are asked about an event can change what participants subsequently claim to remember about that event. The classic studies of the misinformation effect, conducted by Loftus and colleagues, examined whether misleading post-event information could alter eyewitness' memories of events they had recently witnessed (Loftus 1979). In two studies by Loftus and Palmer (1974), participants were shown a film of an accident involving two cars. Participants were then questioned to find out how much they could remember about the event. Loftus and Palmer found that the question 'About how fast were the cars going when they *smashed* into each other?' elicited higher estimates of speed than questions in which the verbs *collided, bumped, contacted* or *hit* were used (see also Loftus *et al.* 1978). This is a robust and easily replicated effect although there are still disagreements as to the mechanisms that cause the misinformation effect (e.g. Bekerian and Bowers 1983; McCloskey and Zaragoza 1985; Zaragoza *et al.* 1987; Weingardt *et al.* 1995). Nevertheless it seems that subtle changes in wording can lead participants to report non-existent *details* of events that they have experienced (see also Nourkova *et al.* 2004).

In a novel twist on the misinformation method, Crombag *et al.* (1996) asked participants whether they remembered seeing a film of a plane crashing into a block of flats in Amsterdam. No film of the crash existed so we can be sure that any participants who claimed to have seen it must be mistaken. Nevertheless, 55–66 per cent of the respondents to Crombag *et al.*'s questionnaire claimed to have seen such a film. Participants were so convinced that they had seen the film that they were willing to give details such as the angle at which the airplane hit the buildings, how long before fire broke out and how long it was before the emergency services arrived. Crombag *et al.* (1996) suggest that perhaps the vivid and emotionally charged nature of the event led people to think about the event, picture it in their heads and then subsequently come to misremember the resulting imaginations as if they were real memories. This is referred to as a 'source monitoring' error and occurs when we misremember the source of information (Johnson *et al.* 1993).

Ost *et al.* (2002b) replicated this effect using a different event – the car crash in Paris in which Diana, Princess of Wales, Dodi Fayed and their driver were killed. Whilst no film of the actual event exists, there had been reports in the press that Diana's car was being pursued on motorbikes by paparazzi that were allegedly filming the chase. Ost *et al.* (2002b) therefore asked participants whether they had seen the paparazzis' video recording of the moment of the crash on television. Whilst it has never been established whether indeed such a film exists, it has certainly never been shown on television. Nevertheless, 44 per cent of Ost *et al.*'s participants claimed to have seen it. Furthermore, many participants even went as far as to say on which television channel they had seen the film. Ost *et al.* found that participants who scored higher on a measure of 'eagerness to please' (the self-monitoring scale; Snyder 1974) were more like to claim to have seen the film than participants who scored lower on this measure (for more recent examples see Jelicic *et al.* 2005; Wilson and French, submitted).

In a replication of the Crombag *et al.* study, Granhag *et al.* (2003) asked participants whether they had seen a (non-existent) film of the sinking of the *Estonia* ferry. Again they found that 52 per cent of their participants claimed to have seen the film. They also had a confederate present when the participants completed the questionnaire who either claimed to have seen the non-existent film or claimed not to have seen it. Granhag *et al.* found that participants either increased or decreased their levels of false reporting in line with the social influence exerted by the confederate. We will discuss their study, and a recent replication (Ost *et al*. 2004) in more detail in the section on the effects of support groups below.

Parental misinformation method

The studies mentioned above show that some individuals will, when misled by subtle changes in wording, or by a confederate, come to report that they remember events (or details of events) that they did not witness. However, they are limited in generalizability when applied to cases of allegedly false or recovered memory of childhood events. The events in the Crombag *et al*., Ost *et al*. and Granhag *et al*. studies were all relatively recent, and had occurred whilst the participants in their studies were adults. In contrast most delayed claims of childhood abuse concern events that, by definition, occurred many years beforehand (see Pendergrast 1996). Can individuals be misled to report false events from their childhood?

Loftus and Coan (cited in Loftus and Pickrell 1995) describe a study in which a 14-year-old boy (Chris) was asked to recall details over five days regarding four events involving family members. One of the events was false and three of them were true (as verified by the family). Chris was interviewed in the presence of a sibling (who was a confederate of the investigators) about these events. The sibling provided verbal corroboration that all the events (including the false event) had taken place. Over time Chris began to report more about the four events, even rating the false event (becoming lost in a shopping mall as a child) as more likely to have occurred than all but one of the three true events.

Loftus and Pickrell (1995) replicated this effect with a larger sample of undergraduate students. In this study participants were asked to complete a booklet concerning four events, the third of which was false (becoming lost in a shopping mall). Parents, who confirmed that their child had never become lost in a shopping mall as a child, also provided details of the real events. Participants were interviewed three times over three weeks and also asked, between interviews, to write down in their booklets anything that came to mind about the events. Loftus and Pickrell (1995) found that after three weeks, 6 out of 24 participants (25 per cent) erroneously believed *part or all* of the false event. However, as Pezdek *et al*. (1997) argue, becoming lost in a shopping mall is a fairly common event that many people would have a 'script' (or 'schema') for such an event around which they could construct a convincing narrative. Therefore it would be relatively easy for an individual to create a convincing report of an event like this.[1] Pezdek et al. (1997) argue that an event that is lower in plausibility, and for which we are less likely to have 'script-relevant' knowledge (such as childhood sexual abuse), is less likely to be implanted (although see Scoboria et al. 2004).

Hyman et al. (1995) therefore attempted to suggest to their participants that they had experienced more unusual events. Following the methodology devised by Loftus and Pickrell (1995), they asked their participants to try to remember three events (two of which had occurred and one of which had not). Hyman et al. (1995) conducted two studies in which they suggested that their participants had experienced one of the following false events when they were children:

- An overnight hospitalization with a possible ear infection (study 1).
- A birthday party with a visit by a clown and pizza (study 1).
- Spilling a punch bowl at a wedding (study 2).
- Evacuating a grocery store when the sprinklers went off (study 2).
- Releasing the handbrake of a car in a parking lot and hitting something (study 2).

Their participants were interviewed three times over a three-week period and after each interview participants were asked to think about the events and to try to remember more details before the next session. By the third and final interview 89–95 per cent of the 'real' events were recalled along with 25 per cent of the 'false' events (see also Hyman and Loftus 1997). This demonstrates that participants can be misled to report more unusual events from their childhood. However, critics argue that having a false memory of spilling a punchbowl at a wedding does not compare to having a memory of being abused as a child, as the latter is a much more negative, traumatic and emotionally charged event. Nevertheless one study has examined whether it is possible to mislead adult participants to report that they falsely remember negative, traumatic and emotionally charged events from their childhood.

Porter et al. (1999), using a similar methodology to Loftus and Pickrell (1995) and Hyman et al. (1995), suggested to participants that they had experienced serious negative events as children, such as:

- a serious medical procedure;
- getting lost;

- getting seriously harmed by another child; and
- a serious animal attack.

Porter *et al.* also verbally encouraged their participants to remember the events ('most people are able to retrieve lost memories if they try hard enough'; Porter *et al.* 1999: 522), as well as asking them to think about this for five minutes every night between interviews. By the third and final interview, Porter *et al.* (1999) found that 54 per cent of participants reported a 'full', or 'partial', false memory.[2] Taken together these studies indicate that, when misled by information provided by siblings or parents, participants will report that they remember unusual, negative, emotionally charged and traumatic childhood events.

In all the studies above some kind of verbal instructions were used to encourage participants to try to remember the events (the only exception to this is Hyman *et al.* 1995, experiment 1). However, it is unclear the extent to which, in the case of false reports of childhood events, the behaviour of the interviewer influenced the manner of recall. For example, Loftus and Pickrell (1995: 722) noted that 'the interviewers maintained a pleasant and friendly manner whilst pressing for details'. In order to explore the possible role of social pressure in the development of false memories, Ost *et al.* (in press) followed a similar methodology to these previous studies but trained their interviewers to interview in an appropriate and non-pressuring manner. Participants were asked about both positive and negative false events, similar to those used in previous studies, for example:

- becoming lost;
- a trip to the hospital;
- a serious accident;
- an eventful birthday party; and
- winning a contest.

Levels of social pressure in the interviews were monitored both by the participants (who were asked to rate, amongst other details, how pressured they felt) and by independent judges (who rated videotapes of the interviews). Overall levels of social pressure reported by both participants and independent judges were low. Despite the low levels of social pressure, Ost *et al.* (in press) found that 7 out of 31 participants produced a 'full' or 'partial' report of a childhood event that did not occur. This study suggests that even minimal social pressure and repeated interviewing are sufficient to lead some individuals to come to report events from their childhood that never occurred.

Limitations of parental misinformation studies

There are, however, several criticisms of the above studies that limit their generalizability to cases of delayed reports of childhood trauma. As already noted, Pezdek *et al.* (1997) argue that most of the false events that participants are asked to recall are events for which participants are likely to have a 'script'. An event that is lower in plausibility, and for which participants are less likely to have 'script-relevant' knowledge (such as childhood sexual abuse), is less likely to be falsely reported.

Pezdek *et al.* (1997) tested this hypothesis by suggesting to Jewish and Catholic participants that they had taken part in both a Catholic ritual (receiving Communion) and a Jewish ritual (Shabbot), neither of which had actually occurred. Pezdek *et al.* (1997) argue that the plausibility of having taken part in a Catholic ritual would be low for Jewish participants, that they would have less script-relevant knowledge to draw upon and vice versa. They found, in line with their predictions, that seven of the Catholic participants but none of the Jewish participants reported the false Catholic event and three Jewish participants and one Catholic participant reported the Jewish false event. This shows that participants were more likely to remember the plausible false event than the implausible false event (i.e. Jewish participants were more likely to remember the false Jewish ritual than the false Catholic ritual). In a second experiment, Pezdek *et al.* (1997) replicated the study by Loftus and Pickrell (1995) and extended it by suggesting to participants that they had 1) been lost in a shopping mall (a plausible event); and 2) that they had received an enema as a child (an implausible event). Again, all events were suggested as having occurred by a close relative or sibling who confirmed that no events of this kind had ever occurred to the participants. Pezdek *et al.* (1997) found that whilst 3 out of 20 participants falsely reported becoming lost in a shopping mall, none of the participants falsely reported receiving an enema. These experiments therefore suggest that the probability that participants can be misled to report false events from their childhood is likely to be a function of the plausibility of, or familiarity with, the event concerned (although see Scoboria *et al.* 2004 for a discussion of the differences between plausibility and script-consistency).

However, certain 'scripts' are more familiar in western culture than might at first be imagined. Lynn and Pezzo (1994; cited in Lynn and Kirsch 1996) found that participants were able to construct very convincing narratives of having been abducted by aliens, even when given relatively little warning or further information. Lynn and Kirsch (1996) argue that narratives of alien abduction are so common in western culture that individuals are likely to have access to 'script-relevant' knowledge (see also Arndt and Greenberg 1996). Given the large number of self-help books, media programmes, news articles and the like dealing with abuse, it is not inconceivable that some individuals could construct a narrative of having been abused.

A second limitation of the parental misinformation studies is that they rely on parents or siblings to verify that certain events did, or did not, occur to participants when they were children. This may be unwise. Whilst it is probable that parents will be able to remember events in the lives of their young children with more confidence than the children themselves (see Ost et al. in press), this in itself is no guarantee that they will remember them with great accuracy (Conte 1999). Indeed, in the study by Ost et al. (in press), a few participants stated outright that their parents must have misremembered events, or confused the participant with another sibling. Indeed there is literature to suggest that parents are not the best at remembering events from their children's past (Wenar 1961; Wenar and Coulter 1962; see also Halverson 1988). The problem, then, is that there is no way of knowing the 'ground truth' (i.e. whether indeed an event did, or did not, occur) with any great certainty.

A third, often-cited, limitation with parental misinformation studies is that the events participants are misled to report are not of an abusive or traumatic nature. However, the study by Porter et al. (1999) showed that participants could be misled to report negatively charged and traumatic events (such as being victim to a serious animal attack). Although untestable in the laboratory, the possibility remains that participants in situations other than a psychology experiment could be misled to report abusive events that did not occur (see also Hyman and Loftus 1997). In fact evidence from retractors (individuals who have repudiated their earlier claims of abuse) suggests that this does occur (see de Rivera 1998; Ost et al. 2001, 2002a). Retractors are individuals who have made claims of childhood abuse, only later to claim that those events did not, in fact, occur (hence the term 'retractors'). Studies have shown that these individuals developed what they now believe to have been false beliefs about having been abused as a child, sometimes becoming so convinced of the truth of their false beliefs that they initiated legal proceedings against their alleged abusers (de Rivera 1998; Ost *et al.* 2001, 2002a). Worryingly, retractors reported that they experienced levels of social pressure, and inappropriate questioning techniques, not dissimilar to those that can lead to false confessions in police interrogations (Wrightsman and Kassin 1993; Kassin 1997, 2005; Ost, *et al.* 2001; Gudjonnsson 2003).

A fourth limitation with parental misinformation studies is that it is not clear what degree of social pressure is required in order to lead participants to make false claims about the past (Ost *et al.* in press). For example, Loftus and Pickrell (1995: 722) note that their interviewer 'maintained a pleasant and friendly manner, whilst pressing for details' yet do not provide details of how participants were 'pressed for details'. Porter *et al.* (1999) state that they employed a degree of verbal encouragement ('most people can remember details if they try really hard'; 522) but the specific effects of this part of their methodology are not clear. Malinoski and Lynn (1999) found that positive verbal encouragement led participants to report earlier (and more implausible) memories. Ost *et al.* (in press) found that, even when social pressure was kept to a minimum (by appropriately training interviewers not to pressure participants), a number of participants still came to report false events from their childhood (see also Erdmann *et al.* 2004 for similar findings with child witnesses). The role of social pressure in the genesis and development of false reports of childhood events is an important avenue for future research (Ost *et al.* 2001 in press).

A final limitation with the parental misinformation studies concerns the complexity of the experimental set-up that is required:

> Loftus's research paradigm has little if any applicability to a typical psychotherapy encounter ... the story of an indexed event ... is deliberately planted in scripted detail by a trusted family member. The clinical parallel would require not the naive, inadequately trained, and overzealous therapist suggested by Loftus and others, but rather a highly skilled and malevolent practitioner who is capable of deliberately planting a highly detailed, wholly inaccurate, scripted tale in the suggestible mind of an exceedingly trusting patient (Harvey 1999: 23).

Whilst the limits to generalizability are well noted there are also a number of similarities between the experimental and therapeutic contexts that mean some conclusions can be drawn (Hyman and Loftus 1997; Bekerian and O'Neill 2001; see also Ost 2003). For example, in both cases there are strong social demands to remember, either from a participant's motivation to be a good experimental participant (see Ost *et al*. 2002a), or from a client's motivation to get better from whatever current problems he or she is suffering.

In addition to the social demands to remember in both the experimental and therapeutic contexts, therapists sometimes suggest that certain techniques might help individuals to 'recover' memories of childhood sexual abuse (referred to by Lindsay and Read 1994 as memory recovery therapy, or MRT). Examples of such techniques are: hypnosis; guided imagery; the use of family photographs; instructions to give your imagination free rein; dream interpretation; interpreting physical symptoms; writing/artwork; and participating in support groups with other individuals who have 'recovered' memories of abuse (see also Poole *et al*. 1995; Andrews 2001). Poole *et al*. (1995) surveyed British and North American practitioners and found that over two thirds of them used such techniques in order to assist clients recover suspected memories of childhood sexual abuse. A similar survey by Andrews (2001) found that 67 per cent of a British sample of practitioners reported using such techniques either before, or after, the client reported his or her first memory of abuse although, as Andrews (2001) notes, in only 21.5 per cent of the cases reported in this survey were the techniques used *before* a client reported any memory of abuse. As Hyman and Loftus (1997) note, in some cases such techniques might act as appropriate memory cues in order to help clients recover memories they had not thought about for a long time. However, they also strongly caution that many of the techniques could lead to false memories of abuse by, for example, encouraging clients to imagine abuse occurring. The problem with this, as outlined below, is that it may encourage clients to evaluate their recovered memories using very lax source-monitoring criteria. The following section examines research that has investigated the effects, that various memory recovery techniques have on reports of past events (for another recent review, see Lynn *et al*. 2003).

Memory recovery techniques

Hypnosis

There is a conflict in the literature about the efficacy of hypnosis as a therapeutic tool to help recover 'memories' (Brandon *et al*. 1997). For example, Lynn *et al*. (1997b: 309) note that 'the available evidence provides no warrant for the use of hypnosis as a memory aid'. Surveys of clinicians have shown that the use of hypnotic procedures is reasonably common. For example, Poole *et al.* (1995) found that 25 per cent of qualified clinical psychologists, both in the UK and the USA, routinely used hypnosis as part of their treatment programmes. However, surveys have also revealed that some respondents report beliefs about the power of such procedures that are not supported by any empirical research. Yapko (1994) found, for example, that 18 per cent of his sample believed that it was not possible to lie whilst hypnotized and 28 per cent believed that it was possible to use hypnosis to recover accurate memories of past lives. Suffice it to say that there is no empirical evidence to support these beliefs (Yapko 1994; Spanos 1996).

Research has highlighted a number of factors that are important determinants of what is reported whilst a participant is 'hypnotized'. For example, there is strong evidence to suggest that what people recall whilst hypnotized is strongly influenced by their own expectations and by those of the person hypnotizing them (Spanos *et al.* 1991). Spanos *et al.* (1991) conducted a series of studies of alleged 'past-life regression'. In one experiment, Spanos *et al.* (1991; experiment 2) suggested to one group of participants that their 'past-life' identities were likely to be of a different sex and race from themselves and that they would be likely to live in an exotic culture. When compared to a control group, these participants were more likely to have incorporated this information into their descriptions of their past lives. In another experiment, Spanos *et al.* (1991: experiment 3) informed participants in one condition that children in earlier historical times were more likely to have experienced some kind of abuse or neglect. Again they found that participants in this condition were more likely than controls to report instances of abuse or neglect in the biography of their past-life identities.

Lynn *et al.* (1997a) argue that, although the use of hypnosis increases the amount of information a participant reports about events he or she has witnessed, much of that extra information is erroneous. Newman and Baumeister (1996) also argue that one effect of hypnosis is to increase participants' subjective confidence in both the accurate and inaccurate aspects of their recall. However others argue that such increases in confidence are typically fairly small and cannot be reliably replicated (Lynn and Kirsch 1996). Furthermore, Lynn and Kirsch (1996: 153) argue that 'the production of new memories, accurate or not, is not much different with hypnosis than it is without hypnosis'. Spanos *et al.* (1993), for example, found that the elaborateness of UFO experiences was not correlated with hypnotizability but with the propensity of participants to have unusual bodily sensations and to be fantasy prone. In other words, it may be that a person who is more likely to respond positively to the social demands of hypnotic suggestions is more likely to respond to social demands in other suggestive contexts. McConkey *et al.* (1998) therefore argue that it is not hypnosis *per se* that is the problem. Rather, it is a complex interaction between individual (e.g. his or her 'hypnotizability' or willingness to play the role of a 'hypnotized' participant; Wenegrat 2001), interpersonal (e.g. the relationship between the client and the therapist) and contextual factors (e.g. the beliefs of the client and therapist) that are strong determinants of what is reported during hypnosis. Therefore, whilst hypnosis itself may not lead to the creation of false memories, the use of hypnosis or pseudo-hypnotic procedures (e.g. relaxation, guided imagery) in a context where individuals are trying to recall allegedly 'hidden' memories of trauma may be extremely problematic – people who are more likely to go along with suggestions that they are 'hypnotized' may be more likely to respond positively to other suggestions (see also Wenegrat 2001 for a discussion of how people adopt different 'illness roles').

Guided imagery

Loftus and Ketcham (1994: 157–8) give the following example of a guided imagery exercise suggested as useful to help an individual to recover memories of abuse:

> Take an event in your family history that you can never actually find out about. It could be your father's childhood or the circumstances in your mother's life that kept her from protecting you. Using all the details you do know, create your own story. Ground the experience or event in as much knowledge as you have and then let yourself imagine what actually might have happened.

However, Loftus and Ketcham (1994) criticize such exercises on the grounds that research has shown that giving free rein to our imagination in the context of trying to recall a past event is problematic. For example, Hyman and Pentland (1996) asked participants to imagine childhood events that they could not remember and compared the recall of these participants with a control group who were simply asked to think about events they could not remember. Hyman and Pentland (1996) found that 40 per cent of participants who were asked to imagine the event created a false memory, compared with 15 per cent of participants who were simply asked to think about the event. One possible reason for this, as Hyman and Loftus (1997) argue, is that people generally do not monitor the source of an image that comes to mind. In other words, people may confuse something they imagined for something that actually happened in the past (Johnson 1988). Furthermore, as Hyman and Loftus (1997) note, we usually associate vivid mental images as being indicators of accurate memories (Johnson 1988; Johnson et al. 1988). Indeed Hyman and Billings (1998) found that a self-reported tendency to experience vivid mental imagery (as well as a self-reported tendency to dissociate) was related to the creation of false reports of childhood events.

In fact, people can report very vivid 'memories' that are totally inaccurate even without instructions to imagine. For example, a number of studies have been conducted on so-called 'flashbulb memories', in which individuals claim to have vivid recollections of highly charged events (usually surrounding the death of a famous person such as John F. Kennedy or Princess Diana; see Conway 1995). The results of these studies have shown that, despite claiming to remember them vividly, people sometimes misremember these events. For example, Neisser and Harsch (1992) studied undergraduate students' recollections of how they heard the news about the explosion of the *Challenger* space shuttle in 1986. Over a hundred students completed a questionnaire on the morning after the explosion, which asked them to provide details such as 'where were you', 'who told you' and 'what time was it'. Two and a half years later, 44 of these undergraduates were recontacted and asked to complete the same questionnaire for a second time. Neisser and Harsch (1992) compared participants' responses to these two questionnaires and found that, in fact, only three participants gave the same information on the second questionnaire as they had on the original questionnaire completed on the morning after the explosion. Eleven of the 44 participants were wrong about every single aspect of the information they had provided in their original questionnaire. Neisser and Harsch (1992) then invited 40 of these participants to attend an interview during which their attention was drawn to discrepancies between their responses to the two questionnaires. Many participants were surprised when confronted with their own original reports and the responses they had given to the second questionnaire two years later. One participant was so surprised by the discrepancy between the two accounts that they claimed that their responses to the original questionnaire must have been incorrect. This demonstrates that individuals can come to report vivid and compelling 'memories' about events that, in some cases, are almost completely incorrect (a phenomenon to which even presidents of the USA are not immune; see Greenberg 2004). The studies by Crombag *et al.* (1996), Granhag *et al.* (2003) and Ost *et al.* (2002b, 2004), mentioned earlier, also show that individuals can be misled to report having seen highly charged events that they could not possibly have witnessed. Crombag *et al.* (1996) suggested that participants in their study may have made a source-monitoring error and mistaken a vivid imagination of having seen these events as an accurate memory.

Our ability to imagine can therefore be a powerful tool with which we can trick ourselves. As will now be discussed, research has shown that the mere act of imagining non-perceived events can increase a person's subjective confidence or likelihood that such events did occur.

Imagination inflation

Garry *et al.* (1996) asked participants to complete a life events inventory (LEI) which asked them to indicate the *likelihood* that a list of 40 events had happened to them before the age of 10. Participants were asked to provide a rating for each event on a scale from 1 to 8 (where a score of 1 meant 'definitely did not happen' and a score of 8 meant 'definitely did happen'). The list of 40 events contained such items as:

- got in trouble for calling 911;
- found a $10 bill in a parking lot;
- gave someone a haircut; and
- broke a window with your hand.

Two weeks later participants were asked to picture (i.e. imagine) some of the events and answer questions about them. These events were referred to as 'critical items'. Participants were then asked to complete the LEI again (on the pretext that the original had been lost). Garry *et al.* (1996) found that the *likelihood* ratings were more likely to change for those events that had been imagined compared with those that had not been imagined. In fact, events that participants initially rated as being very unlikely to have happened to them were more likely to be associated with a positive increase in subjective ratings of likelihood. Garry *et al.* (1996) conclude that the act of imagining an event that was reported by participants *not* to have occurred increased their subjective confidence that it had occurred.

This effect is called the *imagination inflation* effect. Although some researchers question whether these findings can be generalized to the debate over false and recovered memories (see Pezdek and Eddy 2001 and the reply by Garry *et al.* 2001), it nevertheless appears to be robust (Goff and Roediger 1998; Heaps and Nash 1999; Thomas and Loftus 2002). One could argue that it is not particularly surprising that participants' ratings of subjective likelihood might change because they are being asked about events that occurred a long time ago. Therefore it might be more difficult for participants to identify the source of their memories. As older memories would be expected to be less vivid and clear, it might be that it is simply more difficult to distinguish between childhood memories and recently imagined childhood events. However, Goff and Roediger (1998) demonstrated that the imagination inflation effect also occurs when participants are asked about recent events. Participants in Goff and Roediger's (1998) study heard descriptions of 96 actions (e.g. sharpen the pencil; bounce the ball; look in the mirror). Some participants then either performed, or imagined performing, some of those actions. At varying intervals ranging from 10 minutes to two weeks, participants were asked to imagine performing the actions one, three or five times. Two weeks after the first session, participants were asked whether they had 'heard', 'performed' or 'imagined' each action. Goff and Roediger (1998) found that the more participants had imagined the events, the more likely they were to report that they had 'performed' those actions. Thomas and Loftus (2002) also found that the imagination inflation effect even occurs when participants are asked to imagine bizarre events (e.g. tap the flower on your forehead; sharpen the shoelace with the pencil sharpener; kiss the magnifying glass).

Dream interpretation

Some forms of therapy suggest that clients keep a diary in which to record their dreams. These dreams are then interpreted by a therapist who searches for hidden meanings and unconscious themes that may be relevant to the client's presenting problem. However, there is no reliable evidence that the content of dreams reflect anything other than an amalgamation of the day's events along with other images and recent thoughts that the person has been having. In a novel twist to the imagination inflation study, Mazzoni and Loftus (1998) examined whether a suggestion made by an 'expert' in dream interpretation would lead participants to change their subjective ratings of likelihood that certain childhood events had occurred to them. In line with previous imagination inflation research, Mazzoni and Loftus (1998) also asked participants to complete a standard life events inventory relating to events from their childhood. The 'critical' items were 'getting lost in a public place', 'being abandoned by parents' and 'finding oneself lonely and lost in an unfamiliar place'. Participants were then asked to return two weeks later to complete the LEI for a second time. However, in contrast to the standard imagination inflation study, participants were not asked to imagine any of the events in the intervening time. Instead, in an apparently separate study, participants took part in a study on sleep and dreaming in which they were required to bring along an example of a recent dream to be analyzed by a clinical psychologist. The clinical psychologist then interpreted the participant's dream as strongly supporting the idea that certain events had happened to the participant as a child (specifically the three critical items mentioned above). Mazzoni and Loftus (1998) found that participants who had had their dreams 'interpreted' were more likely to increase their likelihood ratings of the critical items when they completed the LEI for the second time. For example, they found that the likelihood ratings of the 'getting lost in public place' event increased by 88 per cent in participants who had participated in the dream interpretation, compared with 43 per cent of the non-dream interpretation participants (see also Mazzoni et al. 1999).

Use of family photographs

Therapists sometimes recommend looking through old family photographs as a way of recovering memories of childhood events. On the surface this seems to be a reasonable suggestion. Photographs contain visual cues that can elicit memories of events that have not been thought about for a long time and can therefore be seen as a potentially powerful way of accessing the past (Schacter et al. 1997) Wade et al. (2002) examined whether faked photographs could be used to convince participants that they had experienced events in their childhood that had not occurred. Twenty participants were shown four photographs of themselves, taken when they were between 4 and 8 years old (the photographs had been obtained from family members). One of the photographs showed the participant and another family member taking a ride in a hot-air balloon. However,

Wade *et al.* (2002) had created this false photograph using computer software. After three interviews 50 per cent of participants reported 'partial' or 'clear' false 'memories' of having been taken for a ride in a hot-air balloon.

Although this study demonstrates that photographs are powerful cues that can lead individuals to remember events that did not occur the obvious limitation is that individuals are unlikely to encounter doctored photographs of themselves (especially in a therapeutic context; Lindsay *et al.* 2004). However, even real, undoctored photographs are powerful cues that can lead individuals to recall events that did not occur. Lindsay *et al.* (2004) asked participants about a number of childhood events – one of which was false (putting 'slime' in a teacher's desk). Lindsay *et al.* (2004) showed half their participants a school class photograph (which was taken in the same year as the suggested false event) in order to help them 'jog their memory' for the events. In line with previous research, 27 per cent of participants in the 'no-photo' group were judged to have a false memory for the 'slime' event (e.g. Hyman *et al.* 1995; Loftus and Pickrell 1995; Hyman and Billings; 1998; Porter *et al.* 1999). However, in the 'photo' group, 65 per cent of participants were judged to have developed a false memory for the suggested event (Lindsay *et al.* 2004). This demonstrates that even real, undoctored photographs are, if used in conjunction with misleading suggestions, extremely powerful cues that can lead to the development of false reports of childhood events.

Support groups

Some therapists recommend that one way to help clients recover memories of abuse is to participate in support groups with other people who have also recovered such memories. For example, Herman (1992: 224) states that:

> The group provides a powerful stimulus for the recovery of traumatic memories. As each group member reconstructs her own narrative, the details of her story almost inevitably evoke new recollections in each of the listeners. In the incest survivor groups, virtually every member who has defined a goal of recovering memories has been able to do so.

As Herman's example suggests, participation in group therapy may act as a powerful cue to enable clients to access previously unavailable memories of abuse. However, psychological research also suggests that the social demands of such groups may also act to encourage individuals to report falsely events that did not occur. Consider the example below, provided by a retractor (an individual who came to believe she had been abused, only later to repudiate that belief). She claims that members of her support group, as well as her therapist:

> exerted pressure to remember 'repressed' memories ... I felt pressured to recover memories as a result of hearing all the other people recover their memories ... participating in support groups contributed to making me very dependent on my therapist ... encouraging me to enter group therapy and participate in self-help groups contributed to [me] recovering 'memories' of abuse' (Ost *et al.* 2001: 564).

Yet, what if this individual really had been abused as a child? Would the (presumably) confirmative social influence of the other members of the group have encouraged and enabled her to report more accurately her experiences (Herman and Schatzow 1987) or would it have encouraged her to embellish and possibly confabulate events that did not occur (McNally 2003)? Surprisingly, there is relatively little research that has examined the possible asymmetric effects of social influence on *memory reports* – if the social influence is disconfirmative, rather than confirmative, does this lead people to suppress reports of events that *did* occur (Wright *et al.* in press)? A body of psychological literature that may be able to provide answers to these questions is the research examining the circumstances under which individuals are more likely to go along with (i.e. conform to) the decisions of other people (e.g. Asch 1951; Cialdini 2001; Milgram 1963; Pratkanis in press). For example, participants in Asch's famous conformity studies were asked to make judgments about the qualities of certain perceptual stimuli (e.g. whether a particular line was longer or shorter than those next to it were). Milgram's studies of obedience focused on whether participants would follow the orders of an experimenter to increase the level of an electric shock that was allegedly being administered to another participant (who was actually a confederate of the experimenter). Whilst these studies show that individuals will, under certain circumstances, act in ways that accord with the decisions, or requests, of others they are of limited generalizability because they do not tell us whether people are likely to alter autobiographical memory reports in the same way. In other words, can one person influence another to report that he or she remembers events that did not occur?

There is a growing body of literature that has examined precisely this issue. These studies of what has come to be called *memory conformity* or *social contagion* examine whether other people might be able to influence the memory report of one individual (see Bless *et al.* 2001). For example, Roediger *et al.* (2001) asked participants to study slides of common household scenes and then recall them with a confederate who, unbeknownst to the participant, would occasionally incorrectly recall items from the scene. When participants were subsequently asked to recall the items from the scene, they made errors in their recall that were consistent with the misinformation provided by the confederate. Similar 'social contagion' effects have also been found with other stimulus materials (see Betz *et al.* 1996; Hoffman *et al.* 2001). These effects also appear to be robust when examined with more ecologically valid stimulus material (Wright *et al.* 2000; Gabbert *et al.* 2003; Gabbert *et al.* 2004; Shaw *et al.* 1997). For example, Gabbert *et al.* (2003) found that 71 per cent of witnesses to a video-presented staged crime would incorporate non-witnessed details from a co-witness into their own account. However, the other side of the coin has typically been neglected as only a handful of studies have examined whether post-event information can inhibit memory of witnessed events (Wright *et al.* 2001; Wright *et al.* in press). Only one study has examined whether disconfirmative social influence presented by a confederate can decrease the likelihood that participants will report an event that they have not witnessed (Granhag *et al.* 2003).

Participants in Granhag *et al.*'s (2003) study were asked to complete a questionnaire concerning their recall of a non-televised disaster (the sinking of the cruise ship *Estonia*).[3] In addition, Granhag *et al.* (2003) assigned participants either to a confirmative, disconfirmative or neutral 'social influence' condition. In the 'confirmative' social influence condition a confederate said out loud '*Estonia* – of course I remember that film,' in the 'disconfirmative' social influence condition the confederate said out loud '*Estonia* – I can't remember such a film' and in the neutral (control) condition no confederate was present. In line with previous research (i.e. Crombag *et al.* 1996; Ost *et al.* 2002a), Granhag *et al.* (2003) found that 52 per cent of participants in the control condition reported having witnessed the non-existent film. However, it is their findings regarding social influence that are more relevant here. They found that 76 per cent of participants in the 'confirmative' social influence condition reported witnessing the non-existent film compared with 36 per cent of participants in the 'disconfirmative' social influence condition. Therefore, in addition to demonstrating that *confirmatory* social influence increases the likelihood of 'false alarms', Granhag *et al.* (2003) also demonstrated that *disconfirmative* social influence could act in the opposite direction, leading to more 'correct rejections'. This effect has been replicated using a different target event (the explosion at the Sari nightclub in Bali; Ost *et al.* 2004). Nevertheless, neither of these two studies answers the question of whether confirmative or disconfirmative social influence can lead individuals to increase or suppress reports of ecologically valid events they have witnessed (Williams and Banyard 1999). Furthermore it is not clear whether participants respond in this way due to informative or normative influence. In other words, do participants respond in this way because they want to provide accurate information and assume that the other person (the confederate) has a better memory than they do (informative influence; see Deutsch and Gerard 1955; see also Bless *et al.* 2001), or do they simply not want to appear deviant by contradicting the confederate (normative influence; Asch 1951; Deutsch and Gerard 1955)? A further question concerns whether there are certain characteristics of the confederate that might mediate this effect by, for example, making them seem more credible (Lampinen and Smith 1995; Pornpitakpan 2004). For example, research has demonstrated that misinformation is more likely to be accepted when it is presented by an authority/expert figure (Smith and Ellsworth 1987; Paddock and Terranova 2001; Roper and Shewan 2002), by an interviewer who adopts authoritative verbal, or non-verbal, behaviour (Almerigogna *et al.* 2004; Bain and Baxter 2000; Bull and Curran 2003; Templeton and Hunt 1997; Tobey and Goodman 1992), or even by a confederate wearing dark clothes (Vrij *et al.* 2005).

Conclusion

The psychological research presented in this chapter has shown that, under certain circumstances outside therapy (e.g. repeated suggestive interviewing in a psychological laboratory), some people will come to report that they remember events that did not occur. Further research is still needed to examine what it is about these people, or the circumstances in which they find themselves, that leads them to make false memory reports, which can be vivid and compelling, yet entirely inaccurate. We have seen, for example, that techniques, which are sometimes employed by therapists to help clients access long-lost memories, have also been shown to lead to the creation of false beliefs and false reports about the past. However, we do not yet know if everyone is equally susceptible to the misleading and suggestive nature of such techniques. Finally, a review of recent evidence suggests that participating in support groups may place particularly strong social demands on an individual to alter his or her memory reports in line with the social influence exerted by other people, although aspects of this hypothesis have yet to be directly tested and remain an important avenue for future research. Overall this suggests that using certain techniques to help individuals remember events from their distant, or even recent, past is best approached with extreme caution. At best the resulting report is likely to be a distorted version of what did happen and, at worst, it may well be a compelling and vivid report of an event that never actually occurred. Practitioners and policy makers therefore need to be sensitive to these issues if we are to deal appropriately with cases like Alice's, to prevent future miscarriages of justice, to ensure that genuine victims of abuse receive the support they require and ultimately, to reduce the number of casualties on both sides of the 'memory wars'.

Notes

1. Although, as Loftus (1997: 180) argues, the important point is not that participants might be able to construct a general narrative of such an event but that they report specific details suggested by the experimenter. In these studies participants 'were not asked about ANY experience of being lost. They were asked to remember being lost around the age of five, in a particular location, with particular people present, being frightened, and ultimately being rescued by an elderly person' (Loftus 1997: 180).

2. In the final interview, Porter et al. (1999) also asked participants deliberately to fabricate an account of an event that did not occur. All three types of memory report (real, false and fabricated) were rated using a technique called the memory assessment procedure (MAP) to investigate possible qualitative differences between them. Porter et al. (1999) found that real and fabricated memories were rated as more vivid, more coherent and were given higher confidence ratings than false memories. Fabricated memories were also rated as more stressful and contained more details than both real and false memories (Porter et al. 1999; see also Pezdek and Talyor 2000; Davies 2001; Heaps and Nash 2001; Loftus and Bernstein 2005; Ost et al. 2002b).

3. Granhag et al. (2003) also asked participants about a televised disaster (an airplane crash) but their findings are not discussed here.

References

Almerigogna, J., Bull, R., Ost, J. and Akehurst, L. (2004) 'The effects of state/trait anxiety and interviewer manner on the suggestibility of child witnesses.' Paper presented at the 13th European Association of Psychology and Law conference, 7–10 July, Kraków, Poland.

Andrews, B. (2001) 'Recovered memories in therapy: clinicians' beliefs and practices', in G.M. Davies and T. Dalgleish (eds) *Recovered Memories: Seeking the Middle Ground*. Chichester: Wiley.

Arndt, J. and Greenberg, J. (1996) 'Fantastic accounts can take many forms: false memory construction? Yes. Escape from self? We don't think so', *Psychological Inquiry*, 7: 127–32.

Asch, S.E. (1951) 'Effects of group pressure upon the modification and distortion of judgments', in H. Guetzkow (ed.) *Groups, Leadership, and Men*. Pittsburgh, PA: Carnegie Press.

Bain, S.R. and Baxter, J.S. (2000) 'Interrogative suggestibility: the role of interviewer behaviour', *Legal and Criminological Psychology*, 5: 123–33.

Bekerian, D.A. and Bowers, J.M. (1983) 'Eyewitness testimony: were we misled?', *Journal of Experimental Psychology: Learning, Memory, and Cognition*, 9: 139–45.

Bekerian, D.A. and O'Neill, M.H. (2001) 'Therapeutic techniques, therapeutic contexts and memory', in G.M. Davies and T. Dalgleish (eds) *Recovered Memories: Seeking the Middle Ground*. Chichester: Wiley.

Betz, A.L., Skowronski, J.J. and Ostrom, T.M. (1996) 'Shared realities: Social influence and stimulus memory', *Social Cognition*, 14: 113–40.

Bjorklund, D. (2000) *False Memory Creation in Children and Adults: Theory, Research, and Implications*. Mahwah, NJ: Lawrence Elbaum Associates.

Bless, H., Strack, F. and Walther, E. (2001) 'Memory as a target of social influence? Memory distortions as a function of social influence and metacognitive knowledge', in J.P. Forgas and K.D. Williams (eds) *Social Influence: Direct and Indirect Processes*. Philadelphia, PA: Psychology Press.

Brainerd, C.J. and Reyna, V.F. (1998) 'When things that were never experienced are easier to "remember" than things that were', *Psychological Science*, 9: 484–9.

Brandon, S., Boakes, J., Glaser, D., Green, R., MacKeith, J. and Whewell, P. (1997) 'Reported recovered memories of child sexual abuse: recommendations for good practice and implications for training, continuing professional development and research', *Psychiatric Bulletin*, 21: 663–5.

Brown, D., Scheflin, A.W. and Hammond, D.C. (1998) *Memory, Trauma Treatment, and the Law*. New York, NY: W.W. Norton.

Brown, R., Goldstein, E. and Bjorklund, D.F. (2000) 'The history and zeitgeist of the repressed-false-memory debate: scientific and sociological perspectives on suggestibility', in D.F. Bjorklund (ed.) *False Memory Creation in Children and Adults*. Mahwah, NJ: Lawrence Erlbaum Associates.

Bull, R. and Corran, E. (2003) 'Interviewing child witnesses: past and future', *International Journal of Police Science and Management*, 4: 315–22.

Cameron, C. (1996) 'Comparing amnesic and nonamnesic survivors of childhood sexual abuse: a longitudinal study', in K. Pezdek and W.P. Banks (eds) *The Recovered Memory/False Memory Debate*. San Diego, CA: Academic Press.

Catchpole, Z. (2003) 'Doctor led his patient to make sex claims', *Daily Mail*, 9 September.

Cialdini, R.B. (2001) *Influence: Science and Practice* (4th edn). Boston: Allyn & Bacon.

Conte, J.R. (1999) 'Memory, research, and the law: future directions', in L.M. Williams and V.L. Banyard (eds) *Trauma and Memory*. Thousand Oaks, CA: Sage.

Conway, M.A. (1995) *Flashbulb Memories*. Hove: Lawrence Erlbaum.

Conway, M.A. (1997) *Recovered Memories and False Memories*. Oxford: Oxford University Press.

Crombag, H.F.M., Wagenaar, W.A. and van Koppen, P.J. (1996) 'Crashing memories and the problem of "source monitoring"', *Applied Cognitive Psychology*, 10: 95–104.

Davies, G.M. (2001) 'Is it possible to discriminate between true and false memories?', in G.M. Davies and T. Dalgleish (eds) *Recovered Memories: Seeking the Middle Ground*. Chichester: Wiley.

Davies, G.M. and Dalgleish, T. (2001) *Recovered Memories: Seeking the Middle Ground*. Chichester: Wiley.

Deese, J. (1959) 'On the prediction of occurrence of particular verbal intrusions in immediate recall', *Journal of Experimental Psychology*, 58: 17–22.

de Rivera, J. (1998) 'Relinquishing believed-in imaginings: narratives of people who have repudiated false accusations', in J. de Rivera and T.R. Sarbin (eds) *Believed-in Imaginings: The Narrative Reconstruction of Reality*. Washington, DC: American Psychological Association.

Deutsch, M. and Gerard, H.B. (1955) 'A study of normative and informational social influences upon individual judgment', *Journal of Abnormal and Social Psychology*, 51: 629–36.

Erdmann, K., Volbert, R. and Böhm, C. (2004) 'Children report suggested events even when interviewed in a non-suggestive manner: what are its implications for credibility assessment?', *Applied Cognitive Psychology*, 18: 589–611.

Freyd, J.J. (1998) 'Science in the memory debate', *Ethics and Behavior*, 8: 101–13.

Freyd, J.J. and Gleaves, D.H. (1996) '"Remembering" words not presented in lists: relevance to the current recovered/false memory controversy', *Journal of Experimental Psychology: Learning, Memory, and Cognition*, 22: 811–13.

Gabbert, F., Memon, A. and Allan, K. (2003) 'Memory conformity: can eyewitnesses influence each other's memories for an event?', *Applied Cognitive Psychology*, 17: 533–43.

Gabbert, F., Memon, A., Allan, K. and Wright, D.B. (2004) Say it to my face: Examining the effects of socially encountered misinformation. *Legal and Criminological Psychology*, 9, 215–27.

Gallo, D.A., Roberts, M.J. and Seamon, J.G. (1997) 'Remembering words not presented in lists: can we avoid creating false memories?', *Psychonomic Bulletin and Review*, 4: 271–6.

Garry, M., Manning, C.G., Loftus, E.F. and Sherman, S.J. (1996) 'Imagination inflation: imagining a childhood event inflates confidence that it occurred', *Psychological Bulletin and Review*, 3: 208–14.

Garry, M., Sharman, S.J., Wade, K.A., Hunt, M.J. and Smith, P.J. (2001) 'Imagination inflation is a fact, not an artifact', *Memory and Cognition*, 29: 719–29.

Goff, L.M. and Roediger, H.L. (1998) 'Imagination inflation for action events: repeated imaginings lead to illusory recollections', *Memory and Cognition*, 26: 20–33.

Granhag, P.-A., Strömwall, L. and Billings, F.J. (2003) '"I'll never forget the sinking ferry": how social influence makes false memories surface', in M. Vanderhallen *et al.* (eds) *Much Ado About Crime: Chapters on Psychology and Law*. Belgium: Uitgeverij Politeia.

Greenberg, D.L. (2004) 'President Bush's false "flashbulb" memory of 9/11/01', *Applied Cognitive Psychology*, 18: 363–70.

Gudjonnsson, G.H. (2003) *The Psychology of Interrogations and Confessions*. Chichester: Wiley.

Halverson, C.F. (1988) 'Remembering your parents: reflections on the retrospective method', *Journal of Personality*, 56: 435–43.

Harvey, M.R. (1999) 'Memory research and clinical practice: a critique of three paradigms and a framework for psychotherapy with trauma survivors', in L.M. Williams and V.L. Banyard (eds) *Trauma and Memory* Thousand Oaks, CA: Sage Publications.

Heaps, C.M. and Nash, M. (1999) 'Individual differences in imagination inflation', *Psychonomic Bulletin and Review*, 6: 313–18.

Heaps, C.M. and Nash, M. (2001) 'Comparing recollective experience in true and false autobiographical memories', *Journal of Experimental Psychology: Learning, Memory, and Cognition*, 27: 920–30.

Herman, J.L. (1992) *Trauma and Recovery: From Domestic Abuse to Political Terror*. New York, NY: Basic Books.

Herman, J.L. and Schatzow, E. (1987) 'Recovery and verification of memories of childhood sexual trauma', *Psychoanalytic Psychology*, 4: 1–14.

Hoffman, H.G., Granhag, P.A., Kwong See, S.T. and Loftus E.F. (2001) 'Social influences on reality monitoring decisions', *Memory and Cognition*, 29: 394–404.

Hyman, I.E. (2000) 'The memory wars', in U. Neisser and I.E. Hyman (eds) *Memory Observed: Remembering in Natural Contexts* (2nd edn). New York, NY: Worth Publishers.

Hyman, I.E. and Billings, F.J. (1998) 'Individual differences and the creation of false childhood memories', *Memory*, 6: 1–20.

Hyman, I.E., Husband, T.H. and Billings, F.J. (1995) 'False memories of childhood experiences', *Applied Cognitive Psychology*, 9: 181–97.

Hyman, I.E. and Loftus, E.F. (1997) 'Some people recover memories of childhood trauma that never really happened', in P.S. Applebaum *et al.* (eds) *Trauma and Memory: Clinical and Legal Controversies*. New York, NY: Oxford University Press.

Hyman, I.E. and Pentland, J. (1996) 'Guided imagery and the creation of false childhood memories', *Journal of Memory and Language*, 35: 101–17.

Jelicic, M., Smeets, T., Peters, M.J.V., Candel, I., Horselenberg, R. and Merckelbach, H. (2005) Assassination of a controversial politician: Remembering details from another non-existent film. *Paper presented at the SARMAC VI conference, 5–8 January, Wellington, New Zealand.*

Johnson, M.K. (1988) 'Reality monitoring: an experimental phenomenological approach', *Journal of Experimental Psychology: General*, 117: 390–4.

Johnson, M.K., Foley, M.A., Suengas, A.G. and Raye, C.L. (1988) 'Phenomenal characteristics of memories for perceived and imagined autobiographical events', *Journal of Experimental Psychology: General*, 117: 371–6.

Johnson, M.K., Hashtroudi, S. and Lindsay, D.S. (1993) Source monitoring. *Psychological Bulletin*, 114, 3–28.

Johnston, M. (1997) *Spectral Evidence*. Boulder, CO: Westview Press.

Kassin, S.M. (1997) 'False memories turned against the self', *Psychological Inquiry*, 8: 300–2.

Kassin, S.M. (2005) On the psychology of confessions: Does innocence put innocents at risk? *American Psychologist, 60,* 215–228.

Lampinen, J.M. and Smith, V.L. (1995) 'The incredible (and sometimes incredulous) child witness: Child eyewitnesses' sensitivity to source credible cues', *Journal of Applied Psychology*, 80: 621–7.

Lindsay, D.S., Hagen, L., Read, J.D., Wade, K.A. and Garry, M. (2004) 'True photographs and false memories', *Psychological Science*, 15: 149–54.

Lindsay, D.S. and Read, J.D. (1994) 'Psychotherapy and memories of childhood sexual abuse: a cognitive perspective', *Applied Cognitive Psychology*, 8: 281–338.

Lindsay, D.S. and Read, J.D. (2001) 'The recovered memories controversy: Where do we go from here?', in G.M. Davies and T. Dalgleish (eds) *Recovered Memories: Seeking the Middle Ground*. Chichester: Wiley.

Loftus, E.F. (1979) *Eyewitness Testimony*. Cambridge, MA: Harvard University Press.

Loftus, E.F. (1997) 'Dispatch from the (un)civil memory wars', in J.D. Read and D.S. Lindsay (eds) *Recollections of Trauma: Scientific Evidence and Clinical Practice*. New York, NY: Plenum.

Loftus, E.F. and Bernstein, D.M. (2005) 'Rich false memories: the royal road to success', in A.F. Healy (ed.) *Experimental Cognitive Psychology and its Applications*. Washington, DC: American Psychological Association Press.

Loftus, E.F. and Ketcham, K. (1994) *The Myth of Repressed Memory: False Memories and Allegations of Sexual Abuse*. New York, NY: St Martin's Press.

Loftus, E.F., Miller, D.G. and Burns, H.J. (1978) 'Semantic integration of verbal information into a visual memory', *Journal of Experimental Psychology: Human Learning and Memory*, 4: 19–31.

Loftus, E.F. and Palmer, J.C. (1974) 'Reconstruction of automobile destruction: an example of the interaction between language and memory', *Journal of Verbal Learning and Verbal Behavior*, 13: 585–9.

Loftus, E.F. and Pickrell, J.E. (1995) 'The formation of false memories', *Psychiatric Annals*, 25: 720–5.

Lynn, S.J. and Kirsch, I.I. (1996) 'Alleged alien abductions: False memories, hypnosis, and fantasy proneness', *Psychological Inquiry*, 7: 151–5.

Lynn, S.J., Lock, T.G., Loftus, E.F., Krackow, E. and Lilienfeld, S.O. (2003) 'The remembrance of things past: problematic memory recovery techniques in psychotherapy', in S.O. Lilienfeld, S.J. Lynn and J.M. Lohr (eds) *Science and Pseudoscience in Clinical Psychology*. New York, NY: Guilford Press.

Lynn, S.J., Lock, T.G., Myers, B. and Payne, D.G. (1997a) 'Recalling the unrecallable: should hypnosis be used to recover memories in psychotherapy?', *Current Directions in Psychological Science*, 6: 79–83.

Lynn, S.J., Myers, B. and Malinoski, P. (1997b) 'Hypnosis, pseudomemories, and clinical guidelines: a sociocognitive perspective', in J.D. Read and D.S. Lindsay (eds) *Recollections of Trauma: Scientific Evidence and Clinical Practice*. New York, NY: Plenum Press.

Malinoski, P.T. and Lynn, S.J. (1999) 'The plasticity of early memory reports: social pressure, hypnotizability, compliance, and interrogative suggestibility', *The International Journal of Clinical and Experimental Hypnosis*, 47: 320–45.

Mazzoni, G.A.L. and Loftus, E.F. (1998) 'Dreaming, believing, and remembering', in J. de Rivera and T.R. Sarbin (eds) *Believed-in Imaginings: The Narrative Reconstruction of Reality*. Washington, DC: American Psychological Association.

Mazzoni, G.A.L., Loftus, E.F., Seitz, A. and Lynn, S.J. (1999) 'Changing beliefs and memories through dream interpretation', *Applied Cognitive Psychology*, 13: 125–44.

McCloskey, M. and Zaragoza, M. (1985) 'Misleading postevent information and memory for events: arguments and evidence against memory impairment hypotheses', *Journal of Experimental Psychology: General*, 114: 1–16.

McConkey, K.M., Barnier, A.J. and Sheehan, P.W. (1998) 'Hypnosis and pseudomemory: understanding the findings and their implications', in S.J. Lynn and K.M. McConkey (eds) *Truth in Memory*. New York, NY: Guilford Press.

McNally, R.J. (2003) *Remembering Trauma*. Cambridge, MA: Harvard University Press.

Milgram, S. (1963) 'Behavioral study of obedience', *Journal of Abnormal and Social Psychology*, 67: 371–8.

Neisser, U. and Harsch, N. (1992) 'Phantom flashbulbs: False recollections of hearing the news about *Challenger*', in E. Winograd and U. Neisser (eds) *Affect and Accuracy in Recall*. New York, NY: Cambridge University Press.

Newman, L.S. and Baumeister, R.F. (1996) 'Toward an explanation of the UFO abduction phenomenon: hypnotic elaboration, extraterrestrial sadomasochism, and spurious memories', *Psychological Inquiry*, 7: 99–126.

Nourkova, V., Bernstein, D.M. and Loftus, E.F. (2004) 'Altering traumatic memory', *Cognition and Emotion*, 18: 575–85.

Ofshe, R. and Watters, E. (1994) *Making Monsters: False Memories, Psychotherapy, and Sexual Hysteria*. New York, NY: Scribners.

Ost, J. (2000) 'Recovering memories: convergent approaches toward an understanding of the false memory debate.' Unpublished doctoral thesis, University of Portsmouth.

Ost, J. (2003) 'Seeking the middle ground in the "memory wars". Essay review of Davies and Dalgleish (2001) "Recovered memories: Seeking the middle ground", Williams and Banyard (1999) "Trauma and memory", Lynn and McConkey (1998) "Truth in memory", Conway (1997) "Recovered memories and false memories", Read and Lindsay (1997) "Recollections of trauma: scientific evidence and clinical practice", and Pezdek and Banks (1996) "The recovered memory/false memory debate"', *British Journal of Psychology*, 94: 125–39.

Ost, J., Costall, A. and Bull, R. (2001) 'False confessions and false memories? A model for understanding retractors' experiences?', *The Journal of Forensic Psychiatry*, 12: 549–79.

Ost, J., Costall, A. and Bull, R. (2002a) 'A perfect symmetry? A study of retractors' experiences of making and repudiating claims of early sexual abuse', *Psychology, Crime and Law*, 8, 155–81.

Ost, J., Foster, S., Costall, A. and Bull, R. (in press) 'False reports of childhood events in appropriate interviews', *Memory*.

Ost, J., Hogbin, I. and Granhag, P.-A. (2004) 'Individual differences and false reports of emotionally charged public events.' Paper presented at the BPS annual conference, 15–17 April, London.

Ost, J., Vrij, A., Costall, A. and Bull, R. (2002b) 'Crashing memories and reality monitoring: distinguishing between perceptions, imaginings and false memories', *Applied Cognitive Psychology*, 16: 125–34.

Paddock, J.R. and Terranova, S. (2001) 'Guided visualization and suggestibility: effect of perceived authority on recall of autobiographical memories', *Journal of Genetic Psychology*, 162: 347–56.

Pendergrast, M. (1996) *Victims of Memory: Incest Accusations and Shattered Lives* (2nd edn). Hinesburg, VT: Upper Access, Inc.

Pezdek, K. and Banks, W. P. (1996) 'Preface', in K. Pezdek and W.P. Banks (eds) *The Recovered Memory/False Memory Debate*. San Diego, CA: Academic Press.

Pezdek, K. and Eddy, R.M. (2001) 'Imagination inflation: A statistical artifact of regression toward the mean', *Memory and Cognition*, 29: 707–18.

Pezdek, K., Finger, K. and Hodge, D. (1997) 'Planting false childhood memories: the role of event plausibility', *Psychological Science*, 8: 437–41.

Pezdek, K. and Taylor, J. (2000) 'Discriminating between accounts of true and false events', in D.F. Bjorklund (ed.) *False Memory Creation in Children and Adults: Theory, Research, and Implications*. Mahwah, NJ: Lawrence Erlbaum Associates.

Poole, D.A., Lindsay, D.S., Memon, A. and Bull, R. (1995) 'Psychotherapy and the recovery of memories of childhood sexual abuse: U.S. and British practitioners' opinions, practices, and experiences', *Journal of Consulting and Clinical Psychology*, 63: 426–37.

Pornpitakpan, C. (2004) 'The persuasiveness of source credibility: a critical review of five decades' evidence', *Journal of Applied Social Psychology*, 34: 243–81.

Porter, S., Yuille, J.C. and Lehman, D.R. (1999) 'The nature of real, implanted, and fabricated memories for emotional childhood events: Implications for the recovered memory debate', *Law and Human Behavior*, 23: 517–37.

Pratkanis, A.R. (in press) Social influence analysis: An index of tactics. In A.R. Pratkanis (Ed.), *The science of social influence: Advances and future progress*. Philadelphia: Psychology Press.

Read, J.D. (1999) 'The recovered/false memory debate: three steps forward, two steps back?', *Expert Evidence*, 7: 1–24.

Read, J.D. and Lindsay, D.S. (1997) *Recollections of Trauma: Scientific Evidence and Clinical Practice*. New York, NY: Plenum Press.

Roediger, H.L. and McDermott, K.B. (1995) 'Creating false memories: Remembering words not presented in lists', *Journal of Experimental Psychology: Learning, Memory, and Cognition*, 21: 803–14.

Roediger, H.L., Meade, M.L. and Bergman, E.T. (2001) 'Social contagion of memory', *Psychonomic Bulletin and Review*, 8: 365–71.

Roper, R. and Shewan, D. (2002) 'Compliance and eyewitness testimony: do eyewitnesses comply with misleading "expert pressure" during investigative interviewing?', *Legal and Criminological Psychology*, 7: 155–63.

Salter, A.C. (1998) 'Confessions of a whistle-blower: lessons learned', *Ethics and Behavior*, 8: 115–24.

Schacter, D.L., Koustaal, W., Johnson, M.K., Gross, M.S. and Angell, K.E. (1997). False recollection induced by photographs: A comparison of older and younger adults. *Psychology and Aging*, 12, 203–15.

Scoboria, A., Mazzoni, G., Kirsch, I. and Relyea, M. (2004) 'Plausibility and belief in autobiographical memory', *Applied Cognitive Psychology*, 18: 791–807.

Shaw, J.S. III, Garven, S. and Wood, J.M. (1997) Co-witness information can have immediate effects of eyewitness memory reports. *Law and Human Behavior, 21*, 503–23.

Shobe, K.K. and Schooler, J.W. (2001) 'Discovering fact and fiction: case-based analyses of authentic and fabricated discovered memories of abuse', in G.M. Davies and T. Dalgleish (eds) *Recovered Memories: Seeking the Middle Ground*. Chichester: Wiley.

Smeets, T., Merckelbach, H., Horselenberg, R. and Jelicic, M. (in press) 'Trying to recollect past events: confidence, beliefs, and memories', *Clinical Psychology Review*.

Smith, R.E. and Hunt, R.R. (1998) 'Presentation modality affects false memory', *Psychonomic Bulletin and Review*, 5: 710–15.

Smith, V.L. and Ellsworth, P.C. (1987) 'The social psychology of eyewitness accuracy: misleading questions and communicator expertise', *Journal of Applied Psychology*, 72: 294–300.

Snyder, M. (1974) 'The self-monitoring of expressive behavior', *Journal of Personality and Social Psychology*, 30: 526–37.

Spanos, N.P. (1996) *Multiple Identities and False Memories: A Sociocognitive Perspective*. New York, NY: American Psychological Association.

Spanos, N.P., Cross, P.A., Dickson, K. and DuBreuil, S.C. (1993) 'Close encounters: an examination of UFO experiences', *Journal of Abnormal Psychology*, 95, 21–3.

Spanos, N.P., Menary, E., Gabora, N.J., DuBreuil, S.C. and Dewhirst, B. (1991) 'Secondary identity enactments during hypnotic past-life regression: a sociocognitive perspective', *Journal of Personality and Social Psychology*, 61: 308–20.

Templeton, V. and Hunt, V. (1997) 'The effects of misleading information and level of authority of interviewer on children's witness memory.' Poster presented at the biennial meeting of the Society for Research in Child Development, Washington, DC.

Thomas, A.K. and Loftus, E.F. (2002) 'Creating bizarre false memories through imagination', *Memory and Cognition*, 30: 423–31.

Tobey, A.E. and Goodman, G.S. (1992) 'Children's eyewitness testimony: effects of participation and forensic context', *Child Abuse and Neglect*, 16: 779–96.

Tsai, A., Loftus, E.F. and Polage, D. (2000) 'Current directions in false memory research', in D.F. Bjorklund (ed.) *False Memory Creation in Children and Adults: Theory, Research and Implications*. Mahwah, NJ: Lawrence Erlbaum Associates.

Underwager, R. and Wakefield, H. (1998) 'Recovered memories in the courtroom', in S.J. Lynn and K.M. McConkey (eds) *Truth in Memory*. New York, NY: Guilford Press.

Vrij, A., Pannell, H. and Ost, J. (2005) 'The influence of social pressure and black clothing on crime judgements', *Psychology, Crime and Law*.

Wade, K.A., Garry, M., Read, J.D. and Lindsay, D.S. (2002) 'A picture is worth a thousand lies: using false photographs to create false childhood memories', *Psychonomic Bulletin and Review*, 9: 597–603.

Weingardt, K.R., Loftus, E.F. and Lindsay, D.S. (1995) 'Misinformation revisited: new evidence on the suggestibility of memory', *Memory and Cognition*, 23, 72–82.

Wenar, C. (1961) 'The reliability of mothers' histories', *Child Development*, 32: 491–500.

Wenar, C. and Coulter, J.B. (1962) 'A reliability study of developmental histories', *Child Development*, 33: 453–62.

Wenegrat, B. (2001) *Theatre of Disorder: Patients, Doctors, and the Construction of Illness*. Oxford: Oxford University Press.

Wilkinson, C. and Hyman, I.E. (1998) 'Individual differences related to two types of memory errors: word lists may not generalize to autobiographical memory', *Applied Cognitive Psychology*, 12, S29–S46.

Williams, L.M. and Banyard, V.L. (1999) 'Introduction', in L.M. Williams and V.L. Banyard (eds) *Trauma and Memory*. Thousand Oaks, CA: Sage.

Wilson, K. and French, C.C. (submitted). The relationship between susceptibility to false memories, dissociativity, and paranormal belief and experience.

Winograd, E., Peluso, J.P. and Glover, T.A. (1998) 'Individual differences in susceptibility to memory illusions', *Applied Cognitive Psychology*, 12, S5–S27.

Wright, D.B., Loftus, E.F. and Hall, M. (2001) 'Now you see it; now you don't: Inhibiting recall and recognition of scenes', *Applied Cognitive Psychology*, 15: 471–82.

Wright, D.B., Mathews, S.A., and Skagerberg, E.M. (in press). Social recognition memory: The effect of other people's responses for previously seen and unseen items. *Journal of Experimental Psychology: applied*.

Wright, D.B., Self, G. and Justice, C. (2000) 'Memory conformity: Exploring misinformation effects when presented by another person', *British Journal of Psychology*, 91: 189–202.

Wrightsman, L.S. and Kassin, S.M. (1993) *Confessions in the Courtroom*. London: Sage.

Yapko, M. (1994) 'Suggestibility and repressed memories of abuse: a survey of psychotherapists' beliefs', *American Journal of Clinical Hypnosis*, 36: 163–71.

Zaragoza, M.S., McCloskey, M. and Jamis, M. (1987) 'Misleading postevent information and recall of the original event: further evidence against the memory impairment hypothesis', *Journal of Experimental Psychology: Learning, Memory, and Cognition*, 13: 36–44.

Chapter 14

Investigative interviewing: suspects' and victims' rights in balance

Robert Roy

What are the ethical stakes in police interviewing? Answering this question requires a consideration of ethics. Traditionally, the ethical approach to policing has been based on a code of rules to enforce certain behaviours. Respecting these rules is considered an absolute duty and, consequentially, any derogation becomes a fault and is sanctioned as the code stipulates. One of these rules is, of course, the respect by police officers themselves for the rule of law.

After five years of close and practical involvement with different police institutions in Quebec and Switzerland, I believe we must change this approach and focus on the improvement of moral judgment, for at least two reasons. First, in a rapidly changing world, trying to provide a rule for precisely each situation is not the solution – it is, in fact, part of the problem we are facing in becoming more efficient in policing. Multiplying rules inevitably leads to these rules being put in conflict with the reality in specific situations. In such a context, derogation is the only way out and should no more be automatically considered a fault. Secondly, in such a world, police officers often face situations that did not exist when the law was passed. I do accept that rules are a necessity (they set the bottom line of police professionalism), but they are not the best way to target the best practice in difficult and complex situations.

The ethical concept at work in this chapter is related to one of the trends forming what is known in Quebec as *éthique appliquée*. These trends are unified by a concrete preoccupation for professional and institutional ethical decisions and practices. The ethical framework in use may, however, be quite different from one trend to another. I am actively involved with a trend that relies on deliberation – a philosophical approach to practical judgment. Georges A. Legault has briefly presented the psychological and philosophical backgrounds to this approach (Legault 1999: 225–70). In May 1999, at the 67th annual conference of the Association Canadienne Française pour l'Avancement des Sciences (ACFAS), many practitioners and law, education, health, philosophy, sociology and theology academics gathered to discuss the validity of the methodology and practices put forward by *éthique appliquée*. The presentations were published in May 2000 (Lacroix and Létourneau 2000). I will briefly present the specificity of this approach and outline how it is different from other approaches to moral judgment. To do so, I will first make some comments on moral judgment in general. I will then try to demonstrate how *éthique appliquée*'s concept of such a judgment differs from other ethical frameworks, including Kantian and utilitarian ones.

Moral judgment in general

The act of judging refers to two different activities. We first have to form an opinion and, then, a decision must be made. We form an opinion about a given situation, in a given context at a specific time. The decision is then the starting point of an action. Judging is the mental processing of information emanating from reality and aimed at transforming this reality by an action resulting from a decision. In this chapter we are discussing moral judgment, and morality here refers to an evaluation between right and wrong or fair and unfair.

If we describe moral judgment in a more philosophical way, we can say that at least three different operations are involved:

1. An operation of knowledge, selecting all the *facts* that are relevant.

2. An operation of evaluation that cannot be done without a certain concept of right and wrong or fair and unfair, without referring to some *values* (goals that we consider to be valuable).

3. An operation of will; we must have the *motivation* to put into action the intention we formed at the previous stage. Motivation can be triggered by *emotion*, *reason*, *interest* or a combination of all, or certain, of these elements.

All ethical frameworks are designed in a specific way to consider the relationship between knowledge, concept of good and justice, and motivation. They are also designed differently with regard to the relationship between interest, emotions and reason as triggers of willpower. Behavioural compliance to rules enforced by sanctions supposes that after an officer has gathered proper information the rules always provide a clear concept of rightness or fairness. Moral judgment is here limited to the selection of the appropriate rule for the case. Once the rule is identified, there is no subjective evaluation of rightness or fairness. The duty is now clear, and motivation lies either in the fear of a sanction that can harm the officer's interests or in securing obedience to the rule by virtue of reason and understanding. Such a framework is trying to transform moral judgment into an act of knowledge that requires no subjective evaluation. The only way this could work is to have a rule for each single case and no contradictions amongst the rules. This is completely impossible.

We will now consider well-known ethical frameworks and why *éthique appliquée* departs from these approaches.

Éthique appliquée as an ethical framework

As we saw in the preceding section, any practical judgment is actualizing values (putting in action valuable moral goals). Many ethical frameworks are trying to *discover* which value or principle must be used to *dictate* the action. All these frameworks basically function in a similar way to the rule-oriented framework I have already presented. Just like it, they are trying to reduce moral judgment to an operation of knowledge and the will. In these approaches we do not *choose* the values to put in action, we discover them. The duty is the obligation logically deduced from a moral principle which is considered as a 'universal truth'. These are different from the rule-oriented frameworks because they refer to general principles that must be applied correctly to a situation. Here, moral judgment is not questioning the concept of good or justice, it is using it to clarify the situation. In my view such models have a cognitive approach to moral judgment that pretends to objectivity. *Éthique appliquée* is not such a framework.

In the school of *éthique appliquée* I am referring to, there is no such thing as a 'universal moral truth'. Values cannot be discovered; they are subjective choices made in specific cultural contexts. For such frameworks, moral judgment is not a logical rational operation (one of pure formal logic based upon facts) but a reasonable choice of a subjective preference of values supported by several good reasons that may be accepted by some people but not by others. Such frameworks have no pretension to objectivity – they assume moral judgment is partially subjective. But their pretension to validity rest on a rigorous argument that shows that choices are not arbitrary or partial but are decisions based on principles that can be explicitly presented and that support an argument showing sensible motives for acting in the way chosen. These frameworks develop understandings of good and justice that have no pretensions to universality, even if they are trying to show they are not a door wide open to individual subjectivity. I will call these approaches 'constructionist' because they are trying to set a construction of goodness or fairness that is not universal and eternal. We will now consider how these frameworks of 'constructionism' and cognitivism work in contemporary democracies.

Not so long ago, most western democracies were connected with a Christian concept of morality that was considered the universal foundation of moral judgment. The Holy Book was the ultimate reference of moral principles revealed by God himself. Today, it is generally admitted that a specific faith cannot be the universal foundation of a concept of goodness and fairness. Most democracies recognize freedom of religious expression and admit pluralism as a good thing. Recent political situations in different countries (the USA, Israel and many Islamic states) show that fundamentalism is still alive. Fundamentalism, no matter what faith is involved, is a cognitivist approach to moral judgment. It supposes that fairness and goodness are not a subjective conviction but a fact to be discovered in holy books. These religious principles, when discovered, play exactly the same role as legal or social rules in a rule-oriented framework. Or, if less rigorous, that the faith-oriented framework will lead to a cognitivist approach that will still give undeniable principles that require moral judgments to be implemented logically in specific situations. Such an ethical framework can surely guide personal choices in a democratic society, but it seems too restrictive as a concept of goodness and fairness for a professional, institutional or social ethical framework in a pluralist democratic country. Relying on it as a social framework could harm the rights of people who have different faith perspectives.

Utilitarianism is a common non-faith-based and constructionist ethical framework largely in use in western democracies. Utilitarian concerns relate to the consequences of actions or of the rules that govern actions. The main goal here is to ensure the greatest good for the greatest number. It is a constructionist framework because it has no universal and eternal pretension to define goodness or fairness. Utilitarians take as granted a specific cultural concept of goodness and fairness that is tied to the interest of the majority in a specific society at a given time. Because it is based on collective interest, this framework avoids some of the problems related to the faith-oriented framework. The specific convictions of some individuals are not raised to the level of a social standard. It is certainly more suitable for pluralistic societies since the interests of all members of society are taken into account to define the greatest good for the greatest number. But a utilitarian framework is not a guarantee of individuals' or minorities' rights – it can, and has, led to their complete negation. In a context of rising insecurity, it is very risky to rely only on a utilitarian framework. It can become the political justification for torture or for the massive preventive detention of members of specific communities. Will Kymlicka is critical of an underlying concept of equality that can go some way to explain how a utilitarian framework can lead to such abuses (Kymlicka 1999: 17–59).

In fact, such abuses were so obvious during the Second World War that they gave rise to a strong desire to protect the individual's rights. The horrors of Auschwitz permitted the Kantian approach to human dignity a second birth. Thierry Pech presents a very good analysis of dignity, and he recognizes Kant's major contribution to the matter: 'Kant was the first to set out the idea of human dignity as of invariable value, universal and directly related to the existence of a person, a dignity that cannot be lost even if a person has committed crime and lost his or her civil rights' (2001: 96, my translation). The Kantian framework is definitely cognitivist. Through the power of reason it claims we can find an absolute duty that can be formulated in different ways, one of which is 'not to use an other human being as a simple means to achieve a goal'. In the Kantian ethical framework, being ethical supposes a voluntary obedience (not fear of sanction) to this reasonable duty. This principle is a universal and eternal moral truth, logically produced. Here, also, moral judgment is reduced to an operation of knowledge and willpower.

History has taught us, the hard way, that we cannot just bear in mind the common welfare inherent in an ethical framework, but neither can an idealistic and absolutist version of individual rights be the only preoccupation of an ethical framework. People are not all motivated by reason, the Kantian frameworks suppose – interests and passions are also a motivation to individual actions. Luc Bégin, in an interesting paper, explains how individual rights and freedoms can also interfere with laws and moral principles: 'these norms are setting up individual private life as an inviolable sphere. This situation can be turned by some individuals to their economic or other personal interests somewhat incompatible with common welfare' (2001: 11). *Éthique appliquée* tries to bear all these lessons in mind. At the same time, the ethical framework attempts to avoid:

- setting up individual or specific moral concept as a standard for social practices as faith-oriented frameworks do;

- over-valuing the power of reason, as the Kantian approach does; and

- a mathematical approach to human goodness and fairness that reduces ethics to a calculation of human interest to maximize common welfare, as the utilitarian framework does.

Éthique appliquée puts forward a constructionist and consequentialist approach to good and justice in the same way the utilitarian approach does. But it also gives a role to some moral principles in the same manner as the Kantian framework. We cannot just take into account the collective interest. We have to ponder reasonably individual rights and common welfare on the basis of explicit principles and values. But these principles are not universal duties deduced by pure rationality. Neither are they the values and principles of each individual or of the majority. They are not discovered by a simple application of knowledge. They have to be collectively and reasonably established by an evaluation via a social deliberation. The ethical framework of *éthique appliquée*, as used in the latter analysis, is inspired not only by the Habermassian ethical framework of dialogue (Habermas 1997, 1999) but also by the pragmatic criticism of that approach made by Jacques Lenoble (Lenoble 1994) and co-author Marc Maesschalck (Lenoble and Maesschalck 2003). The general idea put forward by these authors is that we cannot find efficient principles to govern social action if we do not, when they are elaborated, take into account the pragmatic context in which these principles will be applied.

The ability to conduct a dialogue is definitively tied to some attitudes, but *éthique appliquée* does not basically rely on virtues. Virtues are personal qualities that are supposed to dispose a person to do good, and they can be cultivated by good habits. In the framework I am putting forward, all personal qualities favouring dialogue are cultivated, not as a goal in themselves but as a means to achieve a dialogue through which we can identify the relevant sensible principles to guide our actions. An ethical framework focused on virtue, in my opinion, accords too much room to such emotions as compassion and can impair the adequate positioning of reason within moral judgment.

Éthique appliquée is, then, an application of:

- knowledge by the importance given to the concrete analysis of facts and eventual consequences;
- evaluation by the importance given to the social construction of principles and to the selection of values on the basis of sensible motives; and
- motivation by the importance given to the practical context in which the decisions will be implemented. The process of collective deliberation takes into account interests, emotions and reason as a source of motivation to turn intentions into actions since it relies on a collective pragmatic agreement.

This chapter aims to contribute to the social deliberation required by *éthique appliquée* by identifying on the basis of sensible motives:

- the goals and values to pursue; and
- an efficient means legitimately to achieve them.

Therefore, in analyzing the ethical stakes in police interviewing, I will not emphasize the legal limits set for behaviours whilst interviewing. I will first set out some of the principal factors that generate ethical pressures on interviewing. Secondly, I will try to clarify the values that need to be balanced when interviewing a suspect. Finally, I propose some criteria by which to evaluate the legitimacy of interviewing methods.

Factors that generate ethical pressures on interviewing

Ethical pressures on interviewing comes partially from the political, economical and sociological nature of contemporary democratic societies. The rest inhere in certain aspects of police activities in democracies and, in particular, in the importance of a suspect's status and confession in obtaining a conviction.

Political, economical and sociological factors

These factors create ethical pressures on police interviewing because they generate two contradictory social trends. One seeks to increase and the other to decrease the protection of suspects.

The first of these factors is the growth in terrorist attacks and conspiracies. This form of violence can no longer be regarded as a political scapegoat. Terrorism is a real threat, and obtaining information on terrorist activities before crimes occur is an urgent need. Since mass killing is often a consequence of terrorist attacks, some people believe it reasonable to decrease the protection afforded to suspects. Others, however, believe we should increase it. Suspect protection was established because, for example, a person may be wrongly suspected of committing a crime. But when we are dealing with a threat, we are facing the risk of an intention to commit a crime. Hence, we must be extremely cautious, especially since insecurity increases the incidence of racism so that, in the eyes of some people, all members of certain communities are seen as terrorists. Finally, the alleged treatment given to some Iraqi prisoners by the US military also demonstrates that abuses are no longer the province of non-democratic states.

The rise of new forms of gratuitous violence represents the second ethical pressure. 'Wild gunmen' who shoot innocent people are a well-known phenomenon in the USA, and there have been similar experiences in Canada, Scotland, England, Tasmania and Germany. In Canada, there are some street gangs for whom killing or assault is almost an initiation rite. The gravity of the consequences of or threat of such actions works in favour of decreasing suspect protection. However, the rise of intolerance towards all marginal groups can work in the opposite direction: some sectors of society call for an increase in protection. Insecurity can also lead to false allegations or even false testimonies.

The publicity given to violent crimes is a third factor. Sensationalism sells newspapers. The American film-maker, Michael Moore, in his recent picture *Bowling for Columbine*, claims that the media's coverage of violent crime has increased exponentially whilst, at the same time, the rate of these crimes was actually decreasing. It would be interesting to undertake empirical research on this matter to assess it scientifically.

This increase in a sense of insecurity is tied up with these three factors, and it is a real concern that works in favour of restricting suspects' rights and increasing police powers. But the racist or intolerant trend it favours increases the risk of turning some suspects into scapegoats, and thus it works in favour of maintaining or increasing suspect protection. The Wolgang Dascher case that shook Germany in February 2003 shows that the fear of abuses is not just imaginary. In this case, Frankfurt police's number-two chief of police planned to torture a suspect he was interviewing, and he openly threatened him he would do so. The man was suspected of holding an 11-year-old student in a secret hideout. The officer wanted to save the boy's life, and obtain a confession that would lead to the discovery of the boy's body. The officer then surrendered himself to a judge, having recognized his abuse of power. As a defence, he argued that the torture would have been undertaken under medical supervision and would have been done in such a way as to leave no after-effects. In the 25 February electronic issue of Geneva's *Temps* (*Temps.ch*), François Mondoux reported that the president of the German Judge's Association concurred with the officer's defence. In the press, a great many letters referred to the 'inspector's courage' (my translation). The German Interior Minister reaffirmed the complete prohibition of torture, whilst the Conservative Party leader sang the praises of the inspector's 'human and understanding behaviour'.

The last factor I want to present is less obvious but none the less pernicious: the side effects of the increasing number of rules that are employed to enforce respect for human rights. While they are intended to prevent the arrest, detention or conviction of innocent people they are, at the same time, increasing the burden carried by police officers in their fight against organized crime and recidivist criminals because they make it more and more difficult to obtain sufficient evidence that leaves no reasonable doubt of guilt. Suspects' rights are sometimes responsible for the increasing sense of injustice felt by victims. In Canada, some female victims of sexual assault have generated considerable controversy over this issue. They have claimed that suspects' rights have, in fact, transformed the accused's trial into that of the trial of the victim. Such an example amplifies the basic ethical dilemma at the root of all police interviewing, as is discussed in the next section.

The suspect's status

During an investigation, police officers will interview many people (victims, witnesses and suspects), but, in most democratic societies, ethical pressures are at their maximum when they interview suspects. This is the result of three fundamental principles:

1. The separation of legislative, administrative and judicial power.

2. The presumption of innocence.

3. Conviction only occurs when no reasonable doubt remains of the suspect's guilt.

With these principles in place, and no matter at what stage in the investigation the interview occurs, an absolute uncertainty characterizes the suspect's legal status. The burden of suspicion will change from one suspect to another as the investigation progresses, and suspicion will increase or decrease as a result of the information gathered.

The investigator's suspicions may be aroused by simple intuition, by circumstantial proof or by compelling evidence. Intuition is an important quality all investigators should possess. However, basing a moral conviction of guilt merely on intuition is nothing more than prejudice. In Canada, most police work relies on motives and on beliefs that are based on credible evidence. Even if there is no hard evidence, it is clear that the police operate on more than mere intuition. When they evaluate police officers' conclusions, Canadian tribunals use two criteria. The first, which is subjective, requires the police officer to evaluate the weight of the evidence he or she has relied on to take action. In so doing, they must take into account any facts that may invalidate their conclusions. The second criterion, which is more objective, refers to 'any reasonable person's point of view'.

Two Canadian Supreme Court decisions have established the meaning of the latter criterion. According to *Strorrey c. La Reine* ([1990] 1 R.C.S 241), we can say a police officer has reasonable grounds for belief if a reasonable person, in the same situation, also had reasonable grounds to believe. The police officer does not have to rely on concrete evidence to reach this conclusion. *R. c. Collins*, ([1987] 1 R.C.S 265) defines a reasonable person as an average citizen. The court here referred not to the average citizen's opinion but to the average citizen's reasoning abilities. Indeed, even the objective criterion allows for considerable interpretation. One thing is sure, however – police officers do not have to rely on evidence that leaves no reasonable doubt as the only way in which to obtain a conviction.

The legal requirement for such a conviction was set by the Canadian Supreme Court in *R. c. Lifchus* ([1997] 3 R.C.S. 320, para. 36):

- reasonable doubt is inextricably link to the presumption of innocence. So, the burden of proof is always on the accuser and shall never be transfer to the accused;

- a reasonable doubt can never rely on sympathy or prejudice;

- doubt must be logically linked to evidence or lack of evidence;

- the conviction without reasonable doubt cannot be assimilated to an absolute certitude; it's not a certitude beyond any doubt; but neither is it an imaginary or frivolous doubt;

- it takes more than a probability of guilt – if it is no more than the presence of probability, the jury must acquit the defendant.

Following on from these remarks, it is obvious that, even if an investigator (on the basis of testimonies, material proof or confession) is morally completely sure of a suspect's guilt, as a representative of administrative power he or she is not legally responsible for raising queries regarding the suspect's status. This is the legal responsibility of the judge and jury. Where the suspect's status is one where guilt or innocence is not obvious, this factor will be of great importance when the interview's legitimacy is evaluated.

The confession's importance

No matter whether a confession is the explicit or main goal (as in the Reid Technique) or whether it is the welcome side effect of a well prepared interview (as in the PEACE approach), the confession is often the key element in a conviction at trial even if some other factors could lead to a different conclusion. For example, improvements in science and technology may lead us to think that confessions are no longer important. Small, powerful microphones and cameras are used covertly to record conversations. Similarly, we are now able to link a suspect to a crime scene by forensic evidence obtained through the careful analysis of hairs, DNA, finger and footprints, tissues, dust, etc. We are even able to deduce some of the crime's action (distances, the protagonists' positions, etc.) from material evidence left on the scene. Not so long ago, however, an investigator had to rely mainly on testimonies and confessions.

Alternatively, the reliability of testimonies and confessions is frequently challenged, and courts have always been aware of the possibility of lying: swearing on a holy book was more than simply symbolic in countries where faith in God was the rule. Swearing an oath is surely more symbolic today, however, and a suspect who is facing a major sentence will often be willing to risk a perjury conviction to increase his or her chances of an acquittal. Scientific research has also highlighted the great differences that exist in the accuracy and reliability of visual and auditory recollections, along with the existence of selective and even creative memory (Laurence 2004) and people's propensity to give the existence of false confessions even from normal individuals (Scheck *et al.* 2000; St-Yves 2004a). Finally, alleged abuses committed whilst interviewing have also undermined people's trust in the reliability of the confessions and testimonies the police have obtained. Video recording is proof of this lost credibility but, at the same time, is a way to restore it.

Confessions, however, are still very important. First, many investigations rest on circumstantial evidence or on contradictory versions put forward by the victim and suspect. Secondly, confessions often lead to the discovery of new evidence: a body, a weapon, a disguise, etc. Finally, because the suspect's rights are protected by the law, this secondary evidence is often the only way to establish proof beyond reasonable doubt. In these circumstances a confession is a key element for conviction, and the ethical pressures to obtain a confession during an interview continues.

Values to balance whilst interviewing a suspect

Whilst interviewing a suspect, there is a great deal of tension between two general goals. On one hand, there is the legitimate desire to get information from someone who is suspected of a crime or of the intention to commit a crime. But getting information is not a goal in itself – it is only a way to achieve two further valuable goals. The first is to assure the security of persons, institutions and property. Information can prevent or stop an offence such as murder or kidnapping. If the information leads to a conviction, it will also assure justice by punishing the offender, and sometimes, by redressing the damage to a victim, it will restore his or her rights or prevent a mistrial.

On the other hand, there is the legitimate desire (which has been prevalent since the Second World War) to protect individuals who are the targets of the state. At least three reasons explain this. First is the magnitude of the abuses committed by totalitarian regimes. Secondly, there is evidence of police abuses in democratic societies. Finally, scientific progress has demonstrated that miscarriages of justice are more frequent than we thought. Protection is therefore required, first of all, to prevent abusive pressures on persons who may be innocent. The basic right here, as we saw above, is the presumption of innocence. Secondly, even if a suspect is subsequently convicted, we must never forget that we are investigating the behaviour of a person who remains a human being and who must therefore be treated with the dignity he or she deserves.

The ethical pressures on interviewing lie in democratic societies' rejection of the idea that 'the ends always justifies the means'. The key ethical question in police interviewing, therefore, is 'How can we legitimately balance the victim's rights to justice and security with the suspect's rights to dignity and to the presumption of innocence?'

Criteria to evaluate the interviewing method's legitimacy

The ethical legitimacy of interviewing methods is now assessed in relation to the need to balance the suspect's and victim's rights as proposed in the above question. From this point of view, some legal interviewing methods may be ethical but others not, and some ethical methods may be legal but others not.

This evaluation of methods will be conducted at different levels. The legislator creates laws on interviewing practices, whereas police organizations are responsible for conducting investigations, for training and coaching investigators and for conducting interviews. Finally, investigators make important decisions when they are conducting interviews. At each level the question of the legitimacy of interviewing methods may be raised but the ethical issues involved will be different. Differences are also apparent between countries since the ways different countries protect individual rights vary. We should take into account these differences when we evaluate an interviewing method's legitimacy. The contentious question of confessions must also be considered. Since confessions are important in many trials, we must ask ourselves: 'Should obtaining a confession be a goal of interviewing suspects?' We should then be in a position to present some evaluation criteria and to make some remarks on the legal limits to interviewing in Canada.

International differences in enforcing individual rights' protection

The ethical pressures on police organizations and investigators will be different according to the institutional balance between individual rights and the law. Where individual rights are not guaranteed by a constitutional Act, it will be more difficult to enforce them. Laws will have priority over rights. It will also be harder for organizations and individuals to oppose methods they may consider illegitimate from an ethical point of view but that are accepted by law.

In such countries as Canada, where rights are covered by a constitutional Act, things are different. Laws may be challenged and eventually invalidated on the basis of rights. Even in countries that have such Acts, the situation will be different if laws are reviewed before they are passed to verify their compliance with the protection of human rights. In France, for example, all laws are evaluated in this way, but this is not the case in Canada or the USA. In these countries, to avoid a judicial review of legislative activity, laws are passed immediately and the courts will decide their compliance with individual rights only if there is a complaint. This way of doing things places a great deal of pressure on organizations and investigators because it is always possible that a method currently in legal use will be declared unconstitutional because of resulting harms to individual rights. Day-to-day practice is therefore uncertain.

Should obtaining a confession be a goal of suspect interviews?

This was a very contentious question at the 2004 international conference on police interviewing. Representatives from Canada, Quebec and the USA were all using or inspired by the Reid Technique and seemed to agree that confession is one of an interviewer's goals. Representatives from the UK, who are using the PEACE interviewing approach, were opposed to this idea (for a summary of these two approaches, see Landry and St-Yves 2004). What are the views of those who support these opposing stances? Confession supporters focus on the idea that some suspects are intentionally hiding the truth, and they are doubtful that a simple interview will allow them to uncover the truth. No one can contest this. Confession opponents, on the other hand, claim that, if obtaining a confession is the main goal of an interview, this will increase the chances of undue psychological pressures being put on suspects, thus increasing the risk of obtaining a false confession and, perhaps, ultimately of a miscarriage of justice. In my opinion, both supporters and opponents of confession-oriented interviewing underestimate part of the reality of the situation, but not the same part of that reality. Supporters uphold the victim's rights as a goal sufficiently valuable to negate the harm that could be done to the suspect's rights. Opponents uphold suspect's rights and thus negate the harm to the victim's rights. The ethical position, in my view, should aim to balance these rights. Individual rights cannot be considered as absolute principles: in specific situations these rights may be, and often are, in conflict and therefore have to be balanced. The first article of the Canadian Charter of Rights and Freedoms is quite clear on this matter. It 'guarantees the rights and freedoms set out in it subject only to such reasonable limits prescribed by law as can be demonstrably justified in a free and democratic society'.

The Canadian Supreme Court judges – in *Oakes* (*R. c. Oakes*, [1986], 1 R.C.S. 103) – defined a three-step procedure to evaluate these 'reasonable limits'. First, it must be decided if a law or practice is harming a right as recognized by the Canadian charter. Secondly, it must be decided if it is reasonable to harm this right, taking into consideration the specific circumstances of the situation. Finally, it must be decided if the harm done, whilst not respecting the right, is lesser than the harm done if it is respected. With this in mind I will present those criteria with which to evaluate the legitimacy of police interviewing methods.

Criteria to evaluate the legitimacy of police interviewing methods

The interview and the interrogation: a useful distinction
In Quebec, we make a clear distinction between interrogations and interviews. The word 'interview' is used when an investigator wishes to obtain information from a victim, a witness or a person suspected of a crime but only on an intuitive basis. Confession here is not a goal, and the person is not under arrest or in detention. Suspects can refuse to answer questions or can stop doing so. They can leave the interview room or can ask the investigator to leave their house or office, etc. Unlike some countries, in Canada people are not detained on the simple intuition of guilt or involvement with a crime and then interviewed to try to obtain a confession.

To guarantee the presumption of innocence, a suspect can only be interrogated after he or she has been detailed or arrested and both these measures can only be applied if the officers have reasonable grounds to believe (i.e. not merely feelings or intuitions) that a suspect is connected with a crime. This distinction can help to avoid putting undue pressure on those who are guiltless (as the PEACE supporters insist) but permits the protection of victims' rights (as the Reid supporters demand). It permits interviewers to pressurize a suspect when they have some evidence that leads to the reasonable conclusion that the suspect is involved in the crime. However, since investigators are not allowed to arrest or detain a suspect simply to obtain a confession, it is almost impossible to use the Reid Technique legally with people suspected on an intuitive basis. Most suspects who know they can, at any time, put an end to an interview will not participate in the central steps of the Reid Technique. A psychological confrontation with the suspect is almost impossible to achieve if the suspect is not in detention or under arrest. This distinction is not, however, always clear cut. For example, it is not always obvious whether a person is under detention or not, and this situation can only be resolved through a careful consideration of the legislation (see Roy 2004: 428–30). Similarly, it leaves unanswered the question of how much pressure can be legitimately applied to suspects who are being submitted to interrogation.

Criteria to evaluate the legitimacy of police interrogations
When interrogating a suspect, an investigator may face any one of the following scenarios:

1. The suspect is totally innocent and therefore has nothing to say, or does not remember the information the investigator is asking for.

2. The suspect will not reveal information because he or she is in a situation that may lead the investigator to think he or she is guilty when in fact he or she is not. For example, the suspect may have visited the scene before the crime was committed or may have a motive to have committed the crime.

3. The suspect has nothing to do with the crime but will not reveal information because he or she has been threatened by someone.

4. The suspect is innocent but will not reveal information in order to protect a friend or relative.

5. The suspect is innocent of the crime under investigation but committed a crime related to the one under investigation. For example, an accomplice committed a rape or murder that is now under investigation whilst the suspect committed a burglary.

6. The suspect is guilty but cannot recall the events because of shock, alcohol or drug abuse.

7. The suspect is guilty and refuses to reveal information or lies to protect him or herself.

In the first and second scenarios, the suspect is completely innocent. In the third, he or she is innocent and is him or herself the victim of a crime. In the fourth, he or she is not guilty but is hampering progress in achieving justice. In the fifth, the suspect is innocent of the crime he or she is suspected of, but guilty of a different one. In the sixth and seventh, he or she is guilty but will only divulge information as a last resort.

The first question these scenarios raise is: 'Is it legitimate to submit a suspect, who may be totally innocent, to some pressure because we have reasonable grounds to believe he or she is involved in a crime?' To assure the protection of those who are innocent, we should answer 'no'. But, in certain circumstances, such an answer could lead to a complete denial of the victim's rights. For example, the police receive a phone call that bombs have been set along a railway line. The police succeed in tracing the call and arrest the caller because he claims to be the person who placed the bombs. Material and instructions regarding how to build such bombs are found in the house where the arrest was made. The suspect refuses, however, to give details of where bombs are placed. In theory, individual rights are not in conflict but, in practice, they are. Protecting the suspect's rights in such a case places at risk the right to life of many other people. Article 7 of the Canadian Charter of Rights and Freedoms stipulates that 'Everyone has the right to life, liberty and security of the person and the right not to be deprived thereof except in accordance with the principles of fundamental justice'. In reality, complex ethical dilemmas do not oblige us to choose between right and wrong. The choice we have, in such situations, is often to decide which of two positions we would prefer to avoid, and hence creating the less evil. If we admit less evil choice situations exist, the question we now face is: 'When, and up to which point, can we legitimately put pressure on a suspect we have reasonable grounds to believe is involved in a crime? According to Michel St-Yves: 'No matter what the model is we are referring to, one factor is a must: pressure. Should it come from the suspect himself (internal) or from another source (external), this pressure shows that a confession, even if it is sometimes provided by a suspect, is never really free and voluntary' (2004b: 49, my translation). Internal pressure here refers to the suspect's emotions, and external pressure to the legal context, to the quality of the proof or to the relationship with the investigator.

Landry and St-Yves argue that, in the UK, the PEACE approach avoids putting psychological pressures on suspects because pressure was already applied through the legal warning issued at the time of the arrest: 'You are not obliged to say anything. But it may harm your defence if you do not mention when questioned something you later rely on in court. Anything you do say may be given in evidence.' These authors conclude: 'This supports a thesis that claims that some pressure is required, before or during interrogation, to get a confession' (2004: 25, my translation).

The Canadian Supreme Court's position on the legitimacy of police interviewing is largely set out in *R. c. Oickle* ([2000] 2 R.C.S.). The following paragraphs (based mostly on an analysis of that decision) attempt to assess whether the Canadian legal point of view tallies with those ethical preoccupations.

The court was clearly aiming to reconcile rights and obligations from common law rules of confession with those issuing from the Canadian Charter of Rights and Freedoms. Such a reconcilliation had never been attempted by the court since the creation of the charter, and so a great deal of confusion was evident. Hence the judges thought 'It is therefore necessary to broaden the discussion to deal with these issues'. The court first tried to define the scope of the charter: 'it represents a bare minimum below which the law must not fall. A necessary corollary of this statement is that the law, whether by statute or common law, can offer protections beyond those guaranteed by the Charter. The common law confessions rule is one such doctrine.' The judges thought it important to restate the rule for confessions for two reasons. The first was to bring more coherence into courts' decisions. 'Second, and perhaps more important, is our growing understanding of the problem of false confessions.' It is important to understand the main purpose of the rule if we are to judge specific interviewing situations. 'In defining the confessions rule, it is important to keep in mind its twin goals of protecting the rights of the accused without unduly limiting society's need to investigate and solve crimes.' This general goal is compatible with the balance of values I identified previously and, for the judges, the rule is well suited to achieve its 'twin goals' and to prevent false confessions:

> The common law confessions rule is well-suited to protect against false confessions. While its overriding concern is with

voluntariness, this concept overlaps with reliability. A confession that is not voluntary will often (though not always) be unreliable. The application of the rule will by necessity be contextual. Hard and fast rules simply cannot account for the variety of circumstances that vitiate the voluntariness of a confession, and would inevitably result in a rule that would be both over- and under-inclusive. A trial judge should therefore consider all the relevant factors when reviewing a confession.

The relevant factors are grouped into four major categories. As indicated by the above quotation, the focus must be set on the 'voluntariness of a confession'. The moment a judge believes the accused's freedom of will has been overridden, the judge should not accept the confession. The distinction must be made between coercion and voluntariness. Only the first is prohibited by law. Judging by the examples given of what is prohibited and what is not, a confession should be rejected if it is obtained by force rather than persuasion. The examples given are grouped into general categories:

Threats or promises. The court referred here to *Ibrahim* v. *The King* ([1914] A.C. 599). The state's agent must be actively trying to influence using 'fear of prejudice or hope of advantage'. The agent can do so directly or in a veiled manner ('you'd better tell the truth'). Threats to a relative or a person important to the accused are also prohibited. The court considered that moral or spiritual inducements cannot be considered as threats or promises, because relief is not in the hands of the state's agent. The court even tolerates some inducement. The court refers here to *R.* v. *Rennie* ([1981], 74 Cr. App. R. 207 (C.A.), at p. 212):

> Very few confessions are inspired solely by remorse. Often the motives of an accused are mixed and include a hope that an early admission may lead to an earlier release or a lighter sentence. If it were the law that the mere presence of such a motive, even if promoted by something said or done by a person in authority, led inexorably to the exclusion of a confession, nearly every confession would be rendered inadmissible. This is not the law.

Oppression. The court referred here to the general context in which the interview is conducted. Was the suspect questioned for too long or too aggressively? Was the suspect deprived of clothing, food, drink, sleep, medication? Was he allowed to talk to an attorney?

Operating mind. This refers essentially to the agent's ability to understand what the suspect is saying, and that this could be used against the suspect.

Other police trickery. The court referred here to all the tactics investigators may use to obtain information from someone (for example, planting an undercover agent in the same cell or, as in *R. c. Corak* ([1994], 29 C.R. (4ᵗʰ) 388 C.A. C.-B.), where the investigators left a hat found at the scene of the crime well within the suspect's view, hoping he would claim it as his own). The court is clear about this last group of factors: 'Unlike the previous three headings, this doctrine is a distinct inquiry. While it is still related to voluntariness, its more specific objective is maintaining the integrity of the criminal justice system.' The court is not primarily interested in the validity of the confession but in the role the state's agent played to obtain it. It is in this context that the court quoted the often referenced Judge Lamer decision in *Rothman c. Reine* ([1981] 1 R.C.S. 640, 697):

> The investigation of crime and the detection of criminals is not a game to be governed by the Marquess of Queensberry's rules. The authorities, in dealing with shrewd and often sophisticated criminals, must sometimes of necessity resort to tricks or other forms of deceit and should not through the rule be hampered in their work. What should be repressed vigorously is conduct on their part that shocks the community.

Lies are considered by the court as one form of police trickery that cannot be totally prohibited. In another decision (*R. c. Cook*, [1982], 2 R.C.S.), the court recognized that 'policemen must sometimes lie. In many situations, it is not only appropriate but necessary and obviously acceptable' (my translation).

We must always bear in mind that, from a legal point of view, the stress is on voluntariness. Sometimes one factor will be sufficient to vitiate it whilst in another situation, many factors may contribute to the same result. In yet other situations, many small factors will harm voluntariness without being sufficient to vitiate it.

We are now in a position to compare the law with the ethical position as I see it. To do this, I offer eight guidelines. First of all, since we are interviewing a human being, human dignity requires the prohibition of some practices. Because, even in wartime, the international community has agreed to prohibit torture as an acceptable means to achieve a goal, it is obviously reasonable to do the same for suspects facing interrogation – and all the more so when some of them may be totally innocent. I find no disagreement between the ethical and legal views on this matter. This guideline conforms to the rule of confessions as presented in *Oickle* and in Article 12 of the Canadian Charter of Rights and Freedomsm which claims: 'Everyone has the right not to be subjected to any cruel and unusual treatment or punishment.'

The second guideline seeks to prohibit the interrogation of a person who is mentally ill or who is disturbed by alcohol or drug abuse – the risk of obtaining invalid information that may lead to a miscarriage of justice is too great. Again, there is no disagreement here.

The third guideline is always to use the least pressure or as few tricks as possible to obtain the necessary information. Since we are interrogating a person who may eventually prove to be completely innocent, we must do more than preserve dignity – we should conduct the interrogation with the minimum stress possible. However, because we have reasonable grounds to believe the suspect is involved in a crime, it is also reasonable to subject the suspect to stress in order to be sure he or she is not lying or withholding important information. Here also the ethical and legal points of view appear to coincide.

The fourth guideline is to question whether an interrogation is the only way to obtain the required information. If not, and we are not facing an emergency, we should try another method. Realism, however, is important because all investigators know time is against them: some evidence may disappear, witnesses may forget information and the guilty party may have the time to run away or to construct an alibi. *Oickle* did not address this specific issue, but nothing in the law seems to oppose such a precaution. We can even say it respects the spirit of the law.

The fifth guideline is that we must be sure that the harm resulting from not getting information is greater than the one resulting from the stress occasioned to the suspect. Are we trying to obtain information to stop an ongoing crime or to build a body of evidence for a crime that has already been committed? The consequences are not the same when we are interrogating a suspect in relation to a kidnapping if the child is still missing or if the child is safely back home. Are we investigating a crime against property or a crime against a person? Obtaining a conviction for a stolen video camera seems less important than obtaining a conviction for murder or sexual assault.

Here again, we can say this guideline is a concrete example of the general preoccupation of what *Oickle* presented as the 'twin goals' of the rule of confessions.

The sixth guideline is to be aware of psychological distress. It is relatively easy to avoid physical torture because the relationship between physical intervention and physical pain can be anticipated. But, when trying to avoid psychological cruelty, things are not so simple: the same treatment will have different effects on different suspects, and even on the same suspect at different times. The important thing is not to avoid a specific treatment but to observe the suspect's reactions. The ethical and legal implications for each case must be judged on an individual basis.

The seventh guideline is to be wary of lies. If one looks at the literature some important Canadian police organizations follow, there seems to be a tendency to rely on lies. Stella Gabino has made an inventory of the interviewing tricks that seem to be accepted by Canadian courts. Amongst these, we find that police officers have lied about the evidence they have, about witnesses being willing to testify against suspects and about confessions made by accomplices (Gabino 1997). The Montreal Police have cited Gabino and the Canadian Supreme Court (in *R. c. Cook*, [1982], 2 R.C.S.) in literature widely distributed to police investigators as a vindication for the use of such measures. UK laws and PEACE supporters, however, are completely opposed to the use of lies during interviews. Indeed, some research has shown a link between the police's use of lies and false confessions (Scheck *et al.* 2000). Because lying is often the only way to break the 'code of silence' that may exist amongst organized criminals, to abandon lying completely may display a lack of realism. Nevertheless, it should only be used as a calculated risk and not as part of normal practice. A close analysis of the *Oickle* decision shows that this ethical position is also the one proposed by Canada's Supreme Court.

The eighth guideline is to assess whether there are limits to the presumption of innocence and whether these are appropriate. It is this guideline that probably raises the most controversy because of the neat difference between the ethical and legal positions. According to the Canadian Supreme Court, the presumption of innocence is guaranteed to a suspect if, and only if:

- guilt has been established with no reasonable doubt (*R. c. Vaillancourt*, [1987] 2 R.C.S. 636; and *R. c. Starr*, [2000], 2 R.C.S. 144);

- proof, or part of the proof, obliged the suspect to prove his or her innocence (*R. c. Downey*, [1992] 2 R.C.S. 10); and/or

- criminal prosecution was unfair or partial (*R. c. S.* (R.D.), [1997] 3 R.C.S. 484).

Since miscarriages of justice still happen, even with the necessity to establish guilt without reasonable doubt, it would perhaps be too great a risk to change current practice. Earlier comments on the necessity to, cautiously, rely on lies in occasional situations and on victims' and police officers' objections to criminals using suspects' rights to avoid justice are serious enough to require that the legal limits be given a second thought. Because there is an inequality between the individual's and the state's power, the presumption of innocence, actually, requires that the complete burden of proof rests on the state. All the arguments in the *Oickle* decision are based on the principle of voluntariness. In Canada, therefore, it is impossible to place an undercover agent of the state in a suspect's cell and to ask him or her to elicit information from that suspect if the suspect clearly expresses the will to remain silent. To act in this way is to transfer the burden of proof from the state to the suspect because it asks the suspect to incriminate him or herself. For similar reasons, all legal presumptions are now considered unconstitutional. For example, it is now impossible to presume that a person caught with a great quantity of drugs has the intention to traffic in drugs. Is it completely unreasonable, therefore, to assume that a suspect already convicted several times for drug dealing should have the burden of proof that he or she does not intend to traffic the large quantity of drugs he or she has been caught with? Would it, in such circumstances, be completely unreasonable to ask a judge for permission to use an undercover agent to obtain some information, even if this does not respect the suspect's right to remain silent? Whilst it is uncertain whether such restrictions should be changed, questions such as these permit us to examine and restore the legitimacy of these restrictions in the public's mind.

Conclusion

This chapter has tried to demonstrate that all interviews, especially those defined as interrogations, put in question the balance between the victim's right to security and justice and the suspect's right to dignity and the presumption of innocence. This balance is always in question in democracies because a suspect's status, at the time of an interview, is always marked by uncertainty. The contemporary nature of social, economic and political trends is building two contradictory stances. The first favours increasing the suspect's protection whereas the other favours the opposite. The legitimacy of interviewing methods cannot be enforced by instituting uniform procedures for all interviews in all democratic countries. Each country has its own institutions, each investigation is different and each suspect is a unique individual with his or her own psychological profile and past. All these differences must form part of the interview's legitimacy. Such complexity demands that we have a better chance of making the correct decision if we rely on guidelines to analyze a specific situation instead of fixed rules.

This chapter has developed the general idea that interviews must not have confession as a goal, and that they must not rely on tricks, lies or psychological pressure. They should be directed at obtaining information from non-custodial victims, witnesses and suspects who are under investigation on an intuitive basis only. An interrogation, on the other hand, may have a confession as its goal, and may use means prohibited in interviews. Interrogation methods are aimed at getting information from suspects we have reasonable evidence to believe are related to the crime under investigation and, thus, can be held in detention or arrested. But, for the sake of human dignity, interrogations should never rely on physical or psychological torture or on the threat of such, and should only be undertaken if the suspect is in a conscious state of mind. The chapter has also asked for a re-examination of the limits to a suspect's presumption of innocence, especially when the burden of proof always rests on the state's shoulders, no matter what the circumstances or the suspect's criminal past or acquaintances. Such a re-examination would at least restore the public's respect for the presumption of innocence or, at best, avoid the situation where notorious criminals use suspects' rights to escape justice.

References

Bégin, L. (2001) 'L'expansion du pouvoir des juges: enjeux et lieux communs', *Éthique publique*, 3: 7–16.
Béliveau, P. and Vauclair, M. (2000) *Traité général de preuve et de procédure pénales*. Montréal : Éditions Thémis.

Bellemare, J. (1996) *Les pratiques en matière d'enquêtes criminelles au sein des corps de police du Québec. Rapport final déposé au ministre de la Sécurité publique Monsieur Robert Perreault.* Québec: Publications du Québec.

Cournoyer, G. and Ouimet, G. (2002) *Code criminel annoté 2002.* Cowansville: Éditions Yvon Blais.

Division des affaires juridiques de la Police de la Communauté urbaine de Montréal (1995) 'Le droit à l'avocat', *Le conseiller juridique*, 3.

Division des affaires juridiques de la Police de la Communauté urbaine de Montréal (1996a) 'Le droit au silence', *Le conseiller juridique*, 6.

Division des affaires juridiques de la Police de la Communauté urbaine de Montréal (1996b) 'Le policier doit offrir au détenu la possibilité raisonnable de communiquer avec l'avocat de son choix', *Le conseiller juridique*, 8.

Division des affaires juridiques de la Police de la Communauté urbaine de Montréal (1997) 'Le pouvoir de détention', *Le conseiller juridique*, 17.

Division des affaires juridiques de la Police de la Communauté urbaine de Montréal (1998) 'Les motifs raisonnables', *Le conseiller juridique*, 24.

Gabino, S. (1997) *Interrogatoire sur vidéo, aspect légal.* Nicolet: Institut de police du Québec.

Habermas, J. (1997) *Droit et démocratie. Entre faits et normes.* Paris: Gallimard.

Habermas, J. (1999) *De l'éthique de la discussion.* Paris: Champs, Flammarion.

Kymlicka, W. (1999) *Les théories de la justice.* Québec: Éditions du Boréal.

Lacroix, A. and Létourneau, A. (eds) (2000) *Méthodes et interventions en éthique appliquée.* Québec: Fides.

Landry, J. and St-Yves, M. (2004) 'La pratique de l'interrogatoire de police', in J. Landry et M. St-Yves (eds) *Psychologie des entrevues d'enquête: de la recherche à la pratique.* Cowansville: Éditions Yvon Blais.

Laurence, J.-R. (2004) 'Hypnose et mémoire: un bref survol de la littérature scientifique', in J. Landry et M. St-Yves (eds) *Psychologie des entrevues d'enquête: de la recherche à la pratique.* Cowansville: Éditions Yvon Blais.

Leblond, C. (ed.) (2002) *Droit pénal, procédure et preuve. Collection de droit 2001–2002. Volume 10.* Cowansville: Éditions Yvon Blais.

Legault, G.A. (1999) *Professionnalisme et délibération éthique.* Québec: Presses de l'Université du Québec.

Lenoble, J. (1994) *Droit et communication. La transformation du droit contemporain.* Paris: Les éditions du Cerf.

Lenoble, J. and Maesschalck, M. (2003) *Toward a Theory of Governance: The Action of Norms.* The Hague/London/New York, NY: Kluwer Law International.

Modoux, F. (2003) 'Un policier allemand ordonne la torture pour extorquer des aveux à un suspect', *Le Temps.ch*, online, 25 February: 2.

Pech, T. (2001) 'La dignité humaine. Du droit à l'éthique de la relation', *Éthique publique*, 3: 93–120.

Roy, R. (2004) 'Enjeux éthiques des entrevue d'enquête', in J. Landry et M. St-Yves (eds) *Psychologie des entrevues d'enquête: de la recherche à la pratique.* Cowansville: Éditions Yvon Blais.

Scheck, B., Neufeld, P. and Dwyer, J. (2000) *Actual Innocence: Five Days to Execution and Other Dispatches from the Wrongly Convicted*. New York, NY: Random House.

St-Yves, M. (2004a) 'Les *fausses* confessions: comprendre et prévenir', in J. Landry et M. St-Yves (eds) *Psychologie des entrevues d'enquête: de la recherche à la pratique*. Cowansville: Éditions Yvon Blais.

St-Yves, M. (2004b) 'La psychologie de l'aveu', in J. Landry et M. St-Yves (eds) *Psychologie des entrevues d'enquête: de la recherche à la pratique*. Cowansville: Éditions Yvon Blais.

Chapter 15

Regulating police interrogation

David Dixon

Introducing regulation

This chapter considers possibilities and problems in the regulation of police interrogation, drawing for its perspective on my research on the legal regulation of policing (Dixon 1997) and on audio-visual recording of interrogation (Dixon 2004b forthcoming), as well as on recent work in regulatory theory (Baldwin *et al.* 1998; Parker and Braithwaite 2003; Parker *et al.* 2004). The potential connections between policing and regulation have been generally neglected. The growing literature on regulation is predominantly concerned with corporations or privatized utilities.[1] Police are more often seen as those who impose regulation than its recipients, as regulators rather than regulatees. Here, the focus is on police practices in interrogating suspects as the subject of regulation.

This approach to regulation has two general characteristics. First, the term 'regulation' is used broadly. The focus is not just on rules, but on the broader range of resources which are available to control, direct, sanction and influence. Sections below consider aspects of judicial control, rules, training, electronic recording, supervision and management. Regulation here is taken to mean 'the sustained and focused attempt to alter the behaviour of others according to defined standards or purposes with the intention of producing a broadly defined outcome or outcomes, which may involve mechanisms of standard-setting, information gathering and behaviour-modification' (Black 2002: 26). Laws and other types of rules are just one set of tools. As Parker *et al.* suggest, this approach 'incorporates three basic requirements for a regulatory regime: the setting of standards; processes for monitoring compliance with the standards; and mechanisms for enforcing the standards' (2004: 1).

Secondly, this chapter is concerned with the positive potential of regulation. Regulation is all too often identified with negatives – restriction, discipline, sanction. Whilst such forces can be effective when appropriately deployed and are usually a necessary component of a regulatory regime (Parker and Braithwaite 2003: 135), a key lesson of contemporary regulation scholarship is that regulation can be a positive, constitutive force. This is particularly likely if regulation involves persuasive and educative shaping of behaviour, only moving to more coercive methods if resistance is met:

> A large body of empirical sociological and psychological research converges on the finding that non-coercive and informal alternatives are likely to be more effective than coercive law in achieving long-term compliance with norms and coercive law is most effective when it is in reserve as a last resort (Parker and Braithwaite 2003: 134).

It perhaps must be emphasized that this is not a soft or idealistic approach: it includes developing and deploying coercive methods which have a preventative and deterrent effect. Punishment and persuasion, coercion and compliance are not alternatives: 'compliance is optimized by regulation that is contingently cooperative, tough and forgiving'. The 'trick of successful regulation' is their 'synergy' (Ayres and Braithwaite 1992: 51, 25).

A restriction of focus is that my concern is primarily with the interrogation of suspects by public police officers. Whilst acknowledging their importance, I deal with neither the questioning of victims or witnesses nor the interrogation of suspects by other state agencies or private contractors. However, I do draw on some of the current debates surrounding interrogation of 'detainees' captured in Iraq, Afghanistan and elsewhere which vividly illustrate some issues of relevance to regulating police interrogation.

Why interrogate? Why regulate? Why deviate?

A problem which needs to be acknowledged at the outset is the identification of what the goals of interrogation and its regulation are and should be. These have to be considered together: a regulatory regime has to fit with the aims and purposes of the activity to be regulated.

Doing so may seem unnecessary: isn't interrogation obviously about getting a suspect to tell the truth? When police officers are asked to explain their purpose in interviewing suspects, they typically refer to the process as 'a search for the truth'. This is attractive rhetoric. However, it has two flaws. First, it is almost trite to say that any account involves selection and construction. Accounts provided in police interrogations are selected and constructed primarily not because police routinely use ploys to trick suspects (McConville *et al.* 1991), but because this is how memory, recall and account-giving work:

> memory for a complex event is largely constructive. What a person encodes is not recorded in memory ready to be played back like a video-recording. Instead the event is reconstructed using the information the person has encoded about the event and also by using information that the person has about the world in general (Milne and Bull 1999: 17).

Ploys may be used improperly, but it is a mistake to equate doing so with the unavoidable nature of account giving. Even a full, freely given confession is an account constituted by selection, not an unmediated view of reality or 'truth'. More than one account may be available: an adversary system of justice deals in contested versions of reality, not in absolute truths. Police interviewing of suspects involves a very particular form of account construction, 'legalization', which involves the interviewer organizing and 'framing' the suspect's account according to legal criteria (Dixon 1997: 270–4).

Secondly, 'searching for the truth' has too often been the gloss on a method of interrogation which consists of the interrogator seeking the suspect's confirmation of (confession to) an account of events (a truth) to which the interrogator is already committed. Take, for example, these exchanges in the interrogation of George Heron about the murder of Nikki Allen:

> Q Well let's start telling the truth George, I'm just asking you a simple question, right, I believe I know the answer to it and I'm asking you to tell the truth
>
> A I am telling the truth ...
>
> A I didn't kill her

Q   You can keep saying that over and over again but that doesn't mean to me that you didn't do it and you know, sat there, the truth … all the evidence is pointing straight in your direction …

A   I am not admitting to somet't [I didn't do]

Q   We are not asking you to admit that you didn't do, we are asking for the truth about the murder of Nikki Allen.[2]

The interviewing officers' commitment to the 'truth' that Heron was a murderer produced a confession so unreliable that the trial judge excluded it. Heron was acquitted, and Nicki Allen's killer has never been brought to justice. As will be further illustrated below, premature, inflexible 'case theories' (McConville 1989) have been a significant cause of miscarriages of justice (and unsuccessful criminal investigations).

In this respect, the Quebec conference vividly illustrated the divide between approaches to interrogation in the USA and in the UK (and Australia). The Inbau and Reid method, which dominates US policing, focuses on persuading the suspect to confirm an account to which the interrogator is already committed as a result of pre-interrogation interviewing and other investigation (Inbau *et al.* 2001). By contrast, British and Australian police are expected to interrogate with an open mind. The potential for unreliable case theories, hunches and inadequate preliminary inquiries to form the driver of persuasive, psychologically coercive interrogation makes British interrogation experts critical of the Inbau and Reid method (Gudjonsson 2003).

From another perspective, finding the 'truth' may not be a realistic aim. Success in an interrogation may not be marked by the production of a confession. If the prosecution has other evidence, then silence or a supposedly exculpatory statement which police can prove to be a lie may well be more useful than an admission qualified by justification or excuse. In such cases, the statement (or lack of it) will appear in the prosecutor's case, allowing at least the potential for judicial supervision. But in some circumstances, the purpose of the interrogation may not be to produce evidence for use in court. In the extreme case of military intelligence interrogations, success for an interviewer may mean much less than obtaining a confession:

Interrogators find tiny bits of the truth, fragments of information, slivers of data. We enter a vast desert, hundreds of miles across, in which a few thousand puzzle pieces have been scattered. We spend weeks on a single prisoner, to extract only a single piece

– if that. We collect, and then we pass the pieces on, hoping that someone above us can assemble them (Mackey 2004: xxv).

In response to 9/11, 'the interest of investigators has shifted from obtaining viable evidence for prosecution to obtaining credible information for preventing future acts of terrorism' (Strauss 2003: 206).

The implications for interrogation of this shift into a 'forward-leaning' approach (Golden 2004) are likely to go far beyond investigation of terrorism: such experience is increasingly relevant in the broader context of criminal justice. Similar considerations apply in the policing of organized crime, particularly drug trafficking. More generally, informed commentators discern trends in criminal justice (away from its traditional commitments to concepts of guilt, rights, conviction and towards concepts of risk, security, prevention) which will have significant implications for criminal investigation. According to Maguire, current developments 'may prefigure a major shift towards genuinely new strategic and "risk oriented" approaches, driven by threat assessments, prioritisation, forward planning and "problem-solving" objectives' (2003: 364). In England and Wales, a notable expression of this approach is the National Intelligence Model which, if it is able to 'overcome familiar obstacles to translating intentions into reality' (Maguire 2003: 388), may lead to a significant shift away from 'the traditional individualistic, case-based approach' to the investigation of crime (Maguire 2003: 387). For present purposes, the key issue is that if an interrogator has no expectation that the products of interrogation will be presented in court, then methods of regulation other than judicial control will be needed.

If the purpose of interrogation is not always clear, nor is it clear what regulation is intended to achieve. Answers could include:

• maximizing the number of confessions from suspects;
• increasing the reliability of confessions;
• improving the quality of interrogations;
• preserving the integrity of the justice process;
• minimizing miscarriages of justice; and
• protecting suspects' rights.

This list is simply an elaborated version of Packer's familiar distinction between crime control and due process (1968). As in Packer's analysis, it is obvious enough that, in practice, criminal justice will have more than one objective and that some combination of contrary pressures will be required.

Finally, why do problems of police deviance occur in the context of interrogations? This question raises broader issues of reform in policing (Chan 1997; Dixon 1999). Some academic commentators portray the police as dominated by a change-resistant culture, dedicated to crime control and obsessed with the production of confessions (McConville *et al.* 1991). This approach, not surprisingly, leads to the conclusion that attempts to change interrogation practices by rules, supervision and training are doomed and that regulatory pressure for change has to be applied to other parts of the justice process. As explained at length elsewhere (Dixon 1997: 155–69), this approach is excessively pessimistic. Whilst change never comes easily in policing, police culture is not immutable. If police officers are shown how to improve their practices (rather than simply told what not to do), their response is often more positive and diverse than pessimists would allow. Positive regulation can work.

This approach does not mean lurching on the rebound into a naïve optimism. Crucially, change in police culture regarding interrogation (or anything else) will depend substantially on the impact of broader legal, social and political contexts on policing (Chan 1997). So, if police are pressured to operate according to managerialist dogma in which their mandate is narrowly defined as crime control and performance is measured by indicators such as rates of arrests, confessions and clear-ups, pressure on officers to 'perform' can slip (and all too often has slipped) into 'cutting corners ... routine by-passing of suspects' rights or even fabrication of evidence' (Maguire 2003: 379).

In high-profile (particularly homicide) cases, there can be great pressure to produce results. In several notorious miscarriages of justice in Britain, interrogators' urgency to obtain confessions led to wrongful convictions. Some of the regulatory strategies discussed in this chapter have been developed in response to such cases. My focus here is on the positive potential of regulation. If we move beyond the counter-position of suspects' rights and police powers which blights understanding of criminal justice, regulation may be seen as a vital means of ensuring effectiveness and efficiency in policing to the benefit of all concerned. 'Efficiency' means not only convicting the guilty, but also *not* convicting the innocent.

Particular risks in interrogation need to be acknowledged. The relations of power between interrogator and prisoner mean that the temptation to abuse people who are vulnerable and isolated may be hard to resist, particularly when interrogator–prisoner relations are coloured by resentment, hatred, fear or racism. At play are 'the gravitational laws that govern human behavior when one group of people is given complete control over another in a prison. Every impulse tugs downward' (Mackey 2004: 471). The treatment of detainees in Iraq provides the obvious current example: Parry notes that American soldiers 'did not engage in torture solely to assist interrogators. At least some of them tortured for psychological and aesthetic reasons – that is, because they could, because others were doing it, because they enjoyed it, or because they were good at it' (2005: 828). Regulation must seek to constrain the effects of external demands on interrogators, cultural and job-related pressures, and group and individual impulses – and, of course, must appreciate that these are inter-related.

Finally, if police interrogation is to be regulated effectively, a series of myths have to be confronted and dispelled. According to popular (and all too often professional) understanding, typical police interrogations have the following characteristics:

- Suspects resist questioning and interviews are tense, difficult encounters.
- Police dominate interaction in interviews.
- Suspects crack, shifting from denial to full confession.
- Police are expert interviewers.
- Interviews involve a search for truth.
- Interviewers can detect deception from body language.
- Innocent people do not confess to crimes.

The reality of police interrogation is very different: at least in Britain and Australia, these entrenched beliefs bear little relation to empirical reality. In this respect, my research (Dixon 2004b, forthcoming) strongly confirms the findings of other researchers (Baldwin 1993; Pearse and Gudjonsson 1996).

Judicial control as regulation

Perhaps the most familiar mode of regulating interrogation is the authority exercised by judges and magistrates over proceedings before them. Such authority is exercised in various ways. For example, in interpreting the substantive criminal law, judges can indirectly influence police evidence-gathering practices. When courts demand that the prosecution prove beyond reasonable doubt that a defendant intended an act, the police are strongly encouraged to obtain confessions, which provide the direct way of establishing intention.

Of particular relevance here is judicial control over admissibility of evidence of confessions and admissions. Courts can insist that a confession has been obtained by methods which meet standards such as voluntariness, reliability, lack of oppression and fairness. In England and Australia, such standards originated in the common law and have been adapted and developed by statutes. Alternatively, as in the USA, courts may be called upon to interpret rights provided in a written constitution or bill of rights. Increasingly, international conventions on human rights will have to be considered. Judges have potentially potent, but essentially defensive powers with which to regulate police interrogation. However, there are a number of intrinsic limitations stemming from the nature of the judicial function and the actual (rather than the rhetorical) position of judges in the criminal justice process.

First, judicial power focuses on the regulation of court proceedings. A court can regulate how its processes are used, but may not be able to go beyond this to control police activity which is not intended to produce evidence for court. This limitation has been illustrated by recent US Supreme Court cases in which individuals have tried to use constitutional rights, not to have evidence excluded, but as the basis for civil actions against the police. Notably, *Chavez v. Martinez*[3] concerned a police officer's questioning of Oliverio Martinez, a suspect who had been shot five times by another officer. This questioning, over a period of 45 minutes in the ambulance and at the hospital, was apparently intended to get Martinez's account of what happened for the inevitable inquiry into the shooting rather than for a prosecution, because he was not expected to survive his injuries. However, Martinez did survive, was not charged and went on to bring an action against the police for violation of constitutional rights during this interrogation. The significant factor for present purposes is that the Court had not previously ruled on the question of whether the right to due process and the privilege against self-incrimination were substantial or merely procedural: previous cases had all concerned the admissibility of evidence (Strauss 2003: 227). *Chavez v. Martinez* did not resolve the matter: whilst the court indicated that there was a substantive right, its extent and nature were left uncertain by a series of six separate opinions.

Secondly, courts cannot ensure the implementation of changes which they recommend or rule as necessary. The dominance of executive-controlled legislatures in contemporary states makes most judges take a realistically modest view of what they can achieve. For example, in a crucial decision by Australia's High Court, Justices Mason and Brennan refused to interpret the common law so as to provide authority to the police to detain suspects for questioning, arguing that it was the legislature's responsibility to deal with such matters both as a matter of constitutional principle and because it 'is able – as the courts are not – to prescribe some safeguards which might ameliorate the risk of unconscionable pressure being applied to persons under interrogation'.[4]

As a mode of positive, prospective regulation, judicial control is confined by the vagaries of the case law process. Judges have to wait for a case to come before them. In criminal justice processes characterized by heavy reliance on guilty pleas and financial as well as legal barriers in appeal processes, an appropriate vehicle for an attempt at judicial regulation of policing may not come along. When it does, any judicial interest in regulating the police may be tempered by the prospect of acquitting or allowing an appeal by someone they think is factually guilty. This familiar dilemma can be recognized by anyone other than ostrich-like legal formalists. For example, in *Kelly*,[5] the Australian High Court insisted on a narrow interpretation of the phrase 'in the course of official questioning', allowing the police to use in evidence their claim that, after a formal interview had ended, Kelly had made a (very dubious) incriminatory remark which was not electronically recorded. It was no coincidence that there was very strong circumstantial evidence against the defendant (as well as an earlier inadmissible confession, which Kelly agreed to having made, but now repudiated). *Kelly* was a particularly unfortunate vehicle for a crucial statutory interpretation. Even at the highest level, courts have to balance doing justice in the specific case and meeting the general public interest in the broader regulatory implications of the issues raised.

All too often, the result is frustrating for those seeking clear regulatory guidance. Constrained by the case at hand, appeal courts often fail to deal with a topic comprehensively. A legalistic slice through issues which are complex and inter-related is often unsatisfying for those whose concerns go beyond the individual case. Particularly problematic in regard to interrogation is the court's practice of giving the police broad, vague instructions on what they *cannot* do, rather than specific guidance on what they *should* do. Take the key issue of defining 'oppression', the category of behaviour which will render confessional evidence inadmissible under English law. Characteristically, when facing problems of definition, courts say that words should be given their ordinary meaning, and turn to the dictionary.[6] Doing so is unlikely to be much help to an officer planning an interrogation of a difficult suspect. In a much-quoted ruling in *Heron*,[7] Mitchell J said that police questioning can be 'persistent, searching and robust'. But an officer seeking guidance on what this means will be disappointed: 'Where the line is to be drawn between proper and robust persistence and oppressive interrogation can only be identified in general terms.' The interview must be considered as a whole: 'occasional transgressions will not necessarily convert an otherwise properly conducted interrogation into an unfair one, let alone an oppressive one.' The 'age and character' of the suspect will also be relevant. What might lead a court to determine that 'the admission of the evidence would have such an adverse effect on the fairness of the proceedings that the court ought not to admit it'[8] is even less capable of convenient definition. Self-evidently, such rules require judicial and other elaboration. Similar problems are evident in Australia: despite the High Court's hearing of a series of cases about interrogation, 'this has certainly not produced any great clarification of the law. Issues remain unresolved, doctrines imprecise, new uncertainties introduced' (Odgers 1990: 220).

But inadequate coverage is not due only to the legal form. A striking characteristic of judicial decisions on police interrogation at least until the closing decades of the twentieth century was the evident lack of knowledge about how the processes of arrest, detention, questioning, charge and bail worked (Dixon 1997: chs. 4 and 5). If judges were ignorant about policing, then the police were also often ignorant about judicial decisions. The communication of decisions to operational officers has not received the attention that it deserves. Complex appeal court decisions given in a variety of judgments need careful interpretation and translation. If not, the police may simply pick out what they want to hear. In an extreme example involving the police reception of a High Court decision on detention for questioning, the NSW Police based its instructions to officers on the Chief Justice's judgment. The problem was that the Chief Justice had been in a minority of one.[9]

As the *Kelly* case suggests, weak judicial regulation of police interrogation is a matter not just of legal form, or judicial ignorance, but also of judicial politics. Despite the persistent complaints from some police officers and many conservative media commentators about judicial liberalism and 'softness to criminals', the historical record in England and Australia tells a very different story (Dixon

1997: chs. 4 and 5). First, between 1900 and the 1980s, judges stepped back from active regulation of custodial interrogation. Secondly, they often made clear their strong disapproval of defence lawyers who criticized the police. This history was ignored by critics of the statutory reforms of the 1980s and 1990s, who looked back through rose-coloured glasses to common law control of policing.

What impact judicial regulation had on police practice and effectiveness has been the subject of much controversy in the USA. The most convincing interpretation of the extensive research evidence is that heroic Supreme Court cases such as *Miranda* did not significantly reduce police ability to investigate crime, with officers soon finding ways to minimize their impact (Walker 1993: 44–6; Leo 1996: 287). Specifically, they hastened shifts already under way in police interrogation, as techniques of persuasion and psychological coercion were developed in training manuals by Inbau and Reid, and others. However, they did have some beneficial effects: these cases led police organizations to improve their training, supervisory practices and general professionalism (Walker 1980: 229–32; Leo 1994: 114) and encouraged a cultural shift towards the acceptance of accountability and legality. Skolnick writes of a 'legal archipelago...sets of islands of legal values...distributed throughout the broad experience of policing' (1993: 196).

This experience suggests broader lessons about potential judicial contributions to regulation of interrogation. To date, judicial control has shared many of the undesirable characteristics of command/control regulation – it is distanced, unwieldy, non-responsive. If judges want their decisions to have more positive impact, they have to know more about the world they seek to regulate and to express them more clearly and more positively, and with more emphasis on policy and less on the individual case. (Appeal courts, particularly at more senior levels, are obviously more able to do this than are trial judges.) They should be aware of the need to communicate decisions and to participate in processes which review their impact. Attention should be paid to indirect as well as direct effects.

Despite the convenient divisions within this chapter, regulatory measures should not be considered in isolation from each other. Judicial regulation will be affected by other pressures, particularly the structure of rules provided for the detention and interrogation of suspects which are considered in the next section. It is appropriate to point out here that there was a significant shift in judges' approach to the regulation of interrogation following the introduction of the Police and Criminal Evidence Act 1984 (PACE) in England and

Wales. Clearer statements of what was expected contributed here. But a change in rules is unlikely to be enough in itself: in both Britain and New South Wales, new legislation provided the tools, but it was disclosures of police malpractice which impelled judges into a more critical and active regulation of interrogation.[10]

So far, this discussion has assumed an Anglo-American model of adversarial justice, with the judiciary as a notionally distanced referee. There are of course other models, notably the inquisitorial procedure of continental Europe in which judicial officers may be more directly involved in the direction and management of criminal investigation. Problems arise when the messy reality of adversarial systems is compared to an idealized representation of inquisitorial systems. As Hodgson's invaluable empirical research on French criminal justice makes clear, we must compare like with like, and in doing so must be aware of specific legal cultures and systems of state organization. The fact that, in practice, French judicial officers neither attend nor actively supervise interrogations does not mean that such supervision might not be feasible and desirable elsewhere (Hodgson 2001: 359). What is striking about Hodgson's account of police interrogation practices in France is not the contrast between an inquisitorial and an adversarial system, but the similarity between police practices in France and those in England and Australia before the regulatory changes of the 1980s and 1990s. Hodgson's picture of the police single-mindedly trying to get confessions, mistreating suspects and recording only a brief, retrospective, partial account is very familiar. Whilst the principles of inquisitorial justice may provide a valuable alternative perspective, it is not surprising that in France there has been interest in (as well as opposition to) the introduction of PACE-like measures which provide suspects with some protection and are likely to produce more reliable results.

Regulating by rules

The regulation of interrogation has to be placed in a broader context of shifts in the regulation of police investigations. Academic work on the regulation of criminal investigations has been dominated by a critical perspective which has emphasized regulatory failures and patterns of malpractice. Given the history of miscarriages of justice and other misconduct, this is hardly surprising. However, concentration on these crucial matters has tended to draw attention away from some significant trends in the regulation of policing.

As Karl Alderson (2002) demonstrates, the final third of the twentieth century saw the development of a new and distinctive approach to police powers in Britain and Australia. In the mid-twentieth century, such regulation as there was came from common law administered by the courts and from internal police management. The law was anachronistic in crucial areas, failing for example to acknowledge the crucial shift of responsibility in the investigative stages of the criminal justice process from magistrates to the police. As suggested above, those who administered it often displayed ignorance of policing practice. However, by the end of the twentieth century, the law of criminal investigation was a complex structure of laws, subsidiary rules and codes of practice. They provided clear authorization to the police to intrude on individual liberty in various ways – including stop/search, search of premises and detention for investigative purposes. The police had routinely done these things before the new laws, exploiting the gaps and uncertainties in the common law and local legislation, and relying on their targets' ignorance of or inability to enforce their rights. What was new was that the police now had clear authorization for such practices.

It is wrong to focus only on the 'negative' aspects of police powers as increasing power. The provision of powers may also be positive in defining what police may and may not do: law 'has the great virtue of limiting what it grants'.[11] As Finnane suggests, regulation 'of any kind is a two-fold process: it not only constrains but opens up a field of action' (1994: 90). If a police practice is recognized by legal authorization, there may also be recognition that the rights of those subjected to powers need to be formalized and given substance. For example, if it is acknowledged that the police detain suspects for questioning, then specified limits on detention and correlative rights (e.g. to legal advice) become significant issues. Whether the extension of powers is accompanied by positive rights in any particular instance is an empirical matter. The point for present purposes is that it is usually misleading to see power as working in purely a negative way: it may also have positive and unpredictable effects.

Why did such regulatory developments occur? First, they were part of a general shift towards formalization and extension of regulation. Secondly, they accompanied professionalization of policing functions. Thirdly, increasing political interest in matters of crime and crime control pushed them on to the political agenda. Fourthly, there were changes in the status of the objects of police attention: social democratization in the mid-twentieth century meant that 'informality' in dealing with suspects became less appropriate.

Issues raised by the 'authorize and regulate' strategy have been brought sharply into focus in the debate about torture as a tool of interrogation in the wake of 9/11 (e.g. Levinson 2004). Dershowitz attracted a hail of criticism for suggesting the introduction of a 'torture warrant' which would provide judicial authorization for torturing a suspect in particular circumstances. This was not, as is often suggested, advocacy of the *introduction* of torture itself. Rather, Dershowitz claims that 'at least moderate forms of non-lethal torture are in fact being used by the United States' (2003: 277), that 'if we ever confronted an actual case of imminent mass terrorism that could be prevented by the infliction of torture we would use torture' (2003: 277), and that the US already subcontracts torture by 'rendering' suspects to Egypt, Morocco or Jordan (2002: 138; cf. CIHR/CHRGJ 2004). He argues that it is better to acknowledge these realities and to control the practice by bringing it within the law than leaving it outside – in other words, to use the authorize and regulate strategy.[12] If torture is being and will be used, it would be better 'to have such torture regulated by some kind of warrant, with accountability, record-keeping, standards, and limitations' (2003: 277). This is both as a matter of principle (tolerating extra-legal action is unacceptable; we should not rely on the discretion of junior officials to decide when torture should be used) and instrumentally (regulating 'its frequency and severity' might reduce its incidence), whilst not legalizing will allow 'continuing and ever-expanding sub rosa employment of the practice' (2003: 278). Whilst Dershowitz believes that legal regulation would reduce the use of torture, his critics argue that legalizing torture will lead to an increase. His response is 'This, of course, is an empirical claim, which if true, would cause me to reconsider my proposal, since my goal is to cabin the use of torture' (2003: 281).

My point here is to consider in detail neither the use of torture nor the dispute between Dershowitz and his critics,[13] but rather to identify the latter as a sharply focused examination of the authorize and regulate strategy. First, those opposed to authorizing and regulating tend to understate the prevalence of the relevant practice and the problems associated with it. They may well do so not deliberately, but because the practice is not open to public scrutiny. So, for example, pre-PACE opposition to giving the police a power to detain suspects for questioning often assumed that this would be to authorize the police to do something that they did not already do, when in fact, such detention was routine (Dixon 1997: ch.4).

Secondly, they tend to assume that the police will use any power given to the fullest extent legally possible, and will strain to extend it.

'If rules are promulgated permitting torture in defined circumstances, some officials are bound to want to explore the outer bounds of the rules. Having been regularized, the practice will become regular' (Posner, quoted in Dershowitz 2003: 279). Posner was echoing claims made in debates around the introduction of PACE: 'The problem is that if the law is to "inhibit" police officers then it must always diverge to some extent from the rules that officers would write for themselves' (Baldwin and Kinsey 1985: 91). From this perspective if, metaphorically, the police are given authority to drive at 30 mph, they will drive at 35. 'To increase the limit to 35 mph will not close the gap', but will simply lead to 40 mph driving (Baldwin 1985: 21). Such accounts can slip too easily into what Reiner calls 'a law of inevitable increment: whatever powers the police have they will exceed by a given margin' (Reiner 1992: 217).[14] Reiner goes on to provide a good critique of such formulations:

> police abuse is not the product of some overweening constabulary malevolence constantly bursting the seams of whatever rules for regulating conduct are laid down. It is based on pressure to achieve specific results...If the police can achieve their proper objects within the law then one strain making for deviation disappears (Reiner 1992: 217–18).

If there is too great a gap between what police are expected to achieve and the means allowed to them, then they may go beyond the rules, and the rules may follow. Regulatory decline under the weight of 'objectives' is vividly illustrated by a participant's account of interrogation in Afghanistan and Iraq:

> The prohibition on the use of stress positions early in the war gave way to policies allowing their use to punish prisoners for disrespectful behaviour. The rules were relaxed further by those who followed us at Bagram, and within a year stress positions were a formally authorized interrogation technique by the command in Iraq. Rules regarding sleep deprivation, isolation, meal manipulation, and sensory deprivation followed similar trajectories (Mackey 2004: 471–2).

It is often claimed that authorization is a step on to a slippery slope: 'Once torture is available for terrorists in extreme circumstances, someone will inevitably demand it in less extreme circumstances, and then for serial rapists or murderers, or even for those accused of lesser crimes' (Parry 2002: 763). They may well demand this, but law making is not a slippery slope from which escape is impossible. More positively, statutory regulation's provision to officers of an authoritative statement of what is required can be significant symbolically as well as instrumentally. Officers who want to do 'the right thing' are given a resource for use in arguments with others about how suspects should be treated. Similarly, reducing the potential for 'comeback' from a system often experienced as uncertain and capricious is a significant benefit to officers.

The limits of regulation by rules have to be acknowledged. Those favouring legal regulation are often over-optimistic about its likely impact. A wide range of positions are included here, from the simple legalistic-bureaucratic approach of the politician who thinks that passing a law is the remedy for all ills (Dixon 1997: 1–2) to the sophistication of Dershowitz's attempt to make liberal principle connect with empirical reality.

We may not be able to set the limit at 20 mph, even if we want to. So, when Dershowitz says that he hopes 'no torture warrant would ever be issued, because the criteria for obtaining one would be so limited and vigorous' (quoted in Parry 2002: 747) the realism of his approach dissipates. Would no warrant mean no torture – or just torture more carefully hidden in the gulag of America's military bases and the prisons of dependent states?[15] His legalistic faith in the power of law seems quaint: legality has never appeared to be a particularly significant factor in the operations of the CIA. It is hard, for example, to read the American government's list of approved techniques of interrogation without concluding that it is largely for presentational purposes (Department of Defence 2003).

The key lesson is that the impact of rules is contingent, not determined. A review of the extensive literature on legal regulation (Dixon 1997) leads to the conclusion that, whilst the potential of rules should not be overstated, nor should it be underestimated: 'In short, some things work' (Walker 1993: 150). Crucial factors include: the nature of the activity; the degree of commitment to practice; other cultural commitments and factors amongst practitioners; its vulnerability to regulation; the nature of the rules and other regulatory strategies deployed; the commitment of supervisors to implementation; allocation of resources to supervision and accountability; countervailing pressures from institutions on practitioners; and perceptions of the likelihood and weight of punishment for breach. Such factors account for the difference between stop/search and treatment of suspects in police stations in England and Wales. The former involves a low-visibility practice, limited potential for regulation, strong cultural commitment, lack of fit between rules and working norms, and countervailing pressures on patrol officers (to produce arrests). The latter involves potential scrutiny and supervision (not least through a paper trail); allocation of specific responsibility to custody officers; perception that disciplinary action was a real threat; and cultural factors (the tension between uniformed and detective officers).

The impact of a policy of authorizing and regulating depends on contextual factors. Whilst in NSW protection of suspects' rights has been insubstantial and largely rhetorical, in England and Wales some substance was given by the provision of public funding for legal advice in police stations and the organization of lawyers to provide such advice.

Much rule-based regulation of interrogation is, by necessity, indirect because of the nature of the activity. Specific rules are useful at the extremes: a prohibition of torture may require interpretation and application, but there would be widespread agreement about its central meaning. What constitutes 'inhuman and degrading treatment' or (as noted above) 'oppression' or 'unfairness' is more contestable. One way of recognizing such problems is to focus on the regulation of the interrogation's context. So, for example, PACE includes a complex scheme of rules for the questioning of suspects: it should be conducted in a police station so that rules activating other mechanisms (supervision, openness and recording) can operate; the length of detention and interrogation sessions is limited; the welfare of the suspect is covered by rules on access to food, drink and sleep; and access to legal advice and, in the case of vulnerable suspects, appropriate adults such as parents and social workers is available. Interrogation practice can be manipulated by using regulation to change significant features in its context. In addition, the symbolic impact of rules should not be underestimated: if (and this is not necessarily the case) the regulatory change receives strong endorsement from leaders (inside and outside police departments) whom officers respect, then it is more likely to be effective.

There are other rules of which account must be taken. Increasingly, criminal justice has to acknowledge human rights obligations. These are usually written in such general terms allowing exceptions and derogations that their impact on police practice will only come after the courts have developed a jurisprudence of interpretation and application.

Training as regulation

Learning how to interview suspects was long regarded as a matter of absorbing a craft skill, one to be learnt by watching and learning from senior colleagues. An Australian police inspector advised young officers in the following terms:

> Most outstanding interrogators will be able to help you with certain advice, but rarely are they able to define themselves just what makes them so successful in this field. It is an ability developed over the years, coupled with experience of all types of criminals, which enables them to sum up the suspect and ask the right questions at the appropriate time (Crowley 1972: 419–20).

This was not a skill that all could acquire equally well: Innes found that 'at the heart of police notions of "the good detective" was the sense that certain individuals had a particular flair for the work. The most valuable skills were held to be those developed through natural instinct and experience' (2003: 9).

This approach to interviewing has come under increasing criticism. In England, concerns about investigative weaknesses and miscarriages of justice led to scrutiny of the quality of police interviewing. The Royal Commission on Criminal Procedure recommended reform of interview training (Philips 1981: 10.14), but this was 'the neglected recommendation and little was done for nearly ten years to implement it' (Williamson 1993: 92). In this vacuum, police officers who were interested in improving their interviewing skills almost inevitably looked to the USA. American interview training manuals – notably Inbau and Reid's – were a significant influence in some areas, encouraging officers to use persuasive interrogation techniques (Williamson 1993: 92; Milne and Bull 1999: 156). American material was used in training materials, police magazines, and strongly influenced the first British police interview manual, Walkley's *Police Interrogation* (1987). When such approaches to interrogation began to be officially frowned upon, nothing was provided to replace them, and so they continued to form a significant part of an informal curriculum of material distributed amongst police officers.

Research on interrogation practice discovered significant problems:

> Questioning practice could be characterized as bland information
> gathering... The level of questioning skill was quite low, with
> officers capitulating at the slightest obstacle... Many interviews
> appeared chaotic and unstructured. In a significant number the
> allegation was never put to the suspect. In others the questioning
> appeared to lack basic preparation and planning. Many of the
> officers seemed more nervous than the suspect (Williamson
> 1993: 97–8).

Similar assessments were made by Baldwin (1993) and Moston
and Engelberg (1993). Such research had a major impact, directly
influencing a new National Investigative Training Course which was
launched in 1993 (Home Office 1993) and has subsequently been
revised and expanded. The outcome was a large-scale programme in
which police officers in England and Wales received basic training
in investigative interviewing, supplemented by four additional
tiers of training for investigators in more serious cases, specialists
and supervisors (Burbeck 2003: 50). The accredited approach is
'investigative interviewing', which was constructed around the
seemingly inevitable police use of a mnemonic acronym, PEACE.[16]

The new approach to police interrogation training was positively
appraised by the Home Office (McGurk *et al.* 1993), but a much more
critical assessment was provided by Clarke and Milne (2001). Officers
were found to be not using the specific techniques of PEACE: indeed,
there was little difference between the performance of officers who
were trained and those who were not. Whilst the results may be
disappointing, it would be a mistake to adopt Sanders and Young's
conclusion that 'miscarriages of justice... would be more effectively
reduced by preventing confession evidence forming the sole basis of
convictions, and by providing the defence with the same resources as
are provided to the prosecution, than by trying to change interrogation
practices' (2003: 242). Given the poor record of corroboration
requirements and the impossibility of 'equality of arms' in criminal
justice, this seems unfortunately, if characteristically, negative.

The picture is not as bleak as Sanders and Young suggest. Whilst
Clarke and Milne found 'few statistically significant differences
between trained and untrained officers', they rightly note that 'the
possibility of finding an untrained sample that is naïve and has not
been influenced in some way by PEACE interviewing is remote' (2001:
100). As they suggest, it would be more appropriate to compare the
interviews in their sample as a whole with those conducted before
1991. From this perspective, 'there was clear evidence... that since

the introduction of PEACE an improvement in the ethos and ethical approach to interviewing has taken place' (2001: 100) and 'PEACE training has developed the skills used by police officers to interview suspects of crime' (2001: 113). Whilst 'ten per cent of the sample was rated as possibly breaching PACE' (2001: 100), the picture presented is very different from the pervasive misconduct and incompetence found earlier by Williamson, Moston and Baldwin. PEACE is more important for its impact in undermining previously accepted strategies than for the specific techniques of information gathering and checking which it incorporates. At its heart is a simple, but crucial, shift of emphasis: rather than setting out to gain a confession which confirms a case theory to which the officer is firmly committed, the interrogating officer is encouraged to get the suspect's account and then to check its authenticity by questioning and testing it against other evidence.

Responding to perceived problems by seeking to train (or re-train) staff in newly approved techniques (often linked to new rules, guidelines, or codes of practice) is a very familiar regulatory strategy. It is, for example, the approach routinely adopted by university managers who want to change research supervision practices. All too often, insufficient attention is paid to the continuing causes of the problem which the training is intended to rectify. If research supervision is not structured into academic workloads and research students are not culturally integrated into academic schools, training in approved supervision practices is unlikely to have much effect. Similarly, there is no point insisting in PEACE that preparation is vital for good interviewing if officers' workloads are not managed so that time for preparation is available.

The direct effect of training may well be limited. However, training should be seen as a tangible expression of a more significant changing of expectations and values in policing. Whilst police departments are notoriously resistant to change, it would have been surprising if there was no impact from, for example, a royal commission which exposed an endemic process corruption (Wood 1997) or cases so damaging from a crime control perspective as *Heron*[17] or *Paris*.[18] It is better to see PEACE as an expression of and a contributor to a broader change. Whilst officers may not structure their interrogations according to the cognitive methodology of PEACE, more important is the fact that many officers replace inefficient and/or coercive techniques with an approach which incorporates basic elements of effective interviewing in any context, such as asking clear questions, listening to what the interviewee has to say, responding appropriately and treating the interviewee decently. Crucially, new role models for the young officer become available: the tradition of arresting on hunches, interrogating, and giving weak cases a run has been challenged by according status to officers who investigate and collect evidence carefully, find ways of working within the rules, interrogate skilfully and get convictions which are not overturned on appeal (Dixon 1997: 163–4).[19]

From the regulatory perspective adopted here, PEACE is a form of self-regulation induced by sustained external criticism. Whilst it was encouraged by the Home Office, PEACE was developed by the police, working out a way of interrogating that would both withstand judicial scrutiny and would produce results. Rather than imposing rules backed by threat of sanction – the classic command/control mode – PEACE provides a way of doing the job. The challenge was to provide an alternative to established working practices which were connected to cultural norms and values and beliefs – the imperative of obtaining confessions, the working style of the detective, the expectation that suspects will crack under coercive, persuasive questioning. The toehold that PEACE could exploit was the evidence that traditional practices were inefficient, leading to the conviction of the innocent and the evasion of justice by the really guilty. This provided an opportunity for a new approach to interrogation, a partial application of PEACE, to become the standard way of working, to make the crucial transition from externally imposed standard to working norm and self-regulation (Parker and Braithwaite 2003: 137). The need to address existing norms was illustrated well at the Quebec conference by Shaw's and Griffith's insistence that investigative interviewing is not a soft option and that it can incorporate searching and intensive questioning of suspects.[20]

Managerial and supervisory regulation

A corollary of the traditional individualistic approach to criminal investigation which has been discussed above was the lack of positive managerial control or supervision. This was part of a general tendency of police organizations to operate as 'punishment-centred bureaucracies': managers intervened, officers were disciplined and rules were made or revised when things went wrong (Dixon 1997). In our research on the implementation of PACE (Bottomley *et al.* 1991), we found that supervision was seen as an essentially negative process.

In considering the potential role of managerial and supervisory regulation of interrogation, it is particularly important to be clear about the problem (if any) such regulation is intended to counter and the purpose such regulation is intended to achieve. If policy-makers, managers and supervisors are satisfied with their interrogators' performance in what is perceived to be their role of getting confessions and convictions, regulation may well be loose. If however there is concern about over-reliance on interrogation as an investigatory tactic and disquiet about the means of production and reliability of such confessions, regulation will be tighter. A number of possibilities are available. Management may seek to undermine the cultural status of interrogation (and interrogators) by emphasizing other investigative methods. For example, the National Crime Faculty's text on investigative interviewing challenges the traditional concentration on suspects by emphasizing the importance of interviewing victims and witnesses. Accounts given in such interviews provide a 'major source of evidence' and should be fully investigated 'before interviewing any suspect'. Interviews with suspects are given a secondary role: 'An admission from a suspect may go some way to supporting a subsequent prosecution and conviction but should not be solely relied upon to guarantee it' (1998a: 17).

Secondly, managers can affect the way crime is investigated by their deployment of resources. Managers can provide the conditions for change in practice: most obviously, time for the preparation and planning which is intrinsic to PEACE (Clarke and Milne 2001: 99) and which is so often not found by officers. They can routinize good practice by encouraging and requiring the use of standard form interview plan documents. If these are well-designed and include the caution and the wording of notices about recording, legal advice, and the role of appropriate adults they will be attractively useful to interviewers (see, for example, Northumbria Police 1998).

As Innes shows, the traditional structure for the investigation of serious crime was to allocate a case to a senior investigating officer and leave him (or, rarely, her) in charge. Successful as this may often have been, a central flaw was its vulnerability to the senior investigating officer's commitment to a 'case theory' (McConville 1989) which turned out to be mistaken: 'Several of the more experienced officers interviewed were able to recall examples where the officer leading an investigation had developed a theory or "hunch" on a case and became fixated on this, ignoring contradictory evidence or possibilities' (Innes 2003: 84). In this model, the SIO was the only officer with an overview of the inquiry: 'The less senior officers in an inquiry often had only a partial understanding of what they were investigating and, sometimes as a result of their limited knowledge, significant items of evidence were missed' (Innes 2003: 84). There have been numerous documented cases in which officers became convinced of their suspect's guilt and refused to consider or suppressed exculpatory evidence. An Australian example is the Blackburn investigation, which was almost a caricature of the police improperly operating on a case theory. One officer's commitment to his hunch that Blackburn (who was, ironically, himself a mid-ranking police officer) resembled descriptions of a serial rapist led to 'the falsification and distortion of virtually all the evidence brought against him and complete suppression of the evidence pointing to his innocence' (Lee 1990: 473). All this emerged only when the senior investigator was injured in a road accident following the celebration of Blackburn's arrest. The officer who took over exposed the deficiencies in the investigation, and the ensuing scandal led to the establishment of a royal commission.

Unable to rely on car crashes to disrupt case theories, police managers in England have tried to spread responsibility from the senior investigating officer to a group in which, it is hoped, case theories will be more critically assessed. The autocratic model of investigation has been challenged by a 'more systematic and bureaucratic approach' in which knowledge of and responsibility for an inquiry are spread through a team (Innes 2003: 85). If this approach operates as intended, the decision to question a suspect is not that of the SIO following his nose, but the outcome of a considered process. Similarly, the product of an interview will be assessed by more than one person. Indeed, the interrogation itself may be conducted not by an officer previously involved in the case, but by a specialist in interrogating suspects. Whilst other methods may help to limit the impact of case theories during an interrogation, this organization can impact at an earlier stage, preventing inevitable, possibly productive hunches from degenerating into inaccurate, misleading case theories.

Several internal police projects showed that a precondition for successful implementation of the investigative interviewing model is managerial support and active supervision, but that such supervision was often lacking even in forces with supervision policies (Clarke and Milne 2001: 11–14). Having a supervision policy was found to be significantly associated with better interviewing (2001: 117–18). As Clarke and Milne suggest, if having a policy appears to have a desirable effect, then its vigorous implementation should be more beneficial: 'regular and good quality supervision of interviews would lead to a dramatic improvement of skill transference' (2001: 118).

Clarke and Milne's research and the work of key exponents of good interviewing practice at force and national level (such as Gary Shaw, initially in Northumbria Police, now at Centrex) have challenged the individualistic model of criminal investigation by demonstrating the value of active management and supervision of interrogation. This approach is now expressed in a series of ACPO policies and national training strategies which pass on the message that active supervision can improve performance in suspect interviewing (Burbeck 2003: 52). Supervision is to be encouraged by the appointment of 'force champions' for investigative interviewing, and 'interview advisers', whose role is to give advice and assistance on a wide range of matters to investigating officers in complex, volume and serious crime and to improve the quality of interviewing (Centrex 2003: 4–5, 36–7). Crucially, these policies seek to spread best practice which has been developed at operational level. This is an important example of regulation working from the bottom up rather than the top down. Notably, the role of 'interview adviser' was developed by Northumbria Police and then adopted by several other forces before being endorsed by ACPO. Quality is to be tested both by remote monitoring of interrogations as they are being conducted (Home Office 1995) and by emphasizing the importance of the retrospective 'evaluation' required by the PEACE model. The latter should involve sampling of interview records.

At a basic level, the need for such supervision was demonstrated in my research on audio-visual recording in New South Wales, Australia (Dixon 2004b, forthcoming). A random sample of tapes showed that, at some stations, the same technological problem recurred over extended periods. In the worst case, six tapes recorded over a 12-month period in one station suffered from what was apparently the same malfunction, producing a badly blurred visual image. If supervisors were not taking responsibility for simple processes of tape quality control, then *a fortiori* they were not taking advantage of the opportunity offered by audio-visual recording to monitor and improve the interrogation practices of their officers.

As discussed above, police practice may bear little relation to what policy or training requires: but there is now, at very least, an authoritative endorsement of an approach to managerial and supervisory regulation of interrogation which is very different from what went before. The need for active supervision is bluntly expressed:

Information from suspects is vital to any investigation. For this reason, it is not acceptable for investigating or supervisor officers to simply select interviewers and then stand back from the planning and subsequent management of the interview. Investigating or supervisory officers should be influential in developing an interview strategy and must play an active role in its implementation (Burbeck: 2003).

Internal police management and supervision increasingly takes place within a regulatory framework in which the traditional devices of political and legal accountability are replaced by more intrusive managerialist regulation characterized by 'distinct systems of audit, grievance-handling, standard-setting, inspection and evaluation' (Hood *et al.* 1999: 4). For example in England and Wales since the 1990s, a plethora of reports from the Audit Commission, Her Majesty's Inspectorate of Constabulary, the Home Office and the Association of Chief Police Officers has imposed new demands for performance indicators, monitoring, audit, value, efficiency and effectiveness (Dixon 2004a: 123–5). Such regulation – in theory at least – is concerned more with improving performance than using coercive means to enforce compliance (Hood *et al.* 1999: 6). However, positive regulation is still finding its place in policing systems with deeply engrained disciplinary cultures.

Openness and audio-visual recording

Since K.C. Davis's *Discretionary Justice* (1971), the need for openness has been a key theme in public law and regulation: opening official practices to scrutiny, complaint and praise are a vital part of regulation and accountability:

> In the nature of things it is not possible for the cellblock, charge office and interview rooms of a police station to be open to members of the public to come or go as they please. But the procedures should provide satisfactory means of supervision and review, in order that the suspicions of what goes on behind those closed doors can be diminished (Philips 1981: 20).

This was how the (English) Royal Commission on Criminal Procedure expressed the need for openness as one of its three 'standards to be applied to investigative arrangements'. The opening of the investigative process is a notable feature of the last two decades. The secretive world (which I experienced in my early fieldwork in Sydney) into which suspects used to disappear without supervision by senior officers, intimation to a solicitor or family, or contemporaneous recording of interviews have been challenged (at least for those not suspected of terrorist offences) by electronic recording of cell-blocks, 'custody suites' and interrogations rooms (discussed below), and the presence (or potential presence) in stations of appropriate adults, legal advisers, researchers and others. Of course, the station and the interview room are still 'police territory', but the practical and cultural impact of greater openness should not be under-estimated.

Of particular significance in the current context is electronic recording of interrogations. Such recording is frequently presented as a solution to the ills of custodial interrogation. Interest in such recording is not new: there have been calls for its use from the time that recording equipment was widely available. However, the contemporary advocacy of audio-visual recording is more widespread, united and urgent than before.

Notably, calling for the use of electronic recording has become a standard component of proposed programmes to avoid miscarriages of justice in the USA (e.g. Leo 2001; Drizin and Reich 2004). A prominent example was provided in 2003 by the State of Illinois. In response to concern about 13 people who had been convicted and sentenced to death, only to be exonerated by proof (usually DNA evidence) of their innocence, Illinois legislated to require police to record electronically interviews with murder suspects. The reform was designed 'to restore the integrity of the criminal justice system'.[21] All too often, electronic recording is put forward as a panacea. There is little consideration of how or why it will deal with the problem: it is taken for granted that it will.

Criminal justice practitioners and researchers tend to be parochial. In Anglo-American discussions of audio-visual recording, there is little recognition that several Australian jurisdictions have been using audio-visual recording for more than a decade, not just in field trials, research experiments or selected cases, but routinely for questioning about all indictable offences. This is in contrast to England and Wales, where the caution led to a reliance on audiotaping (although the sporadic interest in video is now being revived; Newburn *et al.* 2004). In the USA, audio-visual recording is widespread, but is generally used only for read-backs in the most serious cases (Geller 1992). The Australian experience provides important guidance for other jurisdictions considering the routine, compulsory audio-visual recording of police questioning of suspects.

The key findings of my empirical research (2004b forthcoming) are that the concerns usually expressed about electronic recording have not been substantiated. The interrogator's job has not become impossible: suspects continue to make confessions and admissions. As seems typical, police opinion has shifted from antagonism and scepticism to acceptance and enthusiasm. The removal of the taint of verballing has benefited the criminal justice process, both ideologically by increasing public confidence and instrumentally by reducing the court time spent on challenges to confessional evidence. However, there are problems. Whilst audio-visual recording makes simple verballing impossible, inadequate legal regulation of the process means that recorded interviews are often preceded by unrecorded questioning which may undermine the reliability of any subsequent recorded confession. Secondly, there is a worrying tendency amongst some criminal justice professionals to believe that they can use the recorded image to read the suspect's body language.

Most importantly for present purposes, electronic recording has two principal effects. First, it opens up the previously closed world of the interrogation room – even if, as noted above, this opening is not complete. Secondly, recordings provide officers with an opportunity to see themselves at work. This is usually an excellent way of challenging complacency about interview skills and inducing self-regulation. Once the hurdle of introduction has been jumped, electronic recording has distinct advantages as a regulatory device. Unlike supervisors or, worse, external regulators, the technology can be seen as neutral and unthreatening. Its use becomes the way that the job has to be done.

Conclusion

Looking at the cables of a suspension bridge, my son once asked me 'Why are they holding that bridge down?' I explained that, in fact, they were holding it up. A similar reversal of a commonsense perspective is necessary to understand regulation. Good regulation does not just negatively sanction and discipline: equally importantly, it positively encourages, shapes and directs. The most significant impact of such influences may be indirect: shifting expectations and values may be the long-term contribution of a specific regulatory measure. As suggested throughout this chapter, such influences have to compete with many others: efforts to improve interrogation practices can be undermined by other demands for change in criminal justice.

Regulation should seek positively to foster good policing, not merely to sanction bad practice. A welcome emphasis in the work of writers concerned with regulation is this stress on the positive, for example Braithwaite's identification of what a 'good police service' would look like (1992) or Lacey's emphasis on the need for 'reflection and public debate on the normative political issues of what the role of the police *should* be in a democratic society' (1992: 385). The main objective of the regulation of interrogation is to redefine what is good interrogating.

Police organizations must become as adept at identifying good practice and rewarding officers for carrying it out as they are at creating disciplinary rules and punishing officers for breaking them: 'a programme of "positive discipline" stressing and rewarding integrity is crucial' (Punch 1985: 196). This must involve both individual rewards[22] and organizational recognition (e.g. by the communication of information about successes). Police organizations notoriously rely on negative discipline. It is conventional to include them in Gouldner's category of 'punishment-centred bureaucracies' (1954). The difficulty of change should not be underestimated: Krantz *et al.* found that 'many of the problems associated with the use of negative sanctions also hampers the application of positive incentives' (1979: 61). The fate of reform efforts in the NSW Police shows how external political pressures can stifle fundamental change (Dixon 1999).

This is not to underplay the role of sanction.[23] In a setting where there is pressure for results and the continuing influence of a crime control culture, 'soft regulation' is unlikely to be enough. An appropriate warning can be drawn from Hodgson's analysis of French criminal justice where the non-adversarial approach is expressed in relations of mutual trust and confidence between the police and their supposed judicial regulators which, in practice, promote ineffective supervision and highly undesirable police practices (Hodgson 2004).

Sanction may be hard to apply to individuals when, as in the case of interrogating, norms are uncertain and developing. Whilst punishment for individuals is certainly appropriate in clear cases, it is more important to focus sanctions on the organization. Lessons from corporate regulation are very relevant here. Fining a publicly funded police department for malpractice in interrogation would not be useful. Much more so would be a public shaming of a department through public, media and political criticism. Removing the chief officer and establishing an external inquiry are typical features of such shaming. However, recent experience in England and Australia shows that governments will only tolerate this process for a limited time before criminal justice politics reverts to the rhetoric of crime-fighting and law and order politics (Dixon 1999, 2004a). Just as a corporation may respond to regulation in ways other than the simple compliance assumed by a rational deterrence model (Baldwin 2004), so it is wrong to assume that concerted action to root out misconduct and introduce reform is the only 'rational' response to problems in interrogating suspects.

The conclusion is that regulating police interrogation is no easier – or harder – than regulating many other areas of policing. There are some conditions of successful regulation, only some of which are subject to police control. Research and experience in other regulatory settings indicate that a positive strategy which makes clear what officers should do in order to work efficiently may work. However, its success depends on other factors: if the police are under irresistible pressure to produce results, or if the type of person they question is so stigmatized, or if the process is concerned with risk and security so that justice concepts become irrelevant, then regulation is much less likely to be effective.

Notes

1. For an exception (although not considering policing and using a narrower definition of regulation than that adopted here), see Hood *et al.* (1999).
2. *R* v. *Heron*, unreported, Leeds Crown Court, 1 Nov. 1993; see Dixon (1997: 172–6), Gudjonsson (2003: 96–106).
3. 583 US 760 [1003].
4. *Williams* v. *R* [1986] 66 ALR 385 at p.398.
5. [2004] HCA 12. See now *Nicholls v The Queen, Coates v The Queen* [2005] HCA 1, in which the High Court shifted from narrow legalism to a purposive approach. Continuing conflicts between such modes of judicial reasoning limit the value of case law in regulating police interrogation.
6. See, e.g. *Fulling* [1987] 1 QB 426; *R* v. *Paris et al.* [1993] 97 Cr. App. R. 99.
7. op. cit., n. 2.
8. Police and Criminal Evidence Act 1984 s. 78 (1).
9. Williams op. cit., n. 4. See Dixon (1997: 208–9).
10. In England and Wales, cases involving arrogant and gross misconduct, such as *Canale* ([1990] 91 Cr. App. R.1) and *Paris*, were influential. In NSW, a royal commission into police corruption (Wood 1997) had considerable similar influence.

11. James Boyd White, quoted Krygier (1990: 640). Self-evidently, this depends on the breadth of those limits.

12. A problem for this argument is that the law, in the form of the Geneva Convention against Torture, already deals with torture by imposing a complete ban. Dershowitz argues that the US adoption of the convention was subject to a reservation that the USA is bound 'only to the extent that it is consistent with the Eighth Amendment' (2002: 136).

13. But for the record, I am with the latter. Note particularly Langbein's historical demonstration that 'efforts to accommodate the use of torture within the Western legal tradition have a long history', which included its abandonment because the resulting confessions were unreliable (2004: 93). It seems that we are returning to the Middle Ages in more ways than one.

14. It is strange that Baldwin, who produces some of the best work on regulation, misread PACE so badly; see Dixon (1997: 169–70).

15. Note the limited impact of Israel's attempt to constrain torture by law (Kremnitzer and Segev 2000).

16. PEACE = preparation and planning; engage and explain; account, clarification and challenge; closure; evaluation.

17. op. cit., n. 2.

18. op. cit., n. 6; see also Sekar (1997).

19. Of course, some other less attractive role models are increasingly available – for example, a police officer may feel that 'conversation management' is not enough when harsher methods are officially approved elsewhere (e.g. Department of Defence 2003). Hollywood also contributes – for example, in the casting of Denzel Washington in *Man on Fire*, 'the first authentic American blockbuster in which the hero doesn't just go on a killing rampage but on a torture spree as well' (Cox 2004). Meanwhile, for the counter terrorism unit in the TV series *24*, torture is as routine and morally unproblematic as taking fingerprints.

20. Presentation given at International Conference on Police Interviewing, Nicolet, Quebec, Canada, 9–11 February, 2004.

21. Governor Rod Blagojevich, quoted in 'Ill. Law 1st to order taping murder confessions' (*USA Today* 18 July 2001: 3A). Maine has followed Illinois, with more states to follow. Taping is required in Alaska and Minnesota as a result of court rulings (Drizin and Leo 2004; Drizin and Reich 2004).

22. See, e.g., the stress on the need for supervisors to identify what went well and what could be improved (rather than negative criticism or checking compliance with PACE) in providing feedback on interviews (National Crime Faculty 1998b: 7–8; cf. Audit Commission 1993: 27).

23. In criminal justice, there is, however, no indication of the drift towards punitive regulation which Baldwin (2004) identifies in other fields.

References

Alderson, K (2001) 'Powers and responsibilities: reforming NSW criminal investigation law.' Unpublished PhD thesis, UNSW.

Audit Commission (1993) *Helping with Enquiries*. London: Audit Commission.

Ayres, I. and Braithwaite, J. (1992) *Responsive Regulation*. New York, NY: Oxford University Press.

Baldwin, J. (1993) 'Police interview techniques: establishing truth or proof?', *British Journal of Criminology*, 33: 325–52.

Baldwin, R. (1985) 'Taking rules to excess', in C. Jones and M. Brenton (eds) *The Yearbook of Social Policy in Britain 1984–5*. London: Routledge & Kegan Paul.

Baldwin, R. (2004) 'The new punitive regulation', *Modern Law Review*, 67: 351–83.

Baldwin, R. and Kinsey, R (1985) 'Rules, realism and the Police Act', *Critical Social Policy*, 12: 89–102.

Baldwin, R., Scott, C. and Hood, C. (eds) (1998) *A Reader on Regulation*. Oxford: Oxford University Press.

Black, J. (2002) 'Critical reflections on regulation', *Australian Journal of Legal Philosophy*, 27: 1–35.

Bottomley, A.K., Coleman, C.A., Dixon, D., Gill, M. and Wall, D. (1991) *The Impact of PACE: Policing in a Northern Force*. Hull: Centre for Criminology and Criminal Justice.

Braithwaite, J. (1992) 'Good and bad police services and how to pick them', in P. Moir and H. Eijkman (eds) *Policing Australia*. South Melbourne: Macmillan.

Burbeck, J. (2003) *Standard Entry for ACPO Manuals on Investigative Interviewing from the National Strategic Group on Investigative Interviewing*. London: Association of Chief Police Officers.

Centrex (2003) *Training Curriculum for Tier 5 of the ACPO Investigative Interviewing Strategy*. Bramshill: Centrex.

Chan, J. (1997) *Changing Police Culture*. Melbourne: Cambridge University Press.

CIHR/CHRGJ (2004) *Torture by Proxy: International and Domestic Law Applicable to 'Extraordinary Renditions'*. New York, NY: Committee on International Human Rights of the Association of the Bar of the City of New York and Center for Human Rights and Global Justice, New York University School of Law.

Clarke, C. and Milne, R. (2001) *National Evaluation of the PEACE Investigative Interviewing Course*. Police Research Award Scheme Report PRAS/149.

Cox, A. (2004) 'Column', *Guardian*, 6 August.

Crowley, W.D. (1972) 'The interrogation of suspects', in D. Chappell and P. Wilson (eds) *The Australian Criminal Justice System*. Sydney: Butterworths.

Davis, K.C. (1971) *Discretionary Justice* (2nd edn). Urbana: University of Illinois Press.

Department of Defense (2003) *Working Group Report on Detainee Interrogations in the Global War on Terrorism*. Washington, DC: Department of Defense.

Dershowitz, A.M (2002) 'Should the ticking bomb be tortured?', in *Why Terrorism Works*. New Haven, CT: Yale University Press.

Dershowitz, A.M (2003) 'The torture warrant: a response to Professor Strauss', *New York Law School Law Review*, 48: 275–94.

Dixon, D. (1997) *Law in Policing: Legal Regulation and Police Practices*. Oxford: Clarendon Press.

Dixon, D. (ed.) (1999) *A Culture of Corruption: Changing an Australian Police Service*. Sydney: Hawkins Press.

Dixon, D. (2004a) 'Police governance and official inquiry', in J. Pratt and G. Gilligan (eds) *Crime, Truth and Justice*. Cullompton: Willan Publishing.

Dixon, D. (2004b) 'A window into the interviewing process'? The audio-visual recording of police interviews with suspects in New South Wales, Australia.' Paper presented at the International Conference on Police Interviewing, École Nationale de Police du Québec, February.

Dixon, D. (forthcoming) *Interrogating Images: The Audio-visual Recording of Police Interviews with Suspects*.

Drizin, S.A. and Leo, R.A. (2004) 'The problem of false confessions in the post-DNA world', *North Carolina Law Review*, 82: 891–1008.

Drizin, S.A. and Reich, M.J. (2004) 'Heeding the lessons of history: the need for mandatory recoding of police interrogations to accurately assess the reliability and voluntariness of confessions', *Drake Law Review*, 52: 619–46.

Finnane, M. (1994) *Police and Government*. Melbourne: Oxford University Press.

Geller, W.A. (1992) *Police Videotaping of Suspect Interrogations and Confessions: A Preliminary Examination of Issues and Practices*. Washington, DC: National Institute of Justice.

Golden, T. (2004) 'After terror, a secret rewriting of military law', *The New York Times*, 24 October.

Gouldner, A.V. (1954) *Patterns of Industrial Bureaucracy*. New York: Free Press.

Gudjonsson, G. (2003) *The Psychology of Interrogations and Confessions*. Chichester: Wiley.

Hodgson, J. (2001) 'The police, the prosecutor and the juge d'instruction', *British Journal of Criminology*, 41: 342–61.

Hodgson, J. (2004) 'The detention and interrogation of suspects in police custody in France', *European Journal of Criminology*, 1: 163–99.

Home Office (1993) *Investigative Interviewing: National Training Package*. Circular 7/1993. London: Home Office.

Home Office (1995) *Guidelines for Monitoring of Tape Recorded Interviews with Suspects. Circular 50/1995*. London: Home Office.

349

Hood, C., Scott, C., James, O. and Travers, T. (1999) *Regulation inside Government*. Oxford: Oxford University Press.

Ignatieff, M. (2004) *The Lesser Evil: Political Ethics in an Age of Terror*. Edinburgh: Edinburgh University Press.

Inbau, F.E., Reid, J.E., Buckley, J.P. and Jayne, B.C. (2001) *Criminal Interrogation and Confessions* (4th edn). Gaithersburg, MD: Aspen.

Innes, M. (2003) *Investigating Murder*. Oxford: Oxford University Press.

Krantz, S., Gilman, B., Benda, C., Hallstrom, C.R. and Nadworny, E.J. (1979) *Police Policymaking: The Boston Experience*. Lexington, MA: Lexington Books.

Kremnitzer, M. and Segev, R. (2000) 'The legality of interrogational torture' *Israel Law Review* 34: 509–59.

Krygier, M. (1990) 'Marxism and the rule of law: reflections after the fall of communism', *Law and Social Inquiry*, 15: 633–63.

Lacey, N. (1992) 'The jurisprudence of discretion: escaping the legal paradigm', in K. Hawkins (ed.) *The Uses of Discretion*. Oxford: Clarendon Press.

Langbein, J.H. (2004) 'The legal history of torture', in S. Levinson (ed.) *Torture*. New York, NY: Oxford University Press.

Lee, J.A. (1990) *Report of the Royal Commission of Inquiry into the Arrest, Charging and Withdrawal of Charges Against Harold James Blackburn*. Sydney: Government Printer.

Leo, R. (1994) 'Police interrogation and social control', *Social and Legal Studies*, 3: 93–120.

Leo, R. (1996) 'Inside the interrogation room', *Journal of Criminal Law and Criminology*, 86: 266–303.

Leo, R. (2001) 'False confessions: causes, consequences and solutions', in S.A. Westervelt and J.A. Humphrey (eds) *Wrongly Convicted: Perspectives on Failed Justice*. New Bruswick: Rutgers University Press.

Levinson, S. (ed.) (2004) *Torture*. New York, NY: Oxford University Press.

Mackey, C. with Miller, G. (2004) *The Interrogator's War*. London: John Murray.

Maguire, M. (2003) 'Criminal investigation and crime control', in T. Newburn (ed.) *Handbook of Policing*. Cullompton: Willan Publishing.

McConville, M. (1989) 'Weaknesses in the British judicial system', *Times Higher Education Supplement*, 3 November.

McConville, M., Sanders, A. and Leng, R. (1991) *The Case for the Prosecution*. London: Routledge.

McGurk, B.J., Carr, M.J. and McGurk, D. (1993) *Investigative Interviewing Courses for Police Officers: An Evaluation*. Police Research Series Paper 4. London: Home Office Police Department.

Milne, R. and Bull, R. (1999) *Investigative Interviewing*. Chichester: Wiley.

Moston, S. and Engelberg, T. (1993) 'Police questioning techniques in tape recorded interviews with criminal suspects', *Policing and Society*, 3: 223–37.

National Crime Faculty (1998a) *A Practical Guide to Investigative Interviewing*. Bramshill: NCF.

National Crime Faculty (1998b) *Investigative Interviewing: Supervisor's Workshop and Checklist*. Bramshill: NCF.

Newburn, T. *et al.* (2004). *The Introduction of Visual Recording of Police Interviews with Suspects*. LSE/Kent University, unpublished.

Northumbria Police (1998) *Suspect Interview Plan*. Ponteland: Northumbria Police.

Odgers, S. (1990) 'Police interrogation', *Criminal Law Journal*, 14: 220–48.

Packer, H. (1968) *The Limits of the Criminal Sanction*. Stanford: Stanford University Press.

Parker, C. and Braithwaite, J. (2003) 'Regulation', in P. Cane and M. Tushnet (eds) *The Oxford Handbook of Legal Studies*. Oxford: Oxford University Press.

Parker, C., Scott, C., Lacey, N. and Braithwaite, N. (2004) 'Introduction', in C. Parker *et al.* (eds) *Regulating Law*. Oxford: Oxford University Press.

Parry, J.T. (2002) 'Interrogating suspected terrorists: should torture be an option?', *University of Pittsburgh Law Review*, 63: 743–66.

Parry, J.T. (2005) 'Constitutional interpretation, coercive interrogation, and civil rights litigation after Chavez *v.* Martinez', *Georgia Law Review*, 39: 733–838.

Pearse, J. and Gudjonsson, G.H. (1996) 'Police interviewing techniques at two South London police stations', *Psychology, Crime and Law*, 3: 63–74.

Philips, C. (1981) *Report of the Royal Commission on Criminal Procedure* (Cmnd 8092). London: HMSO.

Punch, M. (1985) *Conduct Unbecoming: The Social Construction of Police Deviance and Control*. London: Tavistock.

Reiner, R. (1992) *The Politics of the Police*. Hemel Hempstead: Harvester Wheatsheaf.

Sanders, A. and Young, R. (2003) 'Police powers', in T. Newburn (ed.) *Handbook of Policing*. Cullompton: Willan Publishing.

Sekar, S. (1997) *Fitted In: The Cardiff 3 and the Lynette White Inquiry*. London: The Fitted In Project.

Skolnick, J.H. (1993) 'Justice without trial revisited', in D. Weisburd and C. Uchida (eds) *Police Innovation and Control of the Police*. New York, NY: Springer-Verlag.

Strauss, M. (2003) 'Torture', *New York Law School Law Review*, 48: 201–74.

Walker, S. (1980) *Popular Justice: A History of American Civil Liberties*. New York, NY: Oxford University Press.

Walker, S. (1993) *Taming the System: The Control of Discretion in Criminal Justice 1950–1990*. New York, NY: Oxford University Press.

Walkley, J. (1987) *Police Interrogation*. London: Police Review.

Williamson, T. (1993) 'From interrogation to investigative interviewing', *Journal of Community and Applied Psychology*, 3: 89–99.

Wood, J.R.T. (1997) *Report of the Royal Commission into the NSW Police Service*. Sydney: Royal Commission.

Conclusion

Tom Williamson

A few months after the first International Conference on Police Interviewing was held in Quebec, Canada in February 2004, pictures of the ill-treatment of prisoners detained by the American military at Abu Ghraib prison in Iraq were circulated around the world. More recently photographs of the ill-treatment of prisoners by British soldiers have also been widely circulated. In both cases courts martial have been held and some of those directly involved have been punished. Amongst the lessons to be learnt from these cases, two seem to have a particular relevance for this book. First, it is difficult to separate the treatment received by the detainees from the broader challenge to human rights currently taking place that is supported at the highest political levels in some democracies.

The notion quickly gained ground that the 'war on terror' represented such a threat to nation-states that it is now appropriate to operate on a means justifies the ends basis, where respect for human rights and judicial safeguards that have been developed over many years can be jettisoned. The rejection of a human rights framework for custodial questioning has serious repercussions for liberal democracies, and we see one consequence of this in the anti-terror legislation and extra judicial arrangements states are currently putting in place.

Slowly but surely the courts in various countries and occasionally government inquiries are looking into the abuses of fundamental human rights that took place in the wake of the attacks in the USA on 11 September 2001. The first 50 years after the Universal Declaration on Human Rights in 1948 was spent on gaining international acceptance of the principle of human rights and it was hoped that the next 50 years could be spent on gaining acceptance of the practice of human rights. It is too early to say what the ultimate price will be for failing to protect human rights in the war on terror. From a utilitarian perspective, will the price be worth it? Is it an effective strategy? It is worth bearing in mind the words of Kofi Anan, Secretary General of the United Nations at the Security Council meeting on 18 January 2002: 'There is no trade-off between effective action against terrorism and the protection of human rights. On the contrary, I believe that in the long term we shall find that human rights, along with democracy and social justice, are one of the best prophylactics against terrorism.'

The second major observation that can be made with regard to custodial questioning is that not enough people are trained to enable them to develop skills in questioning to do the job effectively. There is now sufficient evidence from scientific studies of the key components of effective methods for obtaining information through questioning. There continues to be an over-reliance on confession evidence and this has been a major contributor to miscarriages of justice in many countries, which comes out time and again when these cases attract the attention of a government inquiry. There are different training programmes but many of them contain similar core competencies, such as how to establish rapport. Studies in various countries have shown that humane questioning is more effective than techniques which are abusive. The psychological pressures on someone detained for questioning were identified by the US Supreme Court in *Miranda*, but there continues to be a great deal of ignorance about these psychological processes, and especially when the individual being questioned is vulnerable and may make a false confession. It is important that training programmes provide a greater awareness of the psychology of custody and interrogation as well as demonstrating the skills to obtain information. Psychological research has made an important contribution through developing methods that enable reliable and accurate information to be obtained. It has demonstrated that human memory is fragile and needs to be handled with care.

More enlightened ways of obtaining information through questioning will not of themselves be sufficient. Custodial question has often been an area devoid of supervision and regulation. Rules formulated by judges have been found to be wholly inadequate. As we enter the twenty-first century, the demand for more rigorous regulation will increase. Regulation can be negative or a force for good. For example, the introduction of audio and videotape recording often demonstrates that there is an urgent need for training. The issue is one of competence as well as of safeguarding against deviant behaviour. There are three basic requirements for a regulatory regime: the setting of standards; processes for monitoring compliance with the standards; and mechanisms for enforcing the standards (Parker 2004: 1). In order to produce a broadly defined outcome or outcomes, regulation may require not just mechanisms of standard-setting and information gathering but also programmes that achieve behaviour modification (Black 2002: 26). No practitioner or academic familiar with this area of research would underestimate the size of the challenge if there is to be significant modification of behaviour when it comes to custodial questioning. Our collective experience and the research discussed in the various chapters amply demonstrate that ethical and humane interviewing is also effective interviewing. There is sufficient common ground in the academic and practitioner communities to produce statements of what standards should be set, of what approaches work that would reinforce ethical values and respect for human rights and that increase investigative effectiveness. Publication of such standards and gaining international recognition for them represent the next big challenge for those promoting investigative interviewing.

At one point in the recent past there might have been optimism that investigators in a growing number of countries were learning that ethical ways of eliciting information were also making them individually more effective. A quiet revolution appeared to be underway. Without the imperative of increased effectiveness the interest in investigative interviewing would have withered away. The post-September 11 world has resulted in that ethic being challenged by an ends justifies the means, utilitarian logic. This approach has never been successful in law enforcement and is unlikely to prove successful in the elicitation of information by the military and intelligence communities. In law enforcement it led to numerous miscarriages of justice, some of which resulted in new forms of regulation that set higher standards and required a significant investment to bring about the behaviour modification that was needed. Might it be too naive to dare to hope that some good may similarly come from the various debacles that purported to be custodial questioning? It was not just that what was done was wrong and reprehensible, worse it was stupid and plainly ineffective. We hope that this book may go some way to correcting the appalling ignorance that led to such excesses. Third-degree methods of obtaining information should have no place in democracies in the twenty-first century. Smart investigators are able to demonstrate this through their increased effectiveness, and justice is better served which will contribute to a more stable foundation for democracy in late modernity.

References

Black, J. (2002) 'Critical reflections on regulation', *Australian Journal of Legal Philosophy*, 27: 1–35.

Parker, C., Scott, C., Lacey, N. and Braithewaite, N. (2004) 'Introduction', in C. Parker *et al.* (eds) *Regulating Law*. Oxford: Oxford University Press.

Index

9/11 *see* September 11 terrorist
    attacks
Abu Ghraib prison
    combining the role of guard and
        interrogator 73–4
    interrogation methods 52, 53, 54
        links with interrogation in the
            police environment 74–5
        understanding and
            categorizing 75–80
    use of untrained interrogators
        15
accountability 19
    demand for 6
active listening 93–5
admissibility of evidence 325
admissions, distinguishing between
    confessions and 130–1
advanced interview training 168,
    171–2, 187
    comparison with PEACE 172–4
    research into success 174–81
        using the Griffiths Question
            Map (GQM) 183–5
adversarial criminal justice systems
    148–9, 151
    see also common law criminal
        justice systems

Afghanistan, use of coercive
    techniques 51–2, 130, 332
age
    effect on confession rates 112
    and matching interviewers and
        al-Qaeda-related subjects 32
al-Qaeda-related subjects 23–39
    cultural contexts 25–6
    Jihad and the history of Sunni
        extremism 27–31
    motivation and the importance of
        relationship 26–7
    raport-based interview approach
        see rapport-based interview
        approach
alternative questions 127–8, 200,
    203–4
America *see* US
'analytic interviewing' 230
Anti-terrorism, Crime and Security
    Act (2001) 10, 14, 17–18
anti-terrorism legislation 17–18
    principles 9–10
appropriate adults 141–2, 155–6
Arab culture 25
Asch's conformity studies 279
associative thinking 25, 36
audio-visual recording 341, 354–5

357